China's Coastal Cities

China's Coastal Cities

Catalysts for Modernization

Edited by
Yue-man Yeung and Xu-wei Hu

 University of Hawaii Press • Honolulu

Library of Congress Cataloging-in-Publication Data

China's coastal cities : catalysts for modernization / edited by Yue
-man Yeung and Xu-wei Hu.
    p. cm.
  Includes bibliographical references and index.
  ISBN 0-8248-1373-1
  1. China—Economic conditions—1976- 2. China—Economic
policy—1976- 3. Cities and towns—China. I. Yeung, Yue-man.
II. Hu, Xu-wei, 1928-
HC427.92.C46467   1992
338.951'00914'6—dc20   91-28822
                                              CIP

Designed by Paula Newcomb

CONTENTS

ILLUSTRATIONS

Figures

Tables

PREFACE

THE RESEARCH PROJECT on China's coastal cities from which this volume has stemmed began in 1984 as a collaborative venture between the Institute of Geography under the Academia Sinica in Beijing together with its many branch institutes and geography departments at universities in China. The Department of Geography at the Chinese University of Hong Kong was invited to participate in this project, as well, with the object of broadening the scope to include several other cities outside mainland China with important experience relevant to the future development of cities in China. Consequently, Hong Kong, Macau, Gaoxiong, and Taizhong were included in the project. Altogether twenty-seven coastal cities were included and the volume, a companion to this one, was completed in Chinese in 1988 and published in 1990 by Scientific Press in Beijing.

The senior editor was invited in 1985 to select authors who could translate the chapters into English for wider dissemination. Indeed, authors from universities in many parts of the world began their research work for the English version long before the completion of the Chinese manuscript. As it turned out, however, for many the task proved daunting owing to the lack of data and reference material. The volume presented here represents the fruit of hard labor of those who soldiered on. In almost every case, the senior author of each chapter has the credit for rewriting from the original Chinese manuscript, incorporating the findings of the original as well as additional research, and applying concepts current in Western social sciences and urban studies.

Precisely because of the difficulty in approaching Chinese cities resulting from inadequate information, the project has been a challenge from the outset. At the same time, the intellectual curiosity about China's coastal cities, as well as the demand for more information by planners, administrators, and investors, has grown considerably since the adoption of the open policy in China in 1978. Despite a recent spate of publications on Chinese urbanization and Chinese cities, no book has yet devoted explicit attention to China's coastal cities. This book, in a small way, is a step in this direction.

The book builds its conceptual edifice on the Chinese coastal cities as catalysts in accelerating China's modernization and development programs. There may appear to be an inherent contradiction in the pursuit of a market economic development strategy under the open policy within a staunchly socialist country. Some of these contradictions are unraveled in the chapters which discuss innovative measures. Since the events in Beijing in June 1989, the Chinese government has taken pains to declare time and again that the open policy will not change and that it has every intention of adhering to the path it has cleared. From the signs and signals we have been able to discern so far, we are unable to find any grounds to suspect the veracity of these public pronouncements on the open policy. On the other hand, it would be unrealistic to imagine that China's coastal cities have been totally unaffected by recent events. In all probability, developments have slowed down as a result of internal economic adjustments to the political reverberation and the understandable hesitancy in new foreign investment. The coastal cities, like China itself, are in a state of flux in the short term but will carry on by their own momentum, barring any unpredictable political development. In any case, what is presented in this book remains true and valuable, a useful base upon which future research and understanding can be built.

At this point, it may be in order to address a few stylistic issues. First, the rendition of Chinese names always poses problems, particularly when contributors come from varied cultural traditions and are used to pronouncing their names in Putonghua or Cantonese. The transliteration of contributors' names adopted in this volume is not exactly in the established Pinyin or Wade-Giles format, but rather an amalgam of the two in anglicized form following the habitual spelling of the contributors. Second, the Chinese units of currency, renminbi and *yuan* ($1 = 0.67 *yuan* in December 1990), are used interchangeably. Unless otherwise stated, the US dollar is used in discussions of dollar currency. Third, *shi* and city (in the sense of the total urban region inclusive of rural counties) and *xian* and county are used interchangeably.

Completion of this project makes it incumbent on the editors to thank many who have rendered assistance in one way or another. We wish to thank all the authors who have contributed their expertise, experience, and support to the project. The arduous task of coordinating such an enterprise over long distances and over many years has often taxed the patience and tolerance of many of the English authors, to whom we owe our gratitude. Even to those whose chapters do not appear here, we express our appreciation for their moral support.

This project was supported in part by a grant from the former Centre for Contemporary Asian Studies of the Chinese University of Hong Kong, which is here acknowledged with thanks. Shaw College of the same university also provided partial funding for the senior editor to present some of the findings at the annual meeting of the Association of American Geographers held in Toronto in April 1990. We owe much to Doris Wong and Eric Kwok of the center in providing, respectively, secretarial support and research assistance to the project. Dr. P. Y. Wong, also of the center, offered many bibliographical updates. Janet Wong and C. K. Chou provided most of the assistance in correspondence in English and Chinese respectively. In addition, Chan Man Chee and Lee Pak Kuen of the Geography Department of the university provided helpful research assistance. Jane Wan deserves a special note of thanks for her meticulous and reliable typing and retyping of the manuscript over a long period of time. Credit for the maps and illustrations should go to S. L. Too, the departmental cartographer. Finally, we very much appreciate the constructive comments from two anonymous reviewers, leading to the present more balanced volume. For any remaining imperfection in presentation and representation the editors are largely responsible.

YMY AND XWH

CONTRIBUTORS

REN-QUN CAI, Institute of Geography, Guangzhou, China

SEN-DOU CHANG, Department of Geography, University of Hawaii, United States

HANG CHEN, Institute of Geography, Beijing, China

HAN-XIN CHEN, Institute of Geography, Beijing, China

CHUN-SHING CHOW, Department of Geography, Baptist College, Hong Kong

DAVID K. Y. CHU, Department of Geography, Chinese University of Hong Kong

YU-YOU DENG, Institute of Geography, Guangzhou, China

KA-IU FUNG, Department of Geography, University of Saskatchewan, Canada

XU-WEI HU, Institute of Geography, Beijing, China

DAVID CHUEN-YAN LAI, Department of Geography, University of Victoria, Canada

SI-MING LI, Department of Geography, Baptist College, Hong Kong

YING-MING LI, Department of Geography, Nanjing University, China

XI-XIN LIANG, Department of Geography, Liaoning Normal University, China

C. P. LO, Department of Geography, University of Georgia, United States

CHIU-MING LUK, Department of Geography, Baptist College, Hong Kong

YUE-MIN NING, Department of Geography, East China Normal University, Shanghai, China

XIAO-DI SONG, Department of Geography, Hangzhou University, China

JUN-JIE SUN, Institute of Geography, Beijing, China

KWAN-YIU WONG, Department of Geography, Chinese University of Hong Kong

CHUNG-TONG WU, Department of Urban and Regional Planning, University of Sydney, Australia

ZHONG-MIN YAN, Department of Geography, East China Normal University, Shanghai, China

SHUN-ZAN YE, Institute of Geography, Beijing, China

ANTHONY G. O. YEH, Center of Urban Studies and Urban Planning, University of Hong Kong

YUE-MAN YEUNG, Department of Geography, Chinese University of Hong Kong

LING-XUN ZHAO, Institute of Geography, Beijing, China

XIAN-YAO ZHAO, Department of Geography, Liaoning Normal University, China

HONG-YI ZHENG, Department of Geography, Nanjing University, China

XUN-ZHONG ZHENG, Department of Geography, Fujian Normal University, China

SHI-KUAN ZHOU, Institute of Geography, Beijing, China

China's Coastal Cities

1 China's Coastal Cities as Development and Modernization Agents: An Overview

YUE-MAN YEUNG AND XU-WEI HU

EVER SINCE THE OPIUM WAR that rudely aroused China from its slumber of self-satisfaction and detachment from global change, almost every subsequent government had proudly adopted as a national goal the avowed policy of making the nation strong through modernization and development. The litany of reform failures from the Qing dynasty to the fiasco of the Cultural Revolution is well documented and does not require any recapitulation here.[1] What has lately gripped world attention and directly affected the lives of millions of people has been a series of reform measures that, since 1978, have selectively flung open China's doors again to the world. Scholars, development analysts, and China watchers are particularly intrigued, for in pursuing a set of liberalized economic policy measures with overt capitalistic overtones, contradictions are certain to emerge against the prevailing socialist ideology.[2] An experiment on a gargantuan scale affecting a quarter of mankind is in the making.[3]

The open policy since 1978 has progressively drawn more areas of China into this reform experiment but, to date, it has been confined to the coastal region. The adoption of this new style of development marks not only a radical departure from adherence to self-reliance rooted in socialism, but also a spatial redistribution of development efforts from the interior to the coast—a shift that, since 1949, has been deliberately deemphasized for ideological and strategic reasons. The new development strategy has been assessed as a means of spatial redeployment with renewed emphasis on the coastal region and on its economic efficiency flowing from centuries of sustained human occupancy, cultural florescence, and technological leadership, alongside its geographical endowments.[4] In the process of accelerated development, the role of Special Economic Zones (SEZs) has been the subject of several recent studies.[5] This volume examines the role of coastal cities that clearly have been identified as catalysts of development.[6] As fermenting agents in a context of rapid change, Chinese coastal cities are of immense theoretical and practical interest to the scholars, policymakers, planners, and investors at whom this volume is aimed.

Converging Interests in Chinese Coastal Cities

The term "coastal cities" is used rather loosely in China and lacks any precise definition. On the one hand, since the eleven coastal provinces,[7] Hainan Island, and Taiwan are customarily referred to as the coastal region, it is not uncommon to find some of the cities located in the region, such as Beijing, Shenyang, Shijiazhuang, Jinan, and Nanjing, drawn within the ambit of coastal cities despite their long distances from the coast. On the other hand, even though coastal cities should strictly be used to designate those located along the coast or where rivers empty into the sea, the comprehensive meaning of "city" *(shi)* often included under its jurisdiction rural counties *(xian)* that might be far from the coast. This volume will take the coastal cities under study here in their entire *shi* definition, but it bears mentioning that it is really in the central city and the urban districts that urban functions and characteristics prevail.

Most coastal cities in China are port cities. Indeed, the development of these cities has waxed and waned with the fortunes of the port. It is not true, however, that all coastal cities are ports. Both Dongying and Panshan near the mouth of Huang He and Liao He, respectively, were erected on the basis of oil industries. They both lack favorable factors for port development and are a far cry from the usual coastal port cities. Similarly, Hangzhou, notwithstanding its proximity to Qiantang Jiang, is not a coastal port for like reasons. By the end of 1985, of the 324 cities in China only 32 could be classified coastal port cities.

The first emerging interest in Chinese coastal cities relates to the catalytic role they are destined to play in the nation's recent drive toward modernization and economic development through the adoption of the open policy. More specifically, fourteen coastal cities—namely, Dalian, Qinhuangdao, Tianjin, Yantai, Qingdao, Lianyungang, Nantong, Shanghai, Ningbo, Wenzhou, Fuzhou, Guangzhou, Zhanjiang, and Beihai—were declared open in 1984 (see Figure 1.1). The creation of fourteen open cities is evidence of the determination of the Chinese leadership to seek accelerated economic development after four SEZs were established in 1979. They are all part and parcel of economic devel-

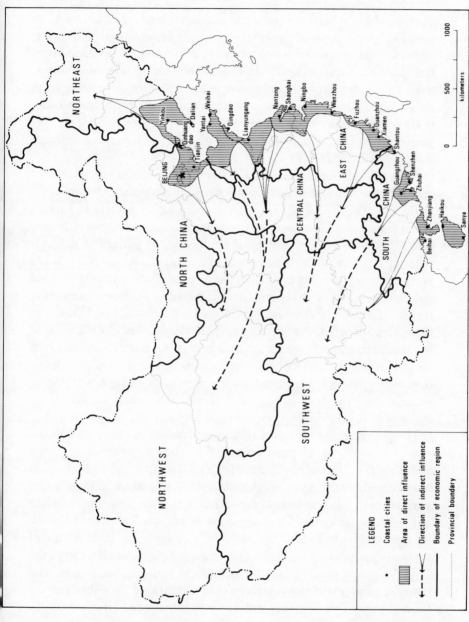

Figure 1.1 The Spread Effects of China's Coastal Cities

opment zones as centers of foreign business investment. Like the SEZs, the open cities are granted special status, which includes the upgrading of their administrative status to the provincial level, the permission to practice flexible economic policies concerning foreign trade and investment, and greater power to offer preferential treatment to overseas investors. Located in economically developed areas and possessed of a relatively strong foundation of industry, science, and technology, these cities are allowed to develop Economic and Technological Development Zones (ETDZs) and science parks with the same generous provision for the corporate profit tax, import and export duties, and other conveniences accorded to the SEZs.[8]

Although the number of coastal port cities in China is just 10 percent of all Chinese cities, their disproportionate importance is clearly reflected in the following set of figures. They account for 16 percent of China's urban population, 20 percent of the nonagricultural labor force, 28 percent of the total value of industrial production, 25 percent of the total value of retailing, and 90 percent of the value of trade export.[9] It has been estimated that approximately 60 percent of the national value of industrial production is concentrated in the cities of the eastern coastal region, of which one-third is again focused on the coastal port cities—in particular, Shanghai, Tianjin, Guangzhou, Dalian, and Qingdao. These key industrial centers account for 26.7 percent of the nation's industrial tax base and exert an overshadowing influence on that sector.[10] In addition, their ranking in commerce, trade, finance, transportation, communication, technology, and cultural activities fully manifests their efficiency as strong, multifunctional, economic centers.

The second interest revolves around the contrasting macrospatial pattern of economic development centered on the coastal region of China and the rest of the country. Economic development in the coastal region has been relatively rapid, notably since 1978, a pattern many analysts attribute to the driving force of the coastal port cities. Since the founding of the People's Republic, a strong sense of pragmatism rather than the innate socialist superiority of spatial balance itself has set the tone of regional development decidedly away from the coastal region. Given the Cold War and a hostile political environment with strained foreign relations for many years, the vulnerability of coastal cities to military attack loomed large. This, together with the well-intentioned objectives of siting industry close to raw materials and new markets, of effecting a degree of regional specialization, and of championing the doctrine of self-reliance, a policy of regional development in favor of the inland and border regions has been in effect since the First Five-Year Plan (1953–1957).[11]

Flowing from this policy of striving for spatial balance in economic development, the coastal region's potential has been deliberately held in abeyance until recently. Kirkby has illustrated that, relative to the inland and border regions, the coastal region suffered a stunted pattern of growth for decades. Indeed, between 1952 and 1982 the coastal region experienced a relative decline of 12.7 percent in the proportion of the total gross value of industrial output (GVIO), 4.2 percent in the proportion of population, 22 percent in the proportion of urban population, and 16.4 percent in the proportion of *shi* population.[12] By contrast, the inland and border regions registered spectacular relative and absolute gains notwithstanding their very small bases at the start. The relative decline of the coastal provinces may be driven home by the fact that their share of China's urban population of 58 percent in 1953 had shrunk to 46 percent by 1981.[13] By and large, therefore, China has achieved a degree of success in the redistributive goals between regions; but for the most part, the relative overall shares of the border and inland regions have not changed drastically. The dominance of the coastal region in industrial production and population persists.

On the basis of different data and regional groupings, Leung's analysis of macrospatial development over the past decades similarly points to the problems of overemphasis on the inland regions and the failure to maximize cumulative regional advantages on the coast. The reorientation of development toward the coast since the mid-1970s is seen as a logical spatial deployment to best serve changing national priorities. Leung further argues that: "For as early as 1956, it had already been fully recognized that the emphasis on the interior must be changed, that China would suffer if insufficient attention was paid to the old industrial bases, that is, the coast area, and that unless the advantages of industrial production in the coast area—inertia, high technology and quality—could be harnessed and further developed, the industrialization of the interior was well-nigh impossible."[14]

A third interest in Chinese coastal cities, in particular the open cities, stems from the uneven development which the open policy would, by design, generate. As part of the national redirection of development centered on the coastal region, the coastal cities are spearheads in a designated region of accelerated growth. There is thus unevenness in the speed of development among the coastal and other cities in the coastal region, as well as between the coastal and the interior regions. From the standpoints of political stability and social equity, there appear to be risks of sharpened disparities in rural/urban conditions within the coastal region and in coastal and inland/peripheral regions of China.

Any trend toward accentuation of internal disparities is cause for concern for planners and decision makers, as the dissatisfaction with the outcome of the urban-based industrialization strategy has in recent years prompted the search for new approaches in development planning. The paradigm of industrial-led growth over the past three decades has led to the following realization: "Although average per capita GNP increased at rates in some cases even greater than targets set by national and international development authorities and experts, the increasing aggregate welfare failed to automatically 'trickle down' beyond the modern industrial sector or over space, and has had little or no benefit to perhaps one-third of the population in the Third World."[15] Indeed, there is evidence to show, in many instances, an absolute decline in income and welfare of the lower 40 percent of the population. This is food for thought for questioning the efficacy of the trickle-down of urban industrial growth to solve the problems of rural/urban disparities and exploring alternative regional development models. The irony is that while the "Chinese model" is often hailed as an inspiration of self-reliance by many development planners and scholars, the Chinese themselves, through their open policy, have been attracted to the conventional wisdom of "redistribution with growth" rather than bear with the snail's space of development which a policy of pulling oneself up by one's bootstraps hitherto entailed.[16]

In opening its doors to the outside, the extent to which China's open cities are incorporated into the international production process and capital accumulation is a point of concern to academics and potential investors alike. The speed of this development will lead directly to varying degrees of unevenness in internal development and hence the need for adjusting regional development policy. Recent studies have provided eloquent evidence that increasingly the forces shaping key cities in Pacific Asia are at least as important internationally as nationally.[17] As China is being drawn into the global economic order, the interdependence of its coastal cities and internationalization of industrial production will increase at the same time.

Finally, China's coastal cities are of immense interest in their own right. For various historical and sociological reasons, Chinese cities (and, for that matter, Chinese coastal cities) have in recent history not been associated with change and industrialization on any large scale, compared, say, with cities in Europe. On the contrary, the treaty port experience gave socialist China every reason not to favor the Western industrial model of concentrated urban growth.[18] The anti-urban sentiments of the key communist leaders in China, born of their revolutionary experience and rustic roots, were reflected in various strands of post-1949 development policy. Until recently, empirical evidence appeared to suggest that the Chinese road to socialism was characterized by anti-urban policies.[19]

Whatever the policy of the Chinese government toward its cities, they have been intense objects of intriguing, if not frustrating, scholarship for decades owing to the paucity of data. The situation, however, has improved immeasurably during the past decade: not only have data source references and other information on Chinese cities become more readily available, but also a certain latitude of field investigation is now possible. As a result, studies on Chinese cities, in both Chinese and English, have appeared with ever-increasing frequency.[20]

The recent availability of data on Chinese cities has certainly facilitated the task of understanding their development, but that in itself does not diminish the enormous complexity with which they are conceptualized and organized, especially with their hinterland in administrative and functional terms. Administrative changes alone have accounted for widely varied urban populations in China. Definitional changes have also contributed to continuing perplexity.[21] In any event, individual coastal cities are little understood in their morphology, structure, pattern, policies, and problems. Thus they form fascinating objects of inquiry given the momentous changes that are taking place in them in coming to terms with the rapid growth occasioned by the open policy. Some of the innovative changes being attempted in these cities are certain to have a far-reaching impact on cities elsewhere in China.

The Changing Role of Chinese Coastal Cities

Ocean transport is the lifeline of Chinese coastal cities. As the past millennium has fully demonstrated, whether the ocean gateway was open or closed has had a profound effect on the development of coastal cities in China. From the Tang dynasty to the early Ming ocean trade was flourishing, with Guangzhou, Quanzhou, and Mingzhou (Ningbo) becoming world-renowned trading ports of their time. Since the late Ming and particularly the Qing dynasty, a closed-door policy led directly to the decline of coastal cities. With the Opium War as a prelude, imperialistic foreign powers forced China to admit the outside world: eighteen trading ports were declared open. Coastal cities that prospered or developed during this period were clearly conditioned by colonialism or semicolonialism, as, for instance, foreign powers enjoyed within their enclaves the rights of extraterritoriality.

Since 1949, the People's Government, in giving a social meaning to the coastal cities, has strengthened their material and technological bases and allowed them to develop according to planned objectives.[22] They have, however, never been able to develop their full potential as gateways to external trade, concentrating, instead, on the domestic market. The severe restriction on foreign trade and technological cooperation can be ascribed to the many political twists and turns, such as the trade embargo stemming from the Korean War, the Sino-Soviet rift, and the leftist extremism during the Cultural Revolution, all inimical to the development of China's coastal cities.[23]

Since 1978, China has adopted an open policy. Under this policy, economic reforms must occur if the new policy is to succeed.[24] In essence, by the adoption of certain measures the open policy encourages the inflow of foreign investment, advanced technology, and management techniques, transforms traditional methods of production, develops an externally oriented economy, and expands foreign trade. Foreign investment may take several forms: direct investment, joint venture, and cooperative management. In every case, infusion of capital and technology—combined with plentiful local labor and other resources—is an effective way of accelerating development. It is also necessary to develop a sound capital market whereby both domestic and foreign investments are effectively pooled. Consequently, international tourism and the service sector are key activities for promoting external exchanges.

The open policy may be structured spatially at six levels: (1) the country, (2) the provinces of Guangdong and Fujian, (3) Special Economic Zones (SEZs), (4) fourteen open cities and Hainan Island, (5) open regions, and (6) export-processing zones. From the viewpoint of investment, the open coastal cities are judged to be most conducive to foreign investment and should be accorded the highest priority for development.[25]

Coastal Cities as Development Catalysts

Under the open policy, the Chinese government has taken a series of steps to speed up development. In 1979 four SEZs were set up in Shenzhen, Zhuhai, Xiamen, and Shantou. Within these delineated zones, special economic policies and management systems would prevail.[26] Although their economies are in theory to depend heavily on foreign investment, their economic activities are regulated by market mechanisms. China is prepared to allow a greater than usual degree of economic autonomy in these zones. Two of these four cities, Shenzhen and Xiamen, are considered in this volume. The creation of a favorable climate to attract foreign investment constitutes one of the development goals of SEZs.

In 1984 the open policy was taken one step further in declaring fourteen coastal cities open. From a geographical viewpoint, the fourteen open cities have formed a coastal belt that is not only important for linkage with foreign markets but also for connection with the massive domestic hinterland. From Dalian to Lianyungang, including the coastal cities in between, they are well located for transportation links with Europe and Northeast Asia, in particular Japan and South Korea. The internal hinterland encompasses Northeast, North, Central, and Northwest China, which may be conceived as direct and indirect zones of influence, as shown in Figure 1.1.[27] Similarly, the open cities south of Nantong to those located on Hainan Island can be seen to play dual roles of providing development impulses to Central and South China and developing foreign trade and attracting investment from countries in Southeast Asia.[28] The open cities consist of some of the finest seaports in the world and, blessed in many cases with sound industrial, cultural, and educational structures, are in a favorable position to import, digest, and transfer advanced technologies and modern scientific information for the country.

The status of an open city may be reflected in two ways. First, such a city would enjoy a higher degree of autonomy so that it has the capacity to pursue externally oriented economic activities. Second, foreign investors would enjoy special privileges for the purpose of using their investment more effectively and importing technologies. Deng has advocated that coastal cities should, as part of a development strategy, concentrate on preserving and expanding the traditional strengths in transportation and trade. At the same time, new technologies and communication should form the bases of new industries and enterprises which, together with the established industrial units, will form the future technological, economic, and social pillars of the country.[29] To create a special investment climate, many coastal cities have established Economic and Technological Development Zones. Indeed, eleven of the fourteen open coastal cities have created such zones.[30] Creating a favorable investment climate entails two interrelated aspects. On the one hand, it involves tangible infrastructural investments such as transport, water and electricity, telecommunication, land use, social facilities, and the like. On the other hand, the intangible aspects are even more important and often more difficult to introduce. These include the quality of cadres and administrators, office efficiency, the legal framework, the nature of the labor force, preferential policies, and so on. Of these crucial dimensions of change, the style and quality of the cadres and administrators rank among the most critical in the open cities.[31]

For open coastal cities to realize their externally oriented economies, structural changes have been effected to improve their production capacity. Based on their natural and economic advantages, many of these cities have readjusted their relative importance in trade, industry, and agriculture. Increased emphasis has been placed on trade with the further development of the harbor. Concomitantly, open coastal cities have generally extended their administrative jurisdiction to rural counties. Thus satellite towns have been developed and have enhanced the centrality and importance of the central city.[32]

In 1985, it was declared that the open policy would be extended to the Chang Jiang (the Yangzi River) Delta, the Zhu Jiang Delta, and the "Golden Triangle" (Xiamen, Zhangzhou, and Quanzhou) in southern Fujian. In these open regions, their relatively more developed economies and superior foreign connections are based on coastal cities which command a host of advantages. Consequently, with the domestic and foreign resources they have access to, these open regions can develop processing and value-added manufacturing according to the demands of foreign trade and become major centers of foreign exports. In recent years, open regions along the coast have continued to expand. They have now essentially embraced the provinces of Guangdong and Fujian and most parts along the coast, including the Shandong and Liaodong peninsulas. Thus the open policy has begun to take on a snowballing effect: from points to surfaces, from outside to inside, from east to west, from the coast to the interior.[33] This is precisely what the proponents of the open policy would

anticipate—that is, the open cities and open regions have become catalysts in accelerating development of the entire country.

Hainan Island was declared open in 1984, but in a move to step up
development the island was established in 1988 as a separate province
independent of Guangdong, under which it previously belonged administratively. The object of such a policy was to make the island more "special" by granting it more liberal policies than those prevailing in the
SEZs. According to planners' thinking, Hainan Island could become the
largest Special Economic Zone or a free-trade zone in China. In any
event, the open policy has been proceeding apace in China, and the
coastal cities have been providing the dynamism for the policy to thrive
and develop. They have also become indispensable agents of change to
translate China's modernization programs into reality.

The theme of open coastal cities as catalysts of development in multiple ways recurs so often in the literature that it is worthy of a little exploration. In terms of commercial activities, coastal cities are seen as, first,
windows in the import of capital, technology, and management skills for
training the local labor force; second, they are seen as beachheads where
advanced technologies and facilities as well as management methods are
absorbed and improved for transfer to their hinterland and where raw
materials and agricultural produce are processed and packaged for the
international market; third, they are seen as hinge points for the vast
domestic market and the international market where they meet in these
cities; and fourth, they are seen as laboratories for a new form of trading
system in China's socialist society.[34] Indeed, the emphasis on attracting
foreign investment and domestic linkage is underlined in all open coastal
cities and is applicable to many facets of development besides commercial activities. There is a widespread belief that the coastal cities are possessed of the requisite technological, production, and educational structures to marry the two objectives so that the optimal results of the open
policy can be realized. Carried to their logical development, the objectives suggest that certain traditional and mature industries could be relocated to the hinterland after benefiting from upgrading through the
import of technologies. In fact, some of the superior, special, high-quality, and new industries could substitute for foreign imports destined for
domestic markets. Conversely, certain raw material and traditional production processes could be relocated to coastal cities for value-added
work and for more ready export to foreign markets.[35]

On the basis of their development patterns, open coastal cities may be grouped in at least three ways. First are the externally oriented economies that are built mainly upon foreign investment and industries with a clear export orientation. The second type refers to the internally oriented structures with an emphasis on improving traditional enterprises with the help of foreign investment and new technologies. The third group of coastal cities is an amalgam of the two varieties: a "two fan surface and one hinge" effect. Production structure is export-oriented; but owing to the relative lack of foreign investment, domestic capital is used to reinforce foreign capital. Generally speaking, open coastal cities have developed comprehensive economic structures with industries as the mainstay and often with multifunctional roles.[36]

In a desirable strategy involving the division of labor between coastal cities and their hinterland, four guidelines have been suggested. First, coastal cities should be allowed to harness their advantages to develop their potential. The benefits so accrued to these cities could be redistributed through economic policy and administrative procedures. Second, immediate and long-term development should be carefully distinguished. In the long run, traditional industries should be gradually relocated to the interior. Third, development should maximize natural and economic advantages inherent in every location without seeking to be "large and complete." Products and enterprises thus developed should complement other economic districts. Fourth, economic development must take into full account the advantages of the overall situation rather than stressing specific factors that lead to unhealthy competition for raw materials and energy among coastal cities to their mutual detriment.[37]

Problems and Prospects

Although China's coastal cities are now in their best ever position to develop, they all appear to follow the path of export-oriented, labor-intensive manufacturing along with knowledge-based industries to enhance their international competitiveness. The question of how each coastal city should be developed effectively and practically is still unresolved. Many coastal cities have not taken into account their relative strengths and weaknesses in pursuing their development objectives. As a consequence, there is a high degree of repetitiveness in their economic activities and little or no attempt at coordination. Some cities would even squander their precious little foreign exchange on import items and duplicate infrastructural investment without any regard of their basic development potential. Such wasteful development policy not only adversely affects the national economy, but also directly hampers the development of the cities in question. In fact, under China's socialist system the speed with which coastal cities can develop is conditioned, on the one hand, by the extent to which a city can pursue its development objectives and, on the other, by the national development policy, in particular the investment policy. Thus one may argue that from the viewpoint of the speed of development and economic efficiency, coastal cities should be the focus of more capital and technological investment by the government in according them a high priority in resource allocation.[38]

Since each coastal city is faced with a different development problem and each has a different mix of natural, social, economic, and technological conditions, the emphasis of development should correspondingly differ. At present, most of the fourteen open cities share a similar predicament. Most of them suffer from poor transportation and outdated telecommunication facilities. Lack of modern equipment also plagues the open cities despite their naturally endowed ports, hindering effective links with their domestic hinterland.[39] Port facilities are so far behind the times that a huge demand and the lack of berthing spaces have resulted in serious congestion of cargo handling in all the fourteen open cities. Moreover, inadequate supplies of water, energy, and electricity have posed additional headaches for the burgeoning urban population. Finally, owing to the foreign exchange factor, the long-standing disparity between domestic and international prices is another cause of problems in development.[40]

In view of these problems, how should the coastal cities proceed? Many practical suggestions have been proffered. These include the restructuring of existing enterprises, acceleration of technological advances, reforming economic activities with a view to achieving higher productivity, and completion of a number of key infrastructural investments. Basic urban facilities—such as the port, railway, highways, water transport, postal service, and telecommunications—must be improved. Equally important, the process should be started for training in technical skills, initiating research, and establishing a maintenance system.[41]

Some scholars have been even more explicit in prescribing development strategies for the coastal cities. At least four strategies have been advanced. First, there is the need for extending capital and resources from the domestic market to the international market, aiming at a combination of the two. Second, from a self-centered one-city/one-location development strategy, there should be a reorientation toward large-scale, regional, and social production. To reach this objective, it is necessary to work closely with other regions of the country, particularly the hinterland. Active steps could be considered for organizing economic districts and for economic cooperation extending over a large area. Third, efforts must be devoted to raising the quality of existing enterprises. In this respect, coastal cities would encounter several basic difficulties: existing enterprises have reached a certain size beyond which expansion is limited by several factors, including the size of the city itself; moreover, it is imprudent to let economic development go large-scale without knowing all of the risks involved; finally, coastal cities face the biggest challenge in both the domestic and foreign markets because many of their manufactured goods lack the competitive edge internationally. And fourth, in recent years coastal cities have raised their technological level largely by their own efforts. In fact, the cities should seriously consider the adoption of technology, with appropriate compensation, from other parts of China or the transfer of technology accompanied by trade.[42]

More fundamentally, in establishing their new production patterns and distribution, coastal cities must discard the traditional and simplistic notion of an industrial city. Each city should, instead, strive for an integrated social and economic entity. Planning must be based on economic, social, and environmental efficiency so that they can plan, implement, and develop in step.[43]

The coastal cities have among themselves much that is in common, such as their coastal location, having a seaport, and having benefited from the open policy. On the other hand, their specific geographical factors, natural endowments, and different hinterlands have given rise to many differences. A comparison between Dalian and Beihai, for example, or between Tianjin and Xiamen, would reveal considerable contrasts in the nature of the city, population size, level of economic development, production structures, social services, overseas connections, infrastructure investment, spatial distribution, and environmental quality. All these development factors and their differences will greatly influence the direction and pace of development of coastal cities.

A Preview of the Chapters

Although the research project from which this book is derived originally included many Chinese coastal cities and several in the neighboring territories of Hong Kong, Macau, and Taiwan, only thirteen cities are considered in this volume. Ten of these are open cities, and Taizhong is the only city outside the mainland. The thirteen chapters which follow will focus on these cities from north to south in consecutive order.

Given the project's common conceptual framework, it is not surprising that many chapters should display similarities in their approach. Most chapters, for instance, present a brief historical background of the city. Most emphasize economic and urban development patterns and policies, as well. One notes that eight of the cities represented here have chosen to accelerate their economic development by providing certain zones with infrastructure, administrative support, and other conveniences to attract domestic and foreign investors. These are Economic and Technological Development Zones, though the terminology may vary from city to city. Within the broad framework of a common focus on the recent development pattern, policies, and problems of the cities, there is an imaginative variety of approaches to the analysis and appraisal of individual cities.

Dalian, an old port and industrial center in North China first developed under Russian and Japanese influences, is studied by Lai, Zhao, and Liang in essentially three parts: port facilities, industrial development, and urban development. Three types of port facilities are noted and their recent development is reviewed. For industrial development, the current status is realistically evaluated. Because of backwardness in production and technology, the city government has actively supported industrial modernization through technical education and imported technology. The urban districts and their functions are also described, especially the Dalian ETDZ. The authors finally point out the problems faced by the city in mounting its development and modernization programs, including transport bottlenecks and a shortage of electricity.

Chang, Hu, and Sun provide a comprehensive and structured account of modern Tianjin full of data and insights. Despite its strategic location as the leading port city in the Bo Hai–Yellow Sea Rim, Tianjin stagnated during the first thirty years after the founding of the People's Republic under the long shadow of Beijing. With its exceptionally well-endowed natural resources in the form of oil, salt, and land for industrial and urban development, Tianjin is well on its way to recapturing its former status as the leading port in North China. The city has developed rapidly under the open policy, registering outstanding success in restructuring its urban economy and improvement in urban infrastructure. Innovation has been exhibited in its approach to urban renewal and housing construction. The chapter, as well, examines Tianjin's development in the broader framework of economic cooperative regions, such as the Beijing–Tianjin–Tangshan Region and the Bo Hai–Yellow Sea Rim Economic Region.

Like Tianjin, Yantai faces Bo Hai and thus shares some of the same locational advantages. Luk and Zhou examine Yantai, however, along a geographical continuum. First, Yantai is studied as a city and its region including the neighboring provinces and municipalities. A composite index on economic development, based on ten variables, is calculated. Second, Yantai is examined in its entire administrative region or *shi*. It has a rich resource endowment and potential for tourism, as well as a good network of small towns vital to Yantai's economy. Third, the city proper is studied with particular reference to the port area, industrial location, and the ETDZ. The chapter ends on a note of increasing competition with other ports in North China and suggests how Yantai should prepare for developing a useful role in the regional setting.

The transformation of Qingdao from a colonial port city to a modern industrial center is traced by Wu, Ye, and Zhou. In examining Qingdao's contemporary development, the authors organize their analysis in three main parts: the urban economy, transportation, and urban development. Within the urban economy, industrial structure, foreign investment, and tourism are spotlighted. It has been noted that the legacy of past industrial development is still discernible today; light industries still predominate. Transport facilities, in particular port and land transportation, are described. Qingdao's urban pattern is studied through an examination of its urban districts, its satellite town development within 50 km of the city center, and the ETDZ. Finally the authors highlight the problems facing Qingdao in its development, notably the comparative inefficiency of its industries, an acute shortage of water, and pollution of the environment. Chemical and metallurgy industries, two of the key economic activities, are the main culprits in water pollution. At the same time, there are many opportunities for planners and policymakers in urban and economic restructuring and urban renewal to rectify some of the past irrationalities in urban land use.

Despite its aquatic and mineral resources in the surrounding areas, Lianyungang's real development potential, as Yeh, Zheng, and Li demonstrate, lies in its huge hinterland. Lianyungang's geographical position as the starting point of the Longhai railway to the interior provinces makes it a convenient exporting port for a region encompassing 40 percent of China's land and one-third of its population. The eleven provinces and autonomous regions in Central and Northwest China are the major producers of grain, cotton, and edible oil and important bases for animal husbandry, mining, and energy production. Lianyungang has actively developed its potential by following a multipronged strategy that is geared to building a modern port with multiple harbors and functions, a new industrial base, a financial center, a base of entrepôt trade, and unique tourist resorts. The city has also developed an ETDZ to assist the interior provinces in making contacts with foreign investors. Issues of development are discussed as a way for Lianyungang to progress.

China's largest city, industrial center, and port—Shanghai—is given thorough scrutiny in the chapter by Fung, Yan, and Ning, especially Shanghai's development with reference to its past, present, and future. Emphasis is placed on an analysis of the city's changing functional and economic importance in relation to policy changes. Since 1949, urban spatial structures have been transformed significantly by the development of satellite towns in the late 1950s and by the establishment of the city region in Shanghai in 1958. These planning strategies, however, have not achieved the objective of absorbing a portion of the population and industry in the central city. The impediments to Shanghai's development include a high concentration of population and industry in the central city area and inadequate transport and communication services. The authors review plans and progress to date on the establishment of the Special Economic Zones of Minhang and Hongqiao in 1982. The need to promote industrial transformation and modernization, to expand tertiary industry, and to initiate urban redevelopment is also underlined.

Ningbo, a city noted for its gifted businessmen and superior geographical location, is discussed in terms of its recent development after a long period of stagnant growth. In examining how new government policy has helped transform Ningbo into an export-oriented, industrial-commercial port city, Lo and Song pay particular attention to the development of a light industrial structure, petrochemical engineering and energy resource industries, external trade and economic technology, village economy and production base for commercial exports, and urban infrastructure for investment purposes. Modern development of Ningbo has focused on the deep-sea port of Beilun and the establishment of an ETDZ. The authors point out two major problems of development: the need for more construction to improve the distribution system of Ningbo's hinterland and the serious lags in infrastructural development. Moreover, the chapter shows how a city like Ningbo not only can survive under the giant shadow of Shanghai but in fact has a viable and complementary role to play as part of the Shanghai Economic Core Area.

Wenzhou, located in southeastern Zhejiang province, is studied by Chow and Chen. In portraying its recent development against its geographical and historical background, they argue that both physical and human factors have prevented Wenzhou from more rapid development to date. The policies adopted since 1978 have not created immediate gains, but the city does possess great potential for future progress, particularly in the exploitation of natural resources and the development of commerce, trade, and tourism. Wenzhou's urban development and morphology are described in unusual detail—especially its suburban growth and industrialization, including the construction of the export-processing zone at Longwan in 1987. The authors optimistically conclude that with economic progress in Wenzhou, many people in that part of the province can derive positive benefits.

Chu and Zheng approach the study of Fuzhou in the conceptual framework of a coastal city in a frontier region. The construct aptly fits its ancient role as the Chinese end of the "Maritime Silk Road" connecting China with West Asia and Europe. Equally, it suits its current role, since 1978, as a frontier coastal city facing Taiwan. There is continuity in Fuzhou's traditional role and function as an administrative center for the development of a frontier province. The importance of overseas Chinese in the city's economic development is highlighted in an examination of Fuzhou's spatial-urban structure. The authors also examine plans and policies designed to make Fuzhou an open city. These include port projects, the ETDZ in Mawei, improvement in transport and communication networks, and increasing the reliability of the energy supply. Fuzhou's frontier role has been further enhanced since 1988, when the Taiwanese authorities dramatically relaxed their policy of no civilian contact across the Straits of Taiwan.

Xiamen shares with Fuzhou many of the characteristics of a coastal city in a frontier province as well as association with overseas Chinese. In this chapter, Li and Zhao stress the role played by overseas Chinese in developing Xiamen in the early part of the present century, especially in transport infrastructure, public utilities, real estate, education, banking, and foreign trade. Xiamen's spatial structure is also considered. Development since 1978 is surveyed with special reference to political and economic reforms. The Special Economic Zone, developed since 1980, is studied in its positive effects on Xiamen's recent economic development. As well, the urban structure is delineated. The authors provide an update on recent progress in building a legal framework for more orderly urban growth that may have relevance for other Chinese coastal cities. They refer, in particular, to the Land-Use Control Regulations of July 1984 and the Land Transfer Ordinance of June 1988.

Guangzhou, China's "southern gateway," is studied by Yeung, Deng, and Chen in a chapter that highlights the thorny problems of effecting change and modernization to a city most susceptible to change by virtue of its geographical location. The authors analyze the urban structure by describing each of its three main parts: the old city, Tianhe, and Huangpu (which is also the site of an ETDZ). Problems that similarly afflict other large Chinese coastal cities—seemingly irrational and inefficient land use, housing shortages, and transportation difficulties—are studied and the reasons probed. The chapter also considers Guangzhou's rural/urban relations and argues that the grain contribution of its rural counties to the central government is an excessive burden on their economy. As well, Yeung, Deng, and Chen highlight the relative failure of satellite towns in fulfilling their stated goal of decentralizing population and economic activities. Finally, the authors introduce various designs for a Guangzhou economic region with the object of enhancing economic efficiency. The future of Guangzhou lies in its quest for a role that will accentuate its centrality and leadership position in a system of thriving urban places in the Pearl River Delta.

As the largest Special Economic Zone having witnessed phenomenal economic growth since 1980, Shenzhen owes its success to its geographical location and social ties to Hong Kong. Wong, Cai, and Chen show in their chapter that Shenzhen is becoming less "special" on account of the proliferation of open cities and regions during the last few years. Specifically, they examine Shenzhen as a model of development from the standpoints of free zones and laboratories for experimentation in modernization. Reference is made to various innovative measures, such as contract labor, a new wage system, and land sale reform—all pacesetting processes in China. Shenzhen's population growth and characteristics are assessed, as well, followed by detailed studies in economic development covering economic structure, manufacturing development, and recent achievements. Finally the authors point out the problems that Shenzhen is facing in its present and future development, including keen competition with other Asian economies and the recent sharp rise in land values.

The port city of Taizhong, located midway in the developed region of western Taiwan, is studied by Yeung and Chu in the framework of its vital stabilizing role in the urban system, regional development, and population redistribution in Taiwan. Taizhong's recent development can be understood by a study of the city itself, Taizhong Harbor, and the Taizhong Export-Processing Zone, all of which are covered in detail. Their difficult spatial relationship, based on regional interests and provincial needs, is then considered. The optimum spatial arrangement of the three units, the authors argue, calls for their full integration as an entity. At least some administrative restructuring should be sought if Taizhong is to aspire to a more important role in promoting economic development.

The final chapter ties the various city studies together in several ways. Special Economic Zones are compared and analyzed—a task made all the more necessary as the volume includes only two cities within these zones. Then the modernization roles assigned to coastal cities are examined from several perspectives, including relative strengths of coastal cities by size, the ETDZ as a development strategy, and comparative statistics. Finally, developments in coastal cities since the events of June 1989 are evaluated—especially the new measures designed to attract foreign investment and Shanghai's plan to develop Pudong (with its anticipated repercussions on other coastal cities and their counterstrategies). The survey concludes on a note of guarded optimism.

Notes

1. For an account and analysis of some of these developments, one may refer to Albert Feuerwerker, *The Chinese Economy 1870–1911* and *The Chinese Economy 1912–1949,* Michigan Papers on Chinese Studies no. 1 and 5 respectively (Ann Arbor: Center for Chinese Studies, University of Michigan, 1968 and 1969); Dwight H. Perkins, *China's Economy in Historical Perspective* (Stanford: Stanford University Press, 1975); and Ramon H. Myers, *The Chinese Economy: Past and Present* (Belmont, Calif.: Wadsworth, 1980). See also Paul A. Cohen, "The Post-Mao Reforms in Historical Perspective," *Journal of Asian Studies* 47(3) (August 1988): 518–540.

2. The new policy could sharpen the contradictions in Chinese society so astutely propounded by Mao Zedong. See Mao Zedong, "On the Ten Major Contradictions," *Collected Works of Mao Zedong,* vol. 5 (Beijing: People's Press, 1977), pp. 267–288 (in Chinese); and J. Gray and G. White (eds.), *China's New Development Strategy* (London: Academic Press, 1982).

3. The experimental nature of the ongoing economic reforms in China has been repeatedly emphasized by Chinese leaders. This tone pervades some recent studies, as in K. Y. Wong (ed.), *Shenzhen Special Economic Zone: China's Experiment in Modernization* (Hong Kong: Hong Kong Geographical Association, 1982).

4. See C. K. Leung, "Spatial Redeployment and the Special Economic Zones in China: An Overview," in Y. C. Yao and C. K. Leung (eds.), *China's Special Economic Zones: Policies, Problems and Prospects* (Hong Kong: Oxford University Press, 1986); and R. J. R. Kirkby, *Urbanisation in China: Town and Country in a Developing Economy 1949-2000 AD* (London: Croom Helm, 1985), chap. 5.

5. A sample of such publications may be represented by Wong, *Shenzhen Special Economic Zone;* D. K. Y. Chu (ed.), *Shenzhen: The Largest Special Economic Zone in China* (Hong Kong: Wide Angle Press, 1983) (in Chinese); K. Y. Wong and D. K. Y. Chu (eds.), *Modernization in China: The Case of the Shenzhen Special Economic Zone* (Hong Kong: Oxford University Press, 1985); Yao and Leung (eds.), *China's Special Economic Zones;* and K. Y. Wong, C. C. Lau, and E. B. C. Li (eds.), *Perspectives on China's Modernization: Studies on China's Open Policy and Special Economic Zones* (Hong Kong: Centre for Contemporary Asian Studies, Chinese University of Hong Kong, 1988).

6. The positive and negative roles played by a city are vividly illustrated in T. G. McGee, "Catalysts or Cancers? The Role of Cities in Asian Society," in L. Jakobson and V. Prakash (eds.), *Urbanization and National Development in South and Southeast Asia* (Beverly Hills: Sage, 1971), pp. 157-181. In this volume, the positive aspects are emphasized.

7. The provinces, comprising 13.4 percent of China's area, are Beijing, Tianjin, Hebei, Liaoning, Shanghai, Jiangsu, Zhejiang, Fujian, Shandong, Guangdong, and Guangxi Autonomous Region.

8. See D. K. Y. Chu, "The Special Economic Zones and the Problems of Territorial Containment," in Yao and Leung (eds.), *China's Special Economic Zones,* p. 35; and Sidney Goldstein, *Urbanization in China: New Insights from the 1982 Census,* East-West Population Institute Papers no. 93 (Honolulu: East-West Center, 1985), pp. 69-70.

9. Statistics may be presented in different ways using different indicators, but the dominance of the coastal region is always clear. See, for example, Li Gan, Zou Feng, and Liu Dongtao, "The Effectiveness of Coastal Cities in China's Strategy of Economic Development," in Li Zhongfan, Xie Wenxia, and Song Tingming (eds.), *Cities and Economic Development Regions* (Fuzhou: Fujian People's Press, 1984), pp. 211-224 (in Chinese).

10. Ibid., p. 213.

11. Kirkby, *Urbanisation in China,* chap. 5.

12. Ibid.

13. Ibid., p. 143.

14. Leung, "Spatial Redeployment," p. 7.

15. Fu-chen Lo, Kamal Salih, and Mike Douglass, "Uneven Development, Rural-Urban Transformation, and Regional Development Alternatives in Asia," paper presented at the Seminar on Rural-Urban Transformation and Regional Development Planning, Nagoya, November 1978, p. 4. See also Johannes F. Linn, *Cities in the Developing World: Policies for Their Equitable and Efficient Growth* (New York: Oxford University Press for the World Bank, 1983), p. 38.

16. See H. Chenery and others, *Redistribution with Growth* (Washington, D.C.: IBRD, 1974), especially "Introduction"; G. H. Helleiner (ed.), *A World Divided* (Cambridge: Cambridge University Press, 1976); and Pugwash Symposium, "The Role of Self-Reliance in Alternative Strategies for Development," *World Development* 5(3) (1977): 257–265.

17. See W. R. Armstrong and T. G. McGee, *Theatres of Accumulation: Studies in Asian and Latin American Urbanization* (New York: Methuen, 1985); and Michael A. Goldberg, *The Chinese Connection: Getting Plugged in to Pacific Rim Real Estate, Trade and Capital Markets* (Vancouver: University of British Columbia Press, 1985).

18. See Rhoades Murphey, *The Treaty Ports and China's Modernization: What Went Wrong?*, Michigan Papers on Chinese Studies no. 7 (Ann Arbor: Center for Chinese Studies, University of Michigan, 1970), and *China Meets the West: The Treaty Ports* (New York: Macmillan, 1975).

19. Kirkby, *Urbanisation in China*, p. 5.

20. Some of these recent publications may be represented by Laurence J. C. Ma and Edward W. Hanten (eds.), *Urban Development in Modern China* (Boulder: Westview Press, 1981); C. K. Leung and Norton Ginsburg (eds.), *China: Urbanization and National Development*, Research Paper no. 196 (Chicago: Department of Geography, University of Chicago, 1980); Christopher Howe (ed.), *Shanghai: Revolution and Development in an Asian Metropolis* (Cambridge: Cambridge University Press, 1981); Martin King Whyte and William L. Parish, *Urban Life in Contemporary China* (Chicago: University of Chicago Press, 1984); Victor F. S. Sit (ed.), *Chinese Cities: The Growth of the Metropolis Since 1949* (Hong Kong: Oxford University Press, 1985); Kirkby, *Urbanisation in China*; and Y. M. Yeung and Zhou Yixing (eds.), "Urbanization in China: An Inside-Out Perspective I and II," *Chinese Sociology and Anthropology* (Spring/Summer 1987 and Winter 1988–89).

21. The complexity of China's urban population in definition and concept is fully revealed in Laurence J. C. Ma and Gonghao Cui, "Administrative Changes and Urban Population in China," *Annals of the Association of American Geographers* 77(3) (1987): 373–395; and Kirkby, *Urbanisation in China*, chap. 3.

22. The Soviet influence was quite noticeable in the development of Chinese cities in the early years after 1949. See, for example, Sit, *Chinese Cities*, p. 9.

23. See Yeung and Zhou (eds.), *Urbanization in China (I)*, pp. 3–7.

24. Many recent studies have dealt with the subject of the open policy and its implications. See several of these reviewed in Yue-man Yeung, "China After Mao: Modernization and Integration with the World Order—a Review Article," *Canadian Journal of Development Studies* 7(1) (1986): 127–131.

25. Zheng Tianxiang and Chen Lijun, "An Evaluation of the Investment Environment of Fourteen Coastal Cities," *Gangao Yanjiu* 1(2) (1986): 83–92 (in Chinese).

26. See note 8.

27. Eighteen coastal cities, including fourteen open cities, are included. They represent the cities studied in this project except Hong Kong, Macau, Taizhong, and Kaoshiung.

28. Liu Weihua, "Several Questions Concerning the Development Strategy in Open Coastal Cities," *Yatai Jingji* 3 (1986): 50–55 (in Chinese).

29. Deng Shoupeng, "China's Special Economic Zones and the Future of Open Coastal Cities," *Kexue Zhichun* 1 (1985): 4–6 (in Chinese).

30. Liu, "Several Questions," p. 44.

31. Ibid.

32. Guo Xiandeng, "An Enquiry into the Externally-Oriented Economic Structure and Development Trends of Open Coastal Cities," *Jingji yu Guanli Yanjiu* [Economic and management research] 4 (1987): 41–43 (in Chinese).

33. Ren Zhiyuan, "On Planning and Development of Special Economic Zones and Economy-Technology Development Zones Along the Coast" (in Chinese), paper presented at the Seminar on Development Planning for the Open Coastal Cities in China, Beijing, October 1986.

34. "Summary of the Viewpoints at the Conference on the Commercial Economy of Open Coastal Cities," *Shangye Jingji Yanjiu* [Commercial economy research] 8 (1986): 30–31 (in Chinese).

35. The importance of domestic links and foreign investment for the better articulation of spatial development is highlighted in Liu, "Several Questions," and Wong and Chu, *Modernization in China*, pp. 8–17.

36. Wang Jian, "Introducing Theoretical Viewpoints About Open Coastal Cities," *Yatai Jingji* 6 (1985): 67–68 (in Chinese). For a systematic categorization of China's coastal cities, see Yang Guanxiong, "The Typology and Structure of Chinese Coastal Port Cities," paper presented at the Seminar on Development Planning for the Open Coastal Cities in China, Beijing, October 1986.

37. Cai Kaozhen and Wu Jinghua, "Strategies of Economic Development in Coastal Cities," *Tianjin Shehui Kexue* [Tianjin social science] 2 (1985): 44–48 (in Chinese).

38. Zhang Runxi and Wang Pupeng, "Views on Developing Special Economic Zones and Opening Fourteen Coastal Cities," *Xueshu Luntan* 1 (1985): 29–32 (in Chinese).

39. Chen Zhaobin, "Guidelines for Open Coastal Cities Based on Shenzhen Special Economic Zone's Experience in Construction," *Yatai Jingji* 1 (1985): 52–57 (in Chinese). See also Li, Zou, and Liu, "The Effectiveness of Coastal Cities," for an account of problems confronting coastal cities in their development.

40. Chen Zhaobin, "On the Strategy of the Formation Structure and Development of China's Coastal Open Policy," *Open Cities and Economic Open Region Economic Research* 3 (1985): 1–21 (in Chinese).

41. Cai and Wu, "Strategies of Economic Development," p. 31.

42. Ibid., p. 33.

43. Guo, "An Enquiry," p. 42.

2 Dalian: Its Industrial Development and Urban Growth

DAVID CHUEN-YAN LAI, XIAN-YAO ZHAO, AND XI-XIN LIANG

IN APRIL 1984 the State Council decided to open up fourteen coastal cities to foreign investment as part of its plans to attract capital and technology from abroad. These cities were permitted to adopt flexible economic policies similar to those being implemented in the four Special Economic Zones in South China. The port of Dalian was one of these open cities designated for foreign investment. In 1984 Dalian was granted economic autonomy and permitted, without the approval of the provincial authority, to implement productive projects with investments of not more than $10 million each. In the following year the State Council gave the city an annual foreign exchange allocation of $100 million as well as provincial status for foreign trade enterprises. In other words, Dalian was permitted to export its own products directly without going through the foreign trade corporations of the provincial government of Liaoning. This chapter studies the geographical setting of Dalian and considers the impacts of China's open policy on the city's industrial, trade, and urban development.

Geographical Setting and Resources

The city of Dalian, on the southern coast of the Liaodong Peninsula between Huang Hai (the Yellow Sea) and Bo Hai, is an important port city of China. It was established on the site of Qingniwa, formerly a small fishing village. During the Manchu dynasty, Qingniwa and its surrounding areas were already a significant transshipment node where goods from Shandong Peninsula and those from Manchuria were exchanged. Commanding the sea entrance to Tianjin and Beijing, the Qingniwa areas were strategically important as well. Since the 1880s the Manchu government had been strengthening the military defense of Luda, the area from the port of Dalian to the port of Lushun at the southern tip of Liaodong Peninsula.

Dalian was first developed in the early 1900s by the Russians and after

1905 by the Japanese as an entrepôt for Manchuria (Heilongjiang, Jilin, and Liaoning provinces). Dalian's harbor is deep, spacious, and silt-free. Its small tidal range varies between 2.3 and 2.9 m. The harbor is basically ice-free, as well. Only part of its water area freezes for about sixty days between January and March, and the ice, varying from 5 to 30 mm in thickness, affects neither navigation nor mooring. Thus Dalian is a very important ice-free port for northeastern China as well as the eastern part of Inner Mongolia. Today Metropolitan Dalian, covering an area of 12,574 sq km, includes six districts of Dalian, the city of Wafangdian, and three counties (Figure 2.1). In 1987 it had a total population of nearly 5 million (Table 2.1).

The metropolitan area of Dalian is endowed with rich local resources which provide the raw materials for some of its industries. Dalian abounds in minerals; its reserves of limestone are estimated at 1.1 billion tons and those of silica, magnesium, quartzite, and dolomite are estimated at over 10 million tons each. Other mineral resources include belonga stone, asbestos, adamas (diamonds), copper, lead, and zinc. Dalian is renowned as China's "home of apples"; its annual production averages more than 400,000 tons. Other types of fruit production include yellow peach, cherry, and grapes. In 1985 it was estimated that Dalian had 35 million fruit trees.

The offshore waters of Dalian are rich in marine products such as shellfish, algae, sea cucumbers, abalones, scallops, mussels, kelps, and prawns. In 1985 the harvest of marine products amounted to 449,000 tons which represented about 6.4 percent of China's total harvest. Dalian, with its 31,000 ha of salt pans, is also one of the chief salt-producing centers in China.

In addition to its rich local resources, Dalian is easily accessible to the rich agricultural, industrial, and mineral resources of its hinterland in Heilongjiang, Jilin, and Liaoning provinces. Today these three provinces, accounting for one-sixth of China's agricultural and industrial output value, still rely on Dalian as the gateway to the outside world.

Development During Foreign Occupations

In 1898 Russia forced the Manchu government to lease Luda for twenty-five years, using Lushun as a naval base and Dalian as a port. Soon after the lease was obtained, the Russians started to construct the South Man-

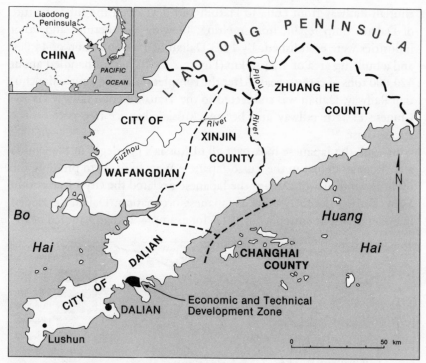

Figure 2.1 The Metropolitan Area of Dalian

Table 2.1   Area and Population of
Metropolitan Dalian: 1985

DISTRICT	AREA (SQ KM)	POPULATION (1,000)
City of Dalian	2,415	2,277
City of Wafangdian	3,576	973
Xinjin county	2,770	792
Zhuang He county	3,656	869
Changhai county	156	76
Total	12,573	4,987

Source: Yearbook of Economic Statistics, Liaoning Province,
1988.

churian Railway from Luda to Harbin and developed the infrastructure of Dalian. Ship repair, iron smelting, brewing, lumbering, and other industries were established. By 1903 Dalian had a population of 44,000 and a built-up area of 4.25 sq km (Figure 2.2). Its harbor handled about 420,000 tons of cargo a year. After the completion of the South Manchurian Railway, Dalian was connected to the Trans-Siberian railway via the Chinese Eastern railway and became Russia's key ice-free port on the Pacific coast.

In 1905 the Japanese took over all of Russia's privileges in Manchuria after Russia's defeat in the Russo-Japanese War. In order to promote the trade and industry of Dalian, the Japanese declared the city a free port in 1906. During the forty years of Japanese occupation, Dalian developed into an important entrepôt. In 1917, for example, Dalian handled nearly

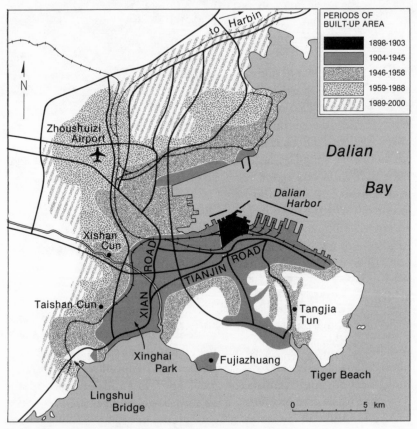

Figure 2.2 The Built-Up Area of the City of Dalian

70 percent of northeastern China's total export and was China's second largest port after Shanghai. By 1939 the harbor handled 10 million tons of cargo. Similar to other treaty ports, Dalian's major export items were minerals, coal, soybeans, and other food products; imports comprised mainly manufactured goods. Light industries were predominant initially, but after 1931 the Japanese government sped up the industrial development of Dalian and emphasized heavy industry. By the mid-1930s the value of Dalian's industrial output exceeded that of Mukden (now Shenyang); thus Dalian became the largest industrial center in Manchuria. The city's urban growth was accelerated, as well, as a result of in-migration. Due to the influx of immigrants from Japan, Korea, Shandong and Hebei provinces, and other areas, the population of Dalian increased from 280,000 in 1930 to 700,000 in 1945, of which 25 percent were Japanese. By 1936, the built-up areas of the city had increased to 45 sq km.

Port Facilities and Trade

The harbors of Metropolitan Dalian can be classified into three types according to their functions. The first type is the military harbor at Lushun; the second comprises the fishing harbors on the northern shore; the third type is the commercial harbor on the western shore of Dalian Bay. The first wharf in Dalian Harbor was built in 1902 by the Russians, and other wharves were constructed later by the Japanese. After 1949, the Chinese government started to revamp the old wharves and built several new ones for sundry goods, coal, hazardous goods, and containers. In 1962 the government constructed a modern fishing harbor at the southern end of Dalian Bay on the site of the Manchu-era naval port; the harbor is now the home of the Luda Marine Products Company.[1]

After the introduction of the open policy in 1978, Dalian's government started to expand its port facilities. Today the port of Dalian has five terminals (Figure 2.3). The Main Harbor Terminal, surrounded by breakwaters, consists of four piers and three wharves with a total of thirty berths. The terminal handles mainly iron and steel, ores, wheat, soybeans, and general cargo. East of the main harbor is the Processed Oil Terminal, which contains two jetty-style wharves and two fuel supply piers. The wharves can accommodate four 10,000-ton tankers at the same time. In the harbor area there are forty-two oil storage tanks with a total capacity of 186,000 cu m.[2] West of the main harbor is the Heizuizi Terminal, which consists of four piers and three wharves. It handles cargo

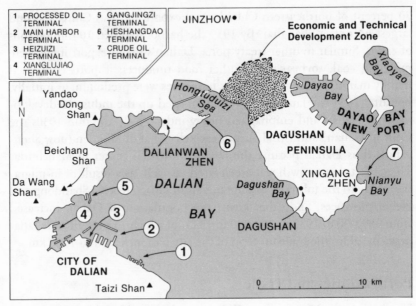

Figure 2.3 Port Facilities of Dalian

with mooring buoys and is used for loading and unloading small coastal craft. Farther west is the Xianglujiao Terminal, used for exporting domestic timber. In 1985 a berth having a capacity of 960,000 tons per year was completed; it is used for handling sundry goods. The fifth terminal, the Gangjingzi Terminal, is especially designed for handling the export of coking coal and other types of coal, vulcanized pitch, cereal, and feed. The terminal has a coal storage capacity of 50,000 sq m and its specialized wharf, 3,000 m long, provides two berths for 10,000-ton ships. In 1985 Dalian Harbor handled 43.8 million tons of cargo.

In addition to these five terminals, the Crude Oil Terminal, built in 1976 in Nianyu Bay at the tip of Dagushan Peninsula, is China's largest deep-water wharf. It consists of two container berths where a 50,000-ton tanker and a 100,000-ton tanker can dock at the same time.[3] The terminal is used to export crude oil which is delivered by pipeline from the Daqing oil field, several thousand kilometers away, at a rate of 70,000 barrels an hour. Another new terminal is being built at Heshangdao for handling 5 million tons of coal a year.

Dalian is China's largest foreign trade port. In 1987, for example, the value of its total export amounted to $5.4 billion, ranking first in China, and the total volume of goods amounted to over 46 million tons (Table

Table 2.2   Total Volume of Goods Handled in
Dalian: 1987

TYPE OF GOODS	WEIGHT (MILLION TONS)	PERCENTAGE OF TOTAL
Crude oil	19.06	41.3
Processed oil	6.59	14.3
Cereal	6.56	14.2
General cargo	5.56	12.1
Iron and steel	2.60	5.7
Ore	2.26	4.9
Timber	0.79	1.7
Coal	0.47	1.0
Others	2.21	4.8
Total	46.10	100.0

Source: Compiled from data of Dalian Statistics Bureau,
1987.

2.2). By 1989 the volume of goods had reached 50 million tons.[4] Dalian
has trade connections with more than a hundred countries and regions
abroad.

In March 1988 Dalian's government started the construction of Dayao
Bay New Port, a key project in China's Seventh Five-Year Plan (1986–
1990). Dayao Bay, about 60 km from Dalian, is a deep, sheltered harbor
having a water area of 33 sq km. The first-phase development of the new
port will cost $83.6 million: $74 million funded by the Chinese government and $9.6 million funded by loan from the World Bank.[5] By 1991,
two 30,000-ton container wharves and two 25,000-ton berths should be
completed. Ultimately the Dayao Bay New Port is planned to have
between seventy and eighty berths for 10,000-ton vessels and a total
annual capacity of 50 million tons serving Dalian's ETDZ. In 1990 a preliminary plan was drawn to develop Dagushan Peninsula as a free port
and transform it into a "Northern Hong Kong."[6]

Industrial Development

Dalian is one of the oldest industrial bases in China. The early industry
included flour milling, vegetable oil refining, sugar refining, and soy-
bean cake manufacturing—general port industries which are operated

with little or no heavy materials and require no special handling facilities for raw materials or products. After 1931 the Japanese started to establish heavy industry in Dalian: special steel, alkaline, cement, machinery, and other factories. Shipbuilding and ship repair continued to expand. By 1934 nearly 70 percent of the 1,835 factories in Dalian were involved in heavy industry.

Since 1949 Dalian has revamped some old industries and developed some new ones such as the manufacture of internal combustion engines, locomotives, roller bearings, special steel, petrochemical products, and electronic equipment. Before 1949, for example, Dalian did not have an electronics industry, but by 1977 it had fifty plants making diverse electronic products such as computers, television sets, video and audio records, and various electronic components.[7] The Dalian Rolling Stock Plant formerly carried out repairs and assembly work. After renovation and expansion, however, it was converted into a locomotive factory producing China's first steam locomotives in 1956 and China's first 4,000-horsepower diesel locomotives in 1969.[8]

The industrial development of Dalian has undergone drastic changes since the open policy was initiated. Dalian's government decided to adopt advanced technology to revamp old enterprises and modernize old equipment without changing their products. In other words, modern technology was used to increase the productivity of the old factories and improve the quality of their manufactured products. For example, the Jinzhou Textile Mill, built in 1923, was equipped with 110,000 spindles which were old and inefficient. After the installation of 30,000 spindles imported in 1980 from Switzerland, the mill could manufacture 45-count yarn and fine terylene cloth, which immediately enjoyed brisk sales on the world market.[9] Similarly, the Dalian Heavy Machine Plant began to produce small steel ingot casting machines after the installation of new equipment supplied by a West German company. From 1979 to 1983, Dalian imported 330 high-technology items using funds gained from foreign investment.[10] In 1983, Dalian's total industrial output was valued at nearly $2.3 billion and the city became the eleventh largest industrial base in China.[11] Nevertheless, most of the industrial products were consumed locally. In 1983, for example, exports of domestic industrial goods accounted for only 28 percent of total exports.

In April 1984 the State Council empowered the city government of Dalian to examine and approve projects to revamp existing factories or build new ones using foreign investment; the approval limit for each project was set at $10 million. Preferential treatment was granted to foreign investors: reduced income tax on foreign enterprises, duty-free imported raw materials, and other incentives. As a result, in 1984 more than a hundred groups of overseas business people came to Dalian to explore the opportunities of investment in harbor construction, hotels, taxi services, and tourist facilities.[12] By the end of that year, 253 transactions of technical importation, valued at $190 million, were concluded; $30 million of this was foreign capital which helped improve the production technique of over 130 enterprises.[13]

Between 1949 and 1985, the industrial growth of Dalian increased at an average rate of 11 percent per year. By 1985 the number of industrial enterprises in Metropolitan Dalian had increased to 2,804, of which 1,357 factories were located in the city proper. The industries are highly diversified, ranging from heavy industry such as shipbuilding, petrochemicals, and diesel locomotives to light industry such as the manufacture of glassware and domestic electrical appliances. By 1986 the city had over 130 types of industries with more than 2,000 industrial enterprises. Machinery, chemical, petrochemical, transport, food processing, and textile industries accounted for 55 percent of the city's total value of industrial output.[14] Industries in the city of Dalian are concentrated in twelve major areas: Zhuan Shan Tun Electronic Industry District, Ronghua Beigang Industrial Warehouse District, Hezuizi Shipbuilding District, Wangjiagou Machinery Industry District, Ganjingzi Petrochemical Industry District, and Paoya Construction Material Industry District; Siergou, Shadong, Wuyi Guangchang, and Nansha are four mixed-industry districts; Youyijie and Yandao are two new industrial estates, the former devoted to textiles and the latter to chemicals (Figure 2.4).

Many of the factories in Dalian, both old and new, are still technologically backward. Most of the work in the machine-building industry is carried out manually, for example, and many factories are still using equipment made in the 1930s.[15] Thus after 1985 the city government began to focus on the technical transformation of about thirty key enterprises and eighteen trades. In the first half of 1985, for example, the city signed 188 contracts worth $117 million; about 70 percent of this was spent on buying technology with the rest accounting for investment funds involved in joint ventures.[16] With foreign investment and imported equipment, the city also planned to build a number of new projects such as a glass processing plant, an ethylene works, and a modern oil refinery with an annual production capacity of 10 million tons.[17] By 1989 Dalian had 364 foreign-invested factories of which 197 were in operation.[18]

The city government has also begun to promote the tourist industry. It

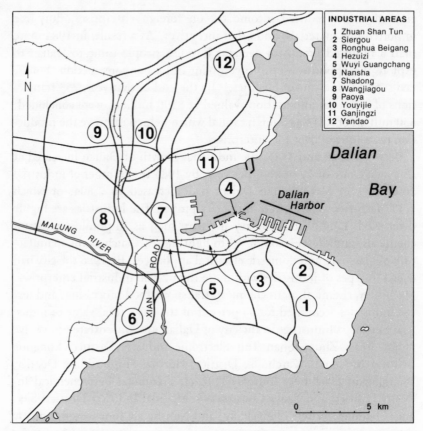

INDUSTRIAL AREAS
1 Zhuan Shan Tun
2 Siergou
3 Ronghua Beigang
4 Hezuizi
5 Wuyi Guangchang
6 Nansha
7 Shadong
8 Wangjiagou
9 Paoya
10 Youyijie
11 Ganjingzi
12 Yandao

Figure 2.4 Industrial Areas of Dalian

is mainly because of the lack of well-equipped hotels that the scenic beaches such as Tiger Beach, Fujia Village, and Xinghai Park on the southern coast of Dalian have not been developed into tourist attractions. In recent years, however, Dalian's government has started the construction of new modern hotels. In 1985, for example, six hotel projects worth about $100 million were signed between Hong Kong investors and the Dalian government; these included the Dalian International, Dalian Furama, and Qing Gang hotels.[19] Dalian Dayang Mansion, a $10 million joint venture between Dalian Co. and Hong Kong Youlian Shipyard, is a 27-story hotel with 300 rooms.[20] It is estimated that during the early 1980s the annual average number of visitors from other parts of China was 300,000 to 400,000; foreign visitors numbered 20,000 to 30,000.

To support its industrial modernization, the city government has paid much attention to technology education. Dalian has more than 50,000 scientists and technicians, sixty-four independent scientific research institutes, another seventy-two research centers affiliated with universities and factories, and a number of universities and professional schools.[21] In recent years Dalian has set up eighteen research and production consortia to tackle technical problems and to quicken the pace at which imported technology is absorbed and applied.

Urban Development

The urbanization of Metropolitan Dalian has been increasing rapidly since 1949. Most of the urban population is concentrated in the City of Dalian, which in 1987 had a population of nearly 2.3 million (46 percent of the Metro's population). The remaining 54 percent were found mainly in the four small cities of Jinzhou, Pulandian, Wafangdian, and Zhuanghe, eleven small towns, and forty-five newly established towns (Figure 2.5). The four small cities had a population between 20,000 and 200,000 each and the small towns had less than 20,000 each; Xingang Zhen and Huatong Zhen are in fact subtowns, having only 2,000 people each. It is obvious that the lack of cities with 200,000 to 900,000 inhabitants represents a break in the urban hierarchy. Future regional planning should be concentrated on the expansion of smaller cities into medium-size cities and subtowns into small cities. The urban expansion of the City of Dalian is expected to follow the northern shore of Dalian Bay to Dalianwan Zhen and the ETDZ, forming a crescent conurbation with Xingang Zhen at the tip of Dagushan Peninsula.

The City of Dalian is divided into six districts, namely Zhongshan, Xigang, Shahekou, Ganjingzi, Xinzhou, and Lushunkou; the last two districts are mostly suburban. After World War II, the old port of Dalian still retained its colonial features. In the former foreign residential areas the avenues were wide and buildings imposing, but in the Chinese residential sectors the roads were muddy and the wooden shacks had neither running water nor sewerage. Indeed, after the war over a thousand families were still jammed together along a stinking ditch in Siergou district.[22] After 1949 the government carried out urban renewal programs and replaced the old dilapidated structures with new apartment buildings. About eighty multistory apartments were built on the former slums in Siergou district, for example. Roads were widened and covered with asphalt. A 27-km-long sewerage system was constructed, taking one-third of the city's treated sewage into the countryside as fertilizer.[23] Today the city has many public parks and small green squares amid tree-lined streets.

The downtown area of Dalian is lively but not crowded. Commercial activities are concentrated on Tianjin and Xian roads (see Figure 2.2). Tianjin Road, including Qingniwa Bridge, is Dalian's commercial spine, a major pedestrian street lined with numerous retailing stores. Since the late 1950s urban expansion has been concentrated in the western part of the city. Xian Road, running from north to south on the western edge of the city, is now a busy commercial axis whose shops cater to customers from the city's western residential and industrial areas. Institutional uses are concentrated in the newly developed areas in Xishan Cun and Ling-shui Hekou on the western fringe of the city.

As Dalian is an old industrial city, its industry is mixed with residential, institutional, recreational, and other uses. Industrial areas, which account for one-quarter of the city's land use, are widely scattered; many of them are intermixed with residential districts and on the leeward side of the prevailing wind. Both Shadong and Wuyi Guangchang industrial areas are situated in residential areas, for example, and have caused serious air and water pollution. A recent survey of 976 factories in the City of Dalian revealed that 346 were established in residential districts. Nansha and certain other industrial areas are within or adjacent to scenic places and detrimental to the development of tourism. Warehouses are scattered throughout the city, although the warehouses for exports are concentrated mainly in Gezhenbao.

In October 1984, the construction of the Dalian ETDZ began near Maqiaoshi Village, which is 33 km from the City of Dalian.[24] (See Figure 2.3.) The first phase of development included the preparation of a site of 3 sq km for technology-intensive enterprises and provision of water, electricity, gas, and other utilities.[25] Bids were invited nationally for the construction of an office building and modern hotels (Figure 2.6).[26] By the end of 1987, some 200 industrial contracts had been signed and about 60 of them are being implemented.[27] In September 1986 the ETDZ had a population of 13,845, of which 5,821 were urban and 8,024 rural. By 1989 an industrial site of 5 sq km had been developed and allocated to over 170 industrial projects valued at $425 million; 130 of these were joint-venture projects valued at $340 million.[28] By 1990 its population had reached 40,000.

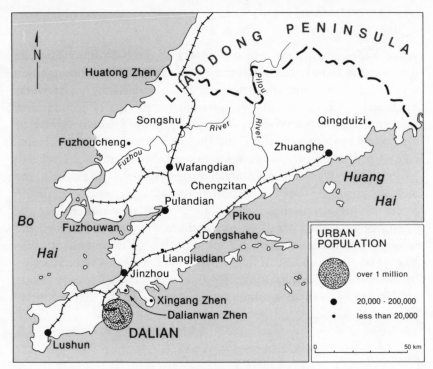

Figure 2.5 Major Urban Centers of Metropolitan Dalian

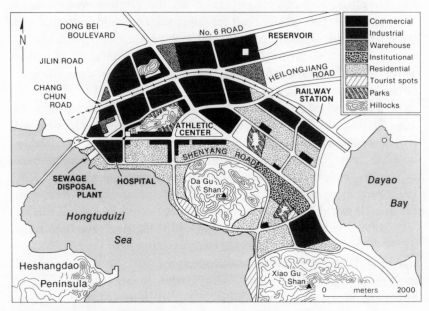

Figure 2.6 Dalian's ETDZ

The ETDZ, eventually covering an area of about 20 sq km, will be developed as an industrial satellite for technically advanced, energy-saving, and pollution-free industries such as the manufacture of precision machinery, precision metallurgy, precision chemical engineering, and modern semiprocessed products. These industries will depend on foreign capital and modern technology. Foreign investors establishing solely foreign-owned enterprises, joint ventures, or other forms of cooperative projects in the ETDZ will enjoy preferential treatment—for example, the income tax will be levied at a reduced rate of 15 percent;[29] legitimate profits of investors after paying income tax will be exempted from tax when being remitted out of China; products manufactured in the zone will be exempted from export tax and consolidated industrial and commercial tax on the industrial link. The zone's shipping is being handled by the Xianglujia General Cargo Terminal until Dayao Bay New Port is completed. By 1988 about thirty factories in the ETDZ were in operation.

Summary

Today Dalian is not only an important entrepôt but also an industrial city. The open policy and the granting of economic autonomy have had a considerable impact on the city's rapid urbanization and industrial and trade development. Between 1979 and 1987, Dalian signed 1,430 contracts valued at about $1.26 billion; 334 of these contracts, valued at $740 million, used foreign capital.[30] Since the early 1980s the city government has been modernizing and expanding the city's infrastructure to keep its rapid urban growth in line with its economic development. In 1984 Zhoushuizi Airport was expanded and the runway widened and lengthened to accommodate jumbo jets such as the Boeing 747. Dalian now has direct air services to Beijing, Shanghai, Qingdao, Guangzhou, and other major cities. Many guest houses and hotels have been revamped, expanded, or newly built. The communication system with the outside world has also been improved. For example, a direct-dialing telephone service from Dalian to Japan and Hong Kong has been instituted. The Shenyang–Dalian 960-channel microwave communication system and the 300-channel coaxial telephone cable project, completed in 1984, are now in operation. The 375-km freeway from Dalian to Shenyang, completed in September 1990, has improved road transport between Dalian and its rich hinterland. The government has started the project of diverting water from the Biliu River to Dalian in order to meet the city's increasing demand for water. In an effort to solve the chronic shortage of electric power, the city government has started construction of a 70,000-kw power station at Heshangdao and the Haicheng–Dalian 500,000-volt transmission and transformer network.[31] The construction of a nuclear power plant is being considered as well.

The prosperity of Dalian still hinges on its trade and industry. The city will continue to boost its exports of cereals, foodstuff, machinery, textiles, and other light industrial products in order to earn more hard currency to fund its imports of technology and modern machinery. In 1987, for example, earnings in foreign exchange of exports totaled $280 million.[32] Tourism is another important means of earning foreign currency. Many beautiful beaches on the irregular coast of Metropolitan Dalian are snuggled into cliffside bays commanding spectacular views of numerous offshore islands and islets. These picturesque coastal spots are potential sites for tourist attraction. The city government has also been trying to develop other new industries such as providing services for the extracting industries of the Bohai and Huanghai oil fields, the manufacture of offshore drilling platforms and facilities for oil jetties, and other enterprises related to offshore oilfield development.

Despite the recent expansion of Dalian's infrastructure and other supporting services, many foreign entrepreneurs still hesitate to invest in the city. For example, it has been reported that Japanese businessmen who arrived to negotiate contracts with the Dalian authorities were frequently put off by the lack of clear answers to their questions about capital cost and profitability (for example, the cost of connecting utilities to plant sites).[33] Another negative factor is the tendency of the Chinese authorities to change the rules applicable to existing investors—such as an abrupt upward revision of the export ratio applied to an established factory. Some investors feel that the joint ventures have a limited life cycle and will then revert automatically to Chinese ownership. The shortage of electricity—attributed to a rapid increase in domestic use of television sets, refrigerators, and other electric appliances—has disrupted construction work on investment projects and operation of factories. Transport bottlenecks in Dalian Harbor are persistent. According to Shen Dequian, manager of the Ports Business Department, ships using the twenty-two berths reserved for international shipping faced delays of up to three-and-a-half months during the busiest season of the year.[34] Until the completion of the new port at Dayao Bay, Dalian's harbor facilities will continue to fall far short of the needs.

Foreign investors have also listed other problems such as insufficient and unsanitary water supplies, overpriced housing, difficulty in obtaining air tickets, and insufficient supply of raw materials. All these complaints have been taken seriously by the city government. Accordingly, in the spring of 1988 the government met with all the foreign investors in Dalian and invited them to express their grievances and make suggestions for improvement.[35] One immediate effect was improved air service between Dalian and Beijing as well as Guangzhou. After the 4 June event in Tiananmen Square in 1989, however, an investment slump set in. The cruise ship trade, for example, which usually brings in some 15,000 high-spending tourists annually, has virtually stopped. Since the beginning of 1990 the Dalian government has been working hard to lure foreign investments again. In February 1990, the Pfizer Company decided to build a $30 million pharmaceutical plant in the ETDZ.[36] This is a major economic boost for Dalian. It should encourage the city government to strive harder to attract foreign investment and technology and continue its economic reform under the open policy.

Notes

1. Chuang Miao, "The Port of Luta: From Colony to Socialist City," *China Reconstructs* 4 (1975): 32.

2. Anon., *Port of Dalian* (Dalian: Dalian Harbor Administrative Bureau, 1985), p. 13.

3. Ibid., p. 12.

4. "Rapid Increase of Exports of Products Manufactured by Dalian Chemical Company," *Shenzhen Special Zone Daily,* 2 January 1990.

5. "The Construction Work on Dalian's Dayao Bay Has Already Begun," *Wah Kiu Yat Pao,* 8 March 1988.

6. "Dalian Is Planning to Build a Free Port on Dagushan Peninsula," *Ta Kung Pao,* 30 December 1989; and "Dalian Is Considering a Northern Hong Kong," *Ta Kung Pao,* 22 April 1990.

7. Lu Dienwen, "Dalian's Growing Electronics Industry," *China's Foreign Trade* 3 (1977): 25.

8. Chuang, "The Port of Luta," p. 29.

9. Ibid.

10. Ibid.

11. Wei Fuhai, "Develop the Advantages of Dalian to Carry Out the Policy of Further Opening," in Lu Yu (ed.), *Fourteen Coastal Cities of the PRC Handbook* (Hong Kong: Guangming Daily and Wah Kwong Newspaper Ltd., 1985), p. 103; and Wei Fuhai, "Dalian, China's Northernmost Gateway," *PRC Quarterly,* January 1985, p. 45.

12. Wei, "Dalian: China's Northernmost Gateway," p. 46.

13. Dalian City People's Government, *Introduction to Dalian*, 1985, p. 5.

14. Various official statistics, State Statistical Bureau, Dalian.

15. Du Zuji and Wang Liu, "Dalian—Northernmost Gateway to China," *Beijing Review* 43 (1984): 6.

16. "Dalian Hotel Projects Get Local Backing," *South China Morning Post*, 15 August 1985.

17. Wei, "Dalian: China's Northernmost Gateway."

18. "Interview with Mayor Wei Fuhai," *Ta Kung Pao*, 28 April 1990.

19. "Dalian Hotel Projects Get Local Backing," *South China Morning Post*, 15 August 1985.

20. "Youlian Shipyard Invests Again and Is Building a Hotel in the City Center of Dalian," *Wen Wei Po*, 27 March 1985.

21. Du and Wang, "Dalian—Northernmost Gateway to China," p. 27.

22. Chuang, "The Port of Luta," p. 33.

23. Ibid.

24. "Dalian Is the First City of the Fourteen Open Coastal Cities to Start the Development of an Economic and Technical Development Zone Today," *Ta Kung Pao*, 16 October 1984.

25. "The Construction of an Industrial Satellite Starts Today in China's First Economic and Technical Development Zone," *Ming Pao*, 16 October 1984.

26. Du and Wang, "Dalian—Northernmost Gateway to China," p. 28.

27. "The *Sanlai Yibao* Meeting Will Be Held in Early March," *Ta Kung Pao*, 22 January 1988.

28. *Shenzhen Special Zone Daily*, 2 January 1990.

29. "Dalian's Economic and Technical Development Zone Ranks First in China's Total Industrial Investment," *Wen Wei Po*, 9 October 1984.

30. "*Sanlai Yibao* Cooperation Talk Will Be Held in March in Dalian," *Wen Wei Po*, 30 January 1988; Gao Guo Zhu, "Persist in the Policy of Opening to the World, Welcome Foreign Companies to Invest in Dalian," *Dalian Foreign Trade*, June 1988, p. 10.

31. State Statistical Bureau, *China Urban Statistics, 1986* (Hong Kong: Longman Group (Far East) Ltd., 1987), p. 34.

32. Gao, "Persist in the Policy."

33. Charles Smith, "The Ties That Bind," *Far Eastern Economic Review*, 23 April 1986, p. 75.

34. Ibid., p. 77.

35. "Spring Comes Early to Dalian," *Shenzhen Special Zone Daily*, 5 June 1988.

36. "Pfizer in US$30m Move into Dalian," *South China Morning Post*, 5 February 1990.

3 Tianjin: North China's Reviving Metropolis

SEN-DOU CHANG, XU-WEI HU, AND JUN-JIE SUN

TIANJIN IS THE LARGEST port city in North China in terms of population. It is one of the three largest cities in China under the direct jurisdiction of the central government and has an administrative status equivalent to a province. Located at the confluent point of the Hai He drainage system and 130 km southeast of Beijing, Tianjin enjoys a strategic position for urban development. The urban districts of Tianjin had a population of 5,543,700 in 1987. If the five rural counties under the city's jurisdiction are included, however, Tianjin's population was 8,243,400 in 1987 spread over a total area of 11,305 sq km.[1] On either account, Tianjin is the third largest urban center in China in terms of population.

The Gate to Beijing

Coastal cities in North China were developed relatively later than inland cities. Compared with other port cities in China, however, Tianjin has a relatively long history thanks to its proximity to the capital city of Beijing. The emergence of Tianjin in the middle of the twelfth century as a transport center was due mainly to the need of a break-of-bulk point for shipping grain to Beijing. During the Yuan dynasty (1280–1368), the development of both the sea route and the Grand Canal for shipping grain from the south further enhanced the importance of Tianjin, where a number of warehouses for storage of grain were established. In the early fifteenth century, when the Ming moved its imperial capital from Nanjing to Beijing, Tianjin became a walled city—a strong military base for protecting the capital city.[2] In the eighteenth century when the salt industry spread along the Bo Hai coast with the application of solar energy, Tianjin emerged as the collection and distribution center for salt. As inland waterways for navigation were improved, the city's volume of trade steadily increased. Gradually, Tianjin became an important commercial and financial center in North China.

Economic prosperity declined temporarily during the mid-nineteenth century, when European nations trading with China pressed their demands for commercial and diplomatic privileges. The Treaty of Tianjin, which ended the Anglo-French War (1856–1858) against China, authorized the establishment of British and French concessions in Tianjin in 1858. Two years later, as a result of the Peking Treaty, Tianjin was declared an open trading port. Modern industries initiated by both Chinese officials and foreign businessmen were developed. Among the earliest industries were the packing industry, Tianjin Machinery Bureau, Daku Shipyard, and Tianjin Railway Company. After the Sino-Japanese War in 1894–1895, foreign banks and enterprises were established one after another. In 1900, the Boxer Incident led to the occupation of the city by Western forces and the destruction of the old city wall. Between 1895 and 1902, concessions were given to Japan, Germany, Russia, Austria-Hungary, Italy, and Belgium. Tianjin has had more foreign concessions than any other port city in China.

By the turn of the present century, with the construction of the Tianjin–Pukou, Beijing–Shenyang, Beijing–Hankou, and Beijing–Baotou railways, Tianjin had extended its hinterland enormously to cover a large portion of North China and became the second largest port city in the nation in terms of total import-export values and an important ocean shipping center in the western Pacific. Under the Republic of China (1912–1949), Tianjin was a special municipality under the direct administration of the national government. By the early 1930s, Tianjin's export volume of cotton accounted for 47 percent of the nation's total and leather and woolen goods amounted to 60 percent.[3] The major imports were grain, textiles, sugar, paper, and tobacco. The total foreign trade volume in the early 1930s accounted for more than 20 percent of the nation's total. During World War I, Chinese nationals developed modern sectors of industry, such as spinning, looming, chemicals, flour milling, hide processing, iron and steel, machinery, and shipbuilding. By the middle of the 1930s, Tianjin had more than 3,000 enterprises covering fifty sectors. In 1937, the urban population of Tianjin exceeded 1 million, making the city the second largest in China. During the eight years of Japanese occupation (1937–1945), a number of military-oriented industries were developed by the Japanese to meet their wartime needs, including the construction of Tangku New Harbor. During this period and China's civil war in the following years, Tianjin's industries suffered substantial decline, although the urban population had increased to 1,790,000 when the People's Republic was founded in 1949.[4]

A survey of 1950 disclosed that there were about 10,000 industrial enterprises in Tianjin. Among these, only ninety-nine employed more than 200 workers each; the majority had fewer than 10 workers.[5] More than two-thirds of Tianjin's industrial output value was accounted for by light industry, particularly cotton textiles, which contributed about 40 percent of the total output value of light industry. Cotton textile manufacturing was followed in order of importance by flour milling, vegetable oil processing, tobacco, matches, rubber goods, and paper products. During the First Five-Year Plan (1953–1957), efforts were made to develop heavy industries, such as iron and steel, textile machinery, construction machinery, electric equipment, chemicals, and thermal power, utilizing coal, iron ore, and salt produced locally or in the vicinity.

During the period 1953–1979, Tianjin's industry grew at 9 percent annually, a rate that was relatively low compared with the national average of 11.1 percent and Beijing's 14.5 percent.[6] From 1950 to 1980, the central government invested a total of 30 billion *yuan* for industrial infrastructure construction in the Beijing–Tianjin–Tangshan region. Of this amount, 52.2 percent was allocated for Beijing and 30.5 percent for Tianjin, reflecting the government's inclination toward the capital city.[7] For a long time, Tianjin was overshadowed by Beijing in the competition for capital investment. Another factor which constrained Tianjin's industrial growth during this period was the emergence of several textile manufacturing centers in the cotton-producing regions of the North China plain, such as Shijiazhuang, Hantan, and Xintai, so that the supply of raw material to Tianjin was seriously affected.

Physical Environment, Resource Base, and Industrial Location

Situated in the northeastern corner of the North China plain with the Yanshan Mountains in the north and Bo Hai in the east, Tianjin municipality runs 186 km from north to south and 101 km from east to west, occupying a total area of 11,305 sq km, including 330 sq km in the city proper. With Beijing lying 130 km to the northwest and the industrial city of Tangshan 100 km to the northeast, Tianjin commands a nodal position in the Beijing–Tianjin–Tangshan Economic Region, the most important and highly industrialized region in North China. The municipality has six urbanized districts in the city proper, three coastal districts (Tanggu, Hangu, and Dagang), four suburban districts (coinciding with the four cardinal directions), and five rural counties (Jixian, Baodi, Wuqing, Jinghai, and Ninghe).[8] (See Figure 3.1.)

Tianjin Harbor is composed of three ports: Tianjin port, Tanggu, and Xingang. Tianjin port is the oldest port area along the banks of the Hai He and, due to shallowness of the water, is capable of handling only inland steamers and Chinese junks. Tanggu, on the south side of the Hai He estuary, is capable of handling ships up to 5,000 tons. Xingang, situated on the north side of the Hai He estuary, is the principal port of Tianjin and has thirty-five berths, including twenty berths capable of handling ships up to 10,000 tons and one berth of 35,000 tons. Xingang also contains China's largest containerized cargo berth and operates twenty major ocean shipping lines accessible to more than 150 countries and regions. In 1987, Tianjin Harbor handled 17.25 million tons of goods (compared with 16 million tons in 1984). It ranked seventh in the nation in that year in terms of total volume of incoming and outgoing cargo, after Shanghai, Qinhuangdao, Dalian, Qingdao, Huangpu, and Ningbo.[9] As each square meter of berth in Tianjin Harbor has 1,000 sq m of land behind it, the harbor has great potential for expansion. Such an asset is enjoyed by only a few ports in China.

The port city of Tianjin has a vast hinterland that can be divided into two macrozones based on the intensity of interaction. The immediate hinterland, which includes the Beijing–Tianjin–Tangshan Economic Region and the province of Hebei, is linked with Tianjin not only by railways and highways but by drainage systems of the Hai He and various traditional socioeconomic ties. The expressway linking Tanggu and Beijing via Tianjin, completed in 1990, will certainly provide the much needed connection between these two great cities in North China. Tianjin's hinterland extends over an area of 1 million sq km in North China and the northwest to include the bulk of Shanxi province, central and western portions of Inner Mongolia, and the Ningxia Hui Autonomous Region. Railways, such as those linking Beijing–Baotou, Baotou–Yinchuan, and Taiyuan–Shijiazhuang, are the major connections with the extended hinterland. Tianjin's hinterland has been very much a legacy of history, as traditional caravan routes between Tianjin and Inner Mongolia have been largely followed by the railways constructed since the beginning of the present century. This vast hinterland, which covers more than one-tenth of China's territory, comprises 12 percent of China's population, three-fifths of its coal deposits, one-sixth of its oil reserves, one-seventh of its iron ore, and one-sixth of its total industrial output value.

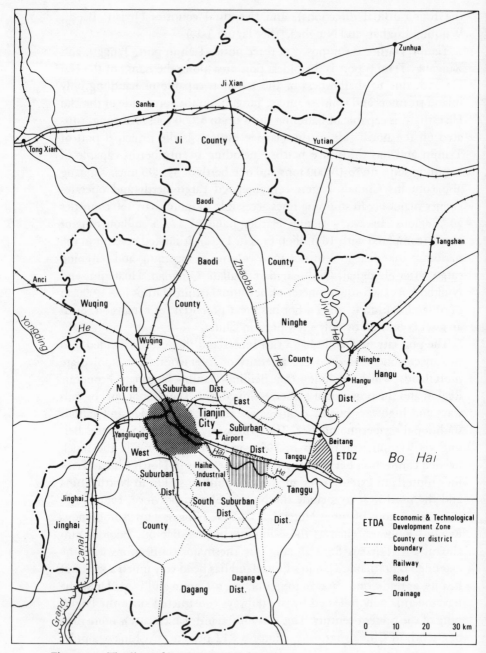

Figure 3.1 Tianjin and Its Geographical Setting

The municipality of Tianjin is abundant in natural resources of economic value, including some minerals and construction materials.[10] Of the fossil fuel reserves, petroleum, natural gas, and coal are almost equally important. The Dagang oil field, lying about 60 km to the southeast of Tianjin city, is one of China's most productive oil and gas fields. It was discovered and operated commercially in 1964 on the barren salt flat. Although the underground oil-bearing plate was broken by faults and no regular pattern could be discerned, the quality of oil is superior to that of Daqing in Heilongjiang, China's largest oil field. (Dagang oil has a sulfur content of 0.08 percent as compared with 2.5 percent for Arabian oil.) The oil-bearing plate extends east to the offshore area to form the Bo Hai oil field, now under intensive exploration. Since its exploitation in 1964, Dagang oil field has produced more than 40 million tons of crude oil and over 9 billion cubic meters of natural gas. In recent years, the field has produced 3 million tons of crude oil and 5,000 million cubic meters of natural gas annually over a controllable oil-bearing area of 250 sq km. The suburban counties of Jixian and Baodi have verified coal reserves of more than 500 million tons, largely unexploited. Tianjin is also well endowed with geothermal resources. The total area with terrestrial heat covers more than 800 sq km, and the total hot water reserves amount to 20 billion tons. The highest temperature of the hot water drawn to the surface reaches 98 °C.

Changlu salt, well known in China, is produced mainly from Tanggu and Hangu salterns in Tianjin. More than 2 million tons of salt is produced in these salterns with a sodium chloride content of up to 98 percent. The huge marble and pottery clay reserves in Jixian county have already become an attraction to foreign investors.

The most valuable resource for Tianjin's industrial and urban development is probably land. The three coastal districts, together with the Southern Suburban District and Ninghe county, share a total area of more than 33,000 ha of seashore and wasteland. Tianjin's long-term urban plan calls for shifting the industrial centers eastward toward the coast. Tanggu is being developed as a modern port city, and with the expected growth of the ETDZ it will be a center of export-oriented enterprises and foreign trade. The lower reaches of the Hai He will be developed as an area of heavy industry with metallurgical processing and warehouses as major economic activities. Dagang is going to become a diversified and comprehensive industrial center, but oil refineries and petrochemical installations will still dominate its landscape. Hangu, located along the coast, is planned to become a chemical and biological industrial center with marine resources as chief raw materials.[11] Seldom in China are the suburban districts of a large city so well endowed with energy, chemicals, marine resources, and extensive land (much of it wasteland that has little value other than for industrial and urban development).

Economic Structure and Urban Infrastructure

Tianjin was originally developed as a trade port to serve the capital city of Beijing. Since the opening of Tianjin as a treaty port in 1860, it was developed to become a major industrial center in North China. During the eighty-eight years between 1860 and 1948, a total of $119 million was invested in the city for industrial development by foreign countries. Prior to 1949, as mentioned previously, Tianjin was essentially a light industrial center processing and manufacturing simple consumer goods.

Although Tianjin's rate of industrial growth in the decades since 1949 has been slower than that of Beijing, the industrial program under the People's Republic has changed the city's industrial structure drastically. As shown in Table 3.1, the first twenty-five years of the People's Republic witnessed a decline in relative importance of both primary and tertiary industries, while secondary industry rose rapidly. Since tertiary industry was long neglected as "unproductive" industry in China, the number of employees declined proportionately. The decline in tertiary industry reached its nadir in the mid-1970s. Since then, this sector has shown signs of recovery, particularly in recent years. By 1982, the percentage distribution of these three sectors in terms of employment was 31.86, 45.30, and 22.84. Although the tertiary industry's share of 22.84 percent was a significant improvement over previous years, it is still low compared with cities in other countries. The low proportion of labor employment in the service sector in Tianjin, as in other large Chinese cities, has been alleviated by the infiltration of an increasingly large floating population from other parts of the country not accounted for in the official urban census and largely engaged in service-related activities.

Compared with other large coastal cities in China, Tianjin's economy has been oriented more toward heavy industry. In 1949, nearly 78 percent of Tianjin's industrial employees were in light industry. By 1970, the number of employees in heavy industry had exceeded that in light industry for the first time. In 1983, the latest figures available, 53.7 per-

Table 3.1 Gross Product of Tianjin Municipality (in million *yuan*):
1952–1987

YEAR	GNP	PRIMARY INDUSTRY		SECONDARY INDUSTRY		TERTIARY INDUSTRY	
		TOTAL VALUE	%	TOTAL VALUE	%	TOTAL VALUE	%
1952	1,280	185	14.5	628	49.1	467	36.4
1957	2,411	247	10.2	1,318	54.7	846	35.1
1962	2,425	212	8.7	1,408	58.1	805	33.2
1965	3,596	351	9.8	2,296	63.8	949	26.4
1970	5,099	380	7.5	3,580	70.2	1,139	22.3
1975	6,973	437	6.3	5,029	72.1	1,507	21.6
1980	10,352	653	6.3	7,243	70.0	2,456	23.7
1985	17,571	1,295	7.4	11,423	65.0	4,853	27.6
1986	19,467	1,651	8.5	12,249	62.9	5,567	28.6
1987	21,600	1,900	8.8	13,500	62.5	6,200	28.7
Employment in 1982			31.86		45.30		22.84

Source: Sun Lianxi, He Zhongxiu, and Wang Minghao, "Prospects of Tianjin City," paper presented to the International Conference on China's Urbanization, Tianjin, August 1988.

Table 3.2 Industrial Production Values of Tianjin (in million *yuan*
adjusted to 1980 price): 1949–1987

YEAR	TOTAL INDUSTRIAL PRODUCTION VALUE	LIGHT INDUSTRY		HEAVY INDUSTRY	
		PRODUCTION VALUE	%	PRODUCTION VALUE	%
1949	654	577	88.3	77	11.7
1952	1,752	1,474	84.1	278	15.9
1957	3,794	2,780	73.3	1,014	26.7
1962	3,847	2,589	67.3	1,258	32.7
1965	5,935	3,726	62.8	2,209	37.2
1970	9,642	5,303	55.0	4,339	45.0
1975	14,268	7,129	50.0	7,139	50.0
1980	18,836	10,175	54.0	8,661	46.0
1983	22,920	12,997	56.7	9,923	43.3
1985	28,580	15,548	54.4	13,032	45.6
1987	32,586	17,465	51.6	15,121	48.4

Sources: Tianjin Statistical Yearbook, 1986, p. 137; *Tianjin Economic Yearbook,* 1988, p. 681.

cent of Tianjin's industrial employees were engaged in heavy industry versus 46.3 percent in light industry. In terms of industrial output values, however, light industry was still ahead of heavy industry by a small margin, though the gap has been closing in recent years (Table 3.2). The relatively low output value of Tianjin's heavy industry reflects largely the price structure in a socialist country. The low productivity of large state enterprises, as well as antiquated equipment in Tianjin's heavy industry, may also contribute to its low output value.

Another important transformation in Tianjin's industrial structure in the past few decades has been a gradual shift of raw material for light industry from agricultural products to nonagricultural products (Table 3.3), reflecting a shift from food processing and textile manufacturing to durable household consumer goods and appliances such as cosmetic chemicals, sewing machines, watches, television sets, cameras, tape recorders, plastic and metal utensils, and electric appliances. All these consumer goods are relatively new to the Chinese and, with increasing nationwide demand, have been growing at a rate ranging from 20 to 50 percent annually in recent years in Tianjin. Tianjin's consumer goods

Table 3.3   Composition of Light Industries in Tianjin (in million *yuan* adjusted to 1980 price): 1949–1987

		PRODUCTION VALUE			
YEAR	TOTAL	RAW MATERIAL FROM AGRICULTURAL PRODUCTS	%	RAW MATERIAL FROM NONAGRICULTURAL PRODUCTS	%
1949	577	509	88.2	68	11.8
1952	1,474	1,311	88.9	163	11.1
1957	2,780	2,091	75.2	689	24.8
1962	2,589	1,821	70.3	768	29.7
1965	3,726	2,687	72.1	1,039	27.9
1970	5,303	3,565	67.2	1,738	32.8
1975	7,129	4,370	61.3	2,759	38.7
1978	7,768	4,741	61.0	3,027	39.0
1980	10,175	6,491	63.8	3,684	36.2
1985	15,548	8,722	56.2	6,826	43.8
1987	17,465	9,221	52.7	8,244	47.3

Sources: Tianjin Statistical Yearbook, 1986, p. 139; *Tianjin Economic Yearbook,* 1988, p. 681.

industry has contributed substantially to the national market. In 1987, some 15.7 percent of China's bicycles, 5.2 percent of its television sets, and 3.7 percent of its household refrigerators were produced in Tianjin.

Since the mid-1950s, Tianjin has become one of the key heavy industrial centers in North China. During the First Five-Year Plan, much investment was allocated in Tianjin to expand or develop industries of iron and steel, power generators, tractors, chemicals, and machinery such as lathes, looms, spindles, electric motors, and construction machines. In the mid-1960s, with the discovery of Dagang oil field, the city developed oil refinery and petrochemical industries. In recent years, manufacturing and processing have developed rapidly while extraction industries have experienced substantial decline (Table 3.4). Tianjin's heavy industry has gradually shifted to the manufacturing of specialized machinery such as petrochemical machinery, oil drilling equipment, cranes, elevators, light duty trucks, and ship propellers.[12]

For a period of thirty years, Tianjin's industrial development has emphasized heavy industry. Since the early 1980s, city leaders have tried to redress this imbalance by stressing light industry and instituting new policies that promote economic efficiency and self-management. Development plans are now aimed at emerging high-growth industries and

Table 3.4　Composition of Heavy Industries in Tianjin (in million *yuan* adjusted to 1980 price): 1949–1987

		PRODUCTION VALUE					
YEAR	TOTAL	EXTRACTION	%	PROCESSING	%	MANUFACTURING	%
1949	77	14	18.2	28	36.4	35	45.4
1952	278	20	7.2	113	40.6	145	52.2
1957	1,014	46	4.5	484	47.8	484	47.7
1962	1,258	58	4.6	554	44.0	646	51.4
1965	2,209	79	3.6	996	45.1	1,134	51.3
1970	4,339	279	6.4	1,583	36.5	2,477	57.1
1975	7,139	951	13.3	2,420	33.9	3,768	52.8
1978	7,747	1,090	14.1	2,581	33.3	4,076	52.6
1980	8,661	1,350	15.6	2,920	33.7	4,391	50.7
1985	13,032	569	4.4	4,956	38.0	7,507	57.6
1987	15,121	652	4.3	5,846	38.7	8,623	57.0

Sources: Tianjin Statistical Yearbook, 1986, p. 140; *Tianjin Economic Yearbook,* 1988, p. 681.

those sectors in which Tianjin has a resource advantage or industrial expertise. The city is now building on its foundation in chemicals and pharmaceuticals by expanding the processing of marine chemicals and petrochemicals. Priority is also given to textiles, garments, metallurgy, medical technology, food processing, machine building, electronics, and motor vehicle production. Indeed, Tianjin has become one of the bases of China's motor vehicle production since it started to import advanced technology from Japan in 1984 to assemble Daihatsu cars. The Tianjin Auto Company turned out 45,000 vehicles in 1988 and 57,000 in 1989. Its products are mainly light-duty vehicles, with more than 80 percent of the parts produced in China.[13]

Among the coastal cities in China, the gross value of Tianjin's industrial output is second only to that of Shanghai. Compared with other coastal cities in China, Tianjin's industrial structure is relatively balanced between light and heavy as shown in Table 3.5, reflecting the city's comparative advantage for developing both industries in terms of resource availability, progressive urban infrastructure, and skilled technicians and workers. Few coastal cities in China can rival Tianjin in these three aspects of industrial development.

China's urban economy in the past few decades has been characterized by heavy state investment in "productive" sectors (processing and manufacturing) with little input in "unproductive" sectors (urban infrastructure). Such unbalanced urban development has had a negative impact on China's economic performance. The city of Tianjin for many years has been under the shadow of Beijing in competition for resources for urban infrastructure construction. The 1976 Tangshan earthquake further deteriorated Tianjin's urban facilities, as more than two-thirds of the city's buildings either collapsed or were seriously damaged.[14] A total of 200,000 people lost their homes and had to be sheltered in temporary huts on the sidewalks. Starting in 1980, the central government poured 3.7 billion *yuan* into the city for urban reconstruction. In the following year a new mayor, Li Ruihuan (who helped to build the Great Hall of the People in Beijing as a carpenter in the late 1950s), took office and started to tackle the serious housing problem.

During the three years between 1981 and 1983, the new mayor and his staff mobilized all available resources and manpower for the restoration of damaged buildings, infrastructure, and utilities. The demolition of damaged buildings and reconstruction of old urban districts paved the way for the various urban renewal projects Tianjin has become famous

Table 3.5 Production Value of Tianjin's Industry by Sector (in million *yuan* adjusted to 1980 price): 1952–1987

SECTOR	1952	1957	1978	1980	1984	1985	1987	1986–1987 GROWTH RATE
Metallurgical	56	319	1,715	1,897	2,114	2,393	2,938	7.5
Electrical	19	40	331	405	506	552	616	4.2
Coal and coke	—	—	—	—	—	31	56	69.7
Petroleum	1	6	755	945	1,049	1,230	1,407	9.8
Chemical	94	367	2,537	2,923	3,789	4,157	4,659	6.4
Machinery	157	651	4,414	5,103	7,423	9,224	11,164	15.7
Construction material	20	52	310	362	479	585	704	2.8
Lumber	32	91	143	159	214	225	208	-2.3
Food	461	684	1,163	1,501	1,828	1,921	2,127	6.0
Textile	698	1,027	2,310	3,109	4,757	5,021	5,126	2.1
Garment	51	120	408	627	829	877	981	4.6
Leather	12	62	149	258	298	349	386	0.3
Paper	53	129	325	361	384	358	403	6.6
Educational supplies	36	91	468	602	737	874	949	5.3
Others	62	155	487	584	742	785	826	3.7
City total	1,752	3,794	15,515	18,836	25,149	28,580	32,586	8.5

Sources: Tianjin Statistical Yearbook, 1986, p. 141; Tianjin Economic Yearbook, 1988, p. 683.

for in recent years. One of the most difficult problems in urban renewal projects, not only in China but in other developing countries as well, is the provision of temporary accommodations to the residents whose houses are being demolished and rebuilt, Tianjin's designation of a number of public houses for such purposes was quite instrumental in its speedy completion of urban renewal projects. Most projects, to the envy of other large cities such as Shanghai, were completed within a year. Between 1981 and 1987, new residences with a total floor space of more than 23 million square meters were built and fourteen new residential areas constructed in urban districts of Tianjin.[15] Most buildings are four to six-story walk-up apartments, although fifteen to eighteen-story high rises have also been constructed with elevators in more accessible locations in old districts. Inside the housing blocks, individual apartment size varies from one to four rooms, with a total floor space of 15 to 24 sq m.[16] Each family has its own kitchen and bathroom facilities equipped with a simple shower. In contrast to many other Chinese cities where a monolithic style of architecture often dominates residential landscapes, Tianjin's public housing is characterized by diversified architecture and color and is often surrounded by yards or parks, perhaps a tradition inherited from the days of foreign concessions.

In 1983, in spite of local objections based on nationalistic sentiment, the mayor proposed the renovation and repair of all the salvageable old buildings in the nine foreign concessions. In the following three years, repair, remodeling, and repainting of these old structures have made Tianjin a museum of nineteenth-century European architecture and urban landscapes, much to the delight of tourists. During the same period, cultural relics have been restored and renovated. In 1986, a Cultural Street was constructed around the rebuilt Tianhou Temple, the temple of the sea goddess. Nearly a kilometer long and 7 m wide, the street is lined with small gray buildings of the Qing dynasty supported by red columns. The eaves of the buildings carry paintings of stories from the past; the walls are decorated with 500 traditional Tianjin brick carvings. Shop signs are in the old calligraphy, and inside the stores are scrolls describing scenes of ancient Tianjin. Many traditional goods are sold in these shops: folk handicrafts, brushes, ink sticks, marble seals, porcelain, jade, and scrolls of landscape paintings and calligraphy. Following the opening of Cultural Street, a number of service-oriented urban projects were also completed, including a food mall where Chinese delicacies can be tasted, an international market, a garment exhibition center, a youth recreational center, and Hotel Street. All these were part of an urban renewal scheme and have been built in such a way as to preserve traditional Chinese architecture and urban landscapes. Much of this urban renovation with a strong cultural flavor has been imitated in other large cities in China, as exemplified by the new market mall near the Confucius Temple in Nanjing that was completed in the summer of 1987.

Besides innovative programs of housing construction and urban renewal projects, Tianjin has also been known for its improvement in urban utilities and road construction. In 1983, the diversion of water from Luan He, a major drainage system in eastern Hebei, was completed and relieved the city's water shortage for the foreseeable future. The project was rather controversial at the time, however, as it was carried out at the expense of much rural interest in the semiarid regions of eastern Hebei.

In 1984, a huge sewage treatment plant was built at Jizhuangzi. The largest treatment plant at that time in China, it was capable of treating 260,000 tons of wastewater per day, equivalent to one-quarter of the total wastewater in the city, and serving an urban area of 3,770 ha including 650 factories. The wastewater is treated in two stages, including sludge treatment, and is recycled for irrigation of farmland in rural counties. The sludge is used as fertilizer for vegetable gardens as well as an element for generating 3.65 million cubic meters of methane gas, a cooking fuel in nearby households.[17]

In 1985, a new expressway was completed with cloverleaf and overpass systems. Ringing the city, it links fourteen major roads radiating out from the center and connects the new satellite cities. Under construction are two other expressways circling the city proper. In 1986, a four-lane freeway connecting Tianjin, Tanggu port, and the ETDZ was opened. The westward extension of this freeway reached Beijing in 1990. By the end of 1987, a total of 2,900 km of road including 145 bridges had been completed, forming a highway network that integrates intracity routes with intercity trunk lines for Tianjin.

The project of supplying cooking gas to urban residents was accomplished in 1987. As shown in Table 3.6, Tianjin ranks as one of the first cities in China where gas is gradually replacing coal for cooking. During the period of 1981–1987, more than 300,000 sq m of courtyard gardens were added to the urban landscape. The city's parks, gardens, and courtyard greens amounted to a total area of 1,563 ha in 1987, equivalent to 13 percent of the total area of the six urban districts.[18] Although this 13

Table 3.6   Urban Infrastructural Indicators of Tianjin Compared with Other Coastal Cities: 1987

CITY	PER CAPITA HOUSING AREA (SQ M)	% OF HOUSEHOLDS WITH FAUCET WATER	% OF HOUSEHOLDS USING GAS	PAVED ROAD AREA PER CAPITA (SQ M)	TELEPHONES PER 100 PERSONS	SEWAGE PIPELINE LENGTH PER 10,000 PERSONS (KM)
Tianjin	6.08	77.8	26.8	4.6	3.1	3.9
Dalian	5.49	76.4	28.1	3.3	2.9	2.5
Qinhuangdao	5.95	53.9	—	8.8	4.0	6.6
Yantai	7.00	52.9	—	1.8	1.0	2.9
Qingdao	5.80	94.1	8.3	4.4	3.6	4.4
Lianyungang	5.84	59.8	0	1.6	2.2	2.8
Nantong	5.60	93.4	6.9	4.0	3.3	3.5
Shanghai	6.15	100.0	47.0	1.9	4.8	2.2
Ningbo	7.20	52.5	—	2.0	3.9	4.0
Wenzhou	7.79	88.3	—	2.2	2.9	2.2
Fuzhou	7.26	82.5	—	3.0	3.3	3.6
Guangzhou	4.49	87.8	—	1.9	5.2	2.2
Zhanjiang	5.61	45.5	—	2.6	1.7	1.5
Beihai	6.32	59.6	—	4.7	1.7	4.8

Source: China Urban Statistical Yearbook, 1988, pp. 338–356.

Table 3.7   Growth of Tianjin's Urban Infrastructure: 1980–1986

INFRASTRUCTURE	1980	1986	CHANGE (%)	ANNUAL GROWTH RATE (%)
Housing area (1,000 sq m)	22,180	45,240	103.97	17.32
Water consumption (1,000 tons)	233,500	366,530	56.97	9.49
Sales volume of liquefied gas (tons)	29,015	34,801	19.94	3.32
Households using gas (%)	31.21	62.20	30.99	5.17
Paved road area (1,000 sq m)	7,280	12,100	66.21	11.04
Public vehicles (units)	1,373	1,739	26.66	4.44
Sewage (km)	1,160	1,750	56.81	9.47
Sewage discharge (1,000 tons/day)	840	1,200	42.86	7.14
Green area (ha)	508.67	1,432.80	181.68	30.28

Source: Xu Runda, Teng Shaohua, and Ning Shuchen, "The Construction of Tianjin's Infrastructural Facilities," paper presented to the International Conference on China's Urbanization, Tianjin, August 1988.

percent is still small compared with cities of comparable size in the Western world, the figure represents a significant achievement in environmental improvement among cities in North China. Haihe Park, completed in 1983, covers an area of more than 200,000 sq m along the west bank of the river in a belt shape. The park was converted from old slum areas and dumping grounds of foreign concession days and offers innovative recreational and entertainment facilities. A few selected indicators depicting the improvement of Tianjin's urban infrastructure during 1980–1986 are shown in Table 3.7.

Tianjin's Role in China's Coastal Development

Since the economic reform began in the late 1970s, Tianjin has gradually revived as a key metropolis in North China. In the past few years, with the restructuring of its urban economy, the remarkable improvement in urban infrastructure, and the establishment of the ETDZ at Tanggu, Tianjin has emerged as a leading port city in the Bo Hai–Yellow Sea Rim, an economic region which possesses greater potential for comprehensive industrial development than any other coastal region in China, thanks to its well-endowed natural resources of energy and minerals.

Tianjin's ETDZ, initiated in 1984, ranks among the earliest development areas in China. The zone's purpose was to encourage foreign investment by giving preferential treatment in taxes, tariffs, remittance of legal profits, land fees, and entry and exit procedures. The first five years of an international enterprise are tax free with a possible extension of another five years. Land use is based on a leasehold of seventy years, and the lease fee is only 14 *yuan* per square meter per annum.[19] These favorable terms are guaranteed by legislation. Investment in the zone can be made in the form of exclusive foreign enterprises, joint ventures, and cooperative enterprises, as well as compensation trade, leasing, processing with supplied materials, assembling with supplied parts and accessories, and purchasing credit. Projects with advanced technological equipment that will not pollute the environment have top priority.

The development zone is located on a branch of the former Tanggu Salt Flat to the north of the Hai He estuary, about 50 km east of the urban districts of Tianjin. The site was selected because the Beijing–Shanhaiguan railway, one of the most vital lines in China, passes its western edge; the town of Beitang, famous for marine products, lies to the north. In addition, the canal diverting water from the Luanhe into Tanggu passes through the development zone and the Beijing–Tianjin–Tangshan high-voltage power grid is only 2 km away, assuring a steady water and power supply. With the completion of the Beijing–Tianjin–Tanggu Expressway in 1990, one can reach Beijing from the development zone in about one hour. Air transportation from the development zone to other parts of China, including direct flight to Hong Kong, is handled by the recently completed Tianjin International Airport 38 km away. These factors have created favorable conditions for the development of international enterprises. The total area available for industry is over 33 sq km, much of it useless for agricultural purposes. Living quarters are planned to cover 15 sq km, including 2 sq km for foreign residents. The first phase of development, covering an area of 3 sq km, was largely completed in 1988 after a total investment of 160 million *yuan* for infrastructure. This initial setup includes 1.8 sq km for office buildings, 0.2 sq km for service centers, and 0.4 sq km for road construction. As of August 1988, a total of 113 projects had been signed involving foreign investment in one form or other.[20]

Tianjin's development zone is actively seeking investment in three spheres. First, the area is interested in projects aimed at utilizing resources available in Tianjin and its immediate hinterlands for producing goods that can be exported. (It does not exclude, however, projects that import materials and components from abroad and sell the final products overseas.) Second, it is interested in foreign investments that will upgrade the industries in Tianjin. Third, it aims to attract foreign investment that will bring high-tech industries to Tianjin: microelectronics technology, biological engineering, alternative energy resources, engineering information, and marine resources.

The Administrative Commission of the Tianjin ETDZ is the zone's leading administrative organization. It examines and approves applications to establish enterprises that involve less than $30 million in total investment and issues business licenses and certificates for land use. The commission also exercises control over investment, insurance, taxes, import and export trade, foreign exchange, and workers' welfare. Finally, it supervises and coordinates customs, commodity inspections, and public security, protects the legal rights of both Chinese and foreign parties within the zone, and provides facilities and services for overseas investors.

According to policies announced by the Administrative Commission, foreign investment in Tianjin's ETDZ enjoys more preferential treatment than inland provinces of China or even the city of Tianjin itself. The major advantages are as follows: customs duty on export products (excluding those under state export control), raw material, and components imported for production of export goods is exempted; building materials, production equipment, raw material components and parts, means of transportation, and office appliances purchased by the enterprise for its own use are exempted from industrial and commercial consolidated tax; the enterprise income tax is levied at 15 percent and a new enterprise may be exempted from income tax in the first and second profitable years; a reduction on prepaid income tax to 10 percent is allowed (further reduction or exemption depends on technological sophistication and preferential conditions brought in by investors); and, finally, overseas investors enjoy the freedom of remitting their capital and profits abroad, all exempted from tax.[21]

An integrated partner of the Administrative Commission is the Tianjin Economic-Technological Development Area Company (TEDAC). Such an integrated administration is quite common in the newly opened coastal cities and Special Economic Zones. TEDAC is set up to ensure that the development zone will function as an economic entity. As such, TEDAC assumes full responsibility for the development and management of foreign business in the zone. It provides overall coordination and guidance to foreign investors. The company has a number of subsidiary companies which undertake land exploitation, industrial investment, factory building, import and export trade, agents of foreign business, public service, labor service, and social insurance. The biggest subsidiary company, the Public Utility Company, is responsible for the overall coordination of the zone's utility and service requirements. It is followed by the Construction Company, the Industrial Investment Company, and the Import and Export Company. All of these companies are responsible for coordination of their respective activities. They also seek active collaboration with foreign investors.[22]

As part of China's open policy in recent years, a number of economic cooperative regions along the coast have formulated plans for integrated regional economic development. Since these economic regions were designed with various purposes and at different scales, some overlapping has occurred. Two such regions in North China consider Tianjin to be the key port city for linkage with the outside world. These two regions are the Beijing–Tianjin–Tangshan (Jing-jin-tang) Region and the Bo Hai–Yellow Sea Rim Economic Region.

The Beijing–Tianjin–Tangshan Region, part of the National Territorial Development Plan initiated in the early 1980s, combines three major industrial cities and the rural counties under their jurisdiction to form the principal economic nucleus of North China. The plan calls for integration and specialization of urban economy among the three cities through communication and transport links and a socioeconomic system of coordination and cooperation. The region distinguishes itself, compared with other macroeconomic regions in China, by its high proportion of urban population in large cities (96.5 percent), high ratio of nonagricultural population in cities and towns (96.9 percent), and relatively low ratio of nonagricultural population in rural towns.[23] All these characteristics imply that the region has been dominated by large-scale state-run industries, particularly heavy industries, and that rural market towns are relatively underdeveloped. To improve the low economic efficiency of large cities in China, which was partly induced by a repetitive industrial structure among cities, the plan of the Jing-jin-tang Region calls for specialization of urban industries in each of the three cities. The capital city of Beijing, which has been developed excessively as a key industrial center in the past forty years, is to constrain further development of heavy industry—particularly the pollution-prone, weight-losing, and raw material processing industries—and to strengthen tertiary industries and service sectors that would improve the function of a capital city in a more

efficient way. Tangshan, a well-established industrial city with easy access
to energy resources and ferrous minerals in eastern Hebei, is to play its
role as a heavy industrial city to provide machinery, construction materials, and energy to other communities in the region. Tianjin, an industrial and trade center with great potential in North China, is capable of
sharing certain industrial production burdens released by Beijing. With
its well-developed financial institutions, Tianjin can also function as a
commercial and foreign trade center for the region.[24]

The concept of the Bo Hai–Yellow Sea Rim Economic Region, formulated in 1984, is another manifestation of China's open policy with a specific regional organization. The scope of this region is much greater than
the Jing-jin-tang Region and comprises three provinces (Hebei, Liaoning, and Shandong) and two independent municipalities (Beijing and
Tianjin). Unlike the Shanghai Economic Region and the Pearl River
Delta Economic Region, both centered around nucleus cities of Shanghai
and Guangzhou, respectively, the Bo Hai–Yellow Sea Rim Region is an
aggregation of thirteen cities of different sizes of which five have been
designated open cities and have established ETDZs. The region is organized with the goal of promoting mutual assistance and mutual benefit
among all participating cities, as well as developing regional specialization and labor division in economic structure based on comparative
advantages such as unique resource endowments or transport facilities.
The purpose is to integrate economic activities of different cities and
counties, to explore natural resources jointly with pooled technology and
labor, and to share capital, urban and regional infrastructure, and harbor
facilities for export-oriented industrial production.[25] With South Korea's
rising interest in making investments in China in recent years, the prospect of developing this region, which shares the shoreline of the Yellow
Sea with South Korea, looks quite promising.

If the Bo Hai–Yellow Sea Rim Economic Region could be developed
according to the original design and with increasing participation of foreign firms, the city of Tianjin could play a key role in absorbing foreign
capital and technology as well as rendering technical and managerial
assistance to other cities around the rim. Above all, Tianjin could act as a
leading port city to serve the vast hinterland of the region, which covers
the entire area of North China, the bulk of Northwest China, and a part
of Central China. As shown in Table 3.8, Tianjin is indeed the dominant
city in the Bo Hai–Yellow Sea Rim: it has overshadowed all other cities
around the rim in total GVIO, total value of profit and tax, and total
value of imports and exports. Clearly Tianjin appears to be on its way to

Table 3.8 Basic Economic Indicators of Major Cities in the Bo Hai–Yellow Sea Rim Economic Region: 1987

CITY	NONAGRICULTURAL POPULATION (1,000S)	GVIO (BILLION YUAN)	TOTAL VALUE OF PROFIT AND TAX (BILLION YUAN)	TOTAL VALUE OF IMPORTS AND EXPORTS (BILLION YUAN)	TOTAL VALUE OF RETAIL SALE (BILLION YUAN)
Tianjin	4,470.5	34.804	6.431	9.680	7.759
Tangshan	1,295.7	8.627	1.132	—	3.083
Qinhuangdao	425.3	2.040	0.274	1.203	1.042
Cangzhou	242.9	1.637	0.233	—	0.562
Dalian	2,035.5	14.799	2.597	8.142	4.341
Dandong	880.2	5.286	0.660	0.233	1.597
Jinzhou	1,333.4	8.443	1.531	—	2.555
Yingkou	653.6	4.647	0.496	0.081	1.322
Panjin	351.5	2.414	0.385	—	0.580
Qingdao	1,519.9	15.048	2.084	3.028	4.158
Dongying	248.7	4.291	0.972	—	0.633
Yantai	953.0	14.187	1.314	0.321	4.746
Weifang	783.3	11.533	0.854	—	3.359
Total	13,993.5	125.342	19.360	23.488	37.541

Source: Sun Lianxi, He Zhongxiu, and Wang Minghao, "Prospects of Tianjin City," paper presented to the International Conference on China's Urbanization, Tianjin, August 1988.

regaining its position as the leading port of North China. Whether Tianjin can actually recapture such a prominent position will depend on continuation of China's open policy, on the success of China's urban reform, and on its ability to attract investment, technology, and managerial skills from abroad.

Conclusions

Tianjin was the largest urban center in North China and the second largest city in the nation for several decades in the first half of the present century. During the first thirty years of the People's Republic, with the reemergence of Beijing as the national capital and the inland-oriented development policy, Tianjin experienced a period of stagnation under the shadow of Beijing. In the past ten years of China's economic reform, however, particularly since the coastal development strategy initiated in the Seventh Five-Year Plan, Tianjin appears to have regained its vitality as the principal port city in North China. If China's open policy continues, its urban economic reform policy is thoroughly implemented, and its coastal development strategy is still considered a priority in national economic development, Tianjin is destined to become one of the largest metropolises in the western Pacific rim as well as a key city to spread modernization impulses to the vast inland regions of northern China. Such an optimistic conjecture for the city is based mainly on two favorable factors. One is Tianjin's geographical location; the other is Tianjin's success in developing its urban economy as compared with other Chinese cities in the past ten years.

The development of the great port cities of the world has been attributed to their strategic location in relation to their easily accessible hinterland and vast, active foreland. Historically, Tianjin was mainly a riverine port along the Grand Canal. Although Tianjin has conducted foreign trade ever since 1860, when it was first opened as a treaty port, the modern maritime port facility was not constructed until 1940, when Japanese occupation forces started to build an artificial harbor in Tanggu to facilitate the shipping of military supplies. The New Harbor (Xingang) in Tanggu was remodeled soon after the founding of the People's Republic and was opened as the largest man-made harbor in North China in 1952. Tianjin's superior strategic location and its well-endowed resource base can be evaluated in the following terms.

First, Tianjin is located near the northern apex of the triangular North China plain, the most extensive densely populated region in China, and is situated near the tangent zone of three macroregions: North China, Northeast China, and Inner Mongolia. The development of railway systems in the past hundred years has enhanced the role of Tianjin as a nodal point among these three macroregions. Thanks to the inland nature of Bo Hai, Tianjin has often been considered to be closer to the vast inland provinces of the northwest than any other port city in China.

Second, the municipality of Tianjin, which comprises five rural counties, together with its immediate hinterland covering large parts of Hebei and Shanxi and the eastern part of Inner Mongolia, is richly endowed with fossil fuels, ferrous minerals, and other raw materials for industrial development. The geographical aggregation of these essential resources in the vicinity of Tianjin rivals that of central Liaoning province and is much superior to the large coastal cities in South China, including Shanghai and Guangzhou, both of which suffer from a shortage of energy supplies. In the long term, however, a potential constraint for Tianjin's industrial development could be water supply. The Luan He Water Diversion Project may be able to provide water for Tianjin's urban and industrial development by the year 2000 or so. Both water-saving measures in industry and new water resources may be required in the early years of the twenty-first century.

Third, rapid industrial growth and urban expansion in the past decade have contributed markedly to the alarming reduction of China's arable land—an average loss of 1 percent a year in the past few years—which has led to the stagnant performance of agricultural production in China since 1985. As most Chinese cities were originally settlements serving rural areas, they were located usually amidst the region's most productive agricultural land. Thus any expansion of a Chinese city is often at the expense of productive arable land. Tianjin, however, is one of a few large cities in China that are not entirely surrounded by intensively cultivated land. In fact, the land to the east and south of Tianjin is largely composed of sandy flats and salty swamps which are not agriculturally productive. Therefore, there is ample land for urban expansion of Tianjin, particularly the area between the existing urban districts and the Hai He estuary, an area that has already caught the attention of local urban planners for future development.

In the past ten years, with the implementation of economic reforms, many large cities in China have striven to improve their urban facilities and upgrade their urban economy. Few cities in China, however, have been able to match Tianjin's level of urban reconstruction. What were the characteristic features of Tianjin's urban development in the past ten years besides its favorable location and well-endowed resources? First, in a highly centralized authoritarian society like China, the quality of leadership plays a crucial role in designing and implementing innovative policies at city and regional levels. In 1981, the city of Tianjin found a capable mayor in Li Ruihuan, who has provided strong leadership in initiating gigantic programs of housing construction, community development, urban renewal, capital and labor mobilization, and foreign investment.

Second, Chinese cities have long been suffering from inadequate urban infrastructure—the so-called unproductive sector that has been neglected for many years in the political economy. Such neglect of urban infrastructure may have been a cause of the generally low efficiency of China's urban economy. The leadership in Tianjin was among the first to note this problem, however, and during the Sixth Five-Year Plan (1981–1985), allocated 51.7 percent of the total capital investment to the construction of urban infrastructure in order to change the situation.[26] Such a high ratio of investment in urban infrastructure is a rarity among Chinese cities and has drawn severe criticism from the media (representing the views of the central government). As a result of this innovative policy, Tianjin now enjoys a reputation as one of the most desirable cities in China in which to live. Although allotting more than 50 percent of total capital investment to infrastructure might seem excessive, Tianjin's planners insist that the portion for infrastructure and service investment should not be less than 40 percent of the city's total capital investment.[27]

Third, urban renewal projects in the first three decades of the People's Republic have been accompanied by the destruction of many cultural relics of historical significance, as exemplified by the zealous dismantling of city walls and city gates in Beijing, to the dismay of art historians and foreign tourists. The urban renewal projects launched in the early 1980s in Tianjin, however, have tried hard to preserve the historical urban cultures of China, including the restoration of nineteenth-century European architecture in former foreign concessions. Several streets that epitomize the urban architectural style and functional specialization of the late Qing dynasty have become distinguished landmarks in Tianjin and in function resemble the pedestrian shopping malls in many American cities today.

Fourth, among large cities in China, Tianjin started relatively early in modifying its economic structure. During the Sixth Five-Year Plan, its light industry increased from 50 percent of the total industrial output in 1980 to 55 percent in 1985, while the service sector increased from 23.5 percent to 27.6 percent during the same period. In the meantime, Tianjin's GNP, the total social output, the gross value of industrial and agricultural outputs, and the city's national income had increased by 58.1, 62.1, 67.5, and 51.0 percent, respectively. These growth rates, reflecting a more balanced and diversified development of the city's economy, surpassed those of Beijing and Shanghai. The average GNP per worker increased from 2,622 *yuan* to 3,805 *yuan* with an annual growth rate of 7.7 percent. Moreover, Tianjin was able to assign high priority to the construction of major utility and service projects, projects that often had low priority in other Chinese cities. During the period 1981–1985, the investment for energy increased by 61.2 percent, the investment for transportation, post, and telecommunications by 157 percent, for education and scientific research by 321 percent, and for technical innovation by 37.6 percent.

Tianjin's economic growth and urban development over the past ten years have been, indeed, quite remarkable. The city is increasingly facing, however, competition from other port cities in North China, such as Dalian, Qinhuangdao, and even Yantai, in attracting investment from the central government and foreign firms for industrial development as well as for tapping resources (including human resources) and developing regional economy in their hinterlands. The city has also had to face a number of issues pertaining to industrial productivity and economic efficiency. These problems are, to a great extent, related to the current institutional framework of China's development policy and are shared by virtually every city in China. They cannot be easily resolved unless the urban economic reforms proposed in the past few years—including industrial restructuring based on comparative advantages, price reforms, land values, user fees, and initiation of labor markets—are successfully implemented.

Notes

1. *Tianjin Today* (Hong Kong: Man Hai Language Publications, 1988), p. 20.
2. Wang Ling, *Beijing di dongbu menhu—Tianjin* [The eastern gate of Beijing] (Beijing: Beijing Institute of Social Sciences, Department of History, 1983), p. 20.

3. *Tianjin Economic Yearbook 1986* (Tianjin: Tianjin People's Publications, 1986), p. 6.

4. Liang Huashan, *Tianjin jingji zhongxin diwei di yanjiu* [On the economic centrality of Tianjin's location] (Beijing: Academia Sinica Institute of Geography, 1985) p. 2.

5. Sun Jingzi, *Huabei jingji dili* [Economic geography of North China] (Beijing: Science Publications, 1957), p. 80.

6. Sun Junjie, *Huabei jingji zhongxin—Tianjin* [North China's economic center—Tianjin] (Beijing: Academia Sinica Institute of Geography, 1986).

7. Liang, *Tianjin jingji zhongxin diwei di yanjiu*, p. 2.

8. *Tianjin Today*, p. 20.

9. *China Statistical Yearbook 1988* (Beijing: State Statistical Publications, 1988).

10. *Tianjin Today*, p. 20.

11. *The Almanac of China's Urban Economy and Society* (Beijing: China's Urban Economy and Society Publications, 1987), p. 341.

12. *Tianjin Economic Yearbook 1988* (Tianjin: Tianjin People's Publications, 1989), pp. 270–285.

13. *China Daily*, 2 June 1989, p. 2.

14. Xu Runda, Teng Shaohua, and Ning Shuchen, "The Construction of the City's Infrastructure Facilities Acts as a Role in Tianjin's Development," paper presented at the International Conference on China's Urbanization, Tianjin, August 1988.

15. *Tianjin Today*, p. 29.

16. David W. Edgington, "Tianjin," *Cities* 3(2) (1986): 117–124.

17. Data derived from personal interview in Tianjin in August 1988 by the senior author.

18. *Tianjin Today*, p. 28.

19. Information gathered through personal interview in Tianjin's development zone in August 1988 by the senior author.

20. Ibid. See also Zhang Zhaoruo, "The Tianjin Economic and Technological Development Area," *China's Foreign Trade* 3 (1985): 6–22.

21. *Tianjin Today*, p. 129.

22. M. W. Luke Chan, "The Tianjin Economic-Technological Development Area: Some Observations on Its Structure and Foreign Investment Profile," QSEP Research Report no. 174, McMaster University, Faculty of Social Sciences, 1986.

23. Sun Panshou and Ye Shunzan, "City-Town Systematic Structure and the Development of Various Cities and Towns in the Beijing-Tianjin-Tangshan Region," *Economic Geography* (Beijing), 4(3) (1984): 171–177.

24. Ye Shunzan, "Regional Perspective of the Relationship of Development

of two Metropolises: Beijing and Tianjin," *China City Planning Review* 2(1) (1986): 21–32.

25. Huang Gang, "The Bohai Economic Region," *Economic Geography* (Beijing), 7(1) (1987): 33–38.

26. He Zhongxiu, "Transformation and Development of Tianjin City," paper presented at the International Conference on China's Urbanization, Tianjin, August 1988.

27. Ibid.

28. Ibid.

4 Yantai: A Geographical Appraisal of Its Potential

CHIU-MING LUK AND SHI-KUAN ZHOU

THE CONTEMPORARY SIGNIFICANCE of Yantai, one of the fourteen coastal cities the Chinese government decided to open to the outside world, matches its historical importance as one of China's oldest foreign trade outlets. This chapter analyzes the geographical advantages that led to Yantai's rise in prominence. Under the current open policy, the benefits of Yantai's development are not confined to the city alone. The city is expected to generate economic impulses that will lead to development of its hinterland—exactly the catalytic role that the Chinese authorities are hoping to achieve. Therefore, a critical appraisal of its development potential is both timely and significant to those interested in China's regional development.

One way to evaluate the geography of Yantai is to approach it via different geographical scales. The following discussion is therefore organized according to a continuum ranging from an inspection of Yantai at the regional scale down to the internal arrangement of the city proper. First, however, we must outline the essential components of its geography and history. Then Yantai's vicinity will be discussed, as well as the socioeconomic structure of Yantai *shi*.[1] Moreover, we shall examine the internal structure of Yantai city proper. Last of all, we offer an assessment of Yantai's development prospects, especially its catalytic role in coastal development.

Geography and Historical Background

Yantai is situated in the northern part of Jiaodong Peninsula in the northeastern portion of Shandong province. The city faces Bo Hai, one of the most important enclosed seas of China, on which famous cities like Tianjin and Dalian are situated. In 1985,[2] Yantai comprised twelve *xian* plus one *xian*-level city.[3] (See Figure 4.1.) The whole city had an area of about 18,900 sq km with a total population of around 8.2 million in 1985.[4] By 1989, a reduced Yantai *shi* reported a smaller area of 13,507

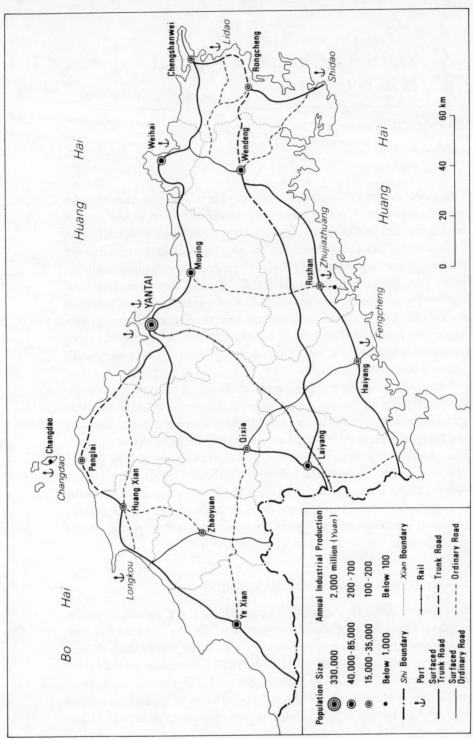

Figure 4.1 The Socioeconomic Structure of Administrative Regions in Yantai *Shi*: 1985

sq km with a total population of 6.2 million. Yantai city proper remains at 835 sq km supporting a population of 778,400 in 1988. Its nonagricultural population in the same year was around 422,500.

Yantai's evolution depends on its port development. The port of Yantai is adjacent to Zhifu, an island in Bo Hai later joined with the mainland because of sedimentation. Indeed, Zhifu has become synonymous with Yantai. Beginning in the first century B.C., Chinese products like silk were shipped to Korea and Japan through here. During the Ming dynasty (thirteenth century), pirates infested the Chinese coast and a series of beacon towers was built to send out the alarm. It was the beacon erected at Zhifu that gave rise to the name Yantai ("beacon tower").

The modern development of Yantai began after the Opium War in the mid-nineteenth century. By the Treaty of Tianjin (1862), Yantai was opened as a trading port for foreigners. As a result, some form of infrastructure was laid down, including wharves and breakwaters. Embassies were set up and customs offices were established. Substantial development of Yantai was carried out between the years 1872 and 1877. Important exports through Yantai were food grains, peanuts, fruit, silk, and traditional handicrafts; the imports included light industrial products like oil and chemicals. Yantai was once the only trading port of Shandong in the early twentieth century. Since then, small-scale industries—wine, flour, canned foods, matches, and the like—were set up. As a result, Yantai emerged as a light industrial base.

Contemporary improvement of Yantai's infrastructure started in the mid-1950s with the construction of a railway connecting Yantai with Jinan. Consequently, its hinterland began to flourish. Since the fifties, Yantai's industries have developed quickly, necessitating port development to facilitate foreign trade. In 1973, large-scale construction of the port was completed, more than tripling its throughput capabilities. Internally, industrial-agricultural growth was impressive. Some estimate its per capita growth at 8.1 percent between 1949 and 1983. From 1983 to 1985, its rate of growth ranked second in the nation. Side by side with these developments, municipal construction was rapid.

Yantai and Its Vicinity

Contemporary theories of regional development suggest the importance of an interdependent system of cities. As China moves ahead in modernization, studies on the development of a single city should not neglect the role played by other cities in its immediate vicinity. Thus one must take a macroview of the neighboring provinces and municipalities to gain insight into Yantai itself.

Yantai is located at the entrance to Bo Hai. In this part of China, five provinces or municipalities are represented: Liaoning, Beijing, Tianjin, Hebei, and Shandong. Because some of the best-developed cities in China are located in this area, suggestions have been made for creating a Bo Hai Economic Ring.[5] To convey a better understanding of Yantai's economic position among various cities in the area, a composite index on economic development was calculated with ten variables representing development level.[6] Data used were *shi* information from *Zhongguo Chengshi Tongji Nianjian, 1985*.[7] Altogether forty-four cities were represented.[8] The index was obtained by dividing the total sum of ranks across all variables for each *shi* by the maximum possible rank sum (44 *shi* × 10 variables = 440). They were then broken down into five categories according to the occurrence of natural breaks in the distribution. Figure 4.2 summarizes the results.

In terms of population size, Yantai is an intermediate city by Chinese standards. In this analysis, it belongs to the second highest category, a finding that justifies the government's policy of choosing Yantai as an open coastal city. Surrounding Yantai are three *shi* with higher development level; more important, both Shandong and Liaoning provinces contain five cities in the second highest category. In Shandong province, Jinan, Zibo, Weifang, and Qingdao are of similar status with Yantai. All are connected by railways which greatly enhance the accessibility of Yantai and strengthen the ties between Yantai city proper and its hinterland. Consequently, there is great potential for Yantai to be an alternative port outlet after Qingdao (no. 28). Direct export to South China seawise may take advantage of Qingdao, but for transshipment to North China, the Bo Hai area in particular, Yantai is the more likely choice.

Liaoning's situation also benefits Yantai. Dalian (no. 16) serves as the outport not only for Liaoning's products but also those of all Northeast China. By means of the excellent rail network in Manchuria, heavy industrial products converge at Dalian. Unless these goods are transported over land, seaward connection is of paramount importance in the Bo Hai area. Since Yantai is only 170 km (90 nautical miles) from Dalian —the shortest distance between Yantai and a comparable city—the interchange of goods from North and Northeast China is frequent at either port. Economic benefit has therefore accrued to both.

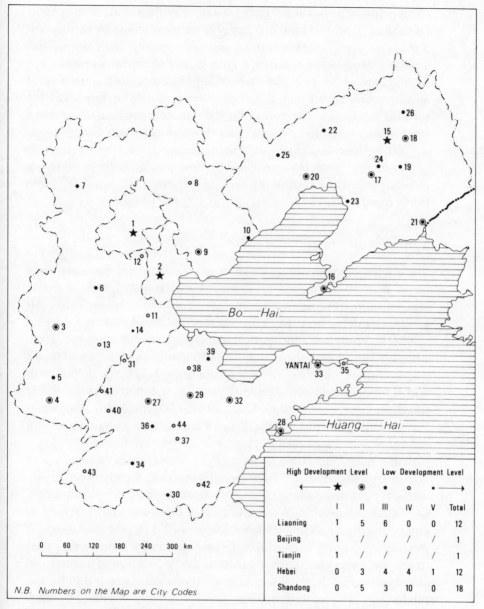

Figure 4.2 The Economic Development Status of Yantai *Shi* and Cities in Neighboring Provinces: 1984

Accessibility with cities in Hebei is less convenient, but no less important. Since Tianjin is only 440 km (240 nautical miles) away, this economic giant also brings benefit to Yantai. Especially when Beijing and Tianjin are considered together, a great variety of products generated in North China converge at the Tianjin outport. Ships dock at Tianjin for loading products and then pay visits to either Dalian or Yantai or both for additional cargo. The port of Yantai reaps substantial advantages as a result. As a whole, then, Yantai's neighbors are important to its prosperity. If they flourish, Yantai will benefit greatly. Given Yantai's situation as a port, the connections with nearby cities are of immense value. As interdependencies intensify, Yantai's development will be all the more firmly based.

Yantai as an Entity

The whole administrative region of Yantai *shi* can be described as its economic hinterland (Figure 4.1). In other words, it includes all the twelve *xian* plus the *xian*-level city of Weihai. Within this region, industrial-agricultural development flourishes. Light industries such as food processing abound. For agricultural products, almost all types are represented. The area's fishery is quite important, as well, for Yantai's coastline (including Weihai *shi*) amounts to 1,359 km dotted with numerous bays and inlets. Besides Yantai, other important ports include Longkou, Changdao, Weihai, Lidao, Shidao, Zhujiazhuang, and Fengcheng. Among all these ports, Yantai's throughput amounted to 50.6 percent of Shandong's total in 1985.

If one treats Yantai *shi* as an entity, it is important to consider its infrastructure to assess its development potential properly. From Figure 4.1, it is clear that Yantai city proper's dominance in industrial production is unquestionable. While the railway that runs southwestward to join eventually with Qingdao is the lifeline of Yantai, the road system is its veins. As the map shows, all of the *xian* capitals are connected by road in one way or another. Special attention should be given to connectivity among *xian* capitals of the second grade (population size and industrial production). In this category one finds Wendeng, Weihai, Muping, Laiyang, and Ye Xian. The surfaced trunk road that runs along the northern coast basically connects the first three cities. Laiyang is connected as well, but Ye Xian suffers from an indirect route. On the whole, the road system has a fair number of east–west and north–south routes.

If Yantai is to develop further, however, the connectivity of the less developed parts of the city must be improved. The immediate vicinity to the south of Yantai city proper is one example.

In terms of resource endowment, Yantai *shi* is quite rich. Different kinds of minerals are found, and their abundance is further helped by widespread distribution. Some estimate that within a circumference of 20 km one can always discover a usable mineral site. This brings in great advantage for the establishment of medium- to small-scale industries like gold smelting, construction materials, and energy extraction. Ocean resources are as vital as land resources for Yantai. Because of the vast expanse of continental shelf that surrounds this peninsula, fishery and marine aquaculture exist in large quantities. Special attention should be given to breeding grounds for prawns, sea cucumbers, abalone, and various algae. Indeed, Yantai is famous for its aquatic products. In terms of prawn production, Yantai accounted for 70 percent of Shandong's share and 10 percent of the whole nation's output.

Yantai's tourist resource is also worth mentioning. To the west of Yantai city proper, Penglai is romantically called a "paradise on earth." To the east, Weihai is famous for its historic role during the first Sino-Japanese War in 1894–1895. Furthermore, the hot springs in Muping, Wendeng, and a few other places possess great medicinal value. Since China recently reopened its doors to the West, tourism in Yantai has been progressing rapidly. Foreign tourists come for sightseeing; domestic visitors come for conferences or for healing purposes. Economic gains as a result of tourism have been increasing steadily.

Within the boundaries of Yantai *shi*, small towns exist in a hierarchy. Before Weihai's elevation to *shi* in 1986, it was a secondary node of Yantai. Generally speaking, the towns in Yantai *shi* are not large in terms of population, as shown by the size of the largest *xian* capitals: Laiyang (68,000), Muping (45,000), Wendeng (39,000), and Ye Xian (38,000).[9] The average size of these *xian* capitals ranges from 15,000 to 35,000; Changdao (9,000) is the smallest. For other small towns administratively defined by the government, populations range from 5,000 to 10,000; some rural market towns have even fewer than 5,000. These small towns are vital to Yantai's economy, for about 80 percent of its industrial production value is derived from them.

The spatial distribution of these towns is worthy of note. On the whole, they spread eastward, westward, and southward from Yantai city proper. Often they are found along railway and highway systems or at their intersection. Therefore, sea and land transport connectivity are determinants of small town locations. Of course, commodity flow patterns and distributions of industries are also influencing factors. Almost a hundred small towns are found in Yantai *shi*. These *xian* capitals are political, economic, and cultural centers of their areas of jurisdiction. Here one finds educational institutions, local industries, and specialized forms of manufacture. For rural/urban commodity exchanges and other transactions, other towns and markets bridge the gap between *xian* capitals and the vast countryside.

Yantai City Proper

This section concentrates on the internal development of Yantai city proper. After conveying a panoramic view of the whole city—including both the inner and outer suburban districts plus the central city (urban district) of Yantai—we consider the port area of Yantai with respect to its growth potential. We then describe the recent establishment of an Economic and Technological Development Zone (ETDZ) outside its core.

From Figure 4.3,[10] one can easily trace the city boundary that separates Yantai city proper from its neighboring *xian* as well as the boundary for its urban district. Within this latter boundary is Yantai's core. Here one finds long stretches of built-up areas and a system of major roads. Note also the port area enclosed within the urban district—known as the "Old City." As later development spread out laterally because of the hills to the south, a "ribbon" type of development appears. Functional specialization at the core is quite clear-cut. At the center are commercial districts, municipal and cultural facilities, as well as the port. To the east are medical and educational institutions. The west is essentially industrial in nature. Also worth mentioning are the two areas outside the urban district: Fushan is an outer suburban industrial district; Fulaishan is the site of the ETDZ.

Industrial locations in the city proper have experienced great changes throughout history. Before 1949, Yantai's industries were basically light ones concentrated in the Old City. With later development of new industrial districts, industries spread especially to the west and south. At the Old City there are light industries plus some machinery manufacture. The western district is a comprehensive industrial area with heavy industries like chemicals, metallurgy, and others leading the production. Besides these two areas, there are isolated industrial zones: to the south is

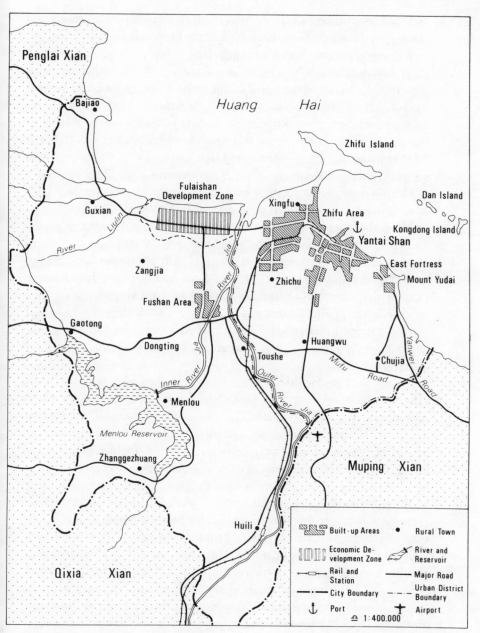

Figure 4.3 City Proper of Yantai *Shi*

one spot, established since the 1970s, which focuses on electronics and textiles; in the north, port-related industries predominate.

Without question, Yantai's growth depends on its port. A closer look at its port facilities helps one to assess Yantai's development potential (Figure 4.4).[11] One of the port's major assets is the long ice-free period. In this part of North China, January temperatures are the lowest; yet snow and ice formation is not severe and no extended delays because of frozen conditions are experienced. An eastern breakwater separates the northern and southern entrances. Large ships can enter through the southern entrance along the internal navigation route. The route is 8.5 m deep—enough for most ships. The western breakwater has been reconstructed as an extended piece of land for wharves.

Altogether there are fifteen wharves available for passengers or goods. Of this number, three can handle ships of over 10,000 tons and twelve are situated on the extended land stretch mentioned earlier. One can see from Figure 4.4 that wharves 5, 6, and 7 can handle larger ships because of their deeper waters. Passenger ships usually dock at wharves 1 or 2 while wharves 11 and 12 are used exclusively for coal shipment. The rest are for manufactured goods of all kinds. Also noticeable are the minor wharves on the right (Taiping Wan area), reserved for docking mechanized boats.

Besides docking facilities, Yantai is also supplied with godowns, storage areas, port railways, and loading and unloading machinery. Since passenger services to Tianjin and Dalian are in high demand, the passenger wharf is equipped with associated facilities like waiting rooms. A variety of general maintenance services are also available: barges, tugboats, ship inspection, emergency rescue teams, and telecommunication networks for the day-to-day running of the port.

Yantai provides a substantial range of services commensurate with its status as a port city. Because of its location, coupled with its infrastructure improvement over the years, Yantai can handle with relative ease both passenger and freight traffic. However, one has to envision a reasonable increase in goods traffic as North China (Hebei in particular) and nearby provinces multiply their export volume. Thus Yantai's plans to handle increased volume should consider an expanded role as Qingdao's alternative port. Moreover, containerization facilities should receive serious consideration if Yantai is to maintain its status as a modern port in North China.

Related to China's modernization is the establishment of an ETDZ on

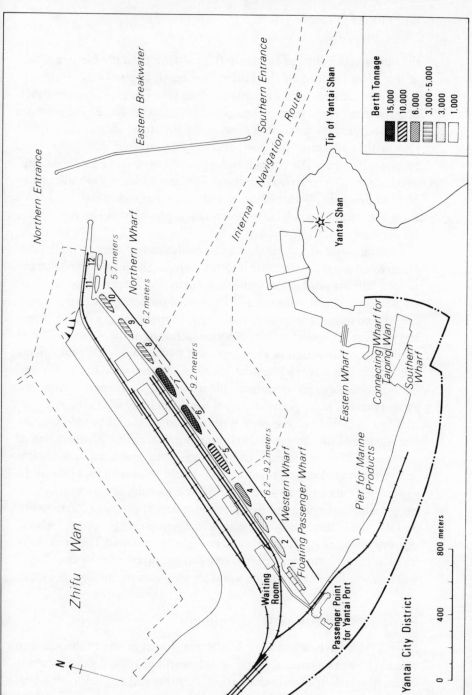

Figure 4.4 The Port of Yantai

the outskirts of Yantai at Fulaishan (Figure 4.5). Basically the area is west of the River Jia, east of the Liulin, and north of the Liuzi. Started in 1984, this zone comprises an area of 20 sq km. The first phase of development, the eastern part, occupied about 10 sq km. The ETDZ possesses several advantages. First, it is close to the industrial districts in the Old City, within 10 km of the port, and only 27 km from Laishan airport. Second, the area is flat enough to be free of engineering problems and, as it is close to electricity transmission lines and within a short distance of Menlou Reservoir, both electricity and water supplies are available. All these infrastructural advantages persuaded planners to choose this site for the zone.

Looking closer at the plan, one can easily see the logic of the layout. Fuhai Road separates the zone into two halves. The plan is to reserve the eastern half for production while its western counterpart is for administration, commercial, cultural, and residential purposes. In contrast to the mixed land uses so common in traditional Chinese cities, a degree of spatial segregation is discernible. Another planning component worthy of note is the construction of greenbelts and parks around the zone, giving the ETDZ much more pleasant environs and also benefiting the residents. A wastewater treatment plant nearby, if properly managed, should prevent water pollutants from being discharged into the sea.

While two-fifths of the zone is devoted to industrial production, the rest is reserved for commercial and residential purposes. The commercial districts are aligned with the arterial roads, thus providing an accessible service network. Residents living there should be able to find jobs in the eastern section of the zone. Employment opportunities are usually connected with processing industries—food, textiles, precision instruments, and the like—since the overall plan is to develop energy-saving, technology-intensive, nonpolluting modern light industries. The idea is to develop these industries by attracting foreign investment so that Yantai will be a window to the outside world for advanced technology.

Prospects for Future Development

Several years have passed since Yantai was chosen as one of the fourteen coastal cities to be opened to the outside world in 1984. To those outside China who lack firsthand information, there are still difficulties in assessing Yantai's performance and development prospects. This section addresses this issue.

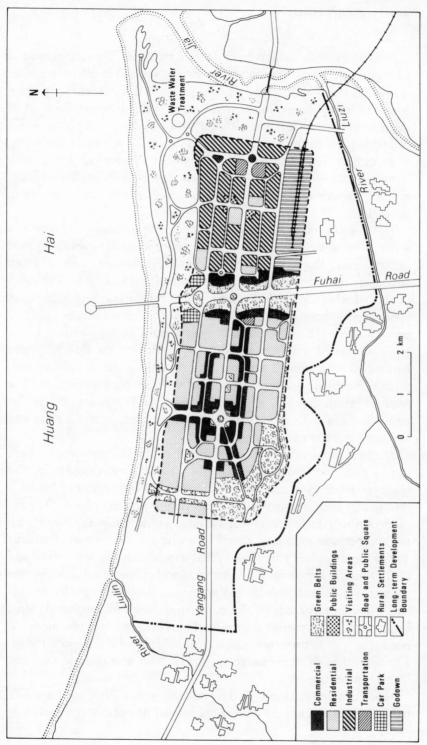

Figure 4.5 Fulaishan ETDZ, Yantai *Shi*

In Chapter 1, the editors have clearly expounded the catalytic role of China's coastal cities. With regard to Yantai, we wish to offer some note-worthy observations. Certainly Yantai possesses advantages that prepare it well for more intense interaction with the outside world. Some of its assets stem from its location within the Bo Hai area. As a port it is in a favorable position for handling transactions in foreign trade and acting as an outport for its hinterland. And with its expanding agricultural-industrial activities plus improvements in its port facilities, Yantai is sig-nificant not only as a port but also as a catalyst to more development in the region.

Yet a regional node requires a number of other factors—for example, a stable political environment and concomitant improvements in regional infrastructure. Moreover, Yantai must improve its port facilities, which are largely traditional and far below international standards. This raises doubts whether the port's present facilities can handle large volumes of goods (or passengers) in an efficient manner. Containerization may be one solution to the problem. However, it must be supplemented by a well-coordinated transport network that speeds up the flow of goods. Particularly important is a freeway system linking the city proper with other *xian* capitals. In other words, a better feeder road system should be planned which connects all the vital parts of Yantai *shi*. When this immediate economic hinterland is fully integrated, Yantai is certain to become a much more important port.

A critical problem for Yantai is the matter of severe competition from nearby ports, for Dalian, Qinhuangdao, Tianjin, and Qingdao are also open coastal cities in this region. Indeed, to a certain extent Yantai is dwarfed by these competitors. For Shandong province alone, Qingdao often outstrips the importance of Yantai in a variety of ways. To deal with the competition problem, several issues have to be tackled. Certainly Yantai must improve education so that its work force is well trained and fit for running a modernized economy. Another important task concerns the status of Weihai. This close ally of Yantai has been upgraded to a *shi* and a development axis on the northern coastline has appeared. More investment in improving transport links between the two nodes is needed to reinforce the connections. (Muping would also benefit.) Thus, a mini-conurbation will emerge to compete with nearby rivals, this time with a competitive edge.

Yantai's traditional hinterland is not large; in fact, Liaodong Peninsula has been Yantai's essential base of operations. As a result, regional trade has predominated over international transactions. Although Yantai has done very well in connecting local economic activities with its port, this advantage may not be repeated in the context of extended openness to the outside world during the current modernization drive. Not only does Yantai fail to attract the attention that is lavished on Guangdong, Fujian, and Shanghai; it also lacks an advanced technological base. The latter shortcoming is particularly noteworthy as China's development strategy is to use coastal cities to introduce up-to-date technologies from abroad. Given such inadequacies, Yantai can best be described as a sub-provincial node. If its authorities truly aspire to upgrade Yantai's status as a coastal city exerting greater economic influence, much more should be done.

For various reasons, therefore, Yantai's catalytic role as a vibrant coastal city in North China is constrained. Nevertheless, the recent establishment of trade liaison offices between China and South Korea has raised new hopes for Yantai.[12] Preferential investment categories for Koreans include agriculture, communications, transportation, and nuclear energy. All these technologies are badly needed in Yantai. Thus it is no exaggeration to say that in order to enhance Yantai's catalytic role, it first requires a catalyst next door.

Notes

1. *"Shi"* literally means "city" in China. According to Chinese definitions, however, a *shi* is an administrative entity which consists of a number of counties *(xian)* surrounding the city proper. Readers should therefore make a distinction between Yantai *shi* and Yantai city proper. Yantai *shi* is much larger in area, of course, and basically rural in character. Unless otherwise stated, "Yantai" refers to Yantai *shi* in the following discussion.

2. These figures were obtained when the first draft of this chapter was written. Since then, however, there have been administrative changes within Yantai that make it impossible to present directly comparable data. I decided to provide the most recent data insofar as circumstances allow. One recent source for Yantai is *Yantai Tongji Nianjian, 1988* [Statistical yearbook on Yantai, 1988] (Yantai Shi Tongji Ju, 1989) (in Chinese).

3. The twelve *xian* are Penglai, Huang Xian, Zhaoyuan, Ye Xian, Laiyang, Qixia, Haiyang, Rushan, Muping, Wendeng, Rongcheng, and Changdao. The *xian*-level city mentioned is Weihai. For each of their locations, see Figure 4.1.

4. Administratively, upgrades of *xian* to *shi* were made since 1985: Huang Xian is now Longkou *shi*, Laiyang is Laiyang *shi*, and Ye Xian is Laizhou *shi*.

Moreover, in 1989 Yantai was reduced in size because of the cession of three *xian* (Rushan, Wendeng, and Rongcheng) to Weihai *shi* in 1986. Thereafter, figures on Yantai *shi* no longer include Weihai's attributes. Readers should be alerted to such a distinction in reviewing figures for Yantai since 1986.

5. See G. Huang, "The Bo Hai Economic Ring," *Jingji Dili* [Economic geography] 7(1) (1987): 33–38 (in Chinese).

6. These variables were (1) proportion of nonagricultural population, (2) agricultural production value, (3) industrial production value, (4) number of telephones, (5) electricity consumption, (6) transaction amount of urban and rural markets, (7) number of technical personnel, (8) number of cinemas and theaters, (9) number of hospital beds, and (10) total wage of workers in the public sector.

7. State Statistical Bureau (ed.), *Zhongguo Chengshi Tongji Nianjian, 1985* [Statistical yearbook on Chinese cities, 1985] (Beijing: Zhongguo Tongji Xinxi Zixun Fuwu Zhongxin and Xin Shijie Chubanshe, 1985) (in Chinese).

8. The cities employed for analysis were coded as follows: (1) Beijing, (2) Tianjin, (3) Shijiazhuang, (4) Handan, (5) Xingtai, (6) Baoding, (7) Zhangjiakou, (8) Chengde, (9) Tangshan, (10) Qinhuangdao, (11) Cangshou, (12) Langfang, (13) Hengshui, (14) Botou, (15) Shenyang, (16) Dalian, (17) Anshan, (18) Fushun, (19) Benxi, (20) Jinzhou, (21) Dandong, (22) Fuxin, (23) Yingkou, (24) Liaoyang, (25) Chaoyang, (26) Tieling, (27) Jinan, (28) Qingdao, (29) Zibo, (30) Zaozhuang, (31) Dezhou, (32) Weifang, (33) Yantai, (34) Jining, (35) Weihai, (36) Taian, (37) Xintai, (38) Binzhou, (39) Dongying, (40) Liaocheng, (41) Linqing, (42) Linyi, (43) Heze, and (44) Laiwu.

9. These are the figures for 1985. More recent population figures for *xian* capitals are not available.

10. Both Figures 4.3 and 4.5 were taken from Q. C. Yin and S. B. Liu, *Yantai* (Beijing: Zhongguo Haiyang Chubanshe; Hong Kong: Zhongwai Chuanbo Shiye Youxian Gongsi, 1986) (in Chinese).

11. Figure 4.4 is adapted from Management Bureau of Marine Transport and Internal Rivers, Ministry of Transport (eds.), "The Port of Yantai," in *Zhongguo Duwai Kaifang Gangkou* [Chinese ports opened to the outside world] (Beijing: Renmin Chubanshe, 1985), chap. 4, pp. 32–37 (in Chinese).

12. As reported in the Chinese edition of *Asiaweek* (14 October 1990), these offices are a tentative arrangement between the two countries to set up eventual diplomatic relations. Business between them amounted to over $3 billion in 1989. Given the many Chinese nationals residing in South Korea, as well as Yantai's close proximity to that country, a rapid surge in trade between them is expected in the near future.

5 Qingdao: From Colonial Port to Export Base

CHUNG-TONG WU, SHUN-ZAN YE, AND SHI-KUAN ZHOU

QINGDAO HAS A DEGREE of recognition at home and abroad which only a handful of other urban centers in China can command. Renowned for its port facilities, its mild climate, and its scenic setting, Qingdao is one of the oldest and largest ports of China and an important tourism destination. Its colonial legacy includes a distinctive architecture and a brewery industry which has established an international following for its products and earned precious foreign exchange. Although the historical development and the colonial history of Qingdao have endowed it with advantages, there are special problems which it now must face to facilitate its transformation into one of the key coastal cities charged with the dual tasks of attracting more foreign investment and developing export trade.

This chapter reviews the historical development of the city, introduces its current economic structure, and surveys the major issues of its urban development in order to assess its prospects as one of China's key open coastal cities. Indeed, Qingdao's attractive location for foreign investment has been an integral part of the city's history and its economic structure has been indelibly influenced by foreign powers. Its present role is vastly different, however, and a new urban structure is being developed to cope with its new role. This developing urban structure raises issues and opportunities which deserve examination.

Located approximately mid-south on the coast of the Shandong Peninsula and fronting the Yellow Sea, Qingdao straddles the east and west of Jiaozhou Wan (Figure 5.1). The entire municipality has an area of 10,654 sq km, a coastline of 730.6 km, and at the end of 1989 a total population of 6,571,600.[1] The urban districts of the municipality occupy an area of 244.4 sq km and a coastline of 177.4 km. The nonagricultural population within the urban district numbered 1.426 million in 1989. In addition to the urban districts, the municipality has under its administration six counties—Laoshan, Jimo, Jiaoxian, Jiaonan, Pingdu, and Laixi—and Jiaozhou city.

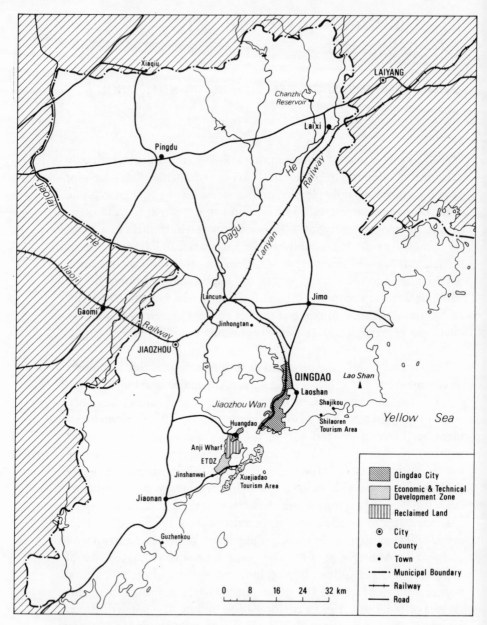

Figure 5.1 Qingdao Municipality

Historical Sketch

Over a thousand years ago, during the Song dynasty, Qingdao had already been transformed from a fishing village to an important anchorage point for ships plying Jiaozhou Wan. By the year 1088, during the North Song era, a municipal admiralty was established in Qingdao. During the Ming and Qing dynasties, Qingdao was considered an important naval base. In 1891, the Qing government established a major military base comprising a governor's mansion, fortifications with naval guns, military wharves, and a telegraph office. Qingdao at the time had a civil and military population numbering 13,000.

Events during the late nineteenth century not only catapulted Qingdao into the international scene but also led to a series of foreign occupiers. In November 1897, the German Empire's forces, using the excuse of the Caozhou Incident, forcibly occupied Jiaozhou Wan. By March 1898, the Qing government was coerced by the German government into accepting the Jiaoao Concessions Treaty, which sanctioned the German occupation of Jiaozhou Wan and ceded the right to build and operate railways and to mine in Shandong province. In 1898, Qingdao was forced to become an "open port" to be developed militarily and commercially. In the following year, customs controls were imposed and concession areas were established.

With the establishment of the open port and the development of commerce and trade, the construction of the city developed apace. Five separate districts were planned: commercial, industrial, residential, hospital, and military. The municipality's infrastructural development included river catchment and waterworks, a drainage system, and electricity generation plants. Among the main industries developed were machinery repair shops, ironworks, a soap factory, a carpet factory, an egg-product factory, a cigarette factory, and the first brewery in China. By 1910, the urban population had reached 160,000.

During and after World War I, Qingdao was occupied by the Japanese for eight years from 1914 to 1922. The Japanese, with the design of further expansion, enlarged the commercial and industrial activities and encouraged the in-migration of Japanese, who, in 1915 alone, totaled 20,000 to 30,000. The Japanese encouraged industrial development in Qingdao, as well, particularly in the spinning and weaving and food processing industries. A 1922 guidebook reveals that the main industries included salt making, aquatic products, spinning and weaving, silk spinning, flour mills, a brewery, food processing (including edible oil), iron works, chemicals, ceramics and glass, tobacco, and canned goods.[2] The textile industry, with at least seven major mills, was considered particularly important. Data for the period 1916–1920 indicate a decline of imported raw materials from Japan, India, and the rest of China as local products became more and more utilized.[3] Japanese investments dominated the industrial sector: all of the major industries having 500,000 *yuan* or more capital investment were Japanese-owned.

Intense industrial development led to urban expansion northward and thus to the establishment of the Sifang and Cangkou industrial districts. Expansion of the harbor, railways, and water plants soon followed. By this time, Qingdao had already become an industrial and commercial city with spinning and weaving as its chief industry. Indeed, by 1922 six of the major mills had a total of 295,000 spindles installed, accounting for one-quarter of the entire nation's mill capacity.[4] Investments in light industry comprised 98 percent of the total industrial investment in the municipality. Qingdao had also become a major import and export center. By 1923, the total population had reached 262,000.

At the end of World War I, the May Fourth movement had created a climate in which the Chinese government could demand the return of Qingdao and the forced purchase of the Jiaoji railways. However, much of Qingdao's economy remained under foreign control. In 1938, the Japanese reoccupied Qingdao. During this period, the industrial sector of the city was still dominated by the spinning and weaving sector though the machinery sector was also being developed. A 1935 tourist guide lists twenty-six major manufacturing concerns variously engaged in the manufacture of soap, noodles, matches, edible oil, tobacco, buttons, textiles, carpets, and other products.[5] By the late 1940s, industrial Qingdao had over 1,000 factories with more than 20,000 workers.

Urban development of the period was largely confined to the construction of a large number of villas along the southern coast and the establishment of parks and related facilities in the same area—for example, in the Taipingjiao, Huiquanjiao, and Baguan Shan areas were established aquariums, beach parks, stadiums, suspension bridges, and other facilities. An official report of the period indicates that a great deal of effort went into the construction and repair of roads—packed earth and gravel roads—and the construction and repair of bridges for both civilian and military purposes.[6] The city government also planted trees, in particular cherry trees, for landscaping and established regulations for the orderly development of the city.

During the 1940s, while the political administration of Qingdao underwent changes, the population of the city remained racially mixed and expanding. The Qingdao Municipality Gazette of January 1942 reported that the total population was 626,234, of which 6.2 percent were citizens of other countries. Among the foreign citizens, 89 percent were Japanese. Individuals of twenty-seven other nationalities were also residing in Qingdao. In 1947, however, the population changes accelerated with upheavals in the rest of China. In January, the municipality reported a population of 754,622; by the end of June, this number had swelled to 799,875—a 6 percent increase in six months.[7] The detailed records of births and deaths show that in-migration amounted to 42,260 during the six-month period—a 5.6 percent population increase through in-migration. When Qingdao was liberated in June 1949, the population was approximately 580,000. By 1980, the total urban population exceeded 1 million.

The Urban Economy

During the early years of the People's Republic, national development policies focused on construction and investment in noncoastal areas. Hence, Qingdao's economic growth was founded largely on the economic base already in place, with heavy reliance on the textile, food processing, machinery, and rubber tire industries. Nevertheless, significant investments were made in steel mills, sodium sulfide plants, fertilizer plants, bicycle factories, and other basic industries, including chemicals, metallurgy, and machinery. The chemical and metallurgy industries together contributed 22.2 percent of the municipality's gross value of industrial output (GVIO) in 1982, compared to a mere 3.2 percent in 1949.

The economy of Qingdao is inextricably linked to its vast hinterland, which includes most of Shandong province, southern Hebei province, as well as central Shanxi province—Qingdao is one of the major ports for the export of Shanxi coal. Shandong province, with some of the nation's most fertile agricultural land, is rich in cotton, food staples, fruits, peanuts, and tobacco. The Jiaoao salt fields are among the four largest in China. Ocean fishery and aquatic products are also plentiful in Shandong; the Yellow Sea is the breeding ground for the renowned Shandong prawns. The Victory oil fields at the mouth of Huang He produce about 20 percent of the nation's crude oil and are expected to become the second largest in the nation, rivaling the Daqing oil fields. Crude oil from the Victory oil fields is transported via pipeline to the Zibo Qilu refineries before being sent to Nanjing. Some of the production is sent overseas via Huangdao harbor in Qingdao. The Zibo Basin's rich alluvia and aluminum oxide deposits represent one-third of the nation's production. Ceramics and fire-resistant materials are also renowned products of the region. The coal fields in the southwestern part of the province, among the largest in the country, have great potential for expansion. These resources constitute favorable conditions indeed for the development of Qingdao's industries and its port activities.

Industries

The legacy of the past industrial structure can still be discerned today, for the key sectors remain largely the same as in the early part of the century and their locations in the city remain relatively unchanged. Light industry still represents the lion's share of the industrial economy of Qingdao. Among the light industries, the textile sector is dominant. Even before 1949, the number of installed spindles in Qingdao was second only to Shanghai. The textile sector constituted 60 percent of the municipality's GVIO in 1949, but this proportion had dropped to 20.8 percent by 1986. This sector boasted of 315 mills, of which 9 are considered large with 542,000 spindles and 13,000 weaving installations.

The food processing industry has expanded rapidly since 1949, and Qingdao now produces about one-third of the province's flour. Peanut oil is an important export. Qingdao beer, 80 percent of which is exported, is part of the industrial legacy. The cigarette industry in Qingdao is ranked number three in all China; the Qingdao Cigarette Factory is the second largest in the nation. Qingdao's chemical industry takes advantage of its coastal location, and the basic materials are often extracted from seaweed and sea salt. The city's rubber tire production is third in the nation; the quality of its products is considered second to none. The machinery sector has experienced exceptionally rapid growth; indeed, Qingdao now has the second largest machinery sector in the province. Since 1953, the Sifang factory has pioneered in the production of tractors and vehicles. It now produces railway engines, vehicles, and power generation machinery.

Qingdao's GVIO has expanded steadily over the years and now holds thirteenth place among the large cities of China. The changes in GVIO and the dominance of light industry are indicated in Table 5.1. Despite its historical dominance in the municipality and its contributions to

Table 5.1   Gross Value of Industrial Output of Urban Qingdao: 1982–1986

INDICATOR	1982	1983	1984	1985	1986
GVIO (10,000 *yuan*)[a]	587,167	628,798	687,008	784,512	875,200[b]
Increase over previous year (%)	—	7.09	9.26	14.2	8.1[b]
Composition of GVIO					
Light industry (%)	65.0	62.8	61.8	63.8	65.9
Heavy industry (%)	35.0	37.2	38.2	36.2	34.1

Sources: Almanac of China's Economy (various years) and *Almanac of China's Urban Statistics* (1987).

[a]1980 prices.

[b]Estimates.

GVIO, the textile sector in Qingdao is not highly competitive nationally. Of the twenty-five key establishments identified in the nation's textile sector, none was located in Qingdao, an indication of its relative inefficiency. In 1984, the State Statistical Bureau cited three key industrial establishments in Qingdao: the Qingdao Tire Factory, the Qingdao Cigarette Factory, and the Qingdao Beer Factory.[8] In fact, the tire and cigarette factories are among the nation's top 200 factories with the highest value of output and are also on the list of the top 200 factories with the largest sales income in 1985.[9]

Detailed data on the sectoral output of Qingdao's urban economy are not available, accounting for discrepancies in published data. (For example, the total GVIO for 1985 reported in the *Statistical Yearbook* is 7.5 percent lower than that given in the *Almanac of China's Economy*.) Nevertheless, close comparison of Qingdao's GVIO with provincial data indicate several important features (Table 5.2):

1. The four largest sectors by value of output are textiles, food (including beverages and tobacco), machinery, and chemicals. Together these four sectors contributed close to 73 percent of the total GVIO in 1985 and 82.7 percent of the total in 1986.[10]
2. Although Qingdao's urban economy is dominated by light industry, two of the four major sectors (machinery and chemicals) are heavy industries. They contributed 36.32 percent of the total municipal

Table 5.2   Urban Qingdao's GVIO by Sector (1980 values in
10,000 *yuan*): 1985 and 1986

SECTOR	1986 QINGDAO[a]	AS % OF PROVINCE	
		1985	1986
Food, beverage, tobacco	96,282	21.6	25.4
Textile	186,203	26.7	29.2
Clothing	24,340	32.8	34.1
Building material and nonmetal products	16,548	13.5	11.4
Ferrous metals	21,810	19.6	19.1
Nonferrous metal	404	4.1	0.8
Metal products	25,694	23.9	24.9
Machinery	85,560	21.3	20.0
Electronic and communication equipment	36,525	43.6	46.4
Leather, furs, and manufactured goods	9,671	23.9	24.6
Papermaking and manufactured goods	9,904	13.8	12.8
Cultural, educational, and sport articles	2,096	27.0	29.7
Power, steam, and hot water	17,955	11.5	11.4
Petroleum	11,718	4.0	5.8
Chemical	70,441	30.2	31.9
Total	530,451	19.22[b]	17.2[b]

Source: Almanac of China's Urban Statistics (1986 and 1987).

[a]Excludes the rural counties.

[b]Represents average percentage.

GVIO in 1985, but this proportion had fallen to just under 30 percent by 1986.

3. In 1985 and 1986, Qingdao produced over 19 percent and 17 percent respectively of the total provincial GVIO. Several of Qingdao's industrial sectors featured prominently within the province. Those representing 20 percent or more of the province's output include the following: electronic and communication equipment; clothing; chemicals; manufacture of cultural, education, and sports equipment; metal products; leather and fur products; textiles; manufacturing of food, beverages, and tobacco products; machinery; and processing of ferrous metals.

4. Indeed, Qingdao leads the rest of the province in the sectors of electronic and communication equipment, chemicals, metal products, and clothing manufacturing. What is remarkable about the electron-

ics sector is that it constitutes a very small proportion of Qingdao's economy, indicating the undeveloped state of this sector in Shandong.

Foreign Investment

The rapid expansion of industries in Qingdao during the early parts of the century was due largely to investment brought in by the foreign occupiers. The legacy of those investments is still evident today in the brewery and textile sectors. Unlike some of the coastal cities, Qingdao was not declared an open city, that is, one where foreigners can invest, until 1980. Consequently, the level of foreign investment in Qingdao—indeed, the whole province—is not as high as in the locations designated earlier.

Data on foreign investment may be found in the *Almanac of China's Foreign Economic Relations and Trade* and the *Almanac of China's Urban Statistics*. The listed investments are agreements only, however, and there is certainly attrition as well as time delays in their implementation. Nevertheless, these agreements furnish at least a set of serious intentions and represent a fairly reliable guide to the sectors which attract foreign investments and the maximum amount of foreign capital which can be expected. Judging by the year the foreign investments were approved, it is clear that Qingdao has had a slow start (Table 5.3). Bearing in mind that most projects have a lead time of one or more years, the impact of these projects would have been felt in the Qingdao economy only recently. Foreign investments have originated from Hong Kong, Macau, Finland, Singapore, Japan, Indonesia, and the United States.

Tourism

Given its history, its geographic setting, and its mild climate, Qingdao is one of the favorite vacation spots among the Chinese. Indeed, its beach

Table 5.3 Foreign Investment in Qingdao: 1981–1986

YEAR	AMOUNT ($10,000)	% OF PROVINCE	UTILIZED FOREIGN INVESTMENT	% OF PROVINCE
1981	20	100.0	na	na
1984	9,761	40.2	40	0.58
1986	3,379	79.7	1,073	60.72

Sources: *Almanac of China's Foreign Economic Relations and Trade* (various years); *Almanac of China's Urban Statistics*.

Table 5.4   Tourism Indicators of Qingdao: 1984–1988

INDICATOR	1984[a]	1985	1986	1988
Number of hotels and hostels	392	458	na	na
Number of beds	28,760	44,000	na	na
Number of tourists (in thousands)[b]	36.192	22.5	24.8	42.7
Percentage of foreign tourists	na	62.67	60.48	52.0
Foreign exchange earnings (million *yuan*)	13.56	14.56	na	na
Number of domestic tourists (in thousands)	na	8.4	9.8	20.2

Sources: *Almanac of China's Economy* (1986); *Statistical Yearbook of China*, 1987, p. 610; 1989.

[a]Data for 1984 calculated from information in the almanac.

[b]Foreigners, overseas Chinese, and Hong Kong/Macau compatriots.

resorts are considered one of its major resources. Numerous guidebooks on Qingdao dating from the early part of the century attest to the historical role that tourism has played. Qingdao's convenient location relative to Shanghai means that it is easily accessible to large numbers of domestic tourists. The area's tourism resources are numerous. In addition to several beach parks, there is the nearby Laoshan Scenic Area, long considered one of the key scenic areas of China. Table 5.4 shows the key tourism indicators.

In the absence of detailed data, the significance of the tourism sector to the economy of Qingdao is unclear. Certainly the expansion of international tourism is an important strategy for the city, and plans have been formulated to establish several major tourist destination areas. South of the Huangdao district is the Xuejiadao tourism area, of which 4.8 sq km is planned for development. This area, only 3 km from the Huangdao ETDZ, is endowed with wide beaches that are several kilometers long. Along with areas on the eastern seacoast, this area is expected to be developed as a major tourism destination area.

Urban Development

Qingdao's urban pattern assumes an "L" shape along the east coast of Jiaozhou Wan, forming a 25-km-long and 2-km-wide ribbon. Two rivers, Haibo He and Licun He, divide the city into three portions. The main urban center is located between the sea and Haibo He. In this main urban center are located the administrative, cultural, and commercial facilities, as well as residential, scenic, and hospital areas. The main north–south artery with the major commercial areas is Zhongshan Road; its southern end starts from the offshore scenic area of Zhanqiao.

The urban districts of Qingdao are centered on the eastern tip of the peninsula guarding the entrance to Jiaozhou Wan. Much of the southeastern coast, separated from the rest of the city by hills, has been developed for villas and a series of beach resorts. The urban center, concentrated around the railway station and the old harbor (see Figure 5.2), stretches northward along the eastern coast of Jiaozhou Wan along the railway line to Jinan, the provincial capital. With the development of industries, the city has expanded northward. To solve the problem of water supply, a major reservoir in Loushan and five sets of pumps were constructed during the late 1950s. Expansion of the harbor also continued apace. The built-up area increased from the 27 sq km of 1949 to over 70 sq km. At present the city is developing toward the southeast and on the southwestern shores of Jiaozhou Wan.

The eastern urban districts, Shidong, Shinan, Taidong, Sifang, and Cangkou, comprising an area of 92.4 sq km, have a population of 1,186,000.[11] The western urban district of Huangdao has an area of 152 sq km and a population of 83,000. Thus in the five main urban districts the average population density is 12,835.5 persons per square kilometer, while it is merely 546 in Huangdao. Across the entrance to Jiaozhou Wan from the main city, Huangdao is in fact the site of the newly established ETDZ. As part of this development, a new harbor and industrial area with oil terminals and an electricity generation plant are being established at Huangdao.

Like all other cities in China, the urban districts are the home of many industrial establishments. Of Qingdao's 2,411 industrial establishments reported in 1985, some 1,062 or 44 percent are located in the five urban districts on the east coast of Jiaozhou Wan. The resulting land-use conflicts and environmental pollution are typical of other major Chinese cities (Table 5.5).

Along the southeastern coast is the cultural and educational district with museums, library, institutes of higher learning, recreation areas, and hospitals. The harbor, located on the southern side of the mouth of Haibu He inside Jiaozhou Wan, is subdivided into the main harbor, middle harbor, and small harbor. The industrial district in this area is dominated by textiles, transport, manufacturing, and processing of aquatic products. The number of establishments in the district is about

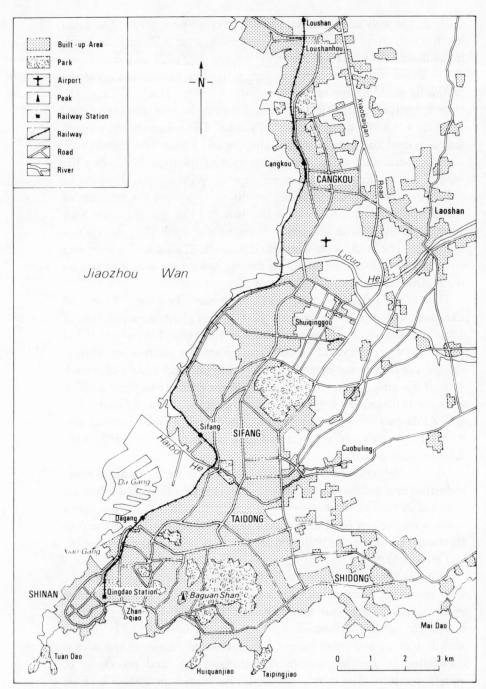

Figure 5.2 Qingdao City

Table 5.5   Selected Urban Indicators for Qingdao: 1982–1988

INDICATOR	1982	1984	1986	1988
Urban population (10,000)[a]	118	122.95	127.30	200.7
Urban nonagricultural population (10,000)[b]	na	114.00	117.7	137.1
Built-up area (sq km)	na	77.0	79.9	83.4
Population density (persons/sq km)[c]	4,836.07	5,038.93	5,217.21	8,211.9
Per capita housing area (sq m)	3.96	4.37	5.60	6.1
Per capita area of paved road (sq m)	3.42	3.84	4.0	4.60
Water reusage rate (%)	72.0	76.0	na	na
Capacity of waterworks (10,000 tons/day)	21	21.3	21.5	33.4

Sources: Almanac of China's Economy (various years) and Almanac of China's Urban Statistics (1985, 1987).

[a]Refers to shiqu renkou.

[b]Refers to shiqu fei nongye renkou (nonagricultural population).

[c]Six urban districts (244 sq km); five urban districts excluding Huangdao have an average density of 12,835.5 persons per square kilometer.

half of the whole municipality, and the gross value of industrial production ranks second within the municipality.

The area from Haibu He to Licun He, including the Sifang, Shuiqinggou, and Cuobuling districts, is industrial as well, mainly spinning and weaving and machinery. Located in these districts are one-third of the city's industrial establishments, large and medium firms predominating. The workers constitute over one-third of the city total, and the gross value of industrial production is the highest among all the urban districts. The density of the factories is high; so too is their interdependency.

Northward from Licun He to Loushanhou is another group of industrial areas largely established since 1949. Chief among these are the ones in Cangkou and Loushan. Within these zones are metallurgy, chemical, and textile industries. Although the number of establishments is only about a tenth of the city's total, the number of workers is about 20 percent of the total and the GVIO is third in the city.

To avoid overconcentration and congestion, several satellite towns were also established in the municipality. These are located within about 50 km of the city center. Licun in Laoshan xian is only 1 km from the built-up areas of the city. It has a population of 25,000 and a GVIO of

180 million *yuan;* its industries are primarily devoted to machinery, textiles, and processing. Licun is too close to the main city, however, and no further large industries will be located there. Jimo town, with a population of 41,000, is located about 20 km from the city center. The gross output-value of its industries—chiefly agricultural machinery, fertilizers, food processing, and marine chemicals—was 290 million *yuan.* Lancun, with a population of 8,000, is located 30 km from the city center; it is where the Lanyan and Jiaoji railways meet and the site of a large railway yard. Shajikou town is located 15 km from the city center; its economy is based largely on handicrafts for the tourist trade and other light textile industries. Linshanwei and Guzhenkou are satellite towns in the southern part of Huangdao district. Linshanwei is dependent on processing of fish and repair of boats; Guzhenkou depends on arts and crafts, clothing, and food processing.

Qingdao and China's Coastal Development

According to the World Bank, congestion of the transport system and energy shortages are two major bottlenecks of China's development.[12] The two problems are inextricably linked since the transportation of coal monopolizes a significant portion of the transport capacity of China. With increasing economic diversification and growth and the consequent mobility of the population, the already stretched transport system is strained to the limit. While much of the transport load and future expansions are dependent on the road and rail systems, water transport is expected to play an important role. Port cities, such as Qingdao, can make significant contributions toward economic development and the promotion of foreign investment and trade. Linked by rail to the coal fields of Shanxi and Shandong provinces, Qingdao has another key role in the transport of energy resources for domestic and foreign consumption.

During the Seventh Five-Year Plan (1986–1990), domestic freight was expected to grow by 45 percent. Increasingly the burden of freight transport is expected to shift from the railways (some 64 percent in 1985) to other modes, chiefly road transport and sea transport. The port subsector was singled out for investment in the Seventh Plan, particularly the updating of technology used in China's ports: palletization and containerization facilities for break-bulk cargo; specialized handling equipment for bulk cargo; and computerization of documentation flow and management information at the berth.[13]

Qingdao, the fourth largest port in China and one of its six major ports which together handle over 80 percent of the freight traffic, is one of the key ports in the expansion and technology drive. Located on the east coast of Jiaozhou Wan, Qingdao has superior natural conditions. Jiaozhou Wan has a relatively narrow mouth of 4.2 km and a north–south width of 18 km at low tide and an area of 446 sq km. Sheltered from the elements, it is a fine harbor with deep navigation channels (between 10 to 15 m) free of siltation and free from ice in the winter.

Present port facilities include nine wharves and forty-nine berths. Since China's import and export trade is dependent largely on sea transport, cities with good harbors are key centers. Table 5.6 details the freight traffic handled by Qingdao's port: the data indicate the increasing importance of international freight.

The chief link for domestic freight is with Shanghai's port. Most of the freight movements from Qingdao to Shanghai are commodities, including table salt, coal, chemicals, peanuts, and tobacco. The freight from Shanghai consists largely of rice and manufactured goods. Qingdao is

Table 5.6   Qingdao Port Freight Traffic (loading and unloading volume in million tons): 1975–1988

YEAR	IMPORTS	EXPORTS	DOMESTIC IN	DOMESTIC OUT	DOMESTIC TOTAL	DOMESTIC %
1975	1.23	1.50	1.07	11.62	15.42	82.3
1976	1.49	1.64	1.25	10.72	15.10	79.3
1977	2.30	1.54	1.69	11.41	16.94	77.3
1978	3.66	2.90	2.16	11.30	20.02	67.2
1979	3.62	4.46	2.00	7.94	18.02	55.2
1980	3.71	4.77	2.04	6.56	17.08	50.4
1981	3.17	4.09	2.02	8.82	18.10	59.9
1982	3.66	4.31	1.87	11.00	20.84	61.8
1983	4.31	5.11	1.89	10.52	21.83	56.8
1984	—	—	—	—	24.22	—
1985	—	—	—	—	26.79	—
1986	—	—	—	—	28.54	—
1987	—	—	—	—	30.28	—
1988	—	—	—	—	31.09	—

Sources: World Bank; *Almanac of China's Urban Statistics* (1986 and 1987); *Almanac of China's Economy* (various years). Data for total freight traffic from World Bank, *Staff Appraisal Report, China: Huangpu Port Project 1987;* data for other years from *Almanac of China's Urban Statistics 1986, 1987* and *Almanac of China's Economy* (various years).

also the center for the provincial coastal shipping and transshipment. The incoming goods include food staples, table salt, peanuts, and aquatic products; the outgoing products include coal, gray cloth, fertilizers, and manufactured goods. Domestic energy transport is an important export from Shandong province to the rest of the country. Coal, and to a lesser extent petroleum products, are shipped to Shanghai and Guangzhou, two manufacturing centers lacking in energy resources.

The harbor along the east coast of Jiaozhou Wan urban district, through refurbishing, dredging, and rebuilding, can be expected to expand its capacity. An eighth wharf with seven deep-water berths and an annual throughput capacity of 4 million tons is under construction. In the long term, a new harbor will be developed in Huangdao–Xuejiadao to satisfy the increasing demand for domestic and international trade. Passenger traffic between Shanghai, Dalian, and Guangzhou is handled by scheduled liners. A separate harbor area accommodates the provincial intercoastal shipping.

Land transport is based largely on the Jiaoji railway, which connects with the national rail network. This railway is being expanded to dual rails with a capacity of 60 million tons. In addition, the Yantai line links the eastern part of Shandong Peninsula. To strengthen the links between Qingdao and the rest of Jiaozhou Wan, a new railway line is being constructed in Jiaoxian through the Huangdao district to the Guzhen railway in Jiaonanxian.

The highway transport system of Shandong province represents one of the densest networks in northeastern China with the most developed vehicular traffic. Within Qingdao, there are 153 highways with a total length of 18,000 km. The major highways go to Yantai on the tip of the peninsula, Shijiazhuang, Lianyuangang, and Jinan. There are plans to construct a highway along Jiaozhou Wan and another along the east coast and Laoshan to strengthen the links between the central urban districts and the surrounding cities and towns. The two highways linking Qingdao to Yantai and Jinan are new first-class national highways.

Qingdao is linked by scheduled flights to nine domestic cities, including Beijing and Shanghai. Recognizing that the expansion of aviation is vital to the development of an open city, the Qingdao Liting airport is being expanded and will be capable of handling large jets. A new heliport is being constructed in the southern part of the city to facilitate links with the ETDZ.

Expansion of Qingdao's port is but one prong of the strategy. The other is to develop Qingdao as a center for foreign investment. This strategy relies on the development of an ETDZ on the western side of Jiaozhou Wan in the Huangdao area. By the end of 1986, some seventy-three agreements had been concluded and six of these had gone into production.[14] As in similar zones in the rest of China, selection of the site is supposed to be based on the following criteria: clear boundaries; links to but independence from the rest of the city; avoidance of usurping arable land; sound geological formation, superior location, natural beauty to create a suitable environment for investment; convenient transport links; use of the existing infrastructure; and potential for future expansion.

Given these criteria, it is clear why the Huangdao site was chosen. Except for the lack of convenient transport links, it has all the other desirable attributes. Consequently, much of the initial investment will be devoted to improving the transport network, particularly the ferry connection with the old urban districts some 4.2 km away. There is an ample electricity supply with a newly constructed 200-megawatt generating plant and another one approved. Since 1984, a harbor has also been planned with six berths and an expected capacity of 17 million to 40 million tons by the year 2000.

The Huangdao ETDZ is also near the Xuejiadao tourism area, but two major drawbacks have emerged. First, the land transport links between Xuejiadao and the rest of the inland area will be less convenient after development of the zone. Second, the first stage involves the resettlement of five villages with 3,261 persons and it is expected that the whole scheme will involve the resettlement of sixteen villages and 8,516 persons.[15]

Unlike the better-known Special Economic Zones, ETDZs are generally smaller in area and attached to a large city already known for its industrial activities. The Huangdao ETDZ is planned to be 1,510 ha in extent. With 27 percent of its land devoted to industrial uses, the ETDZ has within it a diversity of uses which constitute a separate but complete urban area. Due to the distance of the ETDZ site from the existing areas (see Figure 5.1), significant investments have to be made to develop the necessary infrastructure and urban facilities. The total expected infrastructural investment of 607.42 million *yuan* represents an average of 53.8 million *yuan* per square kilometer. The first-stage investment of 377.8 million *yuan* is expected to be composed of 260 million *yuan* plus foreign investment of $120 million.

The planners of the ETDZ have in mind a very different economic structure from the present. The zone is expected to generate close to three-quarters of its industrial output from the electronics and precision instruments sector. In terms of employment, the two key sectors are electronics and textiles, each contributing 30 percent and 28 percent respectively.

The ETDZ is being developed as an integrated area with all urban facilities and residential amenities. The planned population for phase one is 30,000 in 4 sq km; by the year 2000, a population of 100,000 is to be housed in 15 sq km. The population of the Huangdao district was 82,974 in 1984 with a nonagricultural population of 7,469. Thus the ETDZ, in addition to changing the economic structure of Qingdao, will fundamentally alter the population mix and present an urban alternative to further development in the existing urban districts.

Problems and Opportunities

Lack of urban investment and the intrusion of heavy industry into compact urban areas have created a number of problems which characterize Qingdao's urban and industrial patterns today. The future development of Qingdao depends on the successful fulfillment of three roles. First, it is expected to remain a tourist mecca for both international and domestic visitors. Second, as a major port linked to important coal and oil production areas it is expected to serve as an export base for energy resources to both domestic and foreign destinations. Third, as a coastal city it is expected to attract foreign investment and foreign trade. The potential for conflict is ever present, and the city administration must resolve a number of problems if Qingdao is to live up to its potential.

Technological Change and Foreign Investment

That the most important sector of Qingdao's economy, the textile sector, is comparatively inefficient is a salutary reminder of the need for significant technological change in all the industries of the municipality. Further evidence of this need is indicated by the fact that, compared to Dalian, Qingdao lags behind in its investments in technological change in the textile sector. For the first ten months of 1984, for example, the textile industries of Dalian invested over 500,000 *yuan* in microcomputers. For the same period, Qingdao is reported to have spent only 100,000 *yuan*.[16]

The industrial sector of Qingdao is reported to have urgent problems:

20 percent of the installations are of 1950 vintage; more than 8,000 installations require urgent and immediate replacement; over 200,000 sq m of factory space are considered dangerous and require urgent rebuilding. Sixty of the key industries in the municipality, which together contribute close to 50 percent of its GVIO, require investments to bring their facilities to present-day standards. Other sectors, such as the steel industry, have been facing up to the problems of technological renewal. In 1984 alone, the Qingdao Steel Mill was reported to have invested 2.01 million *yuan* to upgrade its refinery, casting, and cutting facilities.

Foreign investment is considered crucial for the process of industrial renewal. Although the new ETDZ is regarded as a key element in this strategy, it is not clear whether foreign investment will find the renewal of existing industries more attractive or would prefer to invest only in the new area.

Water and Energy Shortages

Qingdao is a city with severe water supply difficulties. The common occurrence of granite in Qingdao means that the topsoil is relatively thin, the groundwater level is low, and the watercourses are usually rapid and shallow. Although there are a number of reservoirs, such as Laoshan, Taoyuan, Qianji, and Yicun, their annual capacity is about 88 million cubic meters. This represents a daily supply capacity of 240,000 cu m or approximately three-quarters of daily requirements. Daily per capita water consumption is about 60 liters only.

According to the standards established for the nation, by 1990 the annual water requirement was to be 270 million cubic meters (a daily requirement of 740,000 cu m). By the year 2000, this is expected to be 455 million cubic meters (a daily requirement of 1.25 million cubic meters). To relieve the water shortage, a major project to bring the water of Huang He to supply Qingdao is now under way and was expected to be completed by the end of the Seventh Five-Year Plan (1986–1990). During the dry season (winter and spring), some 100 million cubic meters of water would be diverted from Huang He; 2 million cubic meters would be for the use of the Qingdao urban areas.

The water shortage and other resource limitations such as energy are constraints which must be addressed in planning for the new urban development and the expansion of tourism. Tourists are notoriously wasteful of water and energy. Industrial expansion imposes further demands. For example, the textile industry is vital to the economy of

Qingdao. In 1981, the municipal government decided to increase the capacity of the sector during 1982 to 1985 by 198,000 spindles. Then, in 1982, Factory 7 of the Qingdao National Cotton Textile Corporation decided to expand its production capacity by 13,200 spindles. It is estimated that these two expansion plans would require the daily consumption of 10,000 tons of water, 20,000 kwh of electricity, and 600 tons of coal.[17] Since all of these resources are severely limited, these plans merely exacerbate the already chronic problems.

The new electricity generating plants on Huangdao are expected to ease the energy shortage. Moreover, an additional system to connect Qingdao with the Shandong central distribution network would also help. But as more and more industries are expected to decentralize, the investments in the distribution system and the necessary capacities will require careful planning.

Environmental Pollution

The chemical and metallurgy industries, two of the key industries in Qingdao, are substantial polluters of the environment. According to municipal statistics, the average monthly dust particulate count per square kilometer is 30.7 tons—some 3.4 times the limit set by the national government. The problem is particularly acute in the Loushan-hou, Taidong, and Sifang industrial districts.

Water pollution is another serious problem. It is estimated that the annual discharge of wastewater into Jiaozhou Wan is about 49 million tons, containing some 290,000 tons of heavy metals, petroleum, and other harmful substances. The river courses in the urban districts have become wastewater channels, and Jiaozhou Wan has become the depository of industrial waste and garbage. Although efforts have been made to protect the environment, much is yet to be done and the environment is far from the ideal image of a pristine tourist destination.

Urban Restructuring and Renewal

The comprehensive plan for Qingdao calls for controlling the urban population to around 1.15 million by the end of the century. To accomplish this objective, it will be necessary to decentralize to the small towns and satellite towns in the municipality. However, urban expansion that conflicts with agriculture has always been a problem. Between 1950 to 1979, some 3,840 ha of arable land, one-third of it slopes, was converted to urban usage. Due to the land conversion, rural land per capita, calculated on the basis of the agricultural population only, is less than 0.018 ha in the rural districts near urban areas. At the same time, the population density of the city is around 8,200 persons per square kilometer. Consequently, in the established urban areas expansion is difficult.

Within these urban districts, industrial uses already comprise some 27 percent of the total, or 21.83 sq km. Of this, heavy industry constitutes 62 percent and is considered less efficient in the use of land. Within the old urban districts, therefore, the residential, work-related, transportation, and other public uses all are limited and the old harbor facilities cannot be expanded due to the limited land available in the surrounding area.

Urban renewal will concentrate on ensuring that each district has complete facilities to improve the housing shortage and the level of amenities of the residential areas. Past disregard for the overall planning of the city permitted the eastern industrial districts to develop so that the urban areas are now surrounded on the east and west by industries. The eastern industrial district was also allowed to expand southward into the hospital district. Due to the lack of control and planning, many industrial uses have been allowed to intrude into residential areas. Consequently the dispersal of residential areas became necessary. Thus today many of the residential areas lack adequate municipal or commercial facilities with consequent inconvenience for the residents.

The northern industrial area of Loushanhou, despite its heavy industry and chemical installations, can serve as a reserve area for further industrial development. The Shuiqinggou and Sifang industrial areas are extremely congested. The policy should be to improve the technology, emphasize environmental protection, and decentralize those industries which can be relocated. The eastern part of the Xibaigang Road industrial area, located in the eastern district, is home to numerous plastic and construction material industries; expansion here should be restricted due to the highly polluting nature of these industries. The Cuobuling industrial area is upwind from the city and should be restricted to food processing industries. The Taidong industrial area is largely light industrial and rubber tire industries with a significant impact on the surrounding residential area. These industries too require careful control.

Economic Restructuring

Restructuring land use in a city like Qingdao ultimately involves economic restructuring. In 1981, the State Council approved a plan to develop Qingdao as a tourism and convalescent area with export trade and textiles as its major economic activities. While tourism is still an important element, the basic approach to restructuring the urban economy has been superseded by the development of the ETDZ. Moreover, it is widely recognized that many of the industrial facilities in the urban districts are outdated. Some are polluting industries which can no longer be tolerated among residential areas. Requiring these industries to renovate would involve major investments; relocation would involve even larger investments.

Clearly, some choices will have to be faced in the near future with respect to the restructuring of the urban economy given the economic reforms which are now sweeping China. Enterprises are expected to be more efficient; the residents expect a cleaner and more healthy environment. While both of these goals may be accommodated by some enterprises, others will be unable to do so. Maximizing the tourist attractions of Qingdao may also demand the further decentralization of industrial uses from the urban center. Competing goals will inevitably demand choices to be made about the use of scarce resources such as water and the need to protect the environment. Redesigning the urban structure is integral to restructuring the urban economy. Although the planned development at the Huangdao ETDZ has already initiated these changes, the established urban industries still require attention. The choices are complex and difficult, but they must be faced if Qingdao is to perform its role as a key coastal open city.

Notes

1. State Statistical Commission (ed.), *Almanac of China's Urban Statistics* (Beijing: China Statistical Press, 1990), p. 37.

2. Ye Chunlu, *Qingdao Outline* (Shanghai: Commercial Press, 1922) (in Chinese).

3. Ibid., p. 65.

4. Ibid., p. 66.

5. Zhau Junhao, *Traveller's Guide to Qingdao* (Shanghai: China Travel Co., 1935) (in Chinese).

6. Qingdao Tebishi Gongchu, *Major Events of the Year* (Qingdao, 1940), p. 35 (in Chinese).

7. *Qingdaoshi Zhengfu Gongzuo Baogao* [Report of the Qingdao municipal government], January–June 1947 (in Chinese).

8. Guojia Tongjiju Gongye Jiaotong Muji Tongjizi (ed.), *The Development of*

China's Industry (Beijing: Zhongguo Tongji Chubanshe, 1985) (in Chinese); *Almanac of China's Light Industry* (Beijing: Qinggongye Chubanshe, 1986) (in Chinese).

9. Guowuyuan, *Census of Industries of the PRC 1985* (Beijing, 1987) (in Chinese).

10. *Statistical Yearbook of China,* 1986 and 1987.

11. Chen Chao and Wang Xiguang (eds.), *Handbook of Chinese County Town Administrative Area Information* (Beijing: Ditu Chubanshe, 1986) (in Chinese).

12. World Bank, Staff Appraisal Report, *China: Huangpu Port Project* (Washington, D.C.: World Bank, 1987).

13. Ibid.

14. State Statistical Commission (ed.), *Almanac of China's Urban Statistics* (Beijing: New World Press, 1987), p. 641.

15. Qingdao Jingji Jixue Kaifaqu, *Comprehensive Plan for the Qingdao Economic and Technical Development Zone 1984* (1984).

16. Zhou Yungren and others, "A Preliminary Analysis of the Status and Functions of Qingdao as a Core City," *Shandong Economy* (1985): 18–20 (in Chinese).

17. People's University, Shengcheng Buju Teaching and Research Unit, *Reference and Information on Industry Location* (Beijing, 1983) (in Chinese).

6 Lianyungang: From Coastal Development to Interior Development

ANTHONY G. O. YEH, HONG-YI ZHENG, AND YING-MING LI

LIANYUNGANG, one of China's major ports, is situated in the northern part of Jiangsu province at Haizhou Bay, surrounded by the Yuntai Mountains and facing the Yellow Sea. Located in the southern part of the temperate zone, Lianyungang has a maritime monsoon climate. The average annual temperature is 14 °C, with an average summer temperature of 26 °C and winter temperature of 4 °C. It has 220 frost-free days and an average annual precipitation of 937 mm. Lianyungang municipality is composed of three counties and three urban districts, with a total area of 6,327 sq km and a total population of 3 million in 1985. The three counties are Donghai, Ganyu, and Guanyun; the three urban districts are Xinhai, Lianyun, and Yuntai (Figure 6.1). The total area of the urban districts is 830 sq km with a population of 459,000, of which 288,000 may be classified "urban." The municipal government is located at Xinpu (Lianyungang).

Lianyungang is well endowed with natural resources. With seventeen major rivers and ten reservoirs, the city has an excellent supply of water for both industrial and domestic use. It has more than forty different kinds of minerals and rocks, including phosphatic rock, serpentine, quartz, marble, granite, pottery clay, and freshwater sand. The Jinping phosphate mine is one of the six largest mines in China. The Huaibei saltworks is one of the four largest saltworks in China and has a salt pan of 720 sq km which produces 2 million tons of salt annually. Donghai county is especially famous for its rock crystal. The surrounding area of Lianyungang is rich in agriculture, forestry, animal husbandry, and fishing. The plain produces rice, wheat, and soybeans while the hilly areas produce peanuts, sweet potatoes, and maize. The famous *yunwu* tea used to be offered as tribute to emperors in the past. Haizhou Bay, where the city is located, is one of eight major fishing grounds of China. The annual output of artificially bred fish and shrimps is over 2,100 tons, representing 40 percent of China's total output.

The city offers natural scenery and many historical relics for tourists. It

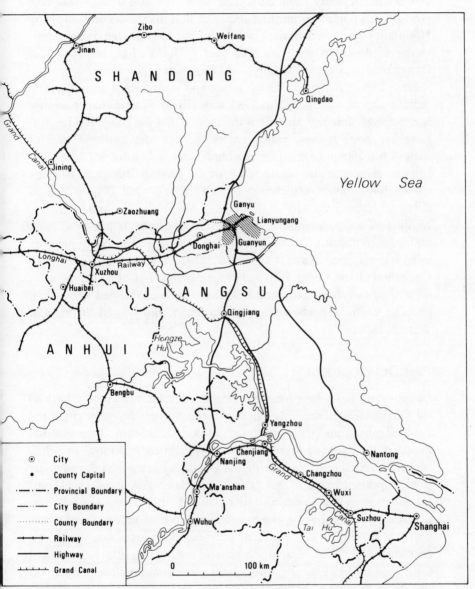

Figure 6.1 The Geographical Location of Lianyungang

has fourteen scenic areas and over one hundred scenic spots, giving the city four distinct features: seascapes, long history, Buddhist spirituality, and calm. The water along Xugou Beach is calm and shallow with fine sand and is a popular swimming area. The Buddha statues on Kongwang Mountain were carved on the cliffs during the Eastern Han dynasty, providing evidence of the "sea silk road." The Yushan hot spring at Donghai attracts a large number of tourists every year.

Lianyungang has good air, rail, water, and sea transport networks. The Baitafu airport was opened in 1985 with flights to Shanghai, Nanjing, and Beijing. Moreover, the city is the terminus of the Longhai (Lianyungang–Lanzhou) railway, which passes through the northern part of Jiangsu and Henan provinces to the border area in Northwest China. The Longhai railway is also connected with the Beijing–Shanghai, Beijing–Guangzhou, Jiaozuo–Zhicheng, Baoji–Chengdu, and Beijing–Baotou railways, linking the city with Beijing, Shanghai, Xuzhou, Bangbu, Nanjing, Tianjin, and other major cities in China. It has four trunk highways connecting Xuzhou, Qingdao, Nanjing, and Nantong. The inland rivers join Chang Jiang (the Yangzi River) and the Beijing–Hangzhou Grand Canal. Its port has nine berths, five of which can cater for 10,000-ton ships. Shipping links have been established with major ports in China and abroad, especially Japan, the United States, and Western Europe.

Past Development

Lianyungang has a long history of seaport development dating back to the Qin dynasty. In the early part of this century, the development of the Longhai railway and the construction of port facilities in Dapu near the mouth of the Jianhong River led to the development of Xinpu, an industrial-commercial town supporting the Dapu port located 5 km away. The three important towns in that period were Haizhou, Xinpu, and Dapu; Haizhou served as the administrative center. In 1933, because of the silting of the Jianhong River, the port at Dapu was abandoned and a new port was developed at the present site near Houyuntai Mountain. This port, backed by Houyuntai Mountain and linking two islands, was called Lianyungang. In 1936, the Dutch built a 1,050-m-long breakwater and two docks capable of berthing 3,000-ton-class ships, and this construction remains the basis for the harbor. The unique pyramidal tower at the railway terminal was built in the late 1930s to commemorate the construction of the port.

The port did not develop much during the period of the Kuomintang government. In 1948, Lianyungang had a population of 107,000 with a built-up area of 7.5 sq km. The industrial base was weak with six mining and industrial enterprises and twenty-nine handicraft factories; the annual cargo handling was just 56,000 tons.

After the founding of the People's Republic, however, the port was reconstructed and expanded several times. It was granted city status in 1950 under the name of Xinhailian but was renamed Lianyungang in 1961. By 1972, the port could handle two 3,000-ton-class ships and two 5,000-ton-class ships; by then, the annual cargo handling was 2.75 million tons, making it the eighth largest seaport in China. The port continued to develop during the next ten years. By 1983, five berths for 10,000-ton-class ships were added and the annual cargo handling had increased to 9 million tons in 1984 (Table 6.1). Of the cargo handled by Lianyungang, 50 percent consisted of exported coal and 25 percent imported food, fertilizers, and steel. The shipment of local products was dominated by sea salt (1 million tons annually).

The total industrial output value of its urban areas in 1983 was 930

Table 6.1   Cargo Handled by Principal Seaports of China
             (in million tons): 1952–1984

SEAPORT	1952	1957	1965	1978	1984
Shanghai	6.56	16.49	31.94	79.55	100.60
Dalian	1.51	5.88	10.57	28.64	40.16
Qinhuangdao	1.81	2.83	4.78	22.19	35.79
Qingdao	1.75	2.21	4.48	20.02	24.22
Huangpu	0.47	1.86	4.70	10.50	16.68
Tianjin	0.74	2.84	5.49	11.31	16.11
Zhanjiang	0.12	0.79	2.20	9.47	11.95
Lianyungang	0.46	1.05	2.65	5.94	9.00
Yantai	0.26	0.48	0.98	4.58	6.74
Ningbo	—	—	—	—	5.97
Basuo	—	0.11	0.99	3.07	4.11
Shantou	0.35	1.30	1.81	1.53	1.77
Haikou	0.16	0.35	0.64	0.76	1.31
Sanya	0.03	0.76	0.29	0.45	0.53
Yingkou	0.18	0.32	0.29	0.33	0.49

Source: Xue Muqiao (ed.), *Almanac of China's Economy 1985/86* (Hong Kong: Modern Cultural Company, 1986), p. 35.

million *yuan*. It had 1,250 enterprises in industries specializing in fields such as textiles, electronics, food processing, engineering, chemicals, building materials, leather processing, and papermaking. Its industrial output is dominated by light industry (65 percent as opposed to 35 percent heavy industry). The city has fairly large chemical engineering, power generating, coal mining, and building material industries. There were 502 heavy industrial enterprises, 12 of which had an annual output of over 10 million *yuan*. The chemical industry is moderately large, as well, producing more than eighty kinds of chemical products such as synthetics, nitrogen, phosphate, potash, and soda ash. Lianyungang is one of China's major alkaline-chemical production centers. The Jinping phosphate mine, producing 300,000 tonnes of concentrated phosphate annually, is China's only phosphorus mining and ore dressing enterprise and provides raw materials for making thirty kinds of phosphorus chemicals. The Huaibei salt field, one of the four largest sea-salt-producing centers in the country, produces 2 million tonnes of crude salt annually. It not only supplies the needs of China but also exports to Japan, Korea, and other countries. The city's food processing industry is rather well developed, with products such as fruit, wine, beer, and canned food. Its output accounted for 34 percent of the city's total industrial output.

Exports, except sea salt, are mainly derived from products of other provinces. Most of the port facilities are geared for long-distance transport and do not have provision for coastal transport. Most of the sea transport involves cargo, not passengers. People going to Shanghai must take a train or bus to Nanjing and then transfer to Shanghai. The development of Lianyungang's port is not integrated with that of the local economy.

Development Potential

The main development advantage of Lianyungang resides in its geographical position and transport services serving a large hinterland. The Longhai railway which starts at Lianyungang—one of the major east-west lines of China—goes through eleven interior provinces and autonomous regions in the central and northwestern parts of China and ends in Lanzhou in Gansu province. These provinces, which constitute over 40 percent of the total area of China with one-third of its total population, are not only major producers of grain, cotton, and edible oil but are also an important base for animal husbandry, mining, and energy production. Their industrial and agricultural output value amounted to 20 percent of the national total, while coal accounts for 48 percent and grain output about 30 percent. Most of these areas rely on the export of raw materials, and Lianyungang is the nearest coastal outlet. It is estimated that by shipping goods via Lianyungang, the transport distance from these provinces can be shortened by 400 km as opposed to going through Shanghai or Qingdao.

With such a vast hinterland, it would be desirable to open up Lianyungang for foreign trade and investment in order to link these areas with the international market. Indeed, the development of Lianyungang is of great strategic importance to the economic development of the interior provinces of China. By attracting foreign investment, it will help to develop Lianyungang as well as these interior areas. Thus, the Longhai railway plays an important role in the present and future development of Lianyungang. At present, goods moved along the Longhai railway account for 90 percent of the cargo handled by the port.

Apart from the advantage of a large hinterland, Lianyungang has rich resources in its surrounding areas, particularly aquatic and mineral resources. As noted earlier, it has an important phosphate mine and salt field. It also has a rich reserve of mineral deposits such as kyanite, serpentine, dolomite, crystal, and quartz. Moreover, Donghai county is an important agricultural area. Not only is it the major soybean-producing area in Jiangsu province, but there are many fruit trees, with an annual production of 25 million kilograms. *Yunwu* tea is one of the four famous teas of Jiangsu province. Aquatic production amounts to 60,000 tonnes a year.

Lianyungang has many tourist resources which are to date largely undeveloped. There are 14 major scenic areas and 116 scenic spots. Among these are primitive rock carvings, ancient Buddhist cliff statues, the Monkey King's home, and a Buddhist monastery of the Tang dynasty. Surrounding the city are many scenic spots and historical sites, including beaches, hot springs, ancient Buddhist pagodas, Paleolithic ruins, and a nature reserve containing many plants found in the temperate zone. Compared with other cities in China, it has abundant water and land resources for urban development.

Despite the potential of Lianyungang, its development has been slow. In fact, its economic development was one of the lowest among Jiangsu's eleven municipalities. In 1982, for example, the per capita industrial and agricultural output of Lianyungang was one-fourth that of Wuxi

Table 6.2   Industrial Structure of
Lianyungang: 1982

INDUSTRY	% OF TOTAL INDUSTRIAL OUTPUT
Food	35.73
Chemical	17.87
Textile	14.60
Machinery	14.13
Electricity	5.21
Building materials	2.53
Paper	1.37
Lumber	0.55
Coal	0.42
Others	7.58

Source: Statistics Department, Lianyungang Planning Committee.

city. Chen cites several reasons for this slow pace of development.[1] First, there is much silting in its harbor, although this problem can be easily overcome with modern dredging technology. Second, the economic base of its surrounding areas is weak because they have been much affected by past flooding and the change of the course of Huang He (the Yellow River). Third, the main transport relies heavily on the Longhai railway whereas coastal and road transport with other areas of Jiangsu province is underdeveloped. Fourth, for historical reasons the city proper at Xinpu is quite far from the port at Lianyun; thus the port lacks the support of urban facilities and the city proper cannot make use of the port's transport network to facilitate development. Finally, Lianyungang's industrial structure relies mainly on food processing, which occupies 35.73 percent of the total industrial output—and 23 percent of this was salt processing (Table 6.2). There is a lack of such industries as ship construction, aquatic food processing, and export processing which can utilize the good harbor facilities and aquatic resources. Although salt and phosphate production is quite significant, chemical industries utilizing these materials are not well developed. There is also a lack of large industries. Apart from the two salt and phosphate plants, most of the industries are small facilities with little horizontal and vertical industrial linkage.

Seaports are main break-of-bulk points which provide a logical focus for development of maritime and processing industries.[2] Although its seaport advantage has not been much utilized, Lianyungang possesses considerable potential for industrial development.

Development Strategy

The State Council has decided that Lianyungang should be gradually built into a new industrial and foreign trade port. It hopes to develop the city as an export outlet and a showroom of products from the interior provinces, serving as a gateway for China's central northwestern provinces and regions. To achieve this goal, the construction of Lianyungang will focus on four major areas.[3]

First is the construction of a modern port with multiple harbors and functions. In addition to the main harbor, which is now under expansion, the city has three river mouths which will be developed into supplementary harbors for inland shipping. The first port is Yanwei harbor at the mouth of Guan He (also known as the second Huangpu River), whose middle and upper courses are linked with the Grand Canal and Chang Jiang. The second port is Xiaoding harbor at the mouth of the Shaoxiang River, which is connected with the Beijing–Hangzhou Grand Canal and Chang Jiang. The third port is Haitou harbor at the mouth of the Zhupeng River, where the water is very deep. When construction of these harbors is completed, there will be a group of harbors centering around the main harbor. The handling capacity of the main port at Lianyun will gradually be upgraded from 10 million tons in 1986 to 20 million tons in 1990 and 60 million tons by the year 2000, when it will have more than a hundred berths.

Second is the development of a new industrial base. Land along the coast will be used for the development of power stations, iron and steel works, petrochemical industries, marine chemical industries, shipbuilding and repair, processing industries, and warehouse facilities. The inland areas will be used for the development of processing and other industries with an emphasis on food, textiles, machinery, electronics, chemicals, and building materials. The aim is gradually to develop the city's inner areas into a new industrial district guided by modern science, technology, and a rational industrial structure with mainly an export orientation.

The third area of focus is building a financial center and base of entrepôt trade. With the expansion of the port and the development of foreign trade, it is hoped that Lianyungang will gradually become a center for finance, trade, and the distribution of goods. The completion of the railway line joining Urumqi with the Trans-Siberian railway in the Soviet Union in 1992 will make the Longhai (Lianyungang–Lanzhou) railway part of the "Eurasian continental bridge" linking the Pacific and the Atlantic oceans (Figure 6.2). Since the Longhai railway will connect all the way to the container port at Rotterdam in the Netherlands, Lianyungang will become the bridgehead in developing Eurasian containerized transport. Thus the city will enjoy the advantages of both sea and rail transport.

The fourth and final focus is the building of unique tourist resorts. The city has a strong potential for tourism development. While keeping the city's basic characteristics of seascapes, long history, spiritual tradition, and calm, efforts will be made to build tourist areas with local features. The plan is to build Xugou Beach into a modern beach, develop Flower Fruit Mountain into a tourist area with a layout modeled after that described in the famous novel *Journey to the West,* develop Kongwang and Shipeng mountains into a tourist area with the cultural features of the Qin, Han, and Song dynasties, develop Sucheng into a mountain village of peach blossoms, develop the area around Dacun reservoir into a vacation resort with Haiqing Temple and Ayuwang Tower as its center, and develop the Yushan hot spring area at Donghai into a tourist resort.

Moreover, the municipal government is planning to build an Economic and Technical Development Zone (ETDZ) with an area of 30 sq km. Located in the Zhongyun (Middle Yuntai) area at the border of the port, the zone is 20 km from the city center at Xinpu, 11 km from the main port, 3 km from the Zhongyun railway station, 42 km from the Lianyungang airport, and 5 km from the Xinxu Canal (Figure 6.3). Two highways will connect the zone with the Linnan Highway. The first stage of construction is a 3-sq-km project. With the port as its main asset, the ETDZ can make use of the water, electricity, roads, and other public utilities of the city. Transport for the zone is very convenient because of its proximity to the port, the railway station, highways, and the airport. Moreover the land is flat, with little need for leveling, and the geological conditions are excellent and will not require much foundation work for building construction. Thus the development cost of the ETDZ is expected to be quite low. The zone will be developed comprehensively with an emphasis on export-processing industries utilizing advanced

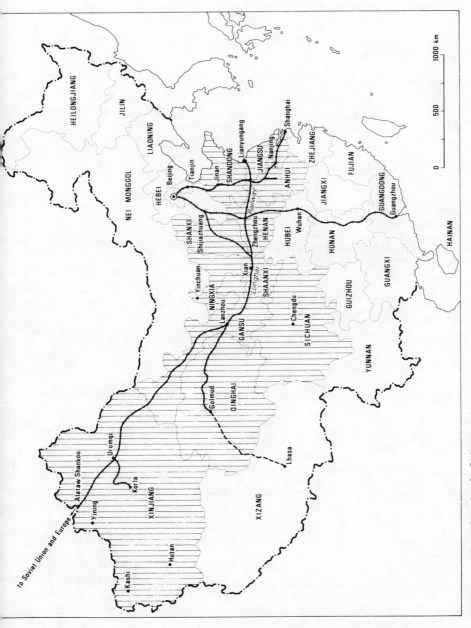

Figure 6.2 The Hinterland of Lianyungang

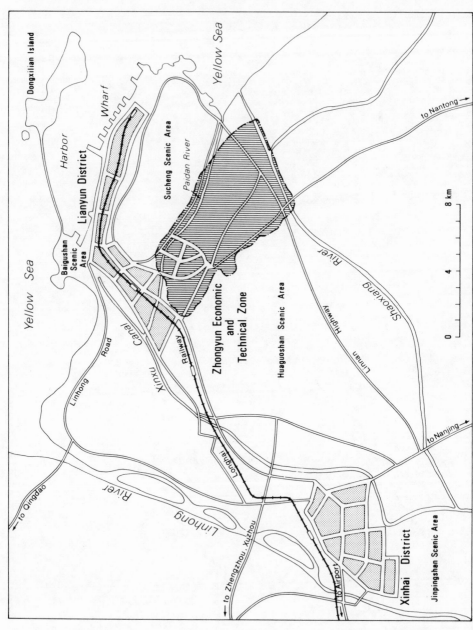

technology. It will also provide facilities for banking, trade, tourism, and scientific and cultural undertakings. The idea is to attract foreign investment and advanced technology to help develop light industry and food processing, as well as electronics, textiles, and machine building.

As in other open cities and Special Economic Zones, preferential treatment of foreign investors has been legislated by the municipal government. A reduced income tax rate of 15 percent will be granted to projects in the zone which apply advanced technology, promote industrial improvement, and produce commodities that can find international markets or substitute imported goods, along with investment in transport, energy development, and port construction. After-tax profits can be remitted abroad without restriction. A land-use fee system similar to the one applicable in Shenzhen SEZ has been established.[4] Land-use fees will be collected for all land used by enterprises, whether it be newly requisitioned or the site of an existing enterprise. These fees will be determined by location, type of business, and term of use. The annual rate charged per square meter of land for industry is 1–5 *yuan,* for commerce 9–14 *yuan,* for commercial residential buildings 4–8 *yuan,* and for tourist facilities 5–10 *yuan.* Land-use fees for agriculture, forestry, animal husbandry, and aquaculture are substantially lower.

The municipal government has allocated an area of 4.5 sq km adjacent to the ETDZ for projects jointly invested by the interior provinces and Lianyungang. This location will provide a base where the interior provinces can trade and make contacts with foreign investors. There will be about a hundred projects—mainly warehouses and other storage facilities, as well as processing factories for export products.

As a first step in attracting foreign investment, the municipal government intends to renovate its existing factories through foreign funds and advanced technology. Priority areas for the future use of foreign capital are as follows.

1. A soda ash plant to be built at the East Sea serpentine mine
2. Two 200-megawatt power generators to be installed at Xinhai electric power plant
3. Upgrading of the eastern section of the Longhai railway during the Seventh Five-Year Plan
4. Development of industries with priority in food processing, packaging, and fodder production
5. Energy development

6. Development of aquaculture and marine processing industries to make full use of coastal resources
7. Development of marine, land, and air transport and communication services
8. Development of a tourist industry with the installation of more facilities in the Huaguoshan (Fruit and Flower Mountain) resort and at Xugou Beach, as well as opening more scenic spots for tourists and building more hotels and restaurants

Various departments have listed more than 300 projects for negotiation with foreign firms. At the end of 1984, thirty-two contracts had been signed involving an investment of $380 million. Six of them have already started construction or have been put into operation. The largest is the brewery jointly funded by the Lianyungang Light Industry Corporation, the China International Trust and Investment Company, and the Jiangsu Provincial International Trust and Investment Company with the Japanese Suntory Company. The annual production is set at 30,000 tonnes of beer and 30,000 tonnes of malt. The total investment, shared equally between China and Japan, was valued at $32 million and the brewery started production in October 1984.

Issues of Development

Silting of the port has been one of the major obstacles to Lianyungang's development. Although Rotterdam has a similar silting problem, because of its large hinterland it has developed into the world's largest seaport through dredging. Since the establishment of the European Economic Community, many import and export goods from Western Europe are handled by Rotterdam. With its large hinterland of interior provinces linked by the Longhai railway (Figure 6.2), Lianyungang too may develop into one of the important ports of China.

There are four major Eurasian railway routes originating in China, namely the Suifenhe, Dalian, Tianjin, and Lianyungang. Although Lianyungang's Eurasian railway is the longest of the four, the part of the railroad within China is 4,134 km, which is the longest among the four; the Lianyungang route should be most beneficial to the development of China (Table 6.3).[5] Most of the Eurasian transport can be handled at China's end of the Eurasian railway. As noted earlier, the connection of the Lanxin (Lanzhou–Urumqi) railway with the Trans-Siberian railway in

Table 6.3   Comparison of China's Four Major Eurasian Railway
Routes

Suifenhe Route
Nachodka[a]—246 km—Ussurijsk[a]—97 km—Suifenhe—548 km—Harbin—935
km—Manzhouli—463 km—Chita[a]—6,128 km—Moscow[a]—1,094 km—Brest[a]
Total: 9,511 km (China = 1,483 km; USSR = 8,028 km)

Dalian Route
Dalian—1,879 km—Manzhouli—463 km—Chita[a]—2,913 km—Novosibirsk[a]—
3,215 km—Moscow[a]—1,094 km—Brest[a]
Total: 9,546 km (China = 1,870 km; USSR = 7,685 km)

Tianjin Route
Tianjin—738 km—Jining—333 km—Erenhot—1,110 km—K'achta[b]—247 km
—Ulan Ude[a]—2,364 km—Novosibirsk[a]—3,215 km—Moscow[a]—1,094 km—
Brest[a]
Total: 9,101 km (China = 1,071 km; Mongolia = 1,110 km; USSR = 6,920 km)

Lianyungang Route
Lianyungang—223 km—Xuzhou—1,536 km—Lanzhou—1,912 km—Urumqi
—240 km—Usu—223 km—Alataw Shankou—304 km—Aktogay[a]—893 km—
Barnaul[a]—231 km—Novosibirsk[a]—3,215 km—Moscow[a]—1,094 km—Brest[a]
Total: 9,871 km (China = 4,134 km; USSR = 5,737 km)

Source: Qi (1989, p. 120).
[a]USSR.
[b]Mongolia.

the Soviet Union in 1992 will create a "Eurasian continental bridge" for
containerized transport with Lianyungang as the bridgehead. The railway connecting Urumqi and Alataw Shankou on the border of China was
completed in October 1990.

The surrounding areas of Lianyungang are not as prosperous as the
Beijing–Tianjin–Tangshan region in the north or the Chang Jiang economic region centered around Shanghai in the south. The potential
development does not rely on its immediate surrounding areas but on
the large hinterland along the Longhai railway. Entrepôt trade and
related industrial development will be the motivating force in developing the local economy. Because Lianyungang is located away from the

main economic areas of Jiangsu province, its development is of lesser importance to Jiangsu than the ports at Shanghai and Nantong. Most of the economic development of Jiangsu province is concentrated in the south along the banks of Chang Jiang. As a consequence, major port developments of Jiangsu have been in Nanjing, Zhenjiang, and Nantong. The open policy, however, has changed the situation. Lianyungang is serving the needs of the provinces along the Longhai railway more than the needs of Jiangsu province to which it belongs administratively. Thus its development is of more strategic value to national development than the regional development of Jiangsu.

The economic base of Lianyungang can be further strengthened if iron and steel industries are developed there. Lianyungang is an ideal place for a steel and iron industry after the Baoshan steel and iron base has been completed in Shanghai.[6] Iron ore can be imported from abroad; limestone can be obtained from Xuzhou; coal can be brought in from the interior provinces along the Longhai railway. Steel manufactured in Lianyungang could supply the needs of the new industrial cities along the Longhai railway, such as Zhengzhou, Luoyang, Xian, Baoji, and Lanzhou. The present flow of goods is unidirectional: most of the trains returning to the interior provinces from Lianyungang have limited cargoes. If a steel and iron complex were developed in Lianyungang, returning trains from Lianyungang could carry steel to the interior provinces, thus increasing the utilization of the Longhai railway. Moreover, ships could be better utilized to export coal and import iron ore. From the viewpoint of industrial distribution on the eastern coast of China, areas north of Lianyungang lack water whereas areas south of it lack coal. Lianyungang is thus an ideal place for establishing an iron and steel complex on the eastern coast.

Lianyungang has considerable potential for developing into a large city or even a sizable city. It is therefore necessary to have a plan to control the growth of the city proper and develop small towns within the boundary of the municipality. The present administrative, economic, and cultural center of Lianyungang is at Xinpu. Future development, however, will focus mainly around the Lianyun port and the ETDZ. It is increasingly felt that it is inconvenient to locate the city government and government departments in Xinpu. Yet the present economic base does not allow relocation of the city government away from Xinpu. In the long run, it may be preferable to separate Xinhai and Lianyun into two cities: the city government of Lianyungang, equivalent to a province, could be located in Lianyun; the newly created county-level government of Xinhai city with Donghai, Ganyu, and Guanyun could be under the administration of Lianyungang. The separation of the seaport at Lianyun from Xinhai may be more advantageous for urban and economic development than the present arrangement.

Foreign trade in China has increased tremendously since the adoption of the open policy in 1978, creating a great demand for port facilities.[7] Like other open cities, Lianyungang hopes to attract foreign investment to speed up its industrialization. But since other open cities and Special Economic Zones are also trying to attract foreign investment, competition is severe. Given the advantage of Longhai railway, an increase in foreign trade could transform Lianyungang into an important entrepôt in China. On the one hand, its port facilities can promote the development of the interior provinces; on the other, entrepôt trade can help develop its industries.

Notes

1. Chen Chuankang, "Eight Measures for Revitalization of Lianyungang," *Acta Geographica Sinica* 41(1) (1986): 59–69 (in Chinese).

2. B. S. Hoyle and D. A. Pinder (eds.), *Cityport Industrialization and Regional Development: Spatial Analysis and Planning Strategies* (Oxford: Pergamon Press, 1981).

3. Economy and Science Press, "Lianyungang," in *China's Open Cities and SEZ* (Hong Kong: Economy and Science Press, 1986), pp. 73–78.

4. Anthony G. O. Yeh, "Physical Planning," in K. Y. Wong and David K. Y. Chu (eds.), *Modernization in China: The Case of the Shenzhen Special Economic Zone* (Hong Kong: Oxford University Press, 1985), pp. 108–130.

5. Qi Yong, "Analysis of Transport by Railways Through Continents," *Scientia Geographica Sinica* 9(2) (1989): 113–121 (in Chinese).

6. Chen, "Eight Measures."

7. T. N. Chiu and David K. Y. Chu, "Port Development in the People's Republic of China: Readjustment Under Programmes of Accelerated Economic Growth," in B. S. Hoyle and D. Hilling (eds.), *Seaport Systems and Spatial Change: Technology, Industry, and Development Strategies* (Chichester: John Wiley, 1984), pp. 199–215.

7 Shanghai: China's World City

KA-IU FUNG, ZHONG-MIN YAN, AND YUE-MIN NING

THE NEW OFFICIAL ENTHUSIASM in the People's Republic for the large metropolitan centers in pursuit of the objectives of the Four Modernizations in the early 1980s is reflected in the State Council's launching of a vigorous campaign to popularize Shanghai's achievements. Shanghai led the nation in the value of industrial output per factory worker, per capita national income, and energy utilization ratio.[1] As China's largest industrial city, in 1981 Shanghai contributed 12.45 percent of the nation's GVIO, far surpassing the combined value of the two Special Municipalities of Beijing and Tianjin (only 8.55 percent). Indeed, the city's remittance to the state in 1981 equaled 16.11 percent of the national revenue.[2]

In 1984, together with thirteen other coastal cities, Shanghai was designated an open port city to serve as a recipient point for capital investment and technology transfer from developed nations. It was hoped that if the economic development of Shanghai succeeded, the economic reforms would trickle down through the entire Yangzi Delta and eventually spread to the lower and middle Yangzi Basin. The prevailing economic climate in China tends to favor active agglomeration and active economic linkages. Shanghai is, therefore, viewed as a catalyst for urban and regional development in Central and East China. The formation of the Shanghai Economic Region was approved by the State Council in 1982. The region included several components: the city region of Shanghai; Suzhou, Wuxi, Changzhou, and Nantong of Jiangsu province; Hangzhou, Jiaxing, Wuzhou, Ningbo, and Xiaoxing of Zhejiang province; as well as fifty-five counties in these provinces. This region was selected as the test case for a national experiment in economic reform.[3] The adoption of these strategies for national economic development by the state government, no doubt, will be a vital catalyst in the growth and development of Shanghai in the coming decades.

This chapter presents a general survey of the leading factors contributing to the city's ascendance from a county town to a world metropolis within several decades. In doing so, we analyze both the potential for its future growth and the challenges it will face in the new era of intense growth and development.

Location and Physical Environment

The city of Shanghai is located at 31°14′N and 121°29′E, and the municipality occupies most of the southern region of the huge Yangzi Delta, including the island of Chongming in the Yangzi estuary. Administratively, it is one of China's three special municipalities. The municipality includes the central city and its urban districts of Huangpu, Nanshi, Luwan, Jingan, Xuhui, Changning, Putuo, Hongkou, Zhabei, Yangpu, and Minhang, the suburban district Baoshan, and the suburban counties of Shanghai, Jiading, Chuansha, Nanhui, Fengxian, Songjiang, Jinshan, Qingpu, and Chongming (Figure 7.1). The total area of the municipality is 6,640.5 sq km: the central city occupies 280.45 sq km (4.4 percent); the suburban district and the suburban counties comprise 6,060.05 sq km (95.6 percent).[4]

The city commands an excellent geographical location. It is situated on the eastern coast of Asia facing the vast Pacific Ocean. Because of its littoral location, Shanghai is China's principal gateway to the outside world. It links China, via maritime shipping, with Japan, the Americas, Southeast Asia, Oceania, and other parts of the world. The metropolis is also strategically located near the midpoint of China's east coast, serving as a link between major port cities in both North and South China. It is 560 nautical miles from Dalian, a major port of the Northeast; 750 nautical miles from Tianjin, North China's economic center; and 910 nautical miles from Guangzhou, the largest city in South China.

Relief

The extensive Shanghai deltaic plain, occupying the southern part of the Yangzi Delta, resembles a half-saucer tilting gently upstream toward the west and the southwest. The formation of this unique physiographic feature is probably due to increasing sedimentation along the eastern coastline in recent times. It is subdivided into three physiographic units: the western part, occupying one-third of the plain, has the lowest elevation (less than 3.5 m above sea level); the eastern part rises gradually toward the shorelines lying to the north, east, and south (average elevation 4.5 m above sea level); the northern part is made up of mainly the estuarine

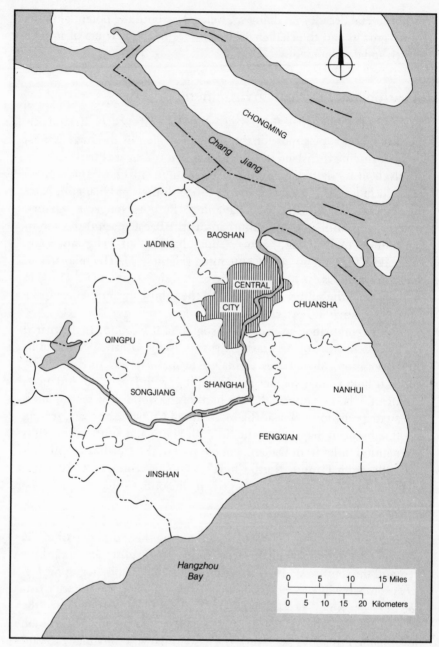

Figure 7.1 The Municipality of Shanghai

deposits of Chongming, Wangsha, and Changxing (elevation ranging between 3.3 and 4.2 m above sea level). Since the formation of Tai Hu (lake) in ancient times, the Shanghai deltaic plain has been expanding eastward. In recent years, the rate of deposition along the coastal areas of the suburban counties of Fengxian and Nanhui has reached 200 m a year.[5] These deltaic deposits may be reclaimed for urban construction and agricultural production in the municipality.

Climate

As Shanghai is located in the mid-latitudes and on the eastern Asiatic coast, it has a subtropical monsoonal climate with distinct seasons. The municipality is under the influence of the cold, dry northwest monsoons from Siberia and Inner Asia in winter and the warm, moist southeast monsoons from the Pacific Ocean in summer. The average annual temperature is 15.7 °C, with an average summer temperature of 27.8 °C in July and an average winter temperature of 3.5 °C in January. The average annual precipitation is 1,151.6 mm. About 60 percent of this amount occurs between May and September.[6] The equable climate in the municipality is highly favorable to agriculture. In addition, Shanghai harbor remains open to maritime shipping in winter when activities at the two major ports of Qingdao and Tianjin in North China are threatened by floating ice.

Hydrography and Hydrology

Huangpu Jiang, the major waterway of the Shanghai deltaic plain, originates from Dingshan Hu southwest of the city. The river drains the suburban counties of Qingpu, Songjiang, Fengxian, Shanghai, Chuansha, and Baoshan before flowing into the Yangzi at Wusong Kou. Its total length measures 113.4 km; its width ranges from 300 to 770 m, its depth from 8 to 18 m. The waterway, which is well sheltered from typhoons and has level terrain along its banks, provides ideal sites for harbor facilities. At present, ships of up to 10,000 dwt with a 7-foot draft may sail up the waterway to Shanghai. At high tide, ships with a draft of 9 feet may still reach the heart of the metropolis. Suzhou He, the major tributary of Huangpu Jiang, flows through the central city. It has a length of 125 km and provides an important link between Shanghai and the rich Tai Hu drainage basin.

Huangpu Jiang and the numerous tidal creeks and canals in the delta provide an annual volume of 498.4 billion cubic meters of water for industrial, domestic, and agricultural use in the municipality. The annual runoff of Huangpu Jiang is 321 cu m per second. It is estimated that the average volume of incoming tide is about 5,100 cu m per second. According to record, the highest tidal volume of the river reached 12,100 cu m per second—fifteen to sixteen times the normal runoff of the waterway.[7]

The city region also has rich groundwater resources. Aquifers occur at five different levels within the alluvial sediments lying beneath the city and its vicinity. Tapping of this natural resource began in 1860 after it was found to be of satisfactory quality for both industrial and domestic uses. Because of its constantly low temperature and good quality, the groundwater has been generally used as a coolant in industries. Overconsumption of groundwater due to rapid industrial development during the 1950s led to slow ground subsidence in the city. In 1965 the sinking reached an alarming 2.37 m in the districts of Yangpu and Putuo. Pumping recycled water back to the substrata has solved the problem.[8]

History in Brief

Recent archaeological finds in the suburban counties of Shanghai indicate that more than 4,000 years ago there were already human habitations in the area of Gangshen lying west and south of the present city. Over the centuries Shanghai gradually increased in importance through, for example, the shift of the gravitational center of China's economic and political development southward in the Sui and Tang dynasties (A.D. 581–905) and its establishment as a county seat in 1074. Large-scale water conservancy projects undertaken in Shanghai since the fifteenth century developed Huangpu Jiang into a major shipping lane. Thus the city became the major port of the Yangzi Delta area and gradually developed into one of China's major seaports—a transport pivot for both domestic and international shipping. As a result of this development, trade and commerce flourished and became the major components of the city's economy.

The conclusion of the Opium War in 1842 ushered in the beginning of profound changes in Shanghai. The city was opened as one of the treaty ports by the Treaty of Nanking of 1842, whereby the British secured rights to station a consul in the British Settlement. In 1848 the Foreign Settlement was officially established. This was followed by the setting up of the American Settlement in 1863, when an agreement was made for the amalgamation of the British and the American settlements, forming officially the International Settlement.[9] After the founding of these foreign enclaves, settlers were busy building roads, residential housing, urban facilities, trading companies, factories, and warehouses. The marshlands and cultivated fields outside the Chinese walled city were soon transformed into thriving urban communities with predominant alien characteristics. Through negotiation with incompetent and corrupt local officials of the Qing government, foreign powers acquired special rights of extraterritoriality for tariff collection—and later the rights for navigating in the East China Sea, the Yellow Sea, and along the Yangzi River, the main transport artery in China. As a result, Shanghai became the beachhead for the economic invasion of China by foreign powers.

Because of the city's orientation to the sea and its excellent accessibility to the Yangzi River, its harbor was thriving with trading and shipping activities. By 1853, the volume of trade in Shanghai had surpassed that of Guangzhou and the city became the largest port in China. The opening of the Shanghai–Hangzhou railway (Huhang Line) and the Shanghai–Nanjing railway (Huning Line) in 1905 and 1908, respectively, greatly improved the city's overland links with a number of major urban centers, and thus the size of the city's hinterland was greatly expanded. Between 1860 and 1930, Shanghai accounted for an average of 68 percent by value of the total reexport of goods within China. In 1933, the foreign trade of Shanghai equaled 1 percent of the world's total. The city also rose to become one of the largest seaports in the Orient in 1936: by then, the total volume of freight it handled had reached 14 million tons, and half of China's foreign trade was conducted through the city.[10]

Following the rapid growth of the port in the late nineteenth century, Shanghai emerged as China's largest economic center, as its urban functions became increasingly diversified, including banking and finance, commerce, and manufacturing. The banking and finance sector in Shanghai, under foreign management, was first established in the mid-nineteenth century. The first foreign bank, set up in 1848, was the British Bank of the Orient. By 1947 the city had 14 foreign banks, 128 government-owned and privately owned banks, 13 trust companies, and 79 money exchangers.[11] With such a large number of financial institutions, representing a high degree of concentration of capital, Shanghai was in a position to control the economy of the entire nation.

After the city was opened as a treaty port, it gradually became the largest commercial center in China. Before World War I, there were more than a hundred foreign firms in the import and export business. The World War I period witnessed a moderate growth of Chinese-owned enterprises. Prior to 1949, according to incomplete statistics, Shanghai had about 181 types of business, with 410,000 employees. In addition, there were over 100,000 small businesses and peddlers. Furthermore, the number of wholesalers comprised one-third of the national total. The city's wholesale market covered practically the entire nation. Most of the city's retail businesses had a long history and close relationships with merchants in other parts of China, particularly in the Yangzi Delta area.

The rise of modern manufacturing in Shanghai was closely linked to the city's shipping industry. In 1851 the establishment of a shipyard by the British marked the beginning of modern industry in Shanghai. The westernization movement in China prompted the gradual development of government-controlled industrial establishments in the city. Among all the modern industries in Shanghai, the production of cotton textiles, flour, silk, and tobacco recorded substantial increases. By the early 1930s, Shanghai's manufacturing industries had attained national prominence. The amount of capital invested in the sector and the total value of production reached almost half of the national total.[12]

China's Largest Multifunctional City

From a paradise for adventurists of the past, Shanghai was transformed into China's most important industrial base by the end of the First Five-Year Plan in 1957. For the last three decades, the city has been providing a great source of strength to the economic development of the nation. Despite vigorous industrial growth in other important cities, such as Beijing, Tianjin, Wuhan, Lanzhou, and Guangzhou, Shanghai still retains much of its industrial and economic primacy. It contributes an annual average of one-tenth of the total national revenue—ranking first among all the cities in China. In 1988 the total value of Shanghai's industrial production was 39.8 percent of the total achieved by the fourteen open coastal cities. The city also has a high productivity in relation to its economic investments, attaining a ratio of 1:2.5.[13] This ratio is 1.5 times higher than the national average. Shanghai also ranks first among all Chinese cities as a center of international and domestic trade, science and technology, and finance. With the government policy to develop the city into a modern metropolis, it will soon emerge as a major center of communication in China.

Several major factors are responsible for the rapid ascendance of Shanghai as the most important multifunctional urban center in the People's Republic. Great cities do not rise by accident. Indeed, Shanghai has a 140-year history of industrial development, and it is the birthplace of the modern sector of China's economy. During the treaty port days, the city's industries included predominantly textile manufacturing and flour processing. The industrial structure of the city underwent drastic changes during the First Five-Year Plan (1953–1957), however. It became more balanced and diversified as a result of the investment policy of the central government, which favored the development of heavy industries. Within the last three decades, Shanghai has developed a comprehensive variety of industries, a high level of industrial skill, and a coordinating system of industrial plants of different sizes. The city's industry has also attained a high degree of sophistication in design and manufacturing.

Among the major industries in Shanghai, textile manufacturing is the oldest and the second largest. It includes the production of cotton, wool, jute (hemp), and silk. In 1988 this sector's annual gross value of production reached 13.89 billion *yuan,* accounting for 13.9 percent of the city's gross value of industrial production. The steel industry, developed during the First Five-Year Plan, is now second only to Anshan, the largest steel production center in China. In 1988 the annual production was 8.6 million tonnes, including 4.73 million tonnes of steel-fabricated materials. The development of the huge and modern Baoshan steel complex in the 1980s further boosted the growth of the city's steel manufacturing industry. With an abundant local supply of steel, the city has become an important production base for a wide variety of metal products. Machinery manufacturing ranks first among Shanghai's industries: the annual gross value of production in 1988 was 33.59 billion *yuan,* which was 33.7 percent of the city's total value of industrial production. Shanghai produces as much as 21.8 percent of China's power generation equipment, 21.7 percent of its ships, 20.2 percent of its watches, 16.9 percent of its bicycles, and 16.5 percent of its cameras.[14] In recent years a variety of new products have been introduced, including new metals, synthetic materials, electronic calculators, precision instruments, scientific gauges, and precision lathes.

In 1988, Shanghai's GVIO reached 99.68 billion *yuan.* The proportion of the value for light industry and heavy industry was 55:45 respectively (excluding the value of rural industries in the city region). The total value accounted for 8.6 percent of the national figure. The city produces a high percentage of China's consumer industrial goods (Table

Table 7.1   Production of Industrial Consumer
Goods in Shanghai: 1988

ITEM	NO. OF UNITS	NATIONAL PERCENTAGE
Television sets	4,728,000	19.0
Color television sets	1,085,600	10.6
Radio and tape recorders	4,220,500	18.0
Washing machines	1,770,400	16.9
Refrigerators	574,500	7.8

Source: *Shanghai Yearbook 1989* (Shanghai: China Statistics Press, 1989), p. 173.

7.1). The amount of industrial profits remitted to the central government equaled one-quarter of the national revenue.

For many years Shanghai's industry has been the national leader in production efficiency. In 1988 the productivity rate per worker in the city's state enterprises reached 33,735 *yuan*—twice the national average. Profits, taxes, and value of production from fixed assets are also higher than the national level, but energy consumption in industry for each 10,000 *yuan* of value of production is far below the nation's average.

For nearly four decades, Shanghai has been making other significant contributions to the modern sector of China's economy. Over 1 million industrial workers and personnel with managerial skills were dispatched to other industrial cities. Since the early 1980s Shanghai's industry has been providing assistance to industrial centers in the interior regions in the form of technology transfer and production cooperation. At the same time, since Shanghai became one of the fourteen coastal cities opened to foreign investment in 1984, economic cooperation with foreign countries has been rapidly developed, greatly facilitating the introduction of advanced technology and production of new types of industrial goods. The export-oriented industries in the city have also reaped the benefit from foreign technology transfer. Modernization of production technology in these industries has increased both production and export. For example, the Jiefang Cotton Textile Mill completed 178 technological changes in recent years. As a result, some of its products surpassed their Japanese counterpart in quality. In 1986 the total profit earned from its export reached $20 million.[15] At present, the number of countries participating in joint ventures with Shanghai's enterprises is on the increase and the scale of cooperation has also been expanded. In 1984–1985 there were altogether 299 direct and indirect investments from foreign countries; the total foreign funds amounted to $1 billion. In 1986 the number of export-oriented project contracts which Shanghai signed with foreign businesses accounted for 60 percent of the total foreign investment —an increase of 20 percent over the total amount in 1985. While restricting foreign investment in the nonproductive sector (which includes hotels, restaurants, and office buildings), the city increased the proportion of foreign investment in industrial projects from 5 percent in 1985 to 35.7 percent in 1988. These projects involved the production of laser products, electronics, chemicals, and new materials.[16]

A Center for Domestic and Foreign Trade

Since the latter part of the nineteenth century, Shanghai has been China's largest commercial center. The service area for the city's wholesale trade covers the entire country. The city's function as a national commercial center has been weakened, however, as many of its trading links with neighboring provinces, municipalities, and administrative districts were severed by the wholesale trade regionalization policy implemented after 1949. Despite this setback, Shanghai still ranks first in China in terms of the size of its internal market and the degree of prosperity in the commercial sector. In 1988 there were 132,420 retail businesses, restaurants, and other service trades (including those in the private sector), with 877,688 employees. The total purchase of the Commerce Department in the same year was valued at 34.24 billion *yuan;* 90 percent of this amount was industrial goods. The total value of industrial products exported from the city reached 15.43 billion *yuan.*[17]

Shanghai is also a city thriving with shopping activities. Consumer goods in the city's stores are renowned for their variety, quality, and style, which have attracted shoppers from all over China. It has been estimated that about one-quarter of the customers of the city's retail businesses come from other parts of the country. In 1988 the total value of consumer goods sold in Shanghai reached 31.35 billion *yuan,* or 4.21 percent of the national figure.[18] To revive Shanghai's role as a major domestic trading center, reforms have been introduced in recent years to the wholesale sector. The first-echelon wholesalers have been amalgamated with their related municipal companies to reduce the amount of administrative work in the commodity distribution process. In addition, the city has established a large trading center for industrial consumer goods, twelve special trading centers, and thirty-eight markets and warehouses for agricultural subsidiary products. The Department of Merchandise Supply has also introduced reforms by establishing the merchandise exchange office, the producer goods markets, the lumber market, and thirty-five special trading centers.

Foreign trade constitutes an important sector in Shanghai's economy, and it has been expanding rapidly since the early 1950s. In 1988 the total value of exports was $4.6 billion, which accounted for 9.7 percent of the nation's total exports.[19] Before liberation, the export commodities were made up mainly of agricultural subsidiary products and light industrial goods, which amounted to 63.9 percent and 35.2 percent, respectively. As a result of the development of the city's economy and the transformation of its industrial structure, the export goods in 1988 were made up of 61.9 percent of light industrial products, 21.8 percent of heavy industrial goods, and 16.3 percent of agricultural subsidiary products.[20] The major exporting items included cotton cloth, cotton yarn, garments, petrochemical products, pharmaceuticals, frozen meats, canned goods, teas, steel products, bicycles, and lathes.

At present, Shanghai trades with over 160 countries and regions: 14,000 traders in all. The major trading partners are Hong Kong and Macau, which together rank first in value of exports; the total value of 1988 exports amounted to $785 million. This was followed by Japan and the United States with a total value of export of $586 million and $559 million, respectively. West Germany, Britain, and Singapore are also important trading partners.[21]

An Advanced Center for Science, Technology, and Education

Besides being China's major commercial center and port city, Shanghai is an important scientific, technological, educational, and cultural center. The vast pool of scientists and technicians in the city have made significant contributions not only to the urban economy but also to the nation's industrialization program. Between 1951 and 1956, of the 240,000 skilled workers assigned to employment in other parts of China, nearly 25,000 were technicians and engineers. These experts provided managerial and technical skills for the construction of turbine factories, boiler plants, antibiotic factories, and textile mills in cities in interior China.[22]

In 1988 there were 795,850 scientific and technological personnel in the city, 426,538 of whom were natural scientists, amounting to 4.4 percent of the national total. Shanghai has fifty-one institutes of higher learning, which produce a large number of scientific personnel and specialists in various fields of study. In 1988 there were 128,163 students enrolled in universities and colleges, 10,332 of them at the postgraduate level, constituting 6.4 percent and 9.6 percent respectively of the national total. In addition, the enrollment in adult education in that year was 81,000.[23]

In recent years, Shanghai's scientists and engineers have made impressive progress in research in microelectronics, bioengineering, new materials, oceanic engineering, lasers, fiber-optic communications, and robotics. A large group of top-ranking scientists in the city are currently conducting one-third of China's scientific research. The results of these research activities will, no doubt, contribute to China's modernization in science and technology, as well as to the economic growth of the nation.

Urban Spatial Structures: Transformation and Development

Since 1949 two changes important to the spatial planning and development of Shanghai took place: one involved the areal expansion of the central city; the other concerned establishment of the city region. In 1949 the city's built-up area was only 82.4 sq km. To meet economic development needs during the First Five-Year Plan, the municipal administration expanded the urban area several times. In 1957 the total urban area reached 116 sq km. During the first half of the 1980s two major changes occurred: the administrative districts of Wusong and Minhang were established and then incorporated (in 1981 and 1982 respectively). As a result, the urban area was further expanded to 351 sq km (Figure 7.2). Early in 1958 the city region of Shanghai was established. The urban administration incorporated the adjacent suburban counties of Baoshan, Jiading to the north, and Shanghai to the south; thus over 863 sq km of territory was added. In December of the same year, the city region further expanded to include the surrounding counties of Chongming, Qingpu, Songjiang, Chuansha, Nanhui, Fengxian, and Jinshan. As a result of the drastic expansion, the total area reached 6,340.50 sq km. In 1988, the district of Wusong and the suburban county of Baoshan were merged into a new administrative district, the suburban district of Baoshan.[24] With the creation of the city region, the

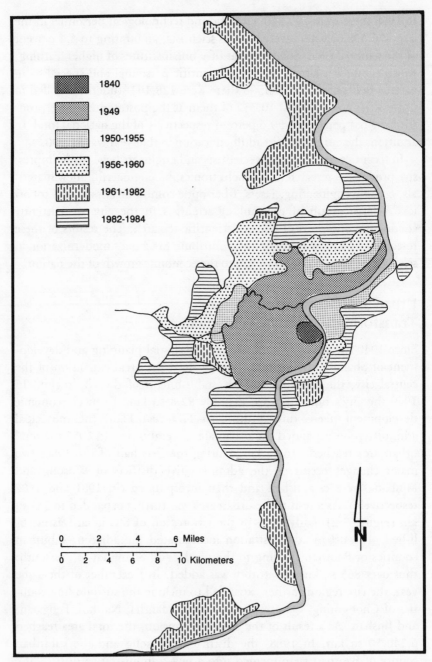

Figure 7.2 The Territorial Expansion of Shanghai: 1840–1984

municipal government was able to implement effective planning on decentralization of industrial activities and dispersal of population from the central city to satellite towns, agricultural land-use management, agricultural production, development and utilization of the local transport system, and mobilization of manpower.

The spatial expansion of Shanghai's built-up area was accompanied by significant changes in its urban form and structure. From a single-nodal center, the city has been transformed into a multinuclear urban settlement. Several notable developments took place in the city region: establishment of near-suburban industrial districts and far-suburban satellite towns; large-scale residential housing construction; formation of a hierarchy of commercial centers; and expansion of harbor facilities.

Owing to the intense development of industry in the latter part of the First Five-Year Plan, the city set up the industrial districts of Pengpu, Beixinjing, Zhoujiadu, and Qingningshi at the urban fringe area. They were soon incorporated as the city's built-up areas. Since 1958 the city has established five industrial districts and seven satellite towns in the suburban areas of the city region, each performing specific industrial functions—the industrial districts of Wujiaochang (general industrial), Gaoqiao (petrochemicals), Taopu (chemicals), Caohejing (electronics and scientific gauges), and Changqiao (construction materials) and the satellite towns of Wusong (iron and steel), Minhang (electrical machinery), Wujing (chemicals), Anting (motor vehicles), Songjiang (light industry), Jiading (scientific research), and Jinshanwei (synthetic fibers). These industrial districts and settlements, with a total area of 56 sq km, have 440 industrial plants and 380,000 employees. The number of permanent residents in these settlements totaled 410,000 in 1982. The total value of fixed assets was one-third of Shanghai's total; the total GVIO amounted to one-sixth that of the city. In 1978 the Baoshan Steel Works and a large satellite town were constructed to the north of Wusong. While development of new industrial districts was under way, changes occurred in the city's old industrial districts due to transformation of the city's industrial structure: Yangpu developed metallurgy and machinery manufacturing, Juxi the electronics industry, and Hunan the metallurgy and construction material industry.

Since 1949 about 140 residential districts have been constructed in Shanghai, adding over 38 million square meters of new residential space. Among the new housing estates, the better-known ones include the Caoyang New Village (Caoyang Xin *cun*) of the 1950s and the Caoxilu high-rise apartment complex of the 1970s. Since the beginning of the 1980s, twelve new residential districts have been added, some of which can accommodate a population of 200,000 to 300,000—the size of a medium-sized city. Because of the overcrowded condition of the urban districts, all these new constructions were erected at the urban fringe areas, which added a new ringlike belt to the city's circular structure.

Prior to liberation, most of the commercial activities were concentrated in the city's central business district and its extensions along some of the arterial roads, such as Nanjing Xilu, Huaihai Zhonglu, and Sichuan Beilu. Since 1949 adjustments have been made to change the spatial distribution of commercial nodes in the city, including upgrading existing business areas and constructing new ones such as those in the districts of Xujiahui, Changshoulu, and Jinganshi. In addition, all new housing developments included shopping facilities. The creation of a three-level hierachy of commercial nodes has enhanced their rational distribution in the metropolis.

After 1949 Shanghai lost its financial center status. This led to the decline of the wholesale trade in the central business district, which was then transformed into a center for retail businesses and government offices. During the Sixth Five-Year Plan (1981–1985), attention was given to the development of tertiary industry and latitudinal economic linkages in the city.

Impediments to Development

Several major problems—including high concentration of population and industry in the central city and inadequate transport and communication services—will affect Shanghai's future development. Unless remedial measures are actively introduced by the city administration, these problems may become more acute with the inevitable increase of economic activities brought about by the open policy.

Despite the rapid rate of urban construction since liberation, the establishment of satellite settlements in its city region, and the recent expansion of its urban area, Shanghai is still facing an extremely high concentration of population and industry in the central city. During the early 1950s, the government of Shanghai adopted several measures to control population increase in the city, measures which greatly restricted in-migration into the urban districts. As a result, the rate of population increase, including natural increase and in-migration, was the lowest among all large cities in China.[25] During the period 1968–1977, there was a net loss of 1,009,000 in the city's population due to the *xiafang* ("sending down") movement.[26]

In recent years, however, Shanghai's population has been on the increase. From 1980 to 1982, the number attributable to natural increase was 323,100, an average increase of 9.3 per thousand per year, which surpasses the average annual increase of 5.2 per thousand in the 1970s. It was estimated that this trend would continue to the second half of the 1980s. Apart from natural increase, in-migration has been contributing to population growth in urban Shanghai. In 1978–1983, in-migration brought an increase of 614,000 persons, which equaled two-thirds of the city's net population growth. This represents an average annual increase of over 100,000 persons.[27] According to the Statistical Bureau of Shanghai, the city's population reached 12,624,000 and that of the central city grew to 7.3 million at the end of 1988.[28] Following the implementation of the open policy, the rate of in-migration is expected to increase. Based on the average increase, the population growth will reach 2.14 million and that of in-migration 1.02 million by the end of the century. The total population of the city by then will be over 15 million.[29]

Despite periodic expansion of the urban area, population density in the central city has been increasing. The average population density in the central city is about 24,781 persons per square kilometer, the highest in the country. In many urban districts, the population density reaches 80,000 persons per square kilometer; the neighborhood of Xiaobeimen in the urban district of Nanshi has the highest density: 230,000 persons per square kilometer![30]

There are other indicators of population congestion in Shanghai. In the central city the gross residential floor space per capita is only 6.3 sq m. The amount of road surface and green space per capita is only 2.3 and 0.96 sq m, respectively, the lowest among the "million-cities" in China.[31]

It should be pointed out that at the end of the First Five-Year Plan, Shanghai established a number of satellite towns in the far suburb of the city region to disperse the high concentration of population and reorganize land use in the central city. After more than three decades, however, these goals have not been achieved. In 1983 the total population of the satellite towns reached 560,000, or 8.7 percent of Shanghai's total urban population. About half of the 430,000 industrial workers in these towns still have their household registration (Hukou) in Shanghai,[32] and a substantial number of workers commute to work daily from the central city. Factories in Minhang, for example, Shanghai's first and largest satellite town, provide transportation to bring over 80,000 of their workers daily from the central city (Figure 7.3).[33]

The high degree of population concentration in the central city has led to serious traffic congestion. There are numerous bottlenecks in the city's transport arteries. Moreover, along the city's periphery roads there are forty-two heavily congested sections and intersections. Vehicle speed has been reduced from 25 km per hour (average speed in the 1950s) to about 15 km per hour. At the busy sections along Wai Bai Du Bridge and Yanan Donglu, the average speed of motor vehicles at peak hours is only 3 to 4 km per hour. The fact that there are only a few north–south arterial roads contributes to the traffic problem.[34]

The satellite town development program of the late 1950s still has not solved the problem of excessive concentration of industry and the mixed industrial/residential land-use pattern in the central city. During the First Five-Year Plan, some factories in the city were relocated in the suburban counties and satellite towns as part of the urban system planning and development. But because of the strong industrial foundation, the scale of economies, and the rapid growth of neighborhood workshops, the central city still has 56.7 percent of all the industrial enterprises in the city region.[35] It is estimated that over 30 percent of the built-up area in the central city is occupied by factories and warehouses.[36] In the urban district of Nanshi, factories occupy 61.6 percent of the total area of 4,175 ha. Further, because of the shortage of space, many workshops use the neighborhood streets for storage, which seriouly affects traffic flow and jeopardizes safety in the area.[37]

Inadequate and outdated transport facilities have caused sluggishness in Shanghai's external linkages, posing serious problems in the city's development as an open port. In recent years the turnaround time in the harbor has been extremely slow, as the outdated facilities have not been able to handle the increasing number of ships and passengers, as well as the growing volume of freight in the sectors of domestic and foreign trade. The city's overtaxed railway system has also posed problems. The carrying capacity of passenger and freight of the Shanghai–Hangzhou railway has reached its limit.

The carrying capacity of the city's civil aviation is insufficient as well— by way of comparison, it is only one-tenth that of the large cities in Southeast Asia. Another problem is the low utilization rate of the out-

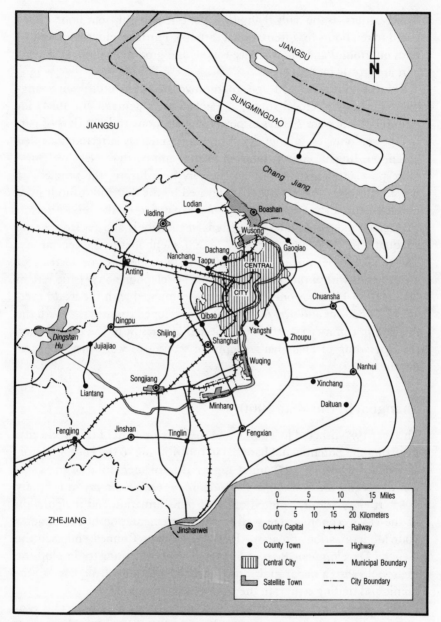

Figure 7.3 Satellite Towns in the Shanghai City Region

dated carriers, as the daily flying time per carrier is only four hours (compared to ten hours for international carriers). Furthermore, the quality of both on-ground and in-air service is poor and ground facilities at the airport are grossly inadequate.[38]

There is an urgent need, too, to improve the public utilities in Shanghai. The city's electrical supply is far below its demand. In 1984, for example, there were 73 days of power interruptions and 114 days of partial power outages in the city. The areas seriously affected included Huangpu, Jingan, Luwan, south of Putuo, and north of Nanshi. Unless more power stations are built in the very near future, the problem of power shortages will be further aggravated by the demands of industrial development, urban construction, and expansion of the service sector. The telephone communication system in the city is also far from being adequate. In 1978 there were only 74,700 telephones in the central city. The total number increased by 6,800 in 1988. Despite the increase of 162,100 sets within the ten-year period, the telephone ownership rate in Shanghai in 1988 was only 3.2 percent—compared with the world average of 12 percent and over 60 percent in developed countries.[39] With the increase in commercial activities expected as a result of the open policy, the upgrading of Shanghai's telephone services to world level is paramount.

Shanghai in the Year 2000

The year 1986 ushered in a new era in the development of this world city. Realizing the potential of Shanghai in contributing to the Four Modernizations drive, the State Council approved implementation of the *General Report on the Strategy to Develop Shanghai's Economy* in February 1985. It emphatically pointed out that transformation and invigoration of the city's economy were vital to the implementation of the nation's Four Modernizations program. In 1986 the State Council endorsed the General Development Plan of Shanghai—the blueprint to develop the metropolis into a major multifunctional city and one of the largest economic and trading centers in the western Pacific region.

As a result, several measures which are vital to the city's rapid economic growth have been introduced since 1986. In essence, these measures include opening the city to foreign investment, establishing of Special Economic Zones and new satellite towns in the city region, transforming traditional industries and developing modern industries, adjusting economic structures and expanding the tertiary sector, and speeding up major urban construction.

To attract offshore investment to the city, measures have been taken by the municipal government to simplify all applications and approval procedures for foreign businesses, to introduce business laws to facilitate and regulate foreign investment, to open the national market selectively to manufactured goods produced by foreign-owned factories and joint ventures in the city, and to provide special tax holidays to foreign business ventures, including exemption from profit taxes levied by the local government until the end of 1985 and exemption from real estate taxes for five years.[40]

Establishment of Special Economic Zones

As part of the open policy, Shanghai established the Special Economic Zones of Minhang and Hongqiao in 1982 (Figure 7.3). The major objectives were to attract foreign investment, to introduce advanced technology, modern equipment, and management skills, and to develop international economic and technological cooperation.

Minhang, located about 30 km south of the central city, is Shanghai's first industrial satellite town. The settlement has excellent external linkages. It is only 27 km from Hongqiao International Airport. Located on the upper reach of Huangpu Jiang, Minhang can be reached by ships up to 3,000 dwt. As well, it can fully utilize all the harbor facilities in the central city, including the container wharf only 47 km from the settlement. The satellite is connected directly with the central city by the Shanghai–Minhang Highway—a four-lane divided highway. A branch of the Huhang Railway links the town with the national railway system. The town's existing industry includes manufacturing of heavy machinery, steam turbines, boilers, industrial water pumps, axles, electrical tools, and prefabricated construction materials. The settlement is well provided with public utilities, including power station, waterworks, sewage treatment plant, and telephone exchange. Located around factory sites are workers' residential housing, stores, police stations, hotels, schools, hospitals, theaters, cinemas, a sports stadium, and parks.

In the northwestern part of Minhang a Special Economic Zone has been set up in close proximity to existing industrial sites. Within the SEZ, 230 ha of land has been designated for industrial purposes. To encourage development of modern industries in the zone, those which utilize advanced technology, such as electronics, scientific instruments, medical equipment, and modern construction materials, have been given a high priority to set up factories.[41] The urban land-use components are as follows: 50 percent for factories, 5.5 percent for warehouses, 5.7 percent for the administrative and service training center, 6 percent for service facilities, 5 percent for roads, and 24 percent for green space. It is claimed that after completion of construction, the SEZ will have a pleasant environment where the building density is only 0.5 to 0.6 percent and the total green space reaches 40 percent—in sharp contrast to the acute shortage of green space in central Shanghai.

Moreover, foreign investors are provided with excellent facilities in the zone. All the trunk roads are four-laned and 30 m wide, while all the secondary roads are two-laned and have a width of 16 m. There are underground sewage systems and supply lines for water, gas, and electricity. The new telephone system has already been installed. The zone also has other facilities such as wharves, waterworks, a sewage treatment plant, and natural gas storage.

The administrative center of the Special Economic Zone houses the customs office, taxation office, foreign trade office, bank, insurance company, and telecommunication facilities. The concentration of services at the center greatly helps foreign investors to conduct business in the zone. As well, there will be a variety of public amenities, such as hotels, offices, guesthouses, restaurants, teahouses, shops, and car rental services. Within designated areas there are luxury apartments and residential houses. Immediately outside the zone, multistory workers' housing has been erected for purchase by joint-venture companies.

Hongqiao, the second Special Economic Zone of Shanghai, is located in the western urban fringe of the city. Its suburban setting provides a pleasant environment, and the range of services facilitates further urban development. The zone is only 6.5 km from People's Square, the geographical center of Shanghai; it is only 5.5 km from Hongqiao International Airport and is well served by transportation.

The planned area of the zone is 65.2 ha. The various urban land-use types in the zone are as follows: land for buildings (46.6 percent), recreation and green space (29.7 percent), and roads (23.7 percent). The entire planned area is divided into three subareas with thirty-four building sites. They have been designated for the construction of high-rise office buildings (such as the Foreign Trade Center), hotels, apartment blocks, foreign consulates and offices, banks, insurance companies, supermarkets, shopping centers, department stores, tennis courts, swimming pool, skating rink, bowling alleys, theaters, parks, schools, medical clinics, and car parks.[42] These facilities should make foreigners feel at home while conducting business in the zone.

Recently the city further established an ETDZ at Caohejing to the southwest of Shanghai, only 7 km from the international airport at Hongqiao. At present, the industrial center is connected with the central city by five transportation routes. Caohejing was the first high-tech development center among the coastal ETDZs approved by the State Council in June 1988. The planned area within the zone is 5 sq km, with pleasant environment, convenient transportation, and a pool of technical experts. There are over ten enterprises involving production of microelectronics, calculators, and aerospace engineering products. Following improvement of the climate for investment, establishment of infrastructure serving foreign businesses, and implementation of preferential policies in the zone, businesses and industrial enterprises have been attracted from Europe, the United States, Australia, Hong Kong, and Japan.[43] These foreign capital investments will, no doubt, make significant contributions to the zone's development.

A multi-billion-dollar project to develop the Pudong area has recently been unveiled by Mayor Zhu Rongji. Approval of the plan has already been granted by the central authorities who made the strategic decision to continue pursuing the economic reform and open policy. According to the plan, 350 sq km of farmland in Pudong will be converted into a "socialist Hong Kong"—a bustling financial, trading, and industrial center. Proponents of Pudong believe the project will revitalize Shanghai, an essential step in China's overall development. They also hope the benefits accrued from the project will trickle down through the entire Yangzi Delta, a key economic zone in eastern China.[44] The initial stage of development (1985–1995) involves construction of bridges and cross-channel tunnels linking Pudong and the central city, as well as the building of urban infrastructures such as roads and public utilities such as power stations, waterworks, and gasworks. The plan also calls for development of 50 sq km of the Gaoqiao area as an export-oriented manufacturing zone. A free port allowing free movement of goods will also be built. During the key construction stage, an area of 170 sq km will be developed to accommodate a total population of 1.7 million.[45] It is hoped that this new development will not only alleviate the acute over-crowding in the central city but also bring economic reforms to the Yangzi hinterland.

Industrial Transformation and Development

Since the founding of the People's Republic, Shanghai's industrial development has been making remarkable progress. The city's industries are still mainly labor-intensive, however, accounting for 49 percent of the total. (The capital-intensive and technology-intensive industries account for only 34 percent and 17 percent, respectively). The present goal is to bring the quality of major industrial goods produced in the city to the world level by 1990. This will be achieved by simultaneously transforming existing industries and developing technology-intensive manufacturing that produces high-valued and small-bulk finished goods requiring only modest amounts of raw materials and energy.

As one of the main objectives of the open policy is to promote the transfer and assimilation of industrial technology, attention has been given to developing coordination among all types of imported technology and building up the microelectronics, bioengineering, and new materials industries. Imports of key technology have focused on strengthening the steel, chemical, and motor vehicle manufacturing.[46] The radical transformation of Shanghai's industries will be favorable to both domestic and international economic development.

Development of Tertiary Industry

In the past, Shanghai's tertiary industries consisted of commerce, finance, communication, science and technology, education, and culture. In 1952 this sector of Shanghai's economy accounted for as much as 42.3 percent of the city's GDP. From the beginning of the First Five-Year Plan (1953–1957), due to the emphasis on industrial production and the neglect of commodity circulation, the tertiary sector in Shanghai's economy steadily declined. In 1972 this sector accounted for only 17.3 percent of the city's GDP. This value is far below that of developed countries such as Japan, whose tertiary industry accounts for 58 percent of its gross national product. Since 1982, however, remarkable changes have been taking place in the sector; its growth rate has started to exceed that of the primary and secondary sectors. This change was brought about mainly by increased investments in the fixed asset of the tertiary sector and the national open policy.

According to international experience, when the per capita value of gross national product reaches about $1,500, the secondary industry will gradually decline and the tertiary industry continue to grow. At present, as the per capita value of Shanghai's gross national product has reached $1,500, it will be appropriate to develop further the tertiary sector, which may stimulate the economy of the city. Plans have been made to increase the proportion of the labor force and the value of the sector's gross national product to 30 percent in 1990 and as much as 60 percent by the year 2000. Special attention will be paid to the rationality of the industry's internal structure, and emphasis will be placed on upgrading technology to enhance further growth of the sector.

Urban Renewal and Construction

Owing to the territorial fragmentation of Shanghai by foreign powers during the treaty port days, there was no standardization in the city's planning and construction. Therefore, urban redevelopment has become a challenging task. As well, the lack of urban planning during the Cultural Revolution has led to a serious shortage of urban facilities which, in turn, has caused serious traffic congestion, overtaxing of the railway system, port facilities, and civil aviation, and very slow development in telecommunications.

To improve the transport system, construction of a new railway station at the Shanghai East Station was begun in 1985 and opened for use in December 1987. This new facility is able to handle up to 22 million passengers a year.[47] A new international port will be built near Wuqing, located at the upper course of Huangpu Jiang. Moreover, a feasibility study will be carried out for port construction both at Luojinggang, at the mouth of Chang Jiang to the north, and at Jinshanwei, on the northern coast of Hangzhouwan to the south. In addition to expanding the facilities at Hongqiao International Airport, construction of a new airport has been planned. To improve traffic conditions in the central city, the outer ring of the Shanghai–Hangzhou Highway has been opened to traffic. Construction of an expressway connecting Shanghai with Nanjing and Hangzhou will soon be undertaken; construction of the two sections between Shanghai and Jiading, and between Xinzhuang and Songjiang, has already been completed. A direct expressway from Wusong, via the central city, to Minhang and Jinshanwei will soon be constructed. Completion of these high-speed motorways will inevitably improve the linkages between the central city and its satellite towns.

The major goals of urban renewal and construction—including construction of urban facilities and residential housing and alleviation of pollution problems—are to improve the livelihood of Shanghai's residents and provide a congenial environment for foreign investment in the city. In 1985 the central government reduced Shanghai's remittance rate from 90 percent to 77 percent. This change has permitted Shanghai to retain more of its revenue for urban construction projects.[48] Currently more than a hundred major construction projects are under way, including energy supply, urban transit, public facilities, environmental protection, and residential housing construction.

According to the statistics of the Shanghai Basic Construction Committee, the investments made by the Shanghai People's Government in urban construction in 1986 increased by 86.8 percent over the same period in 1985.[49] The second tunnel under Huangpu Jiang has been completed. This structure connects Yanan Road East in the central business district and Pudong, an urban district on the eastern bank of Huangpu Jiang. The main tunnel was completed in 1986, and the entire project was finished in 1987. The tunnel measures over 2,000 m in length, 7.5 m in width, and 4.5 m in height.[50] Construction of the 8,346-m-long Nanpu Bridge spanning Huangpu Jiang started in 1988 and was expected to open to traffic late in 1991.[51] These cross-channel projects will contribute to the accelerated development of Pudong and its suburban areas.

Urban renewal projects in the central city will be closely coordinated with the adjustment of the city's economic structure and the development of suburban county towns. The most urgent task involves changing the disproportional land use in the city. At present, as much as one-quarter of the urban land is used for industrial purposes; other activities, such as commerce, culture, amusement, and green space, occupy a relatively small proportion of urban land.

To create a congenial and spacious environment for foreign investment in Shanghai, as well as to transform the city into a socialist, modern, and multifunctional metropolis, it has been proposed to control the outward expansion of the city proper and to change its spatial structure radically by diverting its future growth to satellite towns and Pudong. In particular, future developments will be concentrated in Jinshanwei to the south and Wusong to the north; construction of new urban districts at the city's fringe areas will accelerate. Moreover, bold plans have been made to develop Pudong: the entire urban district will be transformed into a new center for finance, trade, science and technology, culture and education, and commerce; both internal and external linkages of the city will be strengthened when all the trunk roads in the city, the harbor, and the aviation facilities are improved.[52]

Conclusion

Since 1949 a number of large industrial cities have emerged in China. Nonetheless, after more than three decades, the old industrial base of Shanghai still maintains its supremacy as China's largest metropolis and key economic center, due mainly to its superior geographical location, its strong industrial foundation, and its rich human resources. No doubt, the success of Shanghai has been attributed to its favorable physical environment and excellent spatial linkages with the rest of the country via Yangzi Jiang, China's longest river and most important waterway, and two trunk railways (the Huhang and Huning lines). It is significant to note that the vast size and richness of the city's hinterland that includes the Yangzi Delta and the drainage basins of the middle and lower course of Yangzi Jiang have also contributed to the rapid development of the metropolis.

The initial major development of Shanghai in the postliberation years occurred during the 1950s when the state government invested large sums of capital to rejuvenate and restructure the city's industry.[53] The opening of the city as one of China's fourteen centers for foreign capital, advanced industrial technology, and management skills has provided fresh impetus to its future growth and economic development. In recent years, an increasing amount of financial resources has become available, either from the city's own resource base or from foreign sources. Hence the municipal government has been able to initiate several capital construction projects in the central city. These major undertakings are meant to improve the city's energy supply, facilitate cross-channel traffic, and alleviate the chronic housing shortage.

To a great extent, the economic development of Shanghai depends on the modernization of its port. Therefore, it is imperative to upgrade the city's port facilities to world standard, as the outdated loading and unloading equipment, the small and shallow inner harbor for oceangoing vessels, and the persistent silting problems of the waterways leading to the city have posed serious constraints to the expansion of the city's export trade.

The population of Shanghai will continue to grow. Thus the acute overcrowding of population and industry in the central city must be addressed. Several satellite towns were built in the late 1950s with the objective of absorbing a portion of the central city and population. So far this goal has not been achieved. Therefore, more capital investment should be diverted to improve the urban infrastructure and public amenities of these industrial communities, and special wage incentives should be offered to satellite town employees. At the same time, a wide range of employment opportunities should be created to allow all the adults in a family to find suitable employment. Furthermore, plans should be made to develop more satellite settlements in the area to absorb more population from the parent city. The overall success of Shanghai's satellite town program is vital to the city's orderly development and rapid growth in future decades.

Notes

1. *Almanac of China's Economy 1982* (Hong Kong: Almanac of China's Economy Co., 1982), VI:3.

2. *Beijing Review*, 16 August 1982, p. 9 (in Chinese).

3. *Wen Wei Po*, 17 December 1984 (in Chinese).

4. *Shanghai Yearbook 1989* (Shanghai: China Statistics Press, 1989), p. 98 (in Chinese).

5. Shang Xidi and others, *Introduction to the Geography of Shanghai* (Shanghai: Shanghai People's Press, 1974), pp. 2–3 (in Chinese).

6. Ibid., p. 3.

7. *Shanghai Economy 1949–1982* (Shanghai: New China Bookstore, 1983), p. 37 (in Chinese).

8. Shang, *Introduction*, p. 95.

9. *Shanghai Municipal Council Report 1931*, vol. 3, pp. 29 and 45.

10. *A History of Shanghai Port* (Shanghai: Shanghai People's Press, 1979), p. 22 (in Chinese).

11. *A History of Shanghai's Financial System* (Shanghai: Shanghai People's Press, 1978), p. 16 (in Chinese).

12. *Shanghai Yearbook 1934* (Shanghai: Shanghai Commercial Press, 1935), p. 3 (in Chinese).

13. This ratio implies that the total yield from 1 *yuan* of investment is 2.5 *yuan* of profit.

14. *Shanghai Yearbook 1989* (Shanghai: China Statistics Press, 1989), pp. 147 and 173 (in Chinese).

15. *Beijing Review*, 30 March 1987, pp. 31–32.

16. *Beijing Review*, 27 April 1987, p. 20.

17. *Shanghai Yearbook 1989*, p. 332.

18. Ibid., p. 341.

19. Ibid., p. 349.

20. Ibid., p. 351.

21. Ibid., p. 354.

22. *Jiefang Ribao [Liberation daily]*, 24 July 1956.

23. *Shanghai Yearbook 1989*, pp. 386–387.

24. Ibid., pp. 32–33.

25. Chen Wenzi, "Strategy for the Urban Development of Shanghai," in Chen Minzhi and others (eds.), *Research on the Strategy of Shanghai's Economic Development* (Shanghai: Shanghai People's Press, 1985), p. 23 (in Chinese).

26. Sen Anan and W. Chen, "Examination of Large City Population Policy in the Perspective of Thirty Years of Population Changes in Shanghai," in Chen and others, *Research*, p. 55.

27. Ibid., p. 67.

28. *Shanghai Yearbook 1989*, pp. 436 and 450.

29. Da Jin, "Searching for a Policy to Solve the Population Problems in Shanghai," in Chen and others, *Research*, p. 66.

30. Ibid., p. 67.

31. *Shanghai Yearbook 1989*, pp. 436 and 450.

32. Da, "Searching for a Policy," p. 74.

33. Interview with town officials, 10 November 1986.

34. *Ming Pao*, 30 September 1985 (in Chinese).

35. Y. H. Chen, "Planning of Industrial Land Use in Old Urban Areas," *City Planning Review* 6 (1985): 14 (in Chinese).

36. Yan Zhongmin, "Shanghai," in Victor Sit (ed.), *Chinese Cities* (Hong Kong: Oxford University Press, 1985), p. 121.

37. Chen, "Planning," p. 19.

38. *Ming Pao*, 30 September 1988.

39. Ibid.

40. *Beijing Review*, 15 June 1987, p. 12.

41. Interview with Minhang town officials, 10 November 1986.

42. *Wen Wei Po*, 5 November 1984.

43. *Ta Kung Pao*, 23 April 1985.

44. *Ta Kung Pao*, 4 March 1990.

45. *Time,* 24 September 1990, pp. 36–37.

46. *Wen Wei Po,* 25 April 1990.

47. *Beijing Review,* 11–17 January 1988, p. 11.

48. *Ming Pao,* 23 May 1986.

49. Interview with Ku Xian-yun, deputy director of the Urban Planning Institute of Shanghai, 12 November 1986.

50. Ibid.

51. *Wen Wei Po,* 16 November 1989.

52. Interview with Ku Xian-yun.

53. K. I. Fung, "The Spatial Development of Shanghai," in B. C. Howe (ed.), *Shanghai—Revolution and Development in an Asian Metropolis* (Cambridge: Cambridge University Press, 1981), p. 284.

8 Ningbo: East China's Rising Industrial Port

C. P. LO AND XIAO-DI SONG

THE CITY OF NINGBO, whose abbreviated Chinese name is Yong, is located on the south shore of Hangzhou Bay directly opposite the group of islands collectively known as Zhoushan Qundao (Figure 8.1). Administratively the city comprises five city districts, namely Haishu, Jiangbei, Jiangdong, Zhenhai, and Beilun; one county-level city, Yuyao; and five counties, namely Yinxian, Cixi, Fenghua, Ninghai, and Xiangshan—with a total land area of 9,365 sq km and a total population of 4.877 million (see Figure 8.2).[1] The city itself has an area of 1,033 sq km and a population of 1.021 million of which 54 percent is nonagricultural. Thus Ningbo is the largest city after Hangzhou in Zhejiang province.

Ningbo has been the gateway of external economic links for Zhejiang, as well as the political, economic, cultural, and communication center for the eastern Zhejiang region. In recent years, it has been designated by the government as one of fourteen coastal ports opened to the West for trade and also one of the sixty-nine historical and cultural cities in China. With the government policy emphasizing reform of the nation's urban economic system and greater external opening, the development of the port districts of Zhenhai and Beilun signifies the growing importance of Ningbo not only in Zhejiang but in the nation at large.

History of Development

The history of Ningbo's development has been characterized by the role of its port in stimulating the growth of the city. Indeed, the rise and fall of the port have markedly affected the development of Ningbo.

Evolution of the Port/City Relationship

During the Qin dynasty (221–207 B.C.), Ningbo was administratively composed of the three *xian* (counties) of Yin, Mao, and Gouzhang in Huiji *cun* (prefecture). In the Sui dynasty (A.D. 581–618), the three *xian* merged into Gouzhang *xian*, which was renamed Mao *xian* in the Eighth

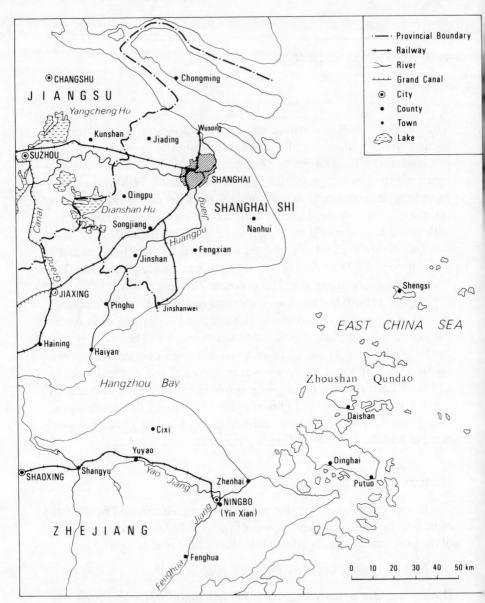

Figure 8.1 The Location of Ningbo City in Relation to Shanghai

Figure 8.2 County Boundaries of Ningbo City

Year of Wudes of the Tang dynasty (A.D. 625). The county seat was located in Xiaoxi (now known as Yinjiang Bridge). In the Sixth Year of Dali of the Tang dynasty (A.D. 771), the county seat was again moved to the confluence of the three rivers: Fenghua Jiang, Yao Jiang, and Yong Jiang—hence its name, Sanjiang Kou (now located inside the old city district of Ningbo). From then on, Ningbo assumed an important role as *xian* political center. In the First Year of Chang Qiang of the Ming dynasty (A.D. 821), the administrative power for Mingzhou was transferred from Xiaoxi to Ningbo, thus making it the political center for the higher-level *zhou* administrative unit. The growth of Ningbo at that time resulted in the establishment of a satellite city to absorb the surplus population. Thus the development of Ningbo can be dated back well over 1,100 years.

The original site of Ningbo basically remained unchanged throughout these years although the city's name changed many times. The reason for transferring the administrative power of Mingzhou from Xiaoxi to Sanjiang Kou was the growing importance of the port of Ningbo as a center of water communication and trade for Mingzhou in the Tang dynasty. At Sanjiang Kou, covering an area along Fenghua Jiang and Yao Jiang, a commercial port was established at that time to collect and distribute commodities from the mountains, agricultural produce from the plains, and dried seafood from Zhoushan Qundao. At the same time, it was also developing into an external trade and cultural exchange center for the southeastern coast of China. For the Tang, Song, and Ming dynasties, Ningbo was China's southern port to Japan and Korea, and the ambassadors from Japan to China during this period all landed first at the port of Ningbo. In the Qing dynasty (A.D. 1644–1911) a customhouse was set up, thus making Ningbo one of the four largest customhouses in China. After the conclusion of the Opium War (1840–1842), Ningbo was opened as one of the first treaty ports. All these developments pointed to the important port boundaries that Ningbo had been able to maintain in the past. The spread effect from the port had stimulated economic development in its surrounding regions.

Why was Ningbo's port able to maintain such importance throughout its historical evolution? One reason for its historical importance is the perennial navigability of Yong Jiang, which flows into the East China Sea. Naturally well endowed with deep water, the port was ice-free and well sheltered and thus could handle ships of all sizes. Moreover, Ningbo's geographical location is superior: it is adjacent to a fertile coastal plain, a rich hinterland of high population density and economic prosperity, and at the confluence of three rivers which help tap the resources of the southern mountain region, the central plain, and the northern coastal islands. Small ships can travel as far as the piedmont zone of the mountain region. Since several settlements along the slope of Siming Shan can be reached directly from the sea by small ships—Yuyao, Tongming, Yinjiang, and Jiangkou—Ningbo became the focus of a water and land network of transportation. It is also possible to link up with Hangzhou–Jiaxing–Taihu plain via Qiantang Jiang and the Grand Canal. Ningbo, therefore, is very well located to facilitate the interchange of goods among the plains, mountains, and sea as well as between the city and the countryside.

Inadequate Port, Ingenious People

During the early treaty ports period, the nine Western Powers, which included Great Britain, France, Germany, and the United States, invaded China and occupied Ningbo as a base for trade development. Leased territories from China were established by the Western Powers along the northern Yong Jiang at Ningbo. All the historically famous produce of the region—silk, textiles, tea leaves, herbal drugs, cotton, construction materials, and handicrafts—became cheap exports overseas.

Because of the great demand in the world market for silk textiles and tea leaves produced in eastern Zhejiang, the region's self-sufficient agricultural economy was gradually transformed into an export-oriented commercial economy. Thus Cixi, Yuyao, and Zhenhai *xian* emerged as specialized production areas for cotton and the "old tea" produced in Pingshui in Huiji Shan became a famous specialty of the region. Although the foreign trade resulted in an influx of rice, edible oil, cloth, and goods from abroad which competed with local produce in the market, it also stimulated the development of local industries. Ningbo is one of the early industrial cities of China.

Beginning in the 1880s, merchants in Ningbo started to establish industries—for example, the Tong Jiu Yuan Cotton Ginning Factory established in 1887, the Cixi Match Factory established in 1889, and the Tong Jiu Yuan Textile Factory in 1896. These industries all made use of local raw materials which were the by-products of agriculture. This development of light industry transformed Ningbo from a mainly commercial city to an industrial-commercial city. Because of the control of capital exercised under the Western Powers, the pace of development was slow.

Ningbo's port facilities lagged far behind those of neighboring Shanghai. The rapid rise of Shanghai's port as the dominant trade hub for all goods in the whole Chang Jiang (Yangzi River) drainage basin had eclipsed Ningbo in its economic development. Both Ningbo and Shanghai were elevated to the status of *shi* (city) in 1927. The population of Ningbo was about 210,000 at that time. By 1980, after more than fifty years of development, it had not exceeded 500,000 and the total volume of goods imported and exported through the port was about 3 million tonnes. Shanghai, whose population was only 200,000 when it was first established as a port in 1843, soared to over 1 million people at the beginning of the twentieth century. By 1980, the population of Shanghai's city area alone was already 6.3 million and the total volume of goods handled by the port had reached 91 million tonnes, making Shanghai the largest port and city in China (exceeding Ningbo in scale by twenty to thirty times). As a result of Shanghai's tremendous growth, foreign merchant offices and consulates originally located in Ningbo were all moved to Shanghai. Even local capital for industrial development was attracted to Shanghai from whence it spread to other regions.

Ningbo has a breed of ingenious people with a special talent for business. Indeed, there is a saying: "There will be no cities without Ningbo people." The old tradition of Ningbo as a port specializing in commerce provided the training ground for shrewd merchants and businessmen who were highly mobile. As they traveled to different parts of China and started businesses and industries, a special fraternity called "Ningbo clansmen" emerged. Since the opening of five treaty ports by China in 1842, commercial activities advanced with great speed and finance and banking developed. At that time in Ningbo, there were over a hundred houses which lent money to businesses in Shanghai, Wuhan, Hangzhou, Wenzhou, and other places in China. By 1876, all the money-lending houses in Ningbo had carried out "account transfers"—a significant development in Chinese banking because it permitted the maximum utilization of capital without resorting to currency for investment purposes. Despite all these human resources and financial services, Ningbo failed to develop into a modern industrial-commercial city because of its inferior port facilities. As a result, Shanghai overtook Ningbo and captured most of its capital. (Some of this capital went to Hong Kong, as well, which also has superior port facilities.) Ningbo people excelled in Shanghai and Hong Kong and could be found in large and medium-size cities throughout China.

Revitalization of the Port

In 1952, train services between Ningbo and Hangzhou began. This important development linked Ningbo with the national railroad net, thus considerably expanding Ningbo's hinterland. In 1971, a wharf was constructed along the coast on Baisha Road in the port zone which served as a sea-land transport connecting point. As a result, the port of Ningbo now provided sea-rail link, a new step in the city's economic development. But as long as the port's navigation conditions remained unchanged, no drastic economic improvement was possible. In fact, the navigation situation was worsened by the construction of a watergate across Yao Jiang in 1959, which reduced the volume of water induced by tidal currents into the navigation channel of Yong Jiang and hence led to the silting up of the river. Even ships of 3,000 tons had to await high tide to sail out of the port, thus greatly restricting the development of the old port of Ningbo.

The year 1974 marked the beginning of an era when all these constraints to the port's development were gradually eliminated. A significant development was the coastal reclamation carried out in Zhenhai which resulted in the provision of new berthing places of 4.3 km in length along the coast for ships up to 10,000 tons. In addition, two special wharves for transporting coal and charcoal, one for 3,000-ton ships and one for 10,000-ton ships, were constructed. Later six wharves, including one for the chemical industry and others for handling different types of goods, were also built. When the construction of all sixteen berthing places was complete, the annual volume of goods handled by the port increased to 12 million tons. The development of Zhenhai port, therefore, had a significant impact on Ningbo's economy, making Ningbo a major gateway of overseas trade for Zhejiang. An important function was its coal and charcoal transshipment along the coast of Zhejiang, a function it shared with the port of Shanghai.

Since 1978 another new development has taken place at the eastern flank of the Yong Jiang estuary—along the southern bank of Jintang waterway—where the major advantage is the deep water. Here a large and modern wharf for mineral transshipment was constructed. Beilun port (so named because of its proximity to Beilun Shan) is an excellent deep-water port in the middle section of the Chinese coastline. The water area in the port exceeds 80 sq km and the length of the deep-water coastline is 13 km. The land area behind the port is 135 sq km. Water remains ice-free and unsilted throughout the year. The Zhoushan Qundao provides an effective wind shelter for the port area. Since the shallowest point of the navigation channel is 17.6 m, ships of 100,000 tons can freely sail in and out of the port and ships of 150,000 tons can enter at high tide. A little dredging of the channel will allow ships of 200,000 to 300,000 tons to sail into the port.

The development of Beilun port has made Ningbo the best seaport in China. The port's development potential is vast, for the coastal areas of Zhoushan Qundao and Jintang Dao in the north can now be linked together. If this linkage materializes, a gigantic deep-water port site will emerge and the dream of an "Eastern Super-Seaport" can be realized. Indeed, some developments have already occurred along this line, including one 100,000-ton and two 25,000-ton wharves for minerals, two 24,000-ton wharves for crude oil, and one 25,000-ton wharf for miscellaneous goods. Now in the planning stage are one 100,000-ton crude oil wharf, one 50,000-ton coal and charcoal wharf, and one 50,000-ton container wharf. In 1985, the total volume of goods handled by the port of Ningbo was 26.7 million tons.

Ningbo is now a port complex comprising the old port district, the Zhenhai port district, and the Beilun port district—symbolizing the integration of small, medium, and large-scale ports. It is also a multifunctional port complex with economic activities in industry, commerce, communications, and fishery. It has excellent potential for developing into a gigantic and versatile international port. The new development of Ningbo into a modern deep-water seaport under the Chinese government's open policy has greatly revived the economy of Ningbo. In recent years, Ningbo's rate of economic growth has already far outstripped that of Shanghai.

Present Conditions

During the 1950s and 1960s, it was government policy to reduce the concentration of industries in the coastal area, a sensitive, national defense frontline. Not only was there no new industrial development in the coastal area, but certain well-established industries were moved to the interior of China. Not until the early 1970s was there port development to be seen in Ningbo.

Despite the late start, Ningbo's economic development proceeded quite rapidly because of its superior hinterland resources and the ingenuity of the city's merchants. In 1980, the total gross value of agricultural and industrial production for the city of Ningbo exceeded that for 1952 by 38.8 times—an average annual increase of 8.5 percent. Out of this, the GVIO increased from 160 million *yuan* to 3,430 million *yuan,* an increase of twenty times. The average annual increase was 11.6 percent.

Since 1978, the adoption of an open policy has been particularly favorable for Ningbo's economic development because of its port revitalization and human resources. From 1980 to 1985, the total gross value of agricultural and industrial production increased 21.3 percent; industrial production alone increased 21 percent. The total GVIO in 1985 was 8,900 million *yuan,* of which the city area accounted for 4,370 million *yuan.*[2] Ningbo ranked sixth among all Chinese coastal ports in terms of GVIO, trailing just behind Shanghai, Tianjin, Guangzhou, Dalian, and Qingdao. Clearly the new government policy has helped to transform Ningbo into a major export-oriented industrial-commercial port city with the following characteristics.

Development of Light Industry

Ningbo has a complete range of industries—in particular, textiles, mechanical engineering, food processing, and chemical engineering. In 1985, there were altogether 7,306 industrial units in Ningbo, of which 1,544 were found in the city district. The total number of employees was 6.24 million (311,000 in the city district). The value of light industrial production was 60.3 percent of the total while heavy industrial production contributed 39.7 percent. Among the light industries, textiles and food processing predominated. Textile production accounted for 32 percent of the total industrial value, making Ningbo one of the principal textile bases of Zhejiang. Textile industries included cotton, wool, silk, chemical fibers, weaving, dyeing, and clothes making—a complete suite of textile industries. The food processing industry was based on local resources, especially in relation to the processing of agricultural by-products, and accounted for 56 percent of the total light industrial value of production. Of the total industrial units in Ningbo, small to medium-scale units accounted for 99 percent; the number of employees and production value were respectively 92 and 86 percent of the total. Of the value of industrial production, processing industries accounted for 85 percent.

The heavy industries in Ningbo focus on automobile assembly, ship-building and repair, production of internal combustion engines, and other mechanical engineering industries. There are also chemical engineering industries which produce chemical fertilizers, insecticides, acids and alkalis, and salt (based on local resources). Ningbo is famous for its traditional handicrafts and arts, such as embroidered clothes, gold and silver embroidery, bone and wood mosaics, gilt and lacquer, reed mats, and bamboo and grass woven products.

Development of Petrochemical Engineering and Energy Industries

The development of Zhenhai port and Beilun port has made possible the introduction of modern industries to Ningbo. The superior conditions of the port are conducive to importing crude oil for petrochemical engineering and related processing industries. Newly completed are a 2.5-million-tonne oil refinery, chemical engineering factories that can produce 300,000 tonnes of synthetic ammonia and 520,000 tonnes of urea annually, and the Zhenhai power plant, which can initially generate 250,000 kw of electricity (and ultimately will be enhanced to generate 1.05 million kw). The first phase of construction of the 1.2-million-kw Beilun power plant has already started.

Thus along the coast of Zhenhai district, just north of Yong Jiang, an area of heavy chemical engineering industries and generating plants has emerged. There are plans to establish a 2.4-million-kw power generating plant, an iron-steel factory, a wood processing factory, a construction material factory, and a shipyard in the Beilun port area. Some of these projects are in an advanced stage of planning. These modern and large-scale industries, if completed, will change the basic economic structure and the spatial distribution of productivity.

Development of External Trade and Economic Technology

Ningbo is Zhejiang's major port for exports and external trade. It is also a transshipment port for some of the nation's minerals, lumber, and crude oil. In 1985 the total value of exports was 290 million *yuan* with 300 varieties of goods. The following local exports are particularly famous in Hong Kong, Macau, and other overseas markets: water meters, diesel electricity generators, copper wire, cotton, yarn, bed sheets, metal products, handicraft products, tangerines, canned peaches, strawberries, naphtha, underwear, frozen geese, *tangyuan* (small balls of stuffed dumplings made of glutinous rice flour), honey, mats, dried scallops, grouper (a reef fish), and prawns.

To meet the growing demands for culture and technology exchange, the government has approved the establishment of an EDTZ in Zhenhai port, a distance of 20 km from Ningbo. The first phase of construction covers an area of 3.9 sq km, but when the last phase is reached the total area will be 10 sq km. This zone is located near the deep-water port of Beilun in the east, only 10 km from the Beilun mineral transshipment wharf, and overlooks Zhenhai port across the river in the west. Nearby Yanggong Shan port district can be used to build piers for the ETDZ. A second-class 20-km-long highway connecting this zone with the old port of Ningbo has already been constructed. An underwater tunnel across the river to link up with Zhenhai port is being built. The major objective of the ETDZ is to attract foreign investment and technology in order to develop small-scale, technology-intensive, export-oriented industries.

Development of a Production Base for Commercial Exports

The total gross value of village production of Ningbo in 1985 was over 8,160 million *yuan,* of which agricultural production accounted for 1,630 million *yuan.* Ningbo's rural economy has provided resources to support the development of the port, city construction, and export trades. Ningbo is located in the eastern part of the Ningbo–Shaoxing plain—agriculturally the most productive region in Zhejiang by virtue of its fertile soils, a dense network of water channels, and a high population density. The mountains to its south and the sea to its north are endowed with abundant land and marine resources. All these advantages tend to favor the development of rural economy in the villages, which has become the production base of Zhejiang for foodgrain, cotton, oil, poultry, cattle, and aquacultural products. The production of foodgrain, cotton, and aquacultural products has reached 10, 50, and 25 percent, respectively, of the whole province's output. In 1985, the total value of industrial production in the villages *(cun)* and below was 2,530 million *yuan.* A sizable proportion of the rural labor force has shifted to secondary and tertiary activities. Those now engaged in the secondary and tertiary sectors exceed 1 million people. The development of commercial economy in rural areas becomes a major impetus for speeding the economic growth of Ningbo city. A consequence of these rural changes is the specialization of foodgrain production by expert grain farmers. To meet the needs of an export-oriented economy, facilities specializing in the production of foodgrain, poultry and cattle, aquacultural products, fruit, mats, herbs, and embroidery are being constructed.

Development of Infrastructure for Investment Purposes

Apart from the port development, Ningbo's infrastructure has been improving. The development focus has been on the eastern part of the city, where a new district with widened roads and new roads has emerged. A number of road widening projects, as in Zhongshan Xi Lu, Ningqiao Dong, and Fuqiao Dong, have been completed. Other projects under construction or in the planning stage include a second-class civil airport, a telecommunication center, a foreign office, and a trade center. Tertiary educational institutions (such as Ningbo University and other postsecondary colleges) and research bureaus have already attained high standards. All these improvements are conducive to foreign investment of capital and technology.

Development Trends and Distribution Pattern

Toward a Modern, Integrated Port City

If Ningbo is to assume the role of a major industrial city of East China, its future development will have to complement the functions of Shanghai economic zone, its neighboring economic giant, and fit in with the overall economic development policy of Zhejiang. Specifically, Ningbo must focus on its port development, the mainstay of its export-oriented economy. Such a development also relies heavily on the area's agricultural production. The blueprint for the future projects Ningbo as a multifunctional, technologically advanced, cultural port city in which care is taken to ensure ecological harmony. It is predicted that by the year 2000, the total population of Ningbo will be between 5.1 and 5.4 million, with 900,000 to 1 million people living in the city area, and the per capita GNP will be 4,000 *yuan* per year. To achieve this objective, the city must utilize to the fullest its advantages and come to grips with the problems of its development.

Maximum Use of Advantages. The three port zones of Ningbo represent three different classes of multifunctional and integrated deepwater ports. Ningbo is now an important seaport serving East China and Zhejiang. Modern railroads and highways, as well as water and electrical utilities, have all been incorporated into the three port zones. As long as engineering work can be carried out to maintain and upgrade the infrastructural facilities, the port will be extremely productive. There is also plenty of space—both on land and in the sea—for the port to expand its transportation, industries, and building construction. Along the coast is nearly 5 ha of marshy land which can be reclaimed. So far 300 ha has been reclaimed for use as industrial land.

The development of the port zone and the city area of Ningbo has pointed to a new path for the future development of Zhejiang. The province is poorly endowed with resources: it is mountainous, lacks arable land, and has a high population density. The resources required for industrial development, namely energy and raw materials, are not present. For the past thirty years, industrial development has relied heavily on renewable agricultural resources. Of the gross value of industrial and agricultural production, industries accounted for 70 percent. Light industries accounted for 70 percent of the GVIO. Within the light industry sector, the gross production value for processing industries utilizing agricultural products and by-products as raw materials also accounted for 70 percent.

These statistics clearly illustrate the importance of agriculture to the economy of Zhejiang. Yet this kind of agriculture-based economy utilizing renewable resources has only limited potential for development. Compounding the difficulty is Zhejiang's high land-use intensity with a multiple cropping index of 260. To increase agricultural productivity per unit area requires input of capital and high technology. Despite the concomitant occurrence of mountains and sea in the province, most of the biological resources have been overutilized or exhausted. Thus a long period of conservation is required before the potential of its land and sea resources can be realized. The development of a port-based, export-oriented, market economy is an important way of boosting the economy of Zhejiang. This explains the rapid development of Ningbo port and the coastal reclamation in the port zone for developing basic industries, in accordance with the central government's open policy, so that Ningbo will become the heavy industrial base and external trade window of Zhejiang province.

Existing Problems and Constraints. The rapid pace of development in Ningbo occurred after a long period of stagnant growth. Its traditional regional economic structure and spatial distribution pattern are obviously outmoded by these new developments.

First, Ningbo is the southern wing of the Shanghai Economic Core Area. As the port extends its functions from the inland area to the coast, Ningbo's role vis-à-vis Shanghai's port functions must be readjusted.

The port of Shanghai has no coastline available for building berthing docks for ships of 35,000 tons or above. In this respect, Ningbo can contribute as a member of the Shanghai economic zone multiport system on the basis of division of labor. But Shanghai port has its own nearby ports, notably Nantong and Zhangjia, both in Jiangsu province, to form an amalgamated port which will have even better coastline resources than Ningbo. Because of their proximity to the central city area of Shanghai, these ports have greater potential than Ningbo, and keen competition exists among them. The hinterland of Ningbo, which has received some improvements in the past, cannot compete with the rich hinterland of Shanghai with its focus on the upper courses of Chang Jiang. In the face of such realities, Ningbo's development strategy will be to build up a coastal industrial base as a means to expand its internal and external markets. The development of coastal industrial zones is the key to Ningbo's future success. There is now an urgent need to expand electricity generation, petrochemical engineering, metallurgical, and other heavy industries and to import raw materials and energy resources for industries. There is also a need to develop the third and fourth generations of container transport to maximize the integrated use of the deep-water port.

Second, water resources development and rational utilization are important to Ningbo's future growth. The major river of Ningbo city, Yong Jiang, has a drainage area of 5,544 sq km and an annual flow volume of 3,600 million cubic meters, or 900 cu m per person per year. Only 30 percent of the water resources are developable. With the rapid economic advances of Ningbo, the shortage of water becomes a prominent problem and it will be necessary to transfer water from the Cao-e Jiang and Fuchun Jiang drainage areas. According to investigations, Ningbo should have enough water to meet the needs of industry and agriculture as well as those of the urban residents during years of average water level, but in the dry or superdry years a shortage of 400 to 600 million cubic meters of water is envisaged. The proposal to transfer water from Cao-e Jiang and Fuchun Jiang has been studied for a long time and is deemed practicable. Only a shortage of funds prevents it from being implemented.

Third, the second express railroad of East China is under construction, construction of the second bridge over Qiantang Jiang has already started, the section of line connecting Hangzhou and Xuancheng in Anhui province on the Changxing–Xuancheng line will be completed at the time of the Seventh Five-Year Plan, and the Shanghai–Hangzhou and Zhejiang–Jiangxi lines are being converted to double tracks. Yet the condition of railroads, highways, and navigation channels leading to these transport pathways in Ningbo badly requires upgrading. Much more construction work is needed to improve the distribution system of Ningbo's hinterland.

Fourth, despite rapid advances in city construction, Ningbo's infrastructure still lags behind the needs brought about by the open policy and the plan for future development. Much needs to be done—notably the readjustment of the spatial structure of the old city area and the opening up of new districts. The major problem in the old city is the overcrowded conditions and the high intensity of land use. Moreover, the use of the coastline is not always rational and basic facilities are still lacking. Measures to control water pollution, to prevent flooding, to preserve the coastline, and to improve city roads must be perfected.

Spatial Distribution and Structure

The development of Ningbo's ports and the changes in its economic structure are reflected in the changes in the city's spatial structure, which are quite considerable. There is a need to modify the city's spatial distribution pattern to fit in with the new regional rhythm of change generated by urban development. Although the development of Ningbo's city and port shares certain common themes with other port cities, it has its own unique aspects. Indeed, its urban development and port distribution are so intimately related that they must be viewed together. In general, the site of the river port has shifted from Sanjiang Kou to the estuary and then to the deep-water seacoast as the volume of goods and raw materials has increased and the ships have become bigger. This shift in location can be gradually carried out toward the lower course of the river and then along the coast; or it can be done discontinuously in a leapfrog manner in accordance with the port's geographical conditions and development stages. The three different port zones of Ningbo are about 20 km apart, and the shifting of the port zone from Sanjiang Kou to the estuary and then along the seacoast took place in less than ten years. The city itself has shifted with the port zone from Sanjiang Kou to the lower course of Yong Jiang around the area called Baisha and then further on to Beilun—thus initially forming a multiple-nuclei city comprising the old city district, Zhenhai district, and Beilun district.

Functional Divisions of the Three Port Zones. The port of Ningbo is a composite port consisting of the old port, the Zhenhai port, and the Beilun port; altogether there are sixteen berthing places. The old port was developed in the last century as a river port and is accessible to ships of 3,000 tons or less. There are abundant berths, but the navigation channel is inferior. Currently, the old port handles passenger ships and freighters distributing and collecting goods from eastern Zhejiang and the old city district. The total volume of goods that can be handled by this port is from 3 to 4 million tonnes.

Zhenhai port is about 29 km from the old city area via waterway (the Yong Jiang navigation channel) and 20 km via highway. Since its establishment in 1974, the port has constructed six berthing docks for ships ranging from 3,000 to 10,000 tons. The ultimate number of docks will be sixteen, thus making it possible to handle the transshipment of the products of Zhejiang, external trade, and large oceangoing passenger liners. Zhenhai port will assume part of the transshipment function of the Shanghai economic zone's composite port.

Beilun port is Ningbo's deep-water port. It has three major roles: a national transshipment port for goods, lumber, and international containers for long-distance (over 3,000 nautical miles) oceangoing ships; the external port of Shanghai economic zone, sharing in the handling of goods from Shanghai and areas in the lower and middle courses of Chang Jiang; and the port serving the local economic development of Zhejiang province as well as the city of Ningbo.

A Three-Tier Economic Structure. Spatially and temporally, the economic structure of Ningbo can be divided into three tiers: the rural economy, the old city's industrial economy, and the coastal area's national industrial economy.

Under the open policy, the rural economy is directed toward export-oriented trade, industry, and agriculture and the demands of city dwellers for food by-products. It will establish diverse commercial agricultural production bases and develop village-town enterprises engaged in secondary and tertiary activities to absorb surplus agricultural labor force.

The old city area clearly reflects an urban economic structure inherited from the past, one which basically utilized local resources and imported raw materials to develop small to medium-scale processing industries. The range of industrial activities is broader and includes manufactured products such as light textiles, food, mechanical engineering, chemical engineering, household electrical appliances, and electronics. Its future development will focus on improving industrial technology and upgrading the quality of products to compete in the market.

The coastal industrial zone is the focus of the new industrial layout plan for Ningbo. From Xiepu in Zhenhai district along the coast west of the Chuanshan Peninsula, the following industrial zones are laid out:

petrochemical industrial zone, economic and technological development zone, energy resources industrial zone, shipbuilding and repair zone, and marine engineering with metallurgical and mechanical engineering industrial zone. Construction of the petrochemical industrial zone is now completed. In the future, apart from increasing its scale of operation, further development will be toward the labor-intensive and resource-integrative objectives. The industrial area behind Beilun port makes use of the large amount of imported raw materials—namely, coal and charcoal, minerals, and lumber—as its basis for developing electricity generating stations, metallurgical, mechanical, and building materials industries, shipbuilding and repair, and marine engineering. The Xiaogang ETDZ, which lies between Zhenhai and Beilun, makes use of foreign capital to introduce new technology to establish technology-intensive processing industries (Figure 8.3).

Structure and Layout of the Urban System. The urban system of Ningbo *shi* is made up of a city district (an old city area and two new city areas), a county-level city *(shi),* five county capitals, and forty-eight established towns *(zhen).* In the process of forming the city area of Ningbo, three spatially separated and socioeconomically independent components of the city have emerged in the form of a triangle: the old city district, the Zhenhai district, and the Beilun district. For long-term development, these three components will eventually merge.

The old city district of Ningbo is the political, economic, cultural, trade, and information center. The need to reconstruct the old city area is urgent. Technological renovation of equipment in the old industries, preservation of historical artifacts, development of education, training, and other services to the populace—all are required. It should also provide strong support to the development of Zhenhai and Beilun districts. The key focus of Zhenhai district is its petrochemical and electricity generating industries. Strengthening the basic infrastructure and social services will nicely complement its development. The development of Beilun district will be based on its deep-water port, heavy industrial district, and the open zone. It is imperative to develop the new city of Beilun and Xiaogang town carefully. In 1985, the nonagricultural population of the old city area was about 500,000; Zhenhai district had nearly 50,000 people; Beilun district, not more than 10,000. It is planned that by the year 2000, the population in the old city will be increased to between 600,000 and 700,000; Zhenhai district, 100,000 to 150,000; and Beilun district, 200,000.

Apart from the city center, the port, and the industrial towns, the

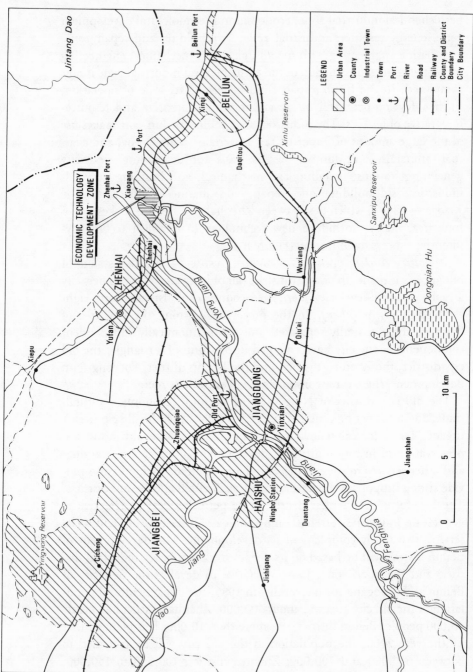

Figure 8.3 The Three Port Areas of Ningbo

LEGEND

▨	Urban Area
◉	County
◎	Industrial Town
●	Town
⚓	Port
	River
	Road
	Railway
	County and District Boundary
	City Boundary

other towns within the city administration of Ningbo have been developed on the basis of a rural commercial economy. The rapid emergence of village and town enterprises has stimulated the growth of small-sized cities, and many new administratively established towns have been sanctioned by the government. A good example is the original Yuyao *xian* located on the upper course of Yao Jiang: it has become a small city at the *xian* level with a nonagricultural population of 170,000 and a GVIO of over 1,000 million *yuan*. In other counties administered by the city, the growth in the commercial production economy and population has also been very fast. The migration of rural population to the small cities has increased. This combination of bottom-up rural urbanization and top-down city, port, and industrial town development is characteristic of Ningbo's urban system, which has its core in the old city area but is composed of town clusters of different functional types and dimensions.

Conclusion

Ningbo is an interesting example of how a city can survive under the giant shadow of Shanghai. Its modern development has focused on a deep-sea port (Beilun) and heavy industries related to oil refining, electricity generating, and chemical fertilizer manufacturing. Another focus of the development stemming from implementation of the open policy has been the establishment of an ETDZ to attract foreign investment and technology which can make use of the port's new facilities. Ningbo's people are famous for their commercial ingenuity, and the city has excellent overseas connections that help boost its export-oriented economy. New infrastructural facilities are also being installed, and a wider hinterland of agricultural products is being tapped by new railroad connections. The future role of Ningbo will complement two major cities in the region: Shanghai, the international port of the nation, and Hangzhou, the scenic spot of the region.

Notes

1. Unless otherwise indicated, the statistics used in this chapter are for the year 1985.

2. This computation is based on the constant price for 1980.

9 Wenzhou: Development in Regional and Historical Contexts

CHUN-SHING CHOW AND HANG CHEN

THIS CHAPTER is concerned with the development of Wenzhou city in its geographical and historical contexts. Wenzhou is located in southeastern Zhejiang province. It is bounded by the East China Sea (Dong Hai) to the east and by the Yandang Mountains (Yandang Shan) to the north, west, and south. The city is situated at a site where Ou Jiang drains into the East China Sea (Figure 9.1).

In premodern times, Wenzhou's location enabled it to benefit by water transportation across the sea and along the river. This made it a desirable locality for the development of a port city. Nevertheless, that Wenzhou was bounded by high mountains on three sides made it difficult to develop land transport there. The railroad era in China began in the late nineteenth century, but the rugged topography surrounding Wenzhou made it exceedingly costly to have the railroad network extended into the city. Even today, Wenzhou is not connected to any other area by rail.

Not only was Wenzhou deprived of rail transportation, but the development of motor roads in the area was slow as well. The first highway connecting Wenzhou to the major trunk road system in Zhejiang was not completed until 1934.[1] The absence of rail transport and the slow development of road networks have left Wenzhou worse off than other port cities, such as Shanghai and Ningbo, which were better served by motor roads and rail. Since the modern era, therefore, Wenzhou has not been able to develop as rapidly as other major cities on the coast. Until the late 1940s, Wenzhou remained a city of moderate size with an urban economy that had not advanced beyond the stage of producing handicrafts and engaging in commerce and trade.[2] Large-scale industrialization had not yet occurred in Wenzhou.

Since the founding of the People's Republic in 1949, the Chinese government has made attempts to transform Wenzhou into an industrial city. Through administrative decisions under the central planning system, the government began in the 1950s to reorganize Wenzhou's pro-

172

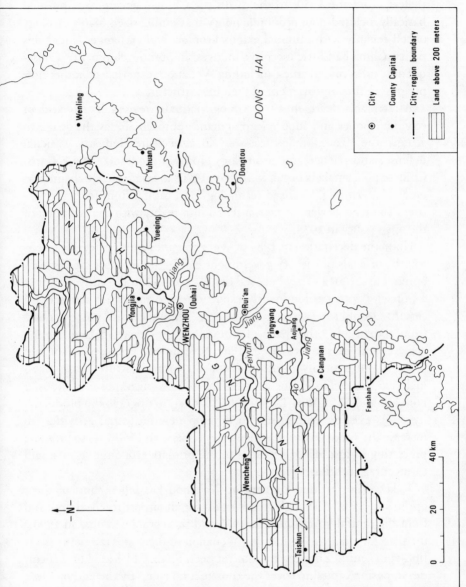

Figure 9.1 Relief of the Wenzhou Region

duction units and establish additional industrial plants, chemical, textile, machine building, and papermaking, in and around the city. Nevertheless, from the 1950s to the 1970s the Chinese government pursued basically a closed-door economic policy that emphasized Mao's ideology of self-reliance with minimal external contact and exchange. Under this policy, China had little incentive to invest in port development.[3] Consequently, most coastal cities, including Wenzhou, experienced rather slow progress in the improvement of their infrastructure.

After Mao's death in 1976, China gradually revised its closed-door economic policy and adopted a pragmatic approach. Today the goal is to achieve the "Four Modernizations" in agriculture, industry, national defense, and science and technology. To help modernize the country, Chinese policymakers began in the late 1970s to acknowledge the importance of absorbing advanced technology and capital from foreign countries. These goals were to be translated into reality with the adoption of the open policy in 1978.

Upon the declaration in 1984 of Wenzhou as one of fourteen open cities, the officials of the city government had high hopes for rapid development in the area. They believed that Wenzhou could readily grow into a port city with predominantly export-oriented industrial activities—a city that would soon serve as a "window" through which entrepreneurs from abroad and other parts of China could interact. To facilitate the achievement of such goals, the city government proposed ambitious plans to substantially improve Wenzhou's infrastructure. Such plans included, for example, the construction of new piers, power stations, a railroad, and an airport. The city also planned to upgrade the productivity of its existing enterprises, to develop new industrial activities, to increase the productivity in agriculture, fishery, and forestry, to promote processing industries for products in the primary economic sectors, and to encourage tourism.[4]

Today, however, development at Wenzhou has fallen short of these optimistic goals. Although construction for an airport received approval from the central government in 1985 and was completed only in 1990,[5] the plan for a railroad connecting Wenzhou to the major rail network via Jinhua in central Zhejiang has not yet been finalized because of difficulties in raising capital to cover the construction cost.[6] By the end of 1987, only a modest amount of foreign capital, $2 million, had been invested in Wenzhou.[7] By December 1988, only twenty-four joint ventures (that is, corporations jointly financed with foreign and local capital) had been established in Wenzhou, engaging primarily in the production of light industrial products such as clothing, shoes, and daily utensils.[8]

Despite the slow progress in Wenzhou's development, city officials are hopeful about the prospects for urban and economic growth in the near future. They are confident that, given the city's strategic location, the rich endowment of natural resources in its vicinity, and new opportunities for development under the open policy, they can speed the pace of progress in Wenzhou if they can manage to streamline the procedures for attracting foreign investment.[9] Whether the city officials' hopes can come true will depend, of course, on subsequent developments in Wenzhou. To assess the potential for future growth in Wenzhou realistically, however, it is necessary to understand the city's development in terms of its historical, geographical, and political contexts.

Wenzhou city itself consists of the central city (the city core or the built-up area) and two suburban districts—Lucheng and Longwan. Lucheng district consists of six *xiang* (administrative villages); Longwan is made up of three *zhen* (towns) and two *xiang*. As an administrative entity, nevertheless, Wenzhou *shi* also means Wenzhou city itself and its city-administered counties, which include Rui'an city (which was upgraded from the status of county in 1987) and eight others: Ouhai, Yongjia, Dongtou, Yueqing, Pingyang, Cangnan, Taishun, and Wencheng (Figure 9.2). To avoid confusion, this chapter refers to the greater Wenzhou *shi* (that is, Wenzhou city, Rui'an, and the eight city-administered counties) as "Wenzhou region" and the city itself (that is, the central city and the two suburban districts) as "Wenzhou city."

Population

In the Wenzhou region, most of the city-administered counties are essentially rural in function and character. This is reflected in the way that the population, particularly the nonagricultural population, is distributed. Table 9.1 portrays the population and population densities of the administrative units in the Wenzhou region as recorded in the 1982 census. In that year, 508,611 inhabitants lived in Wenzhou city and 5,419,717 in its nine subordinate counties, giving a total of 5.9 million in the entire region. Among the various administrative units in the region, Wenzhou city was the most densely populated (3,260 persons/sq

Table 9.1 Population and Population Density by County and City Unit in Wenzhou: 1982

ADMINISTRATIVE UNIT	POPULATION	POPULATION DENSITY (PERSONS/SQ KM)
Wenzhou city	508,611	3,260
Rui'an county[a]	992,889	730
Ouhai county	481,280	736
Dongtou county	112,468	1,125
Yueqing county	879,525	749
Yongjia county	723,784	269
Pingyang county	675,467	641
Cangnan county	933,310	740
Wencheng county	325,722	259
Taishun county	295,272	174
Total	5,928,328	503

Source: PRC State Statistical Bureau, *China Population Statistics Yearbook 1988* (Beijing: Zhongguo Zhenwang Chubanshe, 1988), p. 594 (in Chinese).

[a]Known as Rui'an city after 1987.

km). Other counties were either sparsely populated—such as Taishun (174 persons/sq km), Wencheng (259 persons/sq km), and Yongjia (269 persons/sq km)—or moderately populated, such as Yueqing (749 persons/sq km) and Cangnan (740 persons/sq km). Dongtou county, made up of a number of offshore islands, had the smallest population (112,468); but because of its small area, the population density was relatively high (1,125 persons/sq km) (Figure 9.2).

Table 9.2 shows population statistics compiled through the household registration system in the Wenzhou region for 1987. In that year, the entire Wenzhou region had a population of 6.4 million, of whom only 0.9 million or 14 percent were classified as nonagricultural under the household registration system. Among the administrative units in the region, Wenzhou city had the largest number of nonagricultural people (383,000). In other words, as many as 41.7 percent of the Wenzhou region's nonagricultural population was concentrated within Wenzhou city. In the city-administered counties, the majority of residents were engaged in agricultural activities (Figure 9.3). In Ouhai, for instance, as

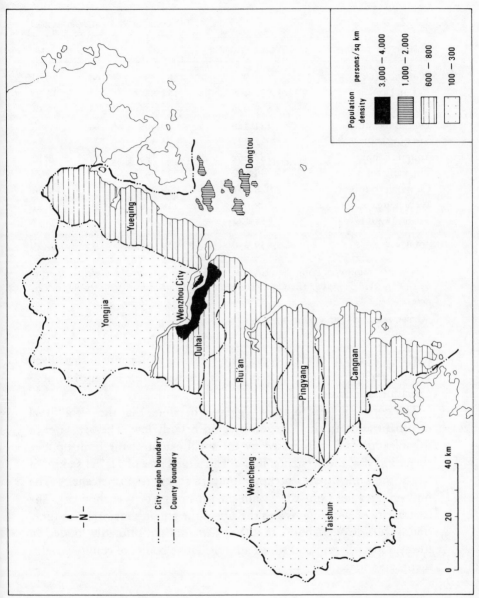

Figure 9.2 Population Density in the Wenzhou Region: 1982

Table 9.2   Population and Nonagricultural Population by County
            and City Unit in Wenzhou: 1987

| ADMINISTRATIVE UNIT | POPULATION | NONAGRICULTURAL POPULATION | |
		NO.	%
Wenzhou city	543,900	383,337	70.48
Rui'an city[a]	1,976,495	153,632	14.27
Ouhai county	509,926	27,246	5.34
Dongtou county	121,328	9,169	7.56
Yueqing county	972,727	73,436	7.55
Yongjia county	789,662	48,173	6.10
Pingyang county	734,542	89,847	12.23
Cangnan county	1,028,153	99,043	9.63
Wencheng county	348,083	19,170	5.51
Taishun county	315,124	16,934	5.37
Total	6,439,940	919,987	14.29

Source: PRC Ministry of Public Security, *People's Republic of China: Population Statistics by County and City, 1987* (Beijing: Zhongguo Ditu Chubanshe, 1988), p. 89 (in Chinese).

[a]Known as Rui'an county prior to 1987.

few as 5.3 percent of the people were classified as nonagricultural. Even in Rui'an city, only 14.3 percent of the residents were engaged in nonagricultural activities.

The population distribution suggests, therefore, that the overall level of urbanization in the Wenzhou region is fairly low. The low level of urbanization is also indicated by the small extent of the built-up area there: in 1986, the Wenzhou region had a total area of 11,784 sq km, of which the built-up area occupied only 18 sq km (0.15 percent).[10] The built-up area lies primarily within the urban core of Wenzhou city. The central city of Wenzhou is also the site of the region's major urban functions. Outside Wenzhou city, urban activities are primarily located in towns, especially those in which administrative bodies of county governments are situated.

Geographical Background

The low level of urban development in the Wenzhou region can be partly attributed to the area's rugged topography and partly to the eco-

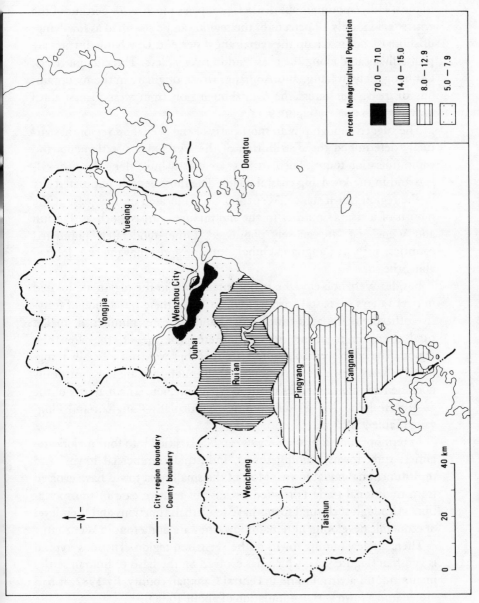

Figure 9.3 Nonagricultural Population by County, Wenzhou City Region: 1987

nomic progress of the entire region. Physiographically, Wenzhou region is made up of hilly/mountainous areas, low-lying areas, and offshore islands. Hilly/mountainous districts occupy as much as 78 percent of the entire region; only 18 percent of the region can be classified as low-lying; offshore islands make up the remaining 4 percent. Low-lying districts are primarily located along the coast and in river valleys. Three major rivers, Ou Jiang, Feiyun Jiang, and Ao Jiang, which originate in the mountainous districts, run across the Wenzhou region from west to east until draining into the sea (Figure 9.1).

The rugged topography in most parts of the Wenzhou region has virtually determined the distribution of the area's major settlements and communication routes. Such artifacts are mostly built along the river valleys and in the low-lying coastal zones. The most densely populated city in the region, for instance, Wenzhou city, is located on the coast at the mouth of a river. Counties in the mountainous areas, such as Taishun and Wencheng, are sparsely populated. Other moderately populated counties, such as Cangnan, Ouhai, Rui'an, and Pingyang, are located along the coast.

Besides Wenzhou city, the major rural towns in the region are located in river valleys or coastal areas as well. In 1985, there was a total of forty-five officially designated towns *(zhen)* and a greater number of smaller rural towns in the nine city-administered counties in the Wenzhou region. The latter were so small in size that they were not officially recognized as *zhen*. Such small rural towns, although they are not statistically documented, are numerous in the Wenzhou region. The majority of the *zhen* were located in coastal counties, particularly Cangnan and Pingyang (Table 9.3).

In terms of function, such towns can be classified into four major categories: rural towns, mining towns, industrial/commercial towns, and multifunctional nodal towns. Most of the small rural towns have evolved from traditional trade fairs sited because of relative ease in transportation. Although such rural towns have few urban functions and their level of economic development remains low, they are numerous in Wenzhou.

There are few mining towns in the Wenzhou region. The most typical is Fanshan (Figure 9.1), which has evolved on the basis of human settlements around a vitriol mine in central Cangnan county. By 1982, it had grown into a town with a population of about 19,000.[11]

Most of the industrial/commercial towns are located on major transportation routes or at the confluence points of such routes. These towns

Table 9.3   Number of Towns by
             County in the Wenzhou
             Region: 1985

COUNTY	NO. OF TOWNS
Rui'an	6
Ouhai	4
Dongtou	1
Yueqing	4
Yongjia	3
Pingyang	12
Cangnan	13
Wencheng	1
Taishun	1
Total	45

Source: Gao Yan and Pu Shanxin (eds.), *Handbook
of Administrative Districts in the People's Republic
of China* (Beijing: Guangming Ribao Chubanshe,
1986), pp. 296–297 (in Chinese).

enjoy better accessibility and can exert larger spheres of influence than
small rural towns. They perform a fair number of nonagricultural functions, such as industrial, commercial, and handicraft manufacturing,
and play a significant role in the rural economy of the counties. They are
also considerably sizable in population: some have developed into towns
of 20,000 to 30,000 each, such as Aojiang (population 23,000 in 1982) in
Pingyang county.[12]

Multifunctional nodal towns are county capitals. These are the political, economic, cultural, and communication centers in the city-administered counties. Industrial activities which are administered by county
governments are often concentrated in such capitals. The population of a
multifunctional nodal town may often exceed the range of 10,000 to
20,000. Chengguan town in Rui'an, for example, has for a long time
had a population of more than 50,000.[13]

All the towns, however, are located in the eastern and southern parts
of the Wenzhou region, especially on coastal plains. Compared with the
low-lying areas, the hilly and mountainous districts in the Wenzhou
region are less densely populated and have fewer town centers. They are
on the whole less developed than the coastal plains. Nevertheless, the

mountainous districts are richly endowed with natural resources, such as timber, orchards, quarries, and metallic as well as nonmetallic mines, especially vitriol and pyrophyllite (both of which are raw materials for fertilizers and related chemical products). In hilly areas, the rapid run-offs in rivers also provide the potential for the generation of hydroelectric power. Such reserves can be profitably exploited when the regional economy of Wenzhou as a whole has become better developed.

Along the river valleys and on the coastal plains, soils are fertile and conducive to intensive agriculture. For long periods of time, the majority of people in the Wenzhou region have lived primarily on agriculture and the exploitation of natural resources in the surrounding mountains. It was in this rural context that Wenzhou city evolved as a major market town in premodern days. Its emergence owed much to its favorable site in a low-lying area on the coast and at the mouth of a major river. Not only does it enjoy greater accessibility than other localities in the region, but its coastal location has enabled it to benefit from long-distance sea transport and to attract the development of port activities in its vicinity.

Nevertheless, for long periods of time Wenzhou city remained an urban center serving the rural hinterland within the Wenzhou region. Because of the rugged topography along the region's mountainous fringes, Wenzhou city was unable to extend its economic influence. Moreover, the rural nature of the Wenzhou region further limited the scope of industrialization in the city. Thus, despite its favorable site for port and urban development, large-scale industrialization did not occur in Wenzhou city before 1949. Even though the People's Republic has attempted to boost urban and industrial development in Wenzhou city since 1949, the city's inherited infrastructure is too weak to support a rapid pace of economic growth. To fulfill the hope of modernizing Wenzhou city and transforming the city into a "window" through which modernization can be diffused into the rest of China, this infrastructure must be drastically improved. To understand why the infrastructure in Wenzhou remains substandard, one must understand the context of how the city has evolved and developed in the past.

Historical Background

Archaeological findings in Wenzhou indicate that people began to settle in this area in prehistoric times. During the periods of the Xia, Shang, and Zhou dynasties (approximately 2100 to 221 B.C.), this part of China was generally known as "Ou" because large numbers of pottery products by the name of Ou (similar to today's bowls) were produced there. In A.D. 138, the dynastic government of the Eastern Han (25–220) set up the administrative organ of a *xian* (county) government in Yongning, which covered the territories of today's Wenzhou and its adjacent Lishui prefecture. Throughout the Han dynasty and its subsequent years, sea transport gradually developed along the China coast. Because of its hilly terrain, Wenzhou was rich in timber resources and by the time of the Three Kingdoms (220–280) it had become a major shipbuilding center in southeastern China.

During the Eastern Jin dynasty (317–420), large numbers of Chinese migrated southward from the Huang He (Yellow River) Basin, thereby intensifying the interactions between Wenzhou and the political and economic centers of China. Such interactions induced rapid development at Wenzhou. Gradually, wet rice farming and the rearing of silkworms were introduced into the territory. To adapt to the agricultural innovations, the people in Wenzhou began to organize themselves for irrigation projects. By A.D. 323, the prosperity of economic activities in this area warranted the establishment of a larger administrative body—the prefecture—and the erection of city walls to protect the prefectural capital there. The prefecture, known as Yongjia, approximately covered the territories of today's Wenzhou and Lishui. The site chosen for its capital later developed into today's Wenzhou city.

In A.D. 622, the government of the Tang dynasty (618–907) officially named this area Wenzhou because of its location south of Wen Mountain. By then, Wenzhou had developed into an important trading port. During the Song dynasty (1127–1278), southern China enjoyed rapid economic growth, especially after the dynastic capital was moved to Hangzhou in 1138. Wenzhou benefited from the overall prosperity in southern China. Improvements in farming techniques, particularly through the utilization of large-scale irrigation projects and the adoption of improved as well as greater varieties of crops, helped increase agricultural production in the Wenzhou region. Nonagricultural activities—boat making, porcelain and chinaware, weaving, lacquer ware, paper mills, breweries, and mining—evolved in the vicinity of Wenzhou city. All these activities induced further development of trade and commerce in Wenzhou city. Traders from foreign countries, who generally traveled to China by sea, were lured to Wenzhou to conduct business. Meanwhile, the Song dynastic government decided to set up customhouses in

Wenzhou city, Guangzhou, Hangzhou, Mingzhou (today's Ningbo), Quanzhou, and Mizhou (today's Jiaoxian county in Shandong province). An administrative organ, the Shi Bo Si, similar to today's customs service, was established to supervise foreign trade, and the policy of stationing the customs office in Wenzhou continued throughout the Yuan dynasty (1271–1368). Wenzhou thus became one of China's major port cities for foreign trade.

During the Ming (1368–1644) and Qing (1644–1911) dynasties, there was further development in agriculture and handicraft production in the Wenzhou region. Sizable settlements also evolved around major mining and quarrying areas, such as the vitriol mines in today's Cangnan county. Nevertheless, since the late Ming dynasty a series of political disturbances had erupted in China and especially along the coast. Such disruptions included, for example, the rampage of Japanese pirates in the coastal provinces during the late Ming dynasty, the prohibition of sea trade during the early Qing dynasty (from 1661 to 1684), the Opium War (1840–1842) and the subsequent invasion of the Western Powers, the Taiping Rebellion (1851–1864), internal warfare during the Warlord Era (1911–1927), the Sino-Japanese War (1937–1945), and the Civil War (1945–1949). Such chaos severely disrupted economic and trading activities along the China coast. Consequently, Wenzhou and its port suffered great instability in economic and urban development.

During World War I, however, because the world's major powers were busily engaged in warfare and badly in need of various supplies, the handicraft and indigenous industries in Wenzhou were able to survive and expand. Contemporary industries such as condensed milk factories, paper mills, and brick works emerged. Production of traditional handicrafts also revived. Nevertheless, such industries had to face severe competition with products from the Western Powers and were unable to develop into enterprises with high levels of sophistication. As a consequence of the serious blows to economic growth caused by frequent political disturbances and warfare over a long period of time, development in Wenzhou remained haphazard and slow. Until 1949, Wenzhou remained a city with an inadequate infrastructure and a low level of industrial development. The built-up area of Wenzhou city was small and constituted only a territory under the administration of Yongjia county.

The new Wenzhou government under the People's Republic was

established in May 1949. Three months later, the central government conferred on Wenzhou the administrative status of a city. Since then, the central and local governments have attempted to reconstruct and expand Wenzhou.

Post-1949 Development

Since 1949, guided by public policy and assisted by direct investment from the government, Wenzhou city has undergone changes in its economic structure. Soon after the liberation of Wenzhou, the government began to rebuild the roads between Wenzhou city, Linhai (in eastern Zhejiang to the north of Wenzhou region), and Jinhua (in central Zhejiang). Such roads had been severely damaged by war. Later, new roads leading to Fujian province via Rui'an county were built. Such works improved the communication and interactive linkages between Wenzhou and other areas, as well as between localities within the district itself.

At the same time, the government invested in a project to dredge Ou Jiang and thus improved the navigability of the waterway to and from the port of Wenzhou city. Nowadays ships with a deadweight capacity of up to 5,000 tons can anchor directly at the urban district of Wenzhou. Subsequent to a series of works to enlarge the seaport, Wenzhou city has by now developed into a port with sixteen berths. Through sea transport, Wenzhou city is well connected to other cities along the China coast. Since 1984, when Wenzhou city was declared an open city for foreign investment, new sea routes have been established to further connect the city with Japan, North Korea, and Hong Kong. Moreover, local ports at Rui'an, Aojiang, Qingshuibu, Panshi, and Shuitonglei have been expanded. Thus a network of waterways and motor roads now radiates from Wenzhou city and leads to Linhai in eastern Zhejiang, Jinhua in central Zhejiang, and Fujian province in the south. Within this network, cargoes are primarily transported by ship and passengers by car.

Despite such works, transport linkages both within Wenzhou and between the region and elsewhere are far from adequate for rapid economic advancement. The plan to connect Wenzhou city by rail to the national network of railroads has yet to materialize. Vast territories in the mountainous portion of the region are not accessible to vehicular traffic. The major motor roads are basically confined to coastal areas and river valleys, but they are often bisected into sections by unbridged rivers. To facilitate economic development in Wenzhou, both the internal and external transport networks will have to be drastically improved.

Urban Development

Within Wenzhou city, developments since 1949 have primarily proceeded on the basis of what the new government has inherited from the past. As mentioned earlier, the city's foundation was laid down some 1,600 years ago. Its morphological structure, therefore, is incompatible with modern urban living. To achieve the goal of transforming Wenzhou into a city contributing to the modernization of China, its inner core will have to be radically rebuilt under the guidance of proper planning.

The original city of Wenzhou evolved at a site that was bound to the north by Ou Jiang. Piers and warehouses were thus located in the northern part of the city. The eastern section was reserved for temples and ceremonial activities. Markets and commercial activities were placed in the south, whereas the western part of the city was primarily for residence. Through years of subsequent development, this early plan of the original city has been blurred and masked over by more recent urban land use. Nevertheless, the city's shape has remained surprisingly intact and is more or less the same as it was years ago.

Nowadays, the built-up area bounded by Ou Jiang to the north, Huancheng Donglu (Circular City Road East) to the east, Renmin Lu (People's Road) to the south, and Jiushan Lu (Nine Mountain Road) to the west is generally considered the urban core of Wenzhou city (Figure 9.4). The entire area covered by the urban core is rather small, only about 10.3 sq km. In 1982, as many as 320,000 inhabitants lived in the urban core, giving an average population density of over 31,000 persons per square kilometer.[14] This was almost ten times the population density in Wenzhou city and sixty times that of the Wenzhou region (see Table 9.1).

The city's major administrative and commercial districts are located in the center of the urban core, along the streets encircling People's Square. Most of the government offices are situated on Guangchang Lu (Square Road), which runs along the southern side of People's Square. Not far from the square is Wenzhou's largest shopping area, which stretches along Wuma Jie (Five Horses Street) and Jiefang Lu (Liberation Road).

Transport facilities, such as piers and bus terminals, are primarily

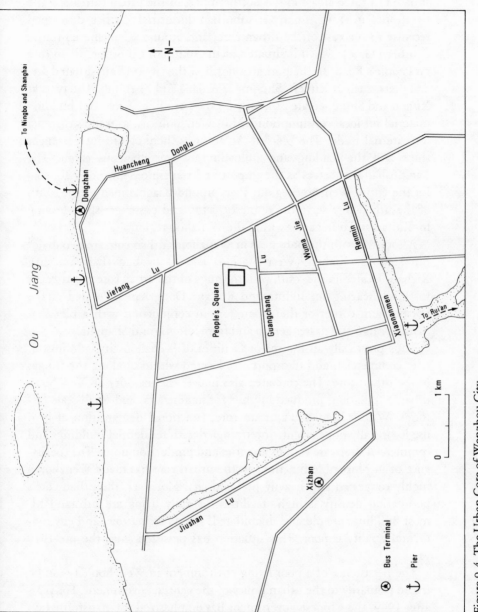

Figure 9.4 The Urban Core of Wenzhou City

located within the urban core or along its fringes. Major port facilities are situated in three areas: in the northern part of the urban core along the riverfront; in Yangfushan, a suburban industrial district developed recently to the east of the urban core; and around Xiaonanmen (Little Southern Gate), which is situated at the southern tip of the urban core on People's Road. In the port area north of the city core are situated several piers, such as Ximen, Shuomen, Anlan, and Zhenhua. The piers at Ximen and Shuomen are primarily for the handling of coal and building material for local consumption within Wenzhou city, as well as material for external trade. The piers at Anlan and Zhenhua are for passenger ships and the loading and unloading of miscellaneous cargo. The Yangfushan pier serves as the import and transshipment center for coal for the entire Wenzhou region. Piers around Xiaonanmen to the south of the urban core serve the domestic cargo and passenger ships leaving for Rui'an and other areas within the Wenzhou region.

Associated with the port areas in Wenzhou's urban core are two major bus stations, Xizhan (West Station) and Dongzhan (East Station). Xizhan, located in the southwestern fringe of the urban core, is primarily for buses leaving for Jinhua and Rui'an. Dongzhan is located at the northeastern corner of the urban core in conjunction with a pier that handles cargo and passengers to and from Ningbo and Shanghai.

Thus practically all the major facilities of Wenzhou city, administrative, commercial, and transport, are located within or along the fringes of the urban core. The core area also houses the majority of Wenzhou's urban population, production units for handicrafts, and small-scale factories. Within Wenzhou's urban core, functional demarcation of land use is virtually nonexistent. Intermingled with residential buildings and commercial shops are various factories and production units. The coexistence of incompatible functions in the urban core has made Wenzhou a highly congested and heavily polluted city. Moreover, the urban core's population density is high, facilities for daily living are substandard, most buildings are old and dilapidated, streets are narrow, and environmental quality is poor. This situation has persisted since the pre-1949 years.

The persistence of a poor living environment in Wenzhou city can be traced primarily to the urban policy of the central government. For years after 1949, the Chinese government has emphasized the transformation of urban areas into "productive" cities through the establishment of industrial and manufacturing activities. The provision of infrastructural projects, however, such as housing, street widening, and urban sewage systems, has been neglected. Such projects have been considered at best "unproductive" or at worst "consumptive" in nature and thus are accorded lower priority.

Suburban Growth

In the 1950s, the Chinese government began to reconstruct the economy of Wenzhou city by preserving its handicraft manufacturing while at the same time establishing large-scale state-operated industrial enterprises. Since then, enterprises in various industries, such as chemicals, machine building, shipbuilding, plastics, leather, papermaking, dairy, textiles, and electronics, have been established in Wenzhou. By the late 1950s, the urban core of Wenzhou city had become so congested that plans had to be made to relocate the major industrial plants in suburban areas. Most of the factories at smaller scale, however, have remained within the urban core.

Since the city core is bounded to the north by the river, suburban expansion has proceeded to its east, south, and west. East of Wenzhou's urban core, a heavy industrial district has evolved at Yangfushan, where enterprises for the metallurgical industry, building materials, and transportation equipment are concentrated. South of the core is a district with primarily machine-building, electric machinery, textile, and food processing industries. West of the core are scattered a number of factories for pottery, porcelain, rubber shoes, and papermaking. About 5 km west of the urban core, an industrial district essentially for chemical industries has developed at Shuangling town.

Associated with the establishment of industrial plants in Wenzhou's suburban areas, a few residential districts have developed along the fringes of the urban core—for example, Huadangtou, Shuangjing, Hongdian, Shibajia, Hehua, and Cuiwei. Nevertheless, infrastructure and social amenities, such as transportation services and educational facilities for children, are inadequate in the new residential districts. Moreover, these suburban developments are small in scale, unable to accommodate large numbers of new residents, and have not relieved the high degree of congestion within the urban core.

Upon the designation of Wenzhou as an open city in 1984, the city government planned to provide more development land away from the urban core, particularly along Ou Jiang and further eastward toward the coast. Such planned development includes the establishment of an export-processing zone with a total area of 18 sq km at Longwan, a small town about 15 km east of Wenzhou's urban core, as well as additional port and industrial districts in Qili Huanghua, an area that stretches along the northern bank of Ou Jiang (Figure 9.5).

Construction for the export-processing zone at Longwan began in 1987. By October 1989, the city government had managed to have two berths with the capacity of 10,000 tons each built in the zone. Other infrastructure projects, such as the installation of telephone lines, had also been completed, and the connection of high-voltage power lines was in progress.[15] The site chosen for the export-processing zone had hardly been developed before 1984. Consequently, developmental work such as site formation and the provision of infrastructure had to begin from scratch. Since the amount of capital involved in the project is considerable and the time span required for its full development will be lengthy, the plan for the export-processing zone cannot reasonably be expected to induce rapid economic growth in Wenzhou city in the immediate future.

While the city government seems overwhelmingly concerned with the generation of new opportunities for foreign investment in newly developed areas such as the export-processing zone, little effort has been made to improve the living environment and the already overstrained infrastructure in Wenzhou's urban core. If the new developmental projects are successful, however, they may generate additional capital and opportunities for the gradual relief of congestion in the urban core.

Economic Activities

Although the central government has attempted to transform Wenzhou into a "city of production" by introducing manufacturing activities into the area, without the benefit of an adequately developed land transport system Wenzhou has remained remote from China's major markets for both raw materials and industrial products. For decades, Wenzhou city suffered from chronic shortages of raw materials and energy resources, such as coal and oil, that are vital for large-scale industrialization. Consequently, economic activities in Wenzhou have to be developed primarily on the basis of the commodities that are locally available in the region. Such commodities include, for example, farm produce, pottery, chinaware, quarries, and other nonmetallic mining products. Thus the level of industrialization that Wenzhou city can achieve has been limited to the

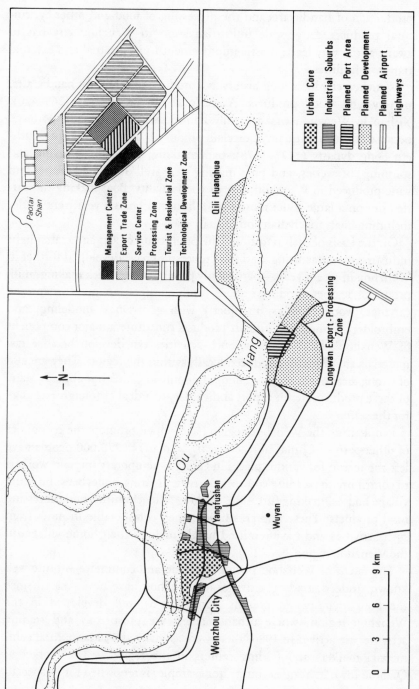

Figure 9.5 Planned Development in Wenzhou City

production of handicrafts and the processing of food and other agricultural products. Large-scale industrialization in Wenzhou city has to await, at the very least, drastic improvement in its internal and external transport facilities.

Wenzhou city has a long history as a production center for handicrafts, pottery, and wood products. As early as the Jin dynasty (265–420), Xishan in Wenzhou was generally known as the "capital of pottery" because of the high-quality porcelain produced there. During the Southern Song dynasty (1127–1278), papermaking, porcelain, weaving and spinning, breweries, and boat making were well developed. Paper and wine produced in Wenzhou were of good quality. Boat making was carried out on a large scale: more than a hundred boats a year were made, including boats for civilian and military uses.

On the basis of such traditions, the production of arts and crafts, light industrial manufacturing, and food processing have developed further in Wenzhou in recent years—particularly papermaking, brick making, milk products, leather products, shoes, umbrellas, rattan mats, soapstone carvings, wood carvings, marquetry with gemstones, modeling, and embroidery. Handicrafts and art products constitute a major component of Wenzhou's local economy. Such activities can develop because raw materials are primarily produced locally within the region. They are also of strong local flavor and are famous not only in China but abroad. Many of these products are for export and gain a great deal of foreign exchange for the state.

People from the Wenzhou region have helped promote the economies of other parts of China. In recent years, as many as 270,000 people have left the region for various places in China as temporary migrant workers to contribute to padding cotton, quarrying, rearing honeybees, building village houses, making furniture, working as blacksmiths, and processing food products. These migrants have earned considerable incomes from such activities and have remitted handsomely to their home villages in the Wenzhou region.[16]

The talent of Wenzhou people for trade and commerce is quite well known. Indeed, trading activities in Wenzhou have never ceased since the Song dynasty. At present, commerce is well developed in the Wenzhou region, where urban markets are prosperous and trading activities are active. In 1986, there were as many as 130 large rural commercial markets and trading centers in the region.[17] The market at Qiaotou town in Yongjia county, for example, is renowned for its specialization in the production and trading of buttons and claims to be the largest button market in Pacific Asia. In 1985, transactions conducted at the ten largest rural markets in the Wenzhou region amounted to as much as 1.15 billion *yuan*.[18]

The development of industrial activities in Wenzhou city has occurred, however, only recently. Before 1949, few industrial activities were of economic significance in Wenzhou. Between 1949 and 1986, the industrial output value in the Wenzhou region had grown by twenty-five times, reaching 4.82 billion *yuan* in 1986.[19] Nevertheless, post-1949 industrial development in Wenzhou has had to be built on the basis of the city's original foundation and has evolved gradually through the reorganization and amalgamation of the pre-1949 small-scale production units. Today the majority of Wenzhou's industrial enterprises are, therefore, under the ownership of collectives and are for light industry, processing, and manufacturing products. Large and medium-sized industrial enterprises owned by the "whole people," that is, the state, are few. In 1986, for example, among the total work force of 481,400 industrial workers in the Wenzhou region, only 69,500 (or 14.4 percent) were employed by state enterprises; whereas 411,900 (or 85.6 percent) were employed by enterprises owned by collectives. Moreover, the region's light industrial output value for the same year was 2.02 billion *yuan*. It exceeded the heavy industrial output value (1.57 billion *yuan*) by 0.45 billion *yuan*.[20]

The major industrial activities in Wenzhou involve machinery, food, textiles, and chemicals. The chemical industry has developed on the basis of the illite and vitriol mines in the region, which provide raw materials for the production of sulfuric acid, fertilizers, insecticides, and other chemical products. Nevertheless, industrial activities related to the generation of energy and the provision of intermediate goods are scanty and weak. Moreover, the people of Wenzhou appear to be content with their traditional modes of production, such as food processing, arts and crafts, stationery, pottery, porcelain, and leather goods. They have made little effort to transform or upgrade the traditional production processes. Thus traditional products continue to play a significant role in Wenzhou's economy.

On the whole, industrial development in Wenzhou has not advanced beyond the stage of processing agricultural products or relying strongly upon locally available raw materials. Furthermore, during the decades when China pursued an inward-looking economic policy, little was done to upgrade the equipment, facilities, and production processes in Wenzhou's industrial plants. Factories established as early as the 1950s still form the majority of the industrial enterprises in Wenzhou. Such establishments suffer from the problems of outdated equipment, inferior production methods, and substandard facilities. In general, the technological level that prevails in the industrial sector of the Wenzhou region is low. Consequently, the productivity of the industrial enterprises remains low. In 1986, for instance, the average labor productivity of the workers in the Wenzhou region's state-owned industrial enterprises was 11,203 *yuan* per person per year—less than one-half that in Ningbo (24,874 *yuan*) or Nantong city (22,480 *yuan*).[21] Even in Xiamen (population 1.04 million in 1986), a city considerably smaller than Wenzhou, the comparable productivity figure for the same year was 22,817 *yuan* per person per year—100 percent higher than that in Wenzhou.[22]

To augment rapid economic development in Wenzhou, it is therefore necessary to improve and modernize the industrial enterprises and other infrastructure. Under the open policy, it is hoped that this can be achieved through the introduction of advanced technologies and foreign capital. In the meantime, however, Wenzhou must continue to develop and strengthen the productivity of its industrial and agricultural sectors.

The natural environment in Wenzhou is favorable for agricultural activities. Labor supply is ample. The people of Wenzhou have been engaged in the exploitation of river plains and coastal areas for such a long time that their techniques in intensive farming are highly advanced. In this region, paddy is the staple crop and its production is abundant. In 1986, the production of grain crops in the Wenzhou region was 1.5 million tons.[23]

Besides paddy and other grain crops, Wenzhou produces a variety of "agricultural sidelines" such as kumquat, sugarcane, mat straw, broad beans, rape, tea, sweet-scented osmanthus, milk, beef, pork, fish, shrimp, and shellfish. In recent years, the reform and open policies have induced more peasants in Wenzhou to be engaged in sideline activities and cash cropping. Between 1985 and 1986, for instance, the output value of sideline activities in the Wenzhou region increased by 27.38 percent, from 528.6 million to 673.3 million *yuan*. Moreover, in 1986 the output value of sideline activities surpassed that of cropping (614.6 million *yuan*) by 58.7 million *yuan* (Table 9.4).

In terms of output value, agricultural activities play a less significant role in Wenzhou's regional economy than industry. In 1986, for exam-

Table 9.4   Agricultural Output Values in the Wenzhou Region:
1985 and 1986

| SECTOR | OUTPUT VALUE (IN MILLION *YUAN*) | | | |
	1985	1986	CHANGE	% CHANGE
Cropping	642.19	614.58	−27.61	−4.30
Forestry	35.09	32.40	−2.69	−7.67
Animal husbandry	244.22	253.13	+8.91	+3.65
Sideline activities	528.60	673.33	+144.73	+27.38
Fishery	102.02	113.05	+11.03	+10.81
Total	1,552.12	1,686.49	+134.37	+8.66

Source: Wang, *Handbook of Coastal Chinese Open Cities,* p. 210.

ple, the total agricultural output value in the Wenzhou region was 1.69
billion *yuan* whereas the total industrial output value was 4.81 billion
yuan. In terms of the numbers of people employed, however, the vast
majority in Wenzhou are engaged in agricultural activities. According to
the household registration records, only 14 percent (920,000 in number)
of the 6.5 million people in the Wenzhou region were classified as nonagricultural in 1987.[24] Of the nonagricultural people, about one-half
(481,400 people in 1986) were employed as industrial workers in state- or
collective-owned factories and enterprises.[25] Although official per capita
data are not available, if the output values by production sector were presented at the per capita level they would show a considerable gap
between the per capita agricultural and industrial outputs.

To encourage more rapid economic development and to enable the
vast majority of the people in the Wenzhou region to generate higher
incomes and thus improve their living conditions, policies should be formulated to induce a proportion of the rural population to transfer from
primary production to the secondary and tertiary sectors. Even though
the open and reform policies that have been put forth in the Wenzhou
region in recent years have not transformed Wenzhou into a modern city
overnight, they appear to be the right strategies. For the benefit of
Wenzhou's people in the long run, such policies will have to stay. Meanwhile, given the low level of urban and economic development that
Wenzhou city has inherited from the past, the authorities and the people
at large will have to be patient with the slow pace of economic advancement.

Conclusion

This chapter has reviewed the developmental process of Wenzhou city in its geographical and historical contexts. We have argued that owing to the combined effects of a series of interrelated factors—political chaos prior to 1949, rugged terrain, inadequate land transport, and the closed-door economic policy of China between the 1950s and 1970s—Wenzhou has not been able to develop as fast as many people would like. Although by now the Wenzhou region has grown into a territory with more than 6 million people, its built-up area remains small; the vast majority of the people live in rural areas and are engaged in agricultural activities. Even within the urban area of Wenzhou city, infrastructure and other social amenities are old and inadequate. Facilities in work units and industrial enterprises are outmoded; consequently productivity remains low.

The open and reform policies have created opportunities for the people in Wenzhou to interact with the outside world, to absorb foreign capital and technologies, and to gradually improve their economic and living conditions. Economic development is, however, a continuous and cumulative process. It has to be built on a certain foundation. Unfortunately, the foundation for economic growth that Wenzhou city has inherited from the past is so fragile that it is unable to support immediate gains from the new open policy. This does not imply, of course, that the open policy should cease in Wenzhou. On the contrary, it means, first, that the people and particularly government officials must be realistic about conditions in the Wenzhou region, be modest with respect to short-range developmental targets, and be patient with the inevitably slow progress in economic advancement. Second, to augment economic growth in the Wenzhou region, the continuation of the open policy is the only possible solution.

Given the present conditions in Wenzhou, the people will have to confront enormous difficulties in rapidly developing the city. Nevertheless, the city and its broader region do possess great potential for future progress, especially in the exploitation of natural resources and the development of commerce, trade, and tourism. This potential cannot be fully developed, however, if Wenzhou's people are deprived of opportunities to generate capital, learn advanced technology, and exchange commodities. The open policy enables such opportunities to prevail.

Moreover, economic development in Wenzhou will not only benefit the city and its region alone but also the vast territories in southern Zhejiang. Wenzhou is located at the converging point of a network of waterways and the East China Sea. It is the center of interaction for people in the drainage areas of Ou Jiang, Feiyun Jiang, and Ao Jiang. It is also the largest center for the concentration and distribution of commodities in southern Zhejiang province. Its economic hinterland covers the Wenzhou region and the Lishui region, as well as the Yuhuan and Wenling districts in the southern part of the Taizhou region, and has a total area of approximately 30,000 sq km (about 30 percent of Zhejiang's total area) and a population of about 9 million (about one quarter of Zhejiang's total population). Economic progress in Wenzhou city can thus serve as a beachhead through which developmental growth can be diffused into the vast territories in southern Zhejiang province and benefit a large number of people there. Such a process, however, will depend on the success of the open policy—and, in the meantime, on people's conviction that the open policy will succeed.

Notes

1. Zhejiang Province, Department of Communications, *History of Zhejiang's Highways,* vol. 1: *Contemporary Highways* (Beijing: Renmin Jiaotong Chubanshe, 1988), pp. 103–108 (in Chinese).

2. Chen Qiaoyi, Zang Weiting, and Mao Bilin, *Geography of Zhejiang Province* (Hangzhou: Zhejiang Jiaoyu Chubanshe, 1985), p. 206 (in Chinese).

3. T. N. Chiu and David K. Y. Chu, "Port Development in the People's Republic of China: Readjustment Under Programmes of Accelerated Economic Growth," in B. S. Hoyle and D. Hilling (eds.), *Seaport Systems and Spatial Change* (New York: John Wiley & Sons, 1984), pp. 199–215.

4. "Wenzhou Plans to Speed Up the Construction of Infrastructure," *Wen Wei Po,* 5 April 1985.

5. "Wenzhou Will Be Open Further with the Construction of 10,000-Ton Berth," *Ta Kung Pao,* 21 March 1985; "Wenzhou Recruited Nine Hong Kong Industrialists and Traders as Economic Consultants," *Ta Kung Pao,* 8 October 1989.

6. "Wenzhou Seeks Taiwan Funds," *South China Morning Post,* 9 December 1988.

7. Yu Ming, "Wenzhou Pays Attention to Facing the World Market," *Outlook Weekly* 45 (9 November 1987): 19 (in Chinese).

8. "Hong Kong's Investment in Wenzhou Accounts for Half of the Number of Foreign Companies," *Sing Dao Jih Pao,* 8 December 1988.

9. "The Mayor of Wenzhou Seeks Autonomous Rights to Set Up Preferential Industrial/Trading District for Taiwanese," *Hong Kong Economic Times,* 11 June 1988 (in Chinese).

10. Wang Wenxiang (ed.), *Handbook of Coastal Chinese Open Cities and Special Economic Zones* (Beijing: Zhongguo Guoji Guangbo Chubanshe, 1988), p. 210 (in Chinese).

11. Zhejiang Province, Department of Surveying and Mapping, *Atlas of Zhejiang Province* (Shanghai: Ditu Chubanshe, 1982), p. 65 (in Chinese).

12. Ibid.

13. Ibid., p. 62.

14. Ibid., p. 58.

15. "Wenzhou Recruited," *Ta Kung Pao,* 8 October 1989.

16. Wu Xiang, "A Discussion on the Developing Rural Commercial Economy in Wenzhou," in Pan Shangeng (ed.), *Wenzhou Experimental Zone* (Beijing: Zhongguo Zhenwang Chubanshe, 1988), pp. 24–33 (in Chinese).

17. Wu Zhengping and Qiu Desheng, "From the Narrowing Down of the 'Three Great Differences' to Look into the Development of 'Wenzhou Economy,' " in Pan Shangeng (ed.), *Wenzhou Experimental Zone* (Beijing: Zhongguo Zhenwang Chubanshe, 1988), pp. 63–68 (in Chinese).

18. Ibid., p. 65.

19. Wang, *Handbook of Coastal Chinese Open Cities,* pp. 209–210.

20. Ibid., p. 210.

21. Ibid., pp. 135, 184, 210.

22. Ibid., p. 466.

23. Ibid., p. 210.

24. PRC, Ministry of Public Security, *People's Republic of China: Population Statistics by County and City, 1987* (Beijing: Zhongguo Ditu Chubanshe, 1988), p. 89 (in Chinese).

25. Wang, *Handbook of Coastal Chinese Open Cities,* p. 210.

10 Fuzhou: Capital of a Frontier Province

DAVID K. Y. CHU AND XUN-ZHONG ZHENG

CHINA IS A COUNTRY with an ancient civilization and a long history. The civilization, which has been dominated by the Han culture, is generally regarded as having originated from the Loess Plateau. It then expanded northwestward and southeastward, constituting two major frontiers.

The Chinese ecumene, according to Whitney, can be subdivided into the core, the intensive ecumenical area, and an extensive ecumenical area. The intensive ecumenical area can be viewed as a direct extension of the national core, except that areal interaction within it is less intensive. Secondary cores can be found inside the intensive ecumenical area. The extensive ecumenical areas are places with poor resources and low interaction. Between the ecumenical and extraecumenical areas are transitional areas where assimilation into and spatial interaction with the ecumene itself occur in varying degrees.[1] Although Whitney's construct is not without its problems, the ideas of ecumene and subecumenical systems are indeed helpful in understanding the Chinese frontiers and frontier towns.

The frontier straddles the ecumene and what lies beyond. It can be defined as a fringe area between political groupings, between settled and relatively unsettled parts of a state, and also between different socioeconomic organizations.[2] Apart from the areal definition, frontiers can also be defined by frontier characteristics, such as the frontier spirit of frontiersmen, inner/outer orientations, and other frontier conditions.

It is the northwestern frontier of China that has been most widely studied.[3] This is perhaps because the area had been fiercely contested among the various ethnic groups like the Turks, the Mongols, the Manchus, and, of course, the Hans. Trading and other cultural interactions on this front were also remarkable. The Great Wall and the Silk Road are famous landmarks intertwined with the history of this part of China. In contrast, China's southeastern frontier has received much less attention although trading and other cultural exchanges can be dated back to 200 B.C.[4] This owes perhaps to the fact that Chinese culture is more land-conscious than sea-conscious and the events on this front were poorly documented. Basically, this frontier was long a settlement frontier for the Hans, marked by the gradual sinicization of the indigenous population.[5] The onset of the sixteenth century, however, marked an abrupt change in the nature of this frontier. The emergence of Japan as a powerful country and the later convergence of the Western Powers on eastern China turned the zone into contested ground between Western and traditional Chinese cultures. Of late, it has become a frontier characterized by competition between the communist and capitalist modes of production and ideological struggles.

The frontier provinces and frontier cities of southeastern China deserve more attention not only because of their transitional character but also for their potential of becoming innovative centers which eventually will modify or even revolutionize the core and the ecumene. According to Friedmann, normally the core region possesses the means for controlling the development of the fringe areas and for extracting from them the resources that will contribute to their own accelerated growth.[6] If the core degenerates because of rigidity and stagnation, however, the fringe areas, as subsystems of the whole, can exploit their relative autonomy and transform themselves into an "upward transitional periphery" for sustained innovation. Mutual interpenetration of different ways of life, value systems, religions, and beliefs help create the necessary innovative spirit if the frontier provinces and cities are allowed sufficient autonomy. On the other hand, acts of war, trade barriers, military curfews, and overwhelming dominance of the core region will destroy the frontier spirit and, subsequently, the associated innovativeness, turning the frontier area into a "downward transitional periphery."

Fuzhou is the capital city of Fujian province, which historically was known as Min, a patch of hilly area in southeastern China between the key economic areas of Guangdong and the Yangzi Delta. This chapter not only focuses on the urban development of Fuzhou but analyzes its development in the framework of frontier movement in the hope that new light may be shed on our understanding of the recent open policy and Special Economic Zones of China.

Fuzhou and the Southeastern Frontier

Is the open policy a new phenomenon to China? Examination of the development of Fuzhou and Fujian reveals that an open policy is not new, at least to the region of southeastern China around Fuzhou. As later paragraphs will show, the exclusion of outside contact in this area was rare. Ample evidence exists to suggest that the area around Fuzhou represents one of the most open throughout Chinese history, especially in its overseas trade.

Fuzhou was the Chinese end of the "Maritime Silk Road" connecting China with West Asia and Europe. It occupied a key position in the Chinese history of seafaring, foreign trade, and cultural exchanges with the outside world. The area around Fuzhou, however, was not conquered by the Hans until the Qin dynasty (221 B.C.), which set up Minzhong county with its capital at the present site of Fuzhou city. Fuzhou has been the political and military center for the region ever since. However, the area remained largely settled by the indigenous population known as the Viets, who, like the other Viets, had a special talent for seafaring.[7] During the Han dynasty (202 B.C.–A.D. 220) a feudal princedom was set up in the county, but the influence of the central government was limited to occasional military intervention in local quarrels among the Viets. From the standpoint of the spread of Han culture, Fujian at that time was no more than a contact zone between the Hans and the Viets.

Only after the fall of the Han dynasty, when the core of the ecumene was destroyed by civil wars and subsequent invasions by tribes from the northern frontier, did waves of Han migration start moving into the area and turn it into a settlement frontier. Fuzhou (known as Jinan at that time) became the first city port of the region and boasted of a prosperous urban economy plus a shipbuilding industry.[8]

Rapid increase in population was witnessed in the subsequent dynasties of Sui (A.D. 589–618) and Tang (A.D. 618–907). The number of households in Fuzhou increased from 12,000 in early Sui times to 91,000 in the middle of Tang. Apart from being an administrative and economic center for the surrounding area, Fuzhou also served as a supporting base for troops and a springboard for delegates and trading parties sent to the Ryukyu Islands and Taiwan (collectively known as Liuqiu at the time). Gradually, Fuzhou and its surrounding area were assimilated partially into the extensive ecumenical area of the Han civilization.

Separatist tendencies and the incomplete sinicization of the indigneous people turned the area into an independent state when the central government was decaying. From A.D. 906 to 945, Fujian was ruled by the Min government. To strengthen its independence, the first Min ruler had actively absorbed new migrants from the core and intensive ecumenical areas, on the one hand, and opened up Fujian to the South China sea trade on the other. Fuzhou and Quanzhou were notable seaports in this trade, but when Fuzhou was attacked by another separatist government from the north, Quanzhou was left to prosper after the attack.[9]

By A.D. 960, the central government had reestablished its control over China. During the Song (1001–1249) and the Yuan (1250–1367) dynasties, Fuzhou was vested with the responsibilities of governing the area and spearheading the development of agriculture and industry (but not overseas trading, which was given to Quanzhou). The customs and excise offices were located in Quanzhou to collect taxes and exert some kind of control over the overseas trade. In other words, Fuzhou was charged with the responsibility of "inclusion" for inland development, whereas Quanzhou had the responsibility of "exclusion" for trade and external exchanges at this stage of frontier development. Characterized by the concentration of Han people and its uniformity with the core area, Fuzhou from the Song dynasty could be regarded as a portion of intensive ecumenical area, with Quanzhou perhaps still at the verge of extensive ecumene.

The Ming dynasty (1368–1644) was the turning point of the Han people's cultural and military supremacy in Fujian and, perhaps, in the southeastern frontier as a whole. The seven oceangoing voyages before and after A.D. 1400 were unprecedented in the world in terms of their range and scale, reaching as far west as East Africa. Led by Zheng He, the fleet reached more than thirty countries and regions, establishing cultural ties and exchanging China's porcelain, silk, and ironware for ivory, precious stones, spices, and cotton. Most of Zheng's armada was launched from the Liujia River near Suzhou, but Fuzhou was a major support base for the missions from shipbuilding to recruitment of sailors. Fuzhou thus resumed part of its frontline functions. Moreover, Quanzhou was gradually silted up so that Fuzhou, together with Xiamen and Zhangzhou, both newly developed seaports in southern Fujian, shared the overseas trade originally handled through Quanzhou. Between 1465 and 1523, the three seaports enjoyed a highly prosperous period.

Toward the end of the Ming dynasty, China experienced its first effective challenge at its southeastern frontier and a maritime prohibition was issued in 1523 lasting almost until 1743. The attack of Japanese pirates along the coast and the occupation of Taiwan by Dutch colonialists posed a formidable challenge to the weak central government, so that the emergence of a competing culture and ethnic group did not turn the

Fujian area into an upward transitional periphery in the first instance. On the contrary, the maritime prohibition turned Fuzhou and its surrounding area into an inwardly oriented and downward transitional periphery. In 1644, the Manchu defeated the Ming government and established the Qing dynasty, though Fuzhou, Xiamen, and the newly recovered Taiwan were still occupied by a Ming general. To facilitate its campaign, the Qing government ordered a retreat of all households along the coast, turning it into a no-man's-land. The maritime prohibition was not relaxed until 1743, when the Ming general was defeated and surrendered. The acts of war and the maritime prohibition eroded the basis of trade and the associated industrial economy of Fuzhou and its surrounding areas, leading to massive poverty and unemployment, but out-migration (characteristic of a long-settled intensive ecumenical area) to Taiwan and Southeast Asia soon turned it back into an extensive ecumenical area.[10] The defeated army and followers of the Ming general in Fujian also migrated to the Philippines. After 1743, Fuzhou was allowed to trade with the Ryukyu Islands and therefore resumed some of its past glories.

This partial openness in terms of overseas trade and cultural exchanges became total after China's humiliating defeat in the Opium War, which was concluded by the Sino-British Treaty of Nanking in 1842. Fuzhou, Xiamen, Ningbo, Shanghai, and Guangzhou became treaty ports. During the period 1858–1893, British colonialists set up three shipbuilding yards in Xiamen and Fuzhou, while Russian interests set up factories for tea processing in Fuzhou. Indeed, Fuzhou rapidly emerged as an important tea market and exporting center. As many as 4,000 lb of tea leaves were exported in 1860 through Fuzhou, 80 percent of Fujian's total export value. Other exports included forestry products, sugar, silk, and handicrafts. In return, massive volumes of cotton textiles, rice and flour, and other manufactured products were imported from Britain, the United States, Germany, and later Japan through Fuzhou and redistributed to other parts of China. For some years the value of imports was equivalent to as many as 1,600 taels of silver. To counteract the colonialists, Fuzhou was chosen by the Qing government to be the first, and the largest, Chinese naval shipyard in 1866. From 1905 to 1945, Fujian came under the sphere of influence of Japan, who controlled Taiwan and used Fujian as a springboard for South China. Exclusive concessions were assigned to the Japanese and Chinese sovereignty was sacrificed.

After the victory of the anti-Japanese war, Chiang Kai-shek's Kuomintang recovered Taiwan and later took refuge there when he was defeated by the Chinese communists. Ironically, the situation was almost a replica of the early Qing situation (1644), when Taiwan was controlled by a defeated general from the former regime of the core and ecumene of mainland China with a few military outposts on the Fujian coast. Right opposite Xiamen is Jinmen, much as Fuzhou faces Mazu, which is still under the control of the Kuomintang army. With the coast of Fujian becoming a military frontier with occasional crossfire, foreign trade and overseas links were severed and the core exerted the strictest control on almost every aspect of life in the frontier province of Fujian lest it become sympathetic to the anticommunist elements. Fuzhou is not only the capital of the province but also the hub of the Fuzhou military region, which covers all of southeastern China.

The reopening of Fujian to the outside world in 1979 came as a surprise. Since 1979, Fujian, like Guangdong, has been granted a special status with greater economic autonomy to trade with the outside world, to experiment with Western management methods, and to absorb foreign investment and technology. Xiamen was chosen as the site of a Special Economic Zone in 1981, and Fuzhou was classified as one of the fourteen open cities in 1984. Under the open policy, Fujian and Guangdong were deliberately allowed to separate themselves from the rigid and outdated economic (and perhaps value) systems prevalent in the core in order to cultivate the necessary innovativeness, a characteristic of the frontier spirit. The subsystem of Fujian is therefore regulated by the provincial government in Fuzhou. The emphasis on ideological purity and the "Chinese way of modernization" is still very much binding, so that the provincial capital is in a more restrictive position than the seaport and the Special Economic Zone of Xiamen. It is thus not surprising that Xiamen displays more innovation, offers more imaginative measures, and attains better results in attracting foreign and Taiwanese investment than Fuzhou. Similarly, Xiamen but not Fuzhou has been chosen as the Special Economic Zone with a lead time of almost four years in opening to the outside.

Spatial-Urban Structure

Fuzhou city exhibits a great continuity of its traditional role and function —to serve as an administrative center for the development of a frontier province. Currently, it is at the same site of the historical town under different names—Ye, Jinan, Jianan, Fuzhou—except that it has evolved in response to its increased population, its thriving urban economy, and the need of shipping and navigation. Right from its inception some 2,190 years ago, the Gulou district, where the present-day government offices are located, was the site of the historical walled city of Fuzhou. We turn now to the reasons for choosing Fuzhou to undertake this special role.

A Sound Geographical Location

Fuzhou is situated next to the Taiwan Strait at the estuary section of the Fuzhou Basin built up by the deposition of Min Jiang (Figure 10.1), the most navigable river in the province. As Fujian is a hilly province, land transport is difficult. Thus a navigable river has been essential to its economic development, especially in the early days. The Fuzhou Basin alone is 17 km wide from east to west and 22 km long from north to south. The average altitude is 6 m above sea level. Since 1955, Fuzhou has been connected with Xiamen and other parts of China through the Yingxia railway; the road network has been improving with time. Fuzhou is therefore accessible by sea, by rail, by road, and by air. Moreover, being at the northern margin of the tropical zone, Fuzhou's average annual temperature is about 19.6°C and the average annual precipitation is 1,342.5 mm; there is a distinct long summer and short winter.

A Sheltered Deep-Water River Port

Min Jiang is short but its annual discharge is voluminous. Although the river basin is only about one-twelfth that of the Yellow River by area, its annual discharge is greater than the Yellow River by 11,000 million cubic meters. Compared with Chang Jiang, its river basin is only 3.56 percent by area but 5.8 percent by annual discharge. Another characteristic is its light sediment loading, only 25 percent that of Chang Jiang, 0.36 percent that of the Yellow River, and 67 percent that of Zhu Jiang. In addition, most of its sediments are deposited in the river channel south of Nantai and Langqi islands, leaving the northern river channel stable, deep-watered, and relatively free of sediment.

The tidal range at the estuary is remarkable, about 4.06 to 4.5 m, facilitating the coming and going of oceangoing vessels. But the estuary is protected by many offshore islands with knolls 200 to 300 m high, so that the effect of strong winds from the northeast and rough waves is to some extent minimized. At Guantou, for example, the average waves are 0.2 to 0.3 m high with the highest at 1.3 m. This serves good anchorage

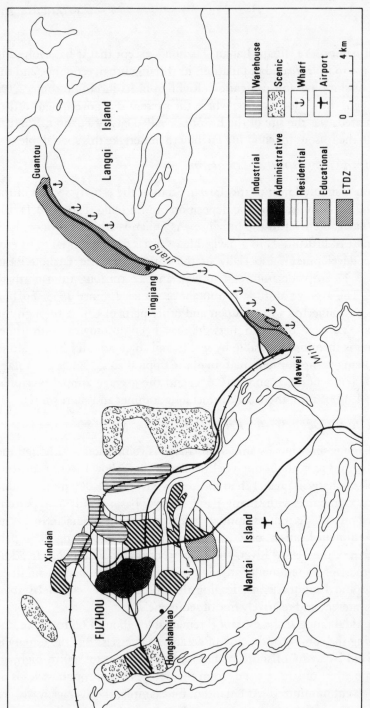

Figure 10.1 The Environs of Fuzhou

Table 10.1   Relative Importance of Fuzhou's Hinterland

HINTERLAND	POPULATION ('000)	AREA (SQ KM)	AGRICULTURAL AND INDUSTRIAL OUTPUT (1,000 YUAN)	INDUSTRIAL OUTPUT (1,000 YUAN)	AGRICULTURAL OUTPUT (1,000 YUAN)
Second tier	4,888.6 (18.01)[a]	11,427.8 (9.42)	5,467,740 (23.14)	3,794,640 (26.95)	1,673,100 (17.53)
Third tier	14,777.1 (54.45)	77,364.5 (63.81)	14,024,270 (59.39)	8,600,660 (61.08)	5,423,610 (56.83)

Source: *Fujian Statistics Yearbook* (1985).

[a]Figures in parentheses are percentage shares of the province.

and midstream loading and unloading of cargo—particularly important for sailing boats and small vessels in the old days.

A Rich Hinterland

The hinterland of Fuzhou may be classified into three tiers. The first tier is the adjacent hinterland covering the suburban Minhou, Changle, and Lianjiang counties. The second tier covers the eight counties under the administration of Fuzhou municipality. The third tier is the largest, covering the whole Min Jiang Basin and northeastern Fujian (Fuzhou, Sanming, Putian *shi,* and Ningde and Jianyang districts). As indicated in Table 10.1, the third tier covers an area of 63.8 percent of Fujian and contains over 50 percent of the population and about 60 percent of the total agricultural and industrial output (two-thirds of the heavy industry and three-fifths of the light industries).

Moreover, the tributaries of Min Jiang run through an important forest of South China. There are 285 million cubic meters reserve of timber in the Fuzhou hinterland, accounting for two-thirds of the province's total reserve (Table 10.2). Tea is another product for export and local consumption. Wuyi Shan and Jiufeng Shan account for 71 percent of the province's tea production. Three-fifths of its grain and four-fifths of its oilseed are also produced here. Table 10.3 shows the relative importance of agricultural produce derived in Fuzhou's hinterland.

Growth of the Urban Area

Many of the considerations noted above were responsible for the choice of Fuzhou as the site for construction of a walled city to administer the region. The walled city set up in the Qin and the Han dynasties at Gulou

Table 10.2   Relative Importance of Fuzhou's Hinterland in
Agricultural Production (percentage shares)

HINTERLAND	FOOD STAPLES	OILSEED	SUGAR	TEA	CITRUS	OLIVE	TIMBER
Second tier	12.7	16.5	8.7	4.9	14.2	38.5	0.7
Third tier	60.0	79.7	36.2	71.0	47.0	73.2	66.2

Source: Bureau of Statistics, Fuzhou Municipality, 1985.

Table 10.3   Relative Importance of Fuzhou's Hinterland in
Agricultural Produce Procured (percentage shares)

HINTERLAND	TOTAL PROCURED	FOOD STAPLES	TEA	FRUITS	PORK	POULTRY	FISHERY PRODUCTS
Second tier	15.8	10.8	5.5	8.2	16.0	13.0	27.0
Third tier	57.2	76.9	68.0	32.7	50.0	25.0	45.2

Source: Bureau of Statistics, Fuzhou Municipality, 1985.

was extremely small and north of the one constructed in the subsequent dynasties (Figure 10.2). Starting from the Jin dynasty, it had grown in response to the larger population within its walls and perhaps the growing volume of commercial activities. During the Song and the Yuan dynasties, the port was in the west outside the walled city at Hongshanqiao. Between Hongshanqiao and Ximen (West Gate) of the walled city, there were places for warehouses and godowns. Ximen Street was the commercial district at that time. Because of gradual silting of the port in the west, the berths and the warehouses were gradually moved to Xiaoqiao, Shanghang Road, and Xiahang Road on the northern banks of Min Jiang south of the walled city. Along Shanghang Road and Xiahang Road transactions of local produce were undertaken.

During the Ming dynasty, the Xiaoqiao area had been silting up and a new port was constructed with dredging so that oceangoing vessels could sail up to Xingang; from there to the walled city stretched the center for foreign trading. Mariners' hostels, Liuqiu (Ryukyu) House, the tribute warehouse, and processing factories were set up in the north of Xingang and around Shuibumen. Further north were the customs and excise authorities. The local commerce, personal services, and restaurants were scattered along Nanjie (South Street), while the craftsmen and their

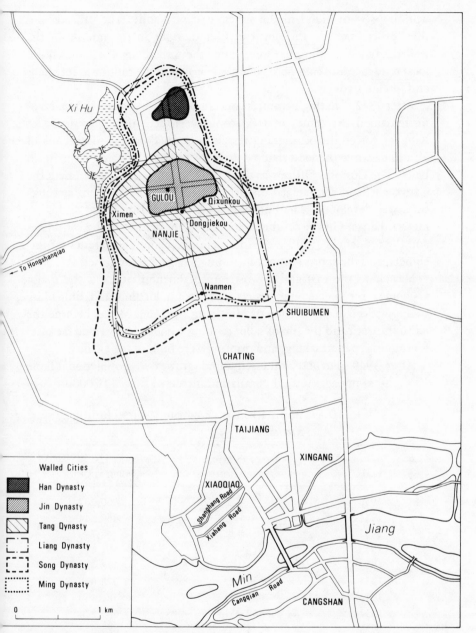

Walled Cities

- ■ Han Dynasty
- ▨ Jin Dynasty
- ▨ Tang Dynasty
- ⬚ Liang Dynasty
- ⬚ Song Dynasty
- ⋯ Ming Dynasty

0   1 km

Figure 10.2 The Evolution of Fuzhou City

workshops were found in the streets east of Nanjie. The officials and their offices were in the north of Gulou, right in the middle of the walled city. From Ming to Qing, then, the walled city was basically for local residence and commerce whereas the area to the south was for aliens and foreign trade.

After 1842, Chating became a concentration of workshops while Nanjie remained the center of local commercial activities. The silting of Xingang forced the oceangoing vessels to berth along the south bank of Min Jiang while the local shallow-draft river vessels moored on the north bank. The Customs Office was set up on the south bank. From here the Cangqian Road commercial district, characterized by Western architecture, was developed. The buildings were occupied by hongs and commercial banks. On the southern slopes of Cangshan were the consulates and the residences of the Westerners, church schools, cemeteries for foreigners, and the sports ground, including a racetrack for horses.

Mawei, to the east and downstream of Fuzhou city, was the major anchorage for oceangoing vessels. Midstream loading and unloading were practiced at this section of Min Jiang. In 1866, Mawei became the naval shipyard and the site of sailor training schools. Many small factories for canning, papermaking, and printing were built in the vicinity.

After 1949, Fuzhou witnessed rapid growth in population (Table 10.4). Total nonagricultural population increased from 341,000 in 1949

Table 10.4   Population of Fuzhou *Shi* (excluding *xian*)

YEAR	NONAGRICULTURAL POPULATION[a]	TOTAL POPULATION[b]
1950	—	460,207
1951	—	469,344
1952	—	474,789
1953	—	501,471
1954	—	578,428
1955[c]	452,622	1,028,068
1956	453,441	581,169
1957	452,251	606,274
1958	471,783	625,613
1959	536,546	671,488

continued

Table 10.4 *Continued*

YEAR	NONAGRICULTURAL POPULATION[a]	TOTAL POPULATION[b]
1960	602,689	746,460
1961	625,775	876,797
1962	617,082	887,111
1963	574,550	843,840
1964	581,063	864,549
1965	586,004	868,626
1966	592,198	877,265
1967	621,906	928,204
1968	629,613	940,314
1969	581,017	868,969
1970	580,563	868,984
1971	549,283	881,181
1972	549,094	872,666
1973	580,147	942,931
1974	587,135	956,911
1975	587,316	1,018,147
1976	600,605	1,035,567
1977	607,192	1,051,926
1978	633,630	1,081,042
1979	662,501	1,109,332
1980	685,327	1,130,499
1981	710,929	1,154,689
1982	731,190	1,180,250
1983	727,024	1,141,969
1984	754,510	1,164,795
1985	784,234	1,189,531
1986	805,546	1,205,040
1987	831,933	1,236,560
1988	846,214	1,251,288

Source: Fujian Province Population Statistical Compendium, 1949–1988 (Chinese Statistical Press).

[a]Includes such population in urban and rural areas.

[b]Includes all populations within urban and rural areas.

[c]The urban population exceeding 1 million in 1955 was the result of changes in administrative boundaries.

to 846,214 in 1988. To house the additional population, the built-up area of Fuzhou city has expanded from 16.57 sq km in 1949 to 45.36 sq km in 1988—which includes the three major urban districts (Gulou, Taijiang, and Cangshan, total built-up area of 38.57 sq km) and three separated patches of suburban industrial areas. Gulou, the oldest district, has predominantly administrative and cultural land uses. Many historical buildings are found there, especially near Dongjiekou. The latest additions in this district are modern hotels and a trade convention center. Taijiang, a mud flat and sandbars with frequent flooding before the Song dynasty, is now a densely populated commercial and light industrial district. Shanghang Road and Xiahang Road are full of shops dealing with tea and local specialties. Chating is noted for its workshops with craftsmen and their families living right behind. The middle section of the Min Jiang frontage is the site of the passenger wharves. The eastern and western sections are occupied by industries: the eastern section is part of the Ofengzhou industrial zone noted for ice making and fish processing; the western section is noted for its food processing industries. Cangshan, an area for storing salt in the Ming dynasty and a westernized district during the treaty port era, has now been transformed into a university and research district; its eastern portion specializes in handicrafts and woodwork.

The city's social structure also reflects to a certain extent its evolution and historical past. The Manchus concentrate at the Qixunkou; they are the descendants of the Qing military personnel and their families. Muslims live next to the Nanmen where the mosque is. The Japanese are found around the Shuibumen area where their ancestors were designated to live during the Ming and Qing dynasties. The westerners and the overseas Chinese who came back before and after 1949 clustered in Cangshan, which had previously been a westernized district.

Overseas Chinese Links and Economic Mainstay

Past history and tradition have provided Fuzhou with many advantages over other cities. Its notable skills in handling forestry products, shipbuilding, tea processing, and navigation have been maintained even though all these enterprises are working with outdated tools and machines. As the administrative center of the province, Fuzhou has many higher learning institutes and a comparatively high level of literacy.

Overseas migration in the past has allowed many people in Fuzhou to have kinship relations with overseas Chinese, especially those living in the Philippines, Singapore, and Malaysia. Their remittance is a source of foreign currency that amounted to $5.30 million in 1985 for the whole Fuzhou municipality. This remittance is still helpful to the urban economy of Fuzhou. The importance of these links might carry even greater weight in the introduction of overseas investment and technology under the open policy.

With the completion of the railway in 1955, many patches of land along the line were designated for storage and warehouses. The railway not only helped to develop the expanding city but also linked the spatially separated functional units of the urban core with suburban industrial zones like Xindian and the outport of Mawei. Fuzhou has since established a diversified industrial base producing an industrial output of 4.79 billion *yuan* (Table 10.5). Xindian is a suburban heavy-industrial district for metallurgy and engineering; the eastern industrial district is for chemical products. Together with the thousand or so small industrial

Table 10.5 The Structure of Fuzhou Industries: 1987

DEPARTMENT	INDUSTRIAL OUTPUT (1,000 YUAN)[a]	%
Wood and bamboo products	700	0.01
Beverage and tobacco	340,950	7.11
Textile	260,370	5.43
Garment	49,190	1.03
Leather and fur products	91,450	1.91
Papermaking and paper products	99,540	2.08
Stationery and sportswear	73,150	1.53
Power generation and supplies	38,950	0.81
Chemical products	316,810	6.61
Construction material and nonmetallic products	94,030	1.96
Ferric metallurgy	61,660	1.29
Nonferric metallurgy	33,980	0.71
Metallic products	131,510	2.74
Engineering	367,190	7.66
Electronic products and communication	936,890	19.54
Total industrial output	4,793,470	100.00

Source: Fujian Statistical Yearbook 1989 (Chinese Statistical Press).

[a]At 1980 constant value.

Table 10.6   Occupational Structure of Urban
Population in Fuzhou

SECTOR	NO.	%
Primary industries	107,100	2.1
Secondary industries	2,728,270	56.79
Manufacturing	(2,425,630)	(48.14)
Tertiary industries	1,961,310	38.90

Source: Bureau of Statistics (1985).

plants, they provide 48 percent of the jobs to the urban working population (Table 10.6).

In other words, Fuzhou is in line with the national policy and has transformed itself into a typical Chinese administrative and industrial center. Its port and gateway function, however, is only a shadow of its past achievement. For example, its export, though growing at 9.4 percent annually from 1979 to 1985, was only 285 million *yuan* in 1985. Its tourist industry attracted only 65,000 foreign visitors in the same year with a foreign currency receipt of only $24 million. Its inner-city port—Taijiang—could only handle small vessels of less than 1,000 dwt with its throughput around 1.48 million tonnes in 1985. Its outport—Mawei—has only two berths for 10,000-dwt oceangoing vessels and another two for 5,000-dwt-class vessels. In 1985, Mawei handled 735 sailings and 2.40 million tonnes of cargo, mainly composed of construction materials, coal, cement, chemical fertilizer, insecticide, and steel. About 33.4 percent (802,000 tonnes) was related to foreign trade. Containerization has had its impact on the port, as well, but the port only handled 10,802 containers (5,495 for import and 5,307 for export) in 1985. Passenger ships were reintroduced in 1982 between Fuzhou and Shanghai. Test voyages have been launched between Fuzhou and Hong Kong, but so far no scheduled service has been introduced.

Thus it is not surprising that there were only 121 joint ventures concluded with a pledged investment amounting to $35 million between 1979 and 1985, when trading with Taiwan was still not allowed. Inside the city urban area, other than a few modern high-rise hotels, it is difficult to find convincing evidence that Fuzhou is a modern city. The historical sites and buildings, including the Kaiyuan Temple, are in a derelict state. They must be rehabilitated if they are to attract tourists and foreign visitors. With such a poor start, it will take a long time to transform

Fuzhou into a modern gateway city—and it needs a new impetus to make it grow faster, as well.

Plans for an Open City

The Fuzhou municipal government has four plans for major improvement in order to develop Fuzhou into one of the fourteen open coastal cities. Essentially these plans address the issues of port development, the Fuzhou ETDZ, the city's transport and communication network, and the reliability of Fuzhou's energy supply.

Port Projects

The existing sites of the berths are poorly chosen, while the navigation channels are not deep enough for 10,000-dwt vessels. The port's backup facilities are badly conceived and poorly coordinated. Modernization of the port system is therefore not only desirable but essential. It is thus planned to ensure that the entrance channel is not less than 6 or 7 m deep and the section between Taijiang and Jiangnan Bridge is not less than 2.5 m deep, so that 1,000 to 1,500-dwt coastal ships can go up to Taijiang and 10,000-dwt oceangoing vessels can enter Mawei at high tide. Apart from fully equipping the existing wharves, six 10,000-dwt berths and two 5,000-dwt berths are to be constructed further downstream at Mawei. Potential sites at Yingyu with its 2,500-m-long deepwater coastline could accommodate another ten 30,000-dwt berths. Several huge container terminals and passenger liner berths are planned so that the modernized port system of Fuzhou can satisfy the demands of an open city.

The Fuzhou ETDZ

To accommodate the targeted foreign-owned or partially foreign-owned export-oriented industries, Fuzhou has set up an Economic and Technological Development Zone (ETDZ) at Mawei. Its total area is as large as 23 sq km and is divided into two portions, Mawei and Tingjiang. Mawei is mainly for export-processing light industries, scientific research, and new product promotion works; it also contains the port zone and a tourist resort. Tingjiang is destined for future heavy industries, including ocean chemistry, petrochemicals, shipbuilding, engineering, and metallurgy. It is projected that by the year 2000 the district as a whole will become a port town of 250,000 people. An immediate plan (Figure 10.3)

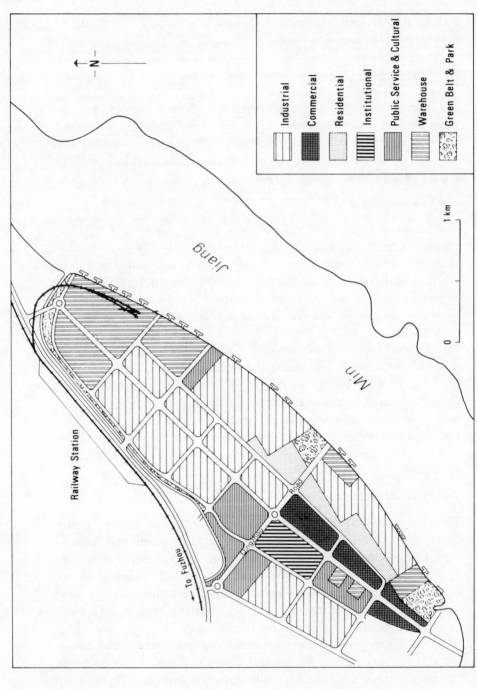

Industrial

Commercial

Residential

Institutional

Public Service & Cultural

Warehouse

Green Belt & Park

0   1 km

N

Railway Station

To Fuzhou

Jiang

Min

Lingnao Road

is to develop a small portion of Mawei. It is subdivided into two sections separated by Qingzhou Road. To the east of Qingzhou Road is the entre-pôt zone, shipbuilding, and other industries, occupying a total area of 2.7 sq km. To the west is a multifunctional zone for the electronics industry, trade and finance, culture and sport facilities, residential quarters, and administrative uses. As many as 150 factories and other enterprises are being built. According to the brief published by the ETDZ authority:

> The zone will import advanced technology, especially new-developed industries of technology and knowledge concentrated. Luoxing section, which will be developed in the near future, will be given priority to the development of electronic industry, including automatic inspecting and gauging instruments, electronic equipment for navigation, broadcasting and communication equipment, and other electronic products. In the meantime, it will develop ship-building industry and its accessories, light industry, food industry, and projects of processing and assembling the materials and parts supplied by foreign customers. Qingzhou section will lay emphasis on building large and medium-sized factories forming an industrial system. Stress will be put on accessory supply of electronic products. Priority will be given to the development of precision machinery, precision instruments, meters, fine chemicals, new building materials, ocean exploitation, port auxiliary facilities, and biological research.[11]

Transport and Communication Network

It is considered that the present railway is not sufficient: a new link between Jiangshan (Zhejiang) and Fuzhou is needed. The Fuzhou–Wenzhou, Fuzhou–Xiamen, and Fuzhou–Gutian roads should be upgraded from second class to first class. Upstream navigation ought to be improved, so that 500-dwt river vessels can reach Nanping. The airport has been improved with scheduled/chartered services between Hong Kong and other major Chinese cities. Telecommunication has paved the way for direct dialing to Hong Kong and the outside world through the completion of a quasi-electronic telephone exchange system.

Reliability of Energy Supply

Shortage of electricity is acute in Fuzhou, especially in the dry season. This is because Fuzhou and the electricity network of northern Fujian depend on the local hydroelectric plants. When the runoff is low (October through April), they must be supplemented by thermal electricity.

Even so, a gap between supply and demand is noticeable. Many factories need to work under capacity because of insufficient electricity. It is thus planned to build a huge hydroelectric plant at Shuikou with a capacity of 140,000 kv and an annual capacity of 4.95 billion kwh. A thermal plant is planned to generate another 2.5 billion kwh with coal imported from Shanxi. To support this thermal plant, the 10,000-dwt tanker and coal berths at Mawei must be completed in time.

Infrastructural improvement alone is not enough. As in other open cities, the Fuzhou government has put forward a package of preferential treatment to foreign investors. Moreover, Fuzhou has set up many customs bonded warehouses (about thirteen by October 1988) and a science park is planned near Fuzhou University. Inside the city, Fuzhou's government is experimenting with the idea of leasing plots of land through public auction and private tenders. All this signifies Fuzhou government's innovative attitude. By introducing modern and tested practices of the market economies, they hope to modernize Fuzhou and take advantage of its status as an open city and provincial capital with great autonomy in economic affairs.

Conclusion

According to the latest indications, the responses to the Fuzhou ETDZ are encouraging. The authorities have approved sixty-eight enterprises, thirty-seven of which are now in production. "To compare the first half of 1988 with 1989," reports the newspaper *Wen Wei Po*, "industrial output increased by 60 percent and export total more than doubled."[12] It is reported that in May 1989 alone, the ETDZ signed up three leather factories with pledged investments of over $1 billion. In addition, two footwear factories and two synthetic textile factories have shown their intention of leasing 4.7 ha of land. The events of June 1989 in Beijing have apparently not affected the stability of Fuzhou. Given the enthusiastic response of the foreign and Taiwanese investors, the administration must now start planning to develop the lower course and estuary section of Min Jiang to meet future needs.

Outside observers may not share the official optimism, but one should not overlook that Fuzhou, despite its slow start, has taken advantage of a frontier situation, particularly a booming Taiwan, which traditionally has had very close trade relations with Fuzhou. Now that Taiwan has become one of the fastest-growing economies in the Pacific Rim, its wage levels and living standards have risen rapidly to erode some of its competitiveness. To lower its costs of production it is now, almost by necessity, looking for a cheap labor backyard—very much similar to the relation between Hong Kong and the Zhu Jiang Delta. Fuzhou and Xiamen are the closest candidates and most likely beneficiaries. The major factors impeding such a transition are the political tension and vast differences in economic organization between the mainland government and the Taiwan authorities. The thaw in relations between the two sides has set the stage for closer cooperation between them. Despite the differences in ideology and economic organization, elimination of the military antagonism would restore peace in the Straits of Taiwan and allow for a more rational approach to economic and social development.

The open policy since 1978 has further allowed Fujian to revise its military frontier outlook and give foreign investors a hearty welcome. A more flexible approach to organizing its economic system by allowing joint ventures and private enterprise has resulted in a mixed economy. Developing further on the basis of market mechanisms cannot be entirely ruled out. Starting from the illegal smuggling trade, contacts between Taiwan and Fujian have gradually been revived. In 1988, Taiwan's government, while maintaining its no-official-contact policy, dramatically relaxed its policy for civilian contact. Taiwanese flocked into Fujian via Hong Kong for family reunions and discussion about indirect trading and investment. The traditional role of Fujian as a frontier and a springboard between Mainland and Taiwan has thus revived. Interpenetration of different ways of life and thinking—from personal contacts to watching Taiwan television broadcasts—is unavoidable, and Taiwan's technology and capital are beginning to have an impact on both Fuzhou and Xiamen.

To conclude, then, the southeastern frontier has been a very active frontier in China since the Ming dynasty when Chinese supremacy ceased on this front. Apart from episodic acts of war, maritime prohibitions, and total stoppages of trade, most of the time this frontier has maintained at least a partial open status for external trade. It is perhaps time for Fuzhou's government to recognize that its heyday as a port in Fujian monopolizing China's maritime trade is long gone. There are, however, a number of historical sites with the potential to be developed into tourist spots in the inner urban districts. What Fujian could now build on is its special geographical and socioeconomic advantages in dealing with Taiwan. At present the interaction between the two sides of the Straits of Taiwan is still impeded by many obstacles.

Looking into the future, closer cooperation and more interaction between China and Taiwan make good economic sense. As Taiwan has already become a regional economic power, inevitably its capital and low-technology industries will have to be transferred to nearby low-cost areas. Fujian is likely to be the first beneficiary of Taiwan's spillovers. The frontier is therefore likely to become an upward transition periphery with regard to the ecumene on the mainland. As provincial capital, Fuzhou is in a favorable position to take advantage of the situation and make itself a leader in this process. Its only real competitor is Xiamen, which enjoys greater flexibility by being not the provincial capital but a Special Economic Zone. A possible solution is to design some kind of division of labor between these two frontier cities. In the course of time, they are likely to work out their differences and reach a compromise.

Notes

1. J. B. R. Whitney, *China, Area, Administration and Nation Building,* Research Paper no. 123 (Chicago: Department of Geography, University of Chicago, 1970).

2. L. D. Kristof, "The Nature of Frontiers and Boundaries," *Annals of the Association of American Geographers* 49(3) (1959): 269–282.

3. See O. Lattimore, *Inner Asian Frontiers of China* (Boston: Beacon Press, 1940). See also R. L. Edmonds, *Northern Frontiers of Qing China and Tokugawa Japan,* Research Paper no. 213 (Chicago: Department of Geography, University of Chicago, 1985); and Whitney, *China, Area.*

4. Wang Gungwu, *South China Seas Trade and South East Asia Chinese* (Hong Kong: Zhonghwa Press, 1988) (in Chinese).

5. H. J. Wiens, *China's March Toward the Tropics* (Hamden, Conn.: Shoestring Press, 1954).

6. J. Friedmann, *Urbanization, Planning and National Development* (Beverly Hills, Calif.: Sage, 1973), pp. 21–34.

7. Wang, *South China Seas Trade,* p. 19.

8. Chen Ji-lin, *An Economic Geography of Fujian* (Fuzhou: Fujian Science and Technology Press, 1984), p. 34 (in Chinese).

9. Wang, *South China Seas Trade.*

10. Edmonds, *Northern Frontiers,* p. 21.

11. Administration Commission, Fuzhou E&TDD, *A Brief Introduction to Fuzhou Economic and Technical Development Districts* (undated).

12. *Wen Wei Po,* 31 July 1989.

11 Xiamen: Regional Center and Hometown of Overseas Chinese

SI-MING LI AND LING-XUN ZHAO

LOCATED ON THE SOUTHEAST coast of Fujian, Xiamen has long been an important seaport serving the Minnan region and the rest of China. It acts as a link between the rich Yangzi floodplains and the Pearl River Delta and serves as a stepping-stone for developing trade and cultural links with Taiwan (Figure 11.1). It is thus not at all surprising that Xiamen was designated as one of five treaty ports under the Treaty of Nanking signed after the Opium War between China and Britain in 1842. Nor is it surprising that the city was conferred the status of Special Economic Zone, together with Shenzhen, Zhuhai, and Shantou (Hainan Island was later added to the list), when China began to reopen its doors in the late 1970s and early 1980s.

The term *shi* (city) in China administratively carries two distinct meanings. First, it may refer to a specific urban area and the suburbs in its immediate vicinity. We may regard *shi* in this sense as a municipality. Second, it may refer to a vast administrative region including not only the urban area but also a number of largely rural counties or *xian* under the city's jurisdiction. In this second sense, *shi* may be viewed as an administrative region. In the first sense, Xiamen comprises the islands of Xiamen and Gulangyu, a number of smaller islands, and the districts of Jimei and Xinglin on the mainland. The total landed area is 554 sq km and in 1987 the population reached 570,000, of which 360,000 were considered nonagricultural. In the second sense, Xiamen *shi* includes Tong'an *xian;* the corresponding total area and population are, respectively, 1,516 sq km and 1.027 million (1985 figure).[1] (See Figure 11.2.) With the designation of Xiamen Island and Gulangyu as a Special Economic Zone in 1984, there is a third sense of Xiamen *shi*—that is, Xiamen Special Economic Zone. In this latter sense, Xiamen includes a total area of 131 sq km and a population of 360,000 (Figure 11.3).[2]

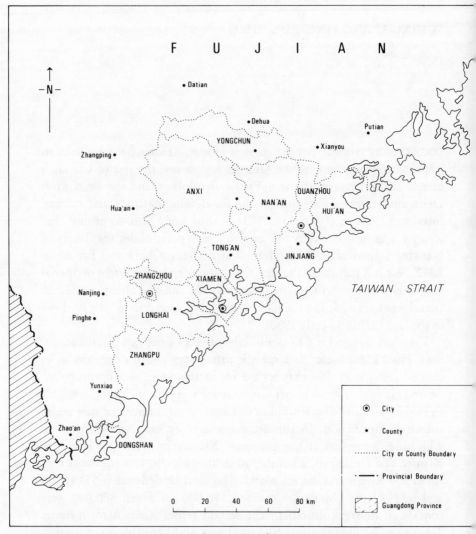

Figure 11.1 The Open Cities and Counties of the Southern Fujian Delta Region

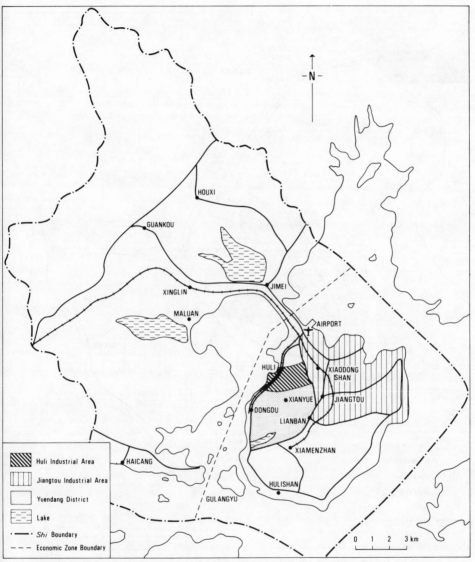

Figure 11.2 Xiamen *Shi*

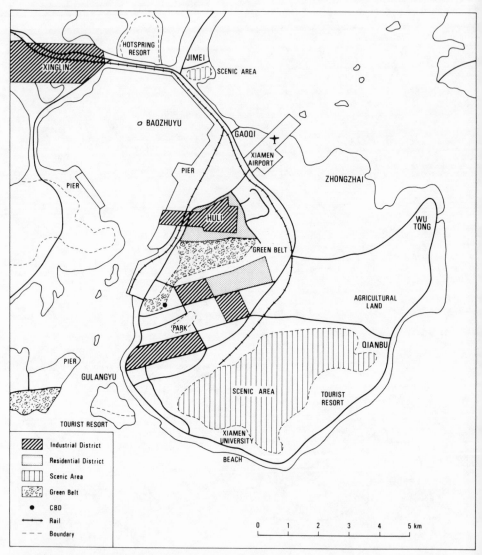

Figure 11.3 The Xiamen Special Economic Zone

History

Early History

The history of Xiamen can be traced back to the Shang dynasty (about 1000 B.C.). Archaeological evidence suggests that Xiamen Island was then inhabited by the ancient tribes of the Min and the Yue. The Han people began to move in during the Tang dynasty (A.D. 618–907). Until the Song dynasty (960–1279), however, Xiamen was no more than a small fishing village administered by Tong'an *xian* of Quanzhou *fu*. *(Fu was then an administrative unit between sheng, or province, and xian.)* Because paddy fields dominated the island's landscape, it was named Jiawoyu, literally Paddy Island. In 1387, the Ming Emperor Hongwu sent General Zhou Dexing to build a fort on the southwestern part of the island in order to defend the Chinese coast against Japanese pirates. Zhou named the fort Daxiamenhu, or Gate of the Mansion. From this time onward Xiamen became an official place name.

The rise and continual development of Xiamen was closely linked to foreign trade and the efforts of overseas Chinese. From the fifteenth century onward, Europeans had been actively promoting trade with the rest of the world. Although the Chinese court prohibited overseas trade because of the pirate problem, Spanish, Portuguese, and Dutch ships made frequent calls on the Fujian coast. The ports of Quanzhou and Zhangzhou, once prosperous trading centers, were then suffering from silting. Xiamen, which had an excellent natural harbor and was close to Quanzhou and Zhangzhou, was favored by European merchants as an unofficial trading post. The fact that Xiamen was an island located off the coast also helped: it was much easier for European traders to circumvent the search of Chinese coastal guards on the island than on the mainland. By the end of the Ming period, Xiamen had become a major port in South China. It was estimated that the Zheng family of Fujian alone had more than 1,000 ships engaged in overseas trade. There were also traders specializing in overseas trade. Exports from Xiamen included tea, ceramics, silk, and sugar; imports included spices, pepper, and precious metals. Foreign trade especially flourished under General Zheng Chenggong, because of the need to generate funds to support the war against the invading Manchus. The volume of foreign trade averaged 4 to 5 million taels of silver during these years.[3]

In 1683, the Qing court reopened the Chinese coast. Xiamen was designated an official port of entry, and a customhouse was set up on the island. In addition, it was official policy that all trading between Taiwan and the mainland had to go through Xiamen. The importance of Xiamen as a trading port grew as a result. By the mid-1700s the volume of trade handled had reached 15 million taels a year. Urban development took place along with the increase in trade. In the year 1838, just before the Opium War, Xiamen was already a sizable city with a population of 140,000.

1842–1949

The designation of Xiamen as a treaty port in 1842 brought about further developments, although Xiamen had then become a base of the imperial powers for the penetration of China's heartland. Banks, trading houses, shipping firms, dockyards, and factories were set up in the concession area. The British also gained control of the customs. A major trading item was opium—up to seven factories were set up to process it. In 1849, import of opium totaled 3,200 *dan;* in 1884, the amount had increased to almost 10,000 *dan.*[4] In 1909, the import of opium accounted for one-third of the year's total import in value terms. In fact, Xiamen was at that time the principal opium trading center in China. The city, however, still suffered from serious trade deficits. Exports were not enough to cover the import of opium alone.

Another important "trading item" of the city was the export of labor. The handicraft industry in the coastal areas collapsed under foreign competition. Life in the rural areas of the Fujian coast was extremely difficult. Many were willing to work overseas as coolies. Firms specializing in the export of labor, known as "piggy houses," sprang up in Xiamen. During the 1840s and 1850s an average of 50,000 workers a year were sent abroad. In some years the number exceeded 100,000. Xiamen, after Guangzhou, was the second largest center of coolie trade. The majority of the workers were sent to Southeast Asia and the Americas. Some went willingly, but many were kidnapped.

Development of manufacturing industries generally lagged behind trading. The first modern manufacturing plant set up in Xiamen was in fact an opium processing plant. At the turn of the present century, there were only a few small factories producing such items as soap, matches, and soy sauce. These might be compared with the more than 1,000 restaurants, trading houses, banks, and casinos and the over 5,000 shops in the city.

Overseas Chinese played an important part in the development of Xiamen, especially in the first half of the twentieth century. In the early days, investments of overseas Chinese tended to concentrate in transport infrastructure, public utilities, and real estate. Examples included the building of the Zhang–Xia railroad in 1905, the establishment of the Xiamen Light and Power Company in 1911, and the founding of the Xiamen Waterworks Supply Company in 1921. It was estimated that during the period, up to 70 percent of the investments in public utilities and real estate came from overseas Chinese. Investments in the manufacturing sector by overseas Chinese were also substantial. These included ceramic plants, food and canning industries, glassware workshops, and sugarcane processing plants. At the outbreak of the Sino-Japanese War in 1937, there were twenty-two factories of various types with a total capital outlay of 5 million *yuan,* of which 90 percent or more had overseas Chinese connections.

In addition to investing in urban infrastructure and industries, overseas Chinese were keen on education. Xiamen University and the prestigious Jimei Middle School were founded and funded by an overseas Chinese, Chen Jiageng. In the 1930s, there were some fifty registered schools, of which eleven were middle or secondary schools, in Xiamen. As many as forty-five of these were either founded or funded by overseas Chinese.

The banking and foreign trade sectors flourished in light of the large-scale investments by overseas Chinese. There were, in the 1930s, more than ten incorporated banks and many more smaller financial institutions. Traffic through the port of Xiamen was increasing at a rapid pace. In 1936, a total of 500,000 passengers including 150,000 overseas Chinese were handled. Throughput in the year amounted to 5 million tonnes—three times that of Fuzhou, the capital of Fujian. It can be said that Xiamen was then the chief industrial and banking center and port in southeastern China. Incorporated in 1933, the city was the first in Fujian to be given *shi* status. By 1936, the population in the urban area had exceeded 200,000.

When the Japanese invading force occupied Xiamen in May 1938, the links between Xiamen and the mainland and overseas Chinese were severed. The city's economy experienced a sharp decline. People escaped the city en masse. Only some 20,000 people remained in the urban area. China's victory in 1945 did not bring about significant improvements. Because of the outbreak of civil war in 1947, the gross industrial output amounted only to 25 million *yuan* per year. Of particular concern was the trade deficit. In both 1948 and 1949, the value of imports was more than ten times that of exports.

Xiamen Under the People's Republic

The First Thirty Years

In 1949, the Kuomintang army fled the mainland to Taiwan. Xiamen became a frontier outpost. The military significance of Xiamen was made all the more pronounced as the Kuomintang army was (and still is) occupying Greater and Lesser Jinmen islands less than 10 km from the city. In 1958, a fierce battle took place in the Jinmen–Xiamen area between the Communist and Kuomintang forces. Both sides continued to exchange artillery shells until the late 1970s. Given Xiamen's frontier position, it might be expected that the central government would refrain from investing in the area in order to minimize the extent of destruction in case of any renewed civil war. However, Xiamen's position was not without its advantages. To facilitate military maneuvers, the Chinese government completed, in 1955, the construction of a causeway linking Xiamen Island to the mainland and completed the Ying–Xia railroad in 1957 connecting Xiamen to the country's railway system.

Industrial growth was extremely rapid despite military threats. In 1950, the gross industrial output was 25 million *yuan;* in 1957, it was close to 80 million *yuan.* In 1965, it was over 200 million *yuan;* and in 1978, it reached 913 million *yuan* (see also Table 11.1).[5] Local resources, especially agricultural products, provided the basis for industrial production. Food and beverages, knitting, tobacco processing, glassware, sugar processing, electrical, machinery, and shipbuilding were among the leading industries in the city.

Developments After 1978

The Third Plenum of the Eleventh (Chinese Communist) Party Congress held in late 1978 marked a watershed in contemporary Chinese history. A wide range of political and economic reforms were adopted. Among these were the adoption of a more accommodating attitude toward private enterprise and foreign investment. After almost thirty years of self-imposed isolation, China reopened its doors to the West. The establishment of Special Economic Zones was a measure designed to attract

Table 11.1   Xiamen: Selected Population and Economic Statistics:
1950–1987

INDICATOR	1950	1978	1980	1983	1985	1987
Population (1,000)						
Administrative region	454	908	934	988	1,027	na
Municipality	263	474	492	521	546	570
Island	169	237	251	271	349	na
Combined agricultural and industrial output (million *yuan*)	62	913	1,134	1,408	2,427	3,246
GVIO (million *yuan*)	25	701	911	1,177	2,585	3,129
Light industry (%)	94.2	70.8	69.0	68.7	68.3	64.4
Heavy industry (%)	5.8	29.2	31.0	31.3	31.7	35.2
GNP (million *yuan*)	na	na	436	599	1,032	1,595
Per capita GNP *(yuan)*	na	na	1,243	1,420	2,529	2,401

Sources: 1950–1983 data from *Yearbook of China's Special Economic Zones*, 1984, p. 404; 1985 data from *Yearbook of China's Special Economic Zones*, 1986, p. 214; 1987 data from *Socioeconomic Profiles of Minnan Delta Area*, 1987, p. 121. The GNP figures reported for the years 1980, 1983 and 1985 pertain only to Xiamen Special Economic Zone (Xiamen Island and Gulangyu); those for the year 1987 pertain to Xiamen municipality.

foreign investment and introduce advanced technical and managerial know-how. In October 1980, the State Council designated the 2.5-sq-km Huli district of northwestern Xiamen as a Special Economic Zone. In March 1984, the zone was extended to cover the entire Xiamen Island and nearby Gulangyu Island. The State Council also allowed Xiamen to adopt certain free-port policies, although it is not at all clear what these policies are.[6]

Developing an adequate infrastructure was the Special Economic Zone's top priority. In the period 1980–1985, some 1,780 million *yuan* worth of infrastructure investments were completed—2.7 times the total completed in the thirty years prior to the establishment of the zone. Of most significant concern was the strengthening of Xiamen's links to the outside world. Four deep-water berths, two for 50,000-dwt ships and two for 100,000-dwt ships, have since been constructed in Xiamen's Dongdu Harbor. One of these berths was designed for container traffic. The newly constructed Xiamen International Airport was opened in October 1983. In the same year, the 220-km Yongan–Xiamen power transmission line (220,000 volts) was completed. Moreover, efforts have been made to upgrade the city's telecommunication system. A digitized telephone exchange was introduced and a microwave telecommunication system was installed. As of 1987, a total of 18,290 telephones had been installed, making Xiamen's telephone ownership rate among the highest in the nation.[7] In addition to improving the city's transport and communication links, of top concern were works on the Huli Processing Zone including site formation and construction of factory premises and residential blocks. An industrial new town of 70,000 inhabitants rapidly sprang up from what were once marshes and paddy fields.

With the gradual improvement in infrastructure and the introduction of a more receptive business environment, foreign capital began to invest in the Special Economic Zone. In the first few years foreign investments were made primarily on an experimental basis. A total of seventeen such investments were made between 1980 and 1983, with a total (planned) capital outlay of $91.78 million, of which $37.15 million was foreign funds.[8] Foreign investment increased drastically in subsequent years. In 1984, eighty-six items were concluded; the total capital outlay amounted to $295 million, of which $150 million were foreign funds.[9] In 1985, the corresponding figures were 105 items, $408 million, and $242.9 million, respectively.[10] More recent data indicate that foreign investment has continued apace in subsequent years. Some 180 investment items with an aggregate investment of $370 million were made in 1988. By the end of 1988, the total number of investment items and the sum of capital outlay involving foreign capital had reached 485 items and $1.6 billion, respectively.[11] Most of the foreign capital was attributable to Hong Kong, although Singapore was also a major source.[12] In recent years, with the gradual relaxation of tension between the mainland and Taiwan, Taiwan capital has begun to be invested in China. Because most Taiwanese are of Fujian origin and speak the same language as the people of Xiamen, a large portion of Taiwan's investments has ended up in Xiamen. By the end of 1988, Taiwanese merchants had invested in more than ninety items, of which some 80 percent were made in 1988 alone. In fact, in that year Taiwan had replaced Hong Kong as the most important source of "foreign" capital in Xiamen.[13]

With the injection of foreign capital and the adoption of more liberal economic policies, Xiamen's economy has taken on a different shape. Industrial growth has been proceeding even faster than before. The gross industrial output rose from 910.6 million *yuan* in 1980 to 3,128.6 mil-

Table 11.2   Industrial Composition in
Xiamen: 1981 and 1985

SECTOR	1981	1985
GVIO (million *yuan*)	1,007	2,141
Composition (%)		
Metallurgy	0.25	0.57
Electricity	1.95	1.07
Chemical	19.63	16.18
Machinery	18.73	39.83
Construction materials	3.68	2.70
Forestry related	1.55	0.80
Food	26.28	20.09
Textile	12.79	9.03
Sewing and knitting	1.84	1.24
Leather	2.11	1.16
Paper	0.74	1.99
Office supplies	3.71	3.54
Others	9.70	1.75

Source: Yearbook of Xiamen Special Economic Zone, 1986,
p. 62.

lion *yuan* in 1987—an annual rate of increase averaging 17.6 percent.
The growth of heavy industry tended to outpace that of light industry.
As a result, the relative contribution of the former increased from 31.0
percent to 35.2 percent, whereas that of the latter decreased from 69.0
percent to 64.4 percent over the period (see Table 11.1). The relative
importance of such traditional industries as food and beverages and textiles declined, whereas that of the modern industries such as machinery
increased (see Table 11.2).

Of particular significance is the reemergence of the service sector.
Although comprehensive information on the performance of the service
sector is not available, there is evidence that it has been experiencing a
growth rate even faster than that of the industrial sector. While the gross
industrial output increased an astonishing 3.44 times in the period
1980–1987, the gross national product, which includes service sector
activities, registered an even bigger increase—3.65 times—over the same
period. Another discernible change is the increasing openness of the
economy, especially its links to the overseas market. Exports, for exam-

ple, increased 2.14 times over the period 1980–1985, an average of 15.2 percent a year. In 1986, exports reached 163.7 million *yuan* or almost double the amount recorded in the previous year.[14]

Xiamen harbor's throughput showed corresponding increases. In 1978, the throughput was 1.5 million tonnes; in 1985, it exceeded 3 million tonnes; in 1987, it reached 4.3 million tonnes. Air traffic also experienced a high rate of growth. At present Xiamen's International Airport ranks eighth in the country in terms of density of flights and volume of traffic. In 1987, some 320,000 passengers used the airport.[15] Despite the efforts made in the early eighties to improve the city's transport infrastructure, the growth in external trade has been so rapid that by 1988 it became clear that Xiamen's Dongdu Harbor and airport were fast reaching their saturation point and were often cited by foreign investors as the main deterrents to further growth.[16]

Spatial Structure of the City

As noted earlier, the term *shi* in China has different meanings, each corresponding to a specific tier in the administration hierarchy. The present discussion focuses on the narrower *shi:* the urbanized area and its immediate vicinity. Figure 11.3 is a sketch map of Xiamen in this narrow sense.[17]

Xiamen's main urban area, located on the western half of the island, covers an area of approximately 66 sq km. Some 280,000 people inhabit the area, making a gross population density of 4,250 persons per square kilometer. The city's old town, located in the southwest corner of the island, was also the city's central business district and civic center. There one finds 70 percent of the city's commercial outlets, the major hotels, parks, and other public facilities. Most streets are narrow and buildings are densely packed. Population density exceeds 20,000 persons per square kilometer. In the vicinity of the old town are the city's cultura' education, and research centers. To the south are Xiamen University, th Third Research Center of the National Ocean Bureau, the Museum of Overseas Chinese, and Nanputuo Monastery. To the east is the Wanshiyan Scenic District. The old port of Xiamen, which nowadays handles mainly passenger traffic, is found in the waterfront of the old town area.

Further northeast is Houjiangdi Industrial District, developed mainly in the 1950s. This is Xiamen's principal industrial zone. Proximity to the rail station is the district's main advantage. Housed there are more than 400 factories, including canning, wine processing, rubber, cigarette, machinery, and precision instrument plants, accounting in 1985 for 70 percent of the city's gross industrial output.

North of the old town, along the shore of Yuandan Lake, is a newly built-up area developed in the 1980s. High-rise commercial and residential structures dot the district. A new town hall to house the city government is planned there. In a few years' time, the district will become the administrative center of Xiamen. Three kilometers north of Yuandan district is Xiamen's outer port, Dongdu Harbor, where the newly constructed 10,000-dwt-class berths are located.

About 8 km north of Yuandan is Huli Export-Processing Zone, the area initially designated as the Special Economic Zone. Developed only after 1980, Huli has now become an important industrial district. Light industry is the backbone: electronics, plastics, and textiles are well represented in the area. By 1985, the district's gross industrial output had reached 320 million *yuan,* accounting for 15 percent of the city's gross industrial output. Most industries in the area have foreign links. In 1985, some 60 percent of foreign-owned enterprises were located there.

On the northwestern side of Xiamen Island bordering Xinglin Bay is Xinglin Industrial District. This is an industrial area developed after the completion of the Ying–Xia railroad in 1957. Represented in the area are glassware, textile, synthetic fiber, sugar processing, and chemical fertilizer factories and an electricity generating plant. One-quarter of the factories there are considered to be large and pivotal. The area's gross industrial output accounts for 10 percent of the city's total.

Located some 700 m off the southwest coast of Xiamen Island is the scenic island of Gulangyu, a small island of 1.8 sq km. Gulangyu, renowned for its beautiful beaches, heavily wooded hills, and buildings with classic architectural design, is one of the nation's most sought-after holiday resorts. Indeed, it is often called the "garden in the sea."

Northwest of Xiamen Island, across the Gaoqi–Jimei Causeway, is the educational and scenic district of Jimei. This is the hometown of Chen Jiageng, one of the most respected overseas Chinese. There one finds the sprawling Jimei Education Complex founded by Chen as well as Guilai Pavilion and Ao Gardens, architectural masterpieces integrating classical and modern designs.

Development Potential

Locational Advantages

Xiamen is blessed with a variety of locational advantages which greatly assist it in realizing its developmental potential. These favorable factors, stemming from its geography, history, external links, and economic structures, may be highlighted as follows.

Favorable Environmental Conditions. Xiamen lies just north of the Tropic of Cancer. Although its winter is much more severe than its latitude might suggest, temperatures never fall below freezing. Moreover, there is an abundance of both sunshine and rainfall: the former averages 2,300 hours and the latter 1,200 mm per year. Such climatic conditions are ideal for the cultivation of subtropical crops, including sugarcane, jute, and diverse subtropical fruits. In addition, the waters in the vicinity of Xiamen are rich fishing grounds. There is considerable potential in developing an export-oriented agriculture and fishery industry.

As a port, Xiamen possesses a number of advantages. First, it is located right between the rich Yangzi and Pearl deltas. The travel distance from Xiamen to Shanghai is 695 nautical miles by sea; to Hong Kong and Guangzhou it is 287 and 390 nautical miles, respectively. Moreover, it lies on many of the South and East China coastal traffic routes and on many transpacific routes. It is not surprising that entrepôt trade has been Xiamen's economic base for a long time. Of course, Xiamen's excellent harbor also plays an important part. There is more than 43 km of deep-water coastline and the harbor is protected by a series of islands including Xiamen itself and the islands of Greater and Lesser Jinmen, Dadan, Erdan, Sandan, and Qingyu. The main channel in the outer harbor has a depth of 12 to 25 m and is able to accommodate ships in the 30,000 to 50,000-dwt class. Even in the inner harbor or old port, the channel depth exceeds 8 m and ships of 10,000 dwt can dock freely. In fact, Xiamen has the best harbor of all the Special Economic Zones.

A Long History of External Trade. Xiamen has a history of more than 600 years of external trade. Although there have been several ups and downs, the city is indisputably one of China's major trading ports. Xiamen's experience in dealing with foreign trade is of immense value to its current drive to develop an external-oriented economy.

The Hometown of Overseas Chinese and Taiwanese. It is estimated that more than 4 million overseas Chinese (including ethnic Chinese holding foreign passports)—roughly one-fifth of the world's overseas Chinese population—have roots in Xiamen and the neighboring Minnan region. The links between Xiamen and overseas Chinese are many and varied. First, many overseas Chinese still have relatives in Minnan. Second, quite a few of them have moved back and settled in their hometown. The presence of such links not only facilitates the flow of information with the outside but also provides an important source of funds for development through remittance and direct investment. Moreover, there is an affectionate element in this financial assistance as epitomized by the case of Chen cited earlier.

What has been said of the overseas Chinese can also be said of the Taiwanese. As noted, most Taiwanese (excluding those who fled to Taiwan from the mainland in 1949 and their descendants) are of Fujian—in particular Minnan—origin and speak the Minnan dialect. The designation of Xiamen as a Special Economic Zone and the adoption of a more accommodating attitude toward external capital certainly help in drawing Taiwanese investors and travelers to the city.

Numerous Tourist Attractions. Gulangyu Island and the Jimei district, described earlier, illustrate this advantage.

A Sizable Pool of Educated Workers. With the support of overseas Chinese, the education system in Xiamen before 1949 was much better developed than the rest of the country. It continued to develop after the communist takeover. There are now six universities and colleges offering higher education, including the highly specialized Institute of Water Resources and College of Physical Education. In addition, there are nine technical colleges offering middle-level technical and professional training. It is estimated that 40 out of every 1,000 people in Xiamen have received higher education, a ratio six times the national average. Xiamen possesses the largest pool of educated workers among the Special Economic Zones.

A Well-Developed Industrial and Commercial Base. The city's commercial and service sectors are among the most developed in the country. Most investors and travelers from abroad would find living in the city a highly enjoyable experience.

Limitations

The further development of Xiamen is constrained by several factors, part geographical, economic, and political.

Limited Hinterland. Xiamen's sphere of influence basically covers the neighboring Minnan and Minxi regions, with a total area of 67,000 sq km and a population of 14 million. As of the mid-1980s the region's combined industrial and agricultural output was valued at some 10 billion *yuan,* of which industrial output accounted for 6 billion *yuan.* This was broadly equivalent to the combined industrial and agricultural output of a middle-ranking city. With the completion of the planned Fujian–Guangdong railway and the Sannan highway (linking southern Fujian, Jiangxi, and Hunan), Xiamen's sphere of influence could reach southern Jiangxi, Hunan, and eastern Guangdong. But still this would cover an area of no more than 200,000 sq km, which is far smaller than the hinterlands of such cities as Shanghai, Tianjin, and Dalian.[18]

Lack of Energy and Water Resources. The Xiamen region does not have any primary energy resources to speak of. As for secondary energy, there are four coal- and oil-fueled power plants. All of them are very small, however, with a total capacity of only 73,000 kw. Power outages are common. This shortcoming acts as an obvious hindrance to industrial and commercial development. Xiamen also lacks a supply of fresh water. Per capita availability of fresh water is estimated to be 710 cu m per year, a figure far below the national average.

Limited Capacity for External Transport. The Gaoqi–Jimei Causeway constitutes the only surface link to the mainland. The causeway is quite narrow, however, with a width of only 19 m, yet it has to accommodate both highway and rail traffic. Each day some 7,000 to 8,000 vehicles make use of the 10-m-wide road spanning the causeway. Traffic jams occur frequently. Moreover, the design standard of the Ying–Xia railway, which runs along the causeway, is rather low and is unable to meet the growing traffic demand. Each year an estimated 5 to 6 million tonnes of needed materials cannot be transported to the city because of the inadequate rail capacity.

Confrontation between Taiwan and the Mainland. Theoretically the Communist and Kuomintang armies are still engaged in a state of civil war, although in recent years the atmosphere in the Taiwan Strait has become much more relaxed. Nevertheless, formal channels of exchange have yet to be developed between Taiwan and the mainland. Meanwhile the importance of Xiamen as a center of economic and cultural interchange between Taiwan and the mainland is very much curtailed.

Prospects

Xiamen has shown remarkable economic progress over the past decade. In a relatively short period of time it has transformed itself from a secluded military outpost into a thriving, externally oriented, commercial and industrial center. Foreign capital has played a significant part in the city's recent development. But this is only possible under a more congenial business environment. A better infrastructure including improved external links is being provided. Taxation concessions are given. And, more important, efforts are being made to build a legal and institutional framework for foreign investment and private enterprise. Of immediate relevance to urban growth and development are two significant measures.

The Land Use Control Regulations announced in July 1984 stipulated the length of land leases and annual land rents for different uses and different locations. A leasehold system was then in an embryonic stage of development. Under this set of regulations, all lands held by individual enterprises will be under the control of a leasehold system. Property rights regarding landholdings are better delineated.

This measure led to the Land Transfer Ordinance enacted in June 1988, which spells out the conditions under which landholdings can be transferred. A leasehold system reminiscent of the one used in Hong Kong is established. Land parcels (the use of which is regulated by land leases) may be bought and sold in the market. A premium amounting to the difference in land values has to be paid for in any change in lease terms, subject to its conforming to the city's master plan. As in Hong Kong, from time to time the city will release land parcels for auction or tender. The first public land auction was held in July 1988; a number of auctions have been carried out since. In all instances, advertisements were placed both within and outside of Xiamen. Foreign firms were successful in a number of such bids. With the formal legitimization of land transfer, it can be expected that the market will begin to assume an allocative function. The use of land (including the age, height, and type of premises built on it) will be determined, at least in part, by its value, although such factors as inertia, high cost of transaction, and the government's housing policies, planning guidelines, strong prices, and wage controls will continue to exert a substantial influence. Users who cannot afford the high land values in the city center will move out. This measure will minimize the extent of wastage arising from a mismatch of land use and land value and from individual enterprises and government units circumscribing large plots of land awaiting future expansion. In addition, spatial differentiation of land use will become more pronounced.

The reforms since 1978 have brought about rapid economic growth not only to the Special Economic Zones but also to the rest of the country. In many respects the growth has been too rapid and has exerted heavy pressure on the nation's transport and energy sectors. Inflation has gone almost out of control. An attempt to free price controls in order to cut down the size of price subsidies and bring about a set of relative prices better reflecting the goods' values in 1988 encountered considerable difficulties. Inflation reached 20 percent a year toward the end of 1988. Moreover, the existence of a two-tier or even a multitier price structure and the mixing of government functions and business provided an opportunity for profiteering and corruption. The government put a brake on the economy in late 1988. These problems led in part to the political events that culminated in June 1989 in Beijing.

Since then, however, the Chinese leaders have been at pains to reiterate that the country's doors, once opened, will not be closed. Policies regarding the coastal cities—the Special Economic Zones in particular—will remain unchanged. Economic development remains the country's top priority. The current emphasis on consolidation in order to bring down the inflation rate, the emphasis on ideology, and the uncertainties regarding the extent to which the country will adhere to a policy of economic (and political) liberalization may bring about temporary difficulties. Nevertheless, it is quite certain that Xiamen, as the largest port on China's southeastern coast, the hometown of overseas Chinese, and the natural recipient of Taiwanese investment and entrepôt handling Taiwan/mainland trade, will be able to overcome these difficulties and continue to prosper in the years to come.

Notes

This research has been supported in part by HKBC research grant FRG 87/88-15.

1. Statistical Bureau of Xiamen, Zhangzhou, and Quanzhou, *Socio-economic Profiles of Minnan Delta Area* (Xiamen, 1986), p. 110; and Editorial Board of Yearbook of Xiamen Special Economic Zone, *Yearbook of Xiamen Special Economic Zone* (Xiamen, 1986), pp. 62–64.

2. Zhang Liseng, Yao Ximao, and Yeh Feng, "Certain Strategic Problems on the Continual Development of Xiamen Special Economic Zone," *Economic Geography* 8(1) (1988): 36–41 (in Chinese).

3. One tael is equivalent to approximately 38 g.

4. One *dan* is equivalent to approximately 60 kg.

5. Yearbook of China's Special Economic Zones Press, *Yearbook of China's Special Economic Zones* (Hong Kong, 1984), p. 404.

6. Gao Peixin, "On the Implementation of Certain Free Port Policies in Xiamen," *Academic Journal of Xiamen University* (Philosophy and Social Science Section), 1 (1989): 34–40 (in Chinese).

7. *Socio-economic Profiles of Minnan Delta Area,* p. 120.

8. Unless otherwise stated, dollars refer to U.S. currency.

9. *Yearbook of China's Special Economic Zones,* p. 267.

10. *Yearbook of Xiamen Special Economic Zone,* p. 92.

11. *Ta Kung Pao,* 1 January 1989; *Sing Tao Il Pao,* 27 December 1988.

12. *Yearbook of Xiamen Special Economic Zone,* p. 93.

13. *Ta Kung Pao,* 13 January 1989.

14. Statistical Bureau of Fujian, *Statistical Yearbook of Fujian* (Fuzhou, 1987), p. 345.

15. *Wen Wei Po,* 22 July 1988.

16. See, for example, *Wen Wei Po,* 22 July 1988.

17. Chen Jilin, *An Economic Geography of Fujian* (Fuzhou: Science and Technology Press of Fujian, 1984); and Fang Wentu, Chen Tianqi, and Gao Zianfeng, *Xiamen: Port, Scenic City and Special Economic Zone* (Beijing: Haiyang Press, 1986).

18. Zhang Ruxiao and Lu Zhangyong, *Regional Economy of Fujian* (Fuzhou: Fujian People's Press, 1986).

12 Guangzhou: The Southern Metropolis in Transformation

YUE-MAN YEUNG, YU-YOU DENG, AND HAN-XIN CHEN

AS THE LARGEST PORT and city in South China and the sixth largest in China, Guangzhou is the political, economic, cultural, and communication center of Guangdong province. Guangzhou *shi,* as of January 1988, consisted of eight urban districts, namely Dongshan, Haizhu, Liwan, Yuexiu, Huangpu, Tianhe, Fangcun, and Baiyun (a suburban district), and four counties *(xian),* namely Huaxian, Conghua, Panyu, and Zengcheng (Figures 12.1 and 12.2).

Traditionally Guangzhou has always been the unrivaled southern metropolis in China. This position has been enhanced under China's recent open policy as Guangzhou ranked highest among the fourteen open cities in its ability to attract foreign capital. To enable Guangzhou to cope with the rapid change that the new economic policy has engendered, the *shi* boundaries were redefined and expanded in 1985 and then further redefined in 1988. The *shi* now encompasses an area of 7,434 sq km of which 1,443 sq km refers to the urban districts and 92.1 sq km pertains to the city proper. By the end of 1988 the total population of the *shi* had reached 5.77 million; 3.49 million were classified "urban," with 2.81 million living in the city proper (Table 12.1).

Historical and Geographical Setting

Guangzhou is an ancient Chinese city dating back some 2,200 years. For centuries Guangzhou's southern location, removed from the incessant warfare of the Northern Plains, provided a favorite destination for population migration as well as a base for steady economic growth. Guangzhou further strengthened its economic base by developing foreign trade as early as the Han dynasty. It became the most important southern trade center, exporting China's silk, tea, and other products and importing pearl, turtle, and other goods from Arabia, India, and Southeast Asia. During the Tang and Song dynasties, Guangzhou witnessed further growth in foreign trade and a concentration of foreign merchants in the

Figure 12.1 Guangzhou and Its Geographical Setting

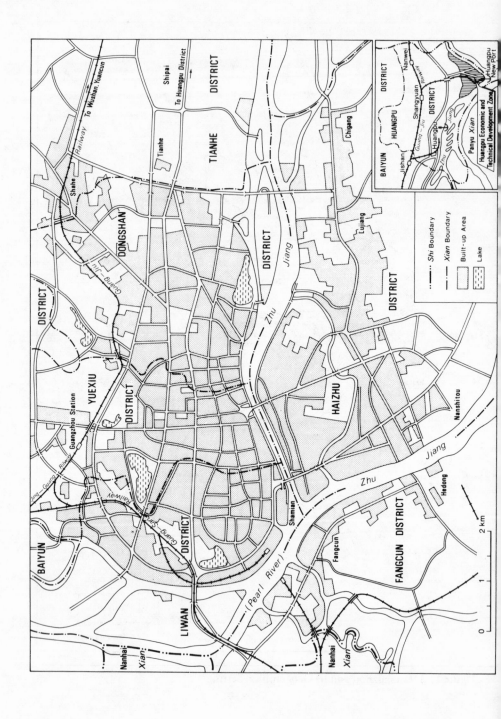

Table 12.1 Population and Area of Guangzhou *Shi:* 1988

SECTOR	TOTAL POPULATION (1,000) (1)	URBAN POPULATION (1,000) (2)	DEGREE OF URBANIZATION (%) (3) = (2)/(1)	AREA (SQ KM) (4)
A. Whole city (B + C + D + E)	5,769.1	3,260.1	56.5	7,434.4
B. Urban district (C + D)	3,490.9	2,811.3	80.5	1,443.6
C. Main city	2,818.5	2,603.9	92.4	321.2
Dongshan	531.3	529.6	99.7	17.2
Haizhu	663.2	601.6	90.6	90.4
Liwan	550.2	548.1	99.6	11.8
Yuexiu	490.4	490.0	99.9	8.9
Huangpu	148.9	102.4	68.8	121.7
Tianhe	296.9	233.6	78.7	108.3
Fangcun	137.6	98.6	71.7	42.6
D. Suburban district (Baiyun)	672.5	207.4	30.8	1,042.7
E. Counties	2,278.2	448.8	19.7	5,990.8
Huaxian	486.6	116.7	24.0	961.1
Conghua	414.3	52.6	12.7	1,974.5
Panyu	737.7	175.7	23.8	1,313.8
Zengcheng	639.7	103.8	16.2	1,741.4

Source: Guangzhou Yearbook, 1989, p. 545.

city under the official policy of promoting maritime trade. Guangzhou reached its pinnacle of development in foreign trade by assuming the foremost place in China; at that time it had a resident foreign population of approximately 10,000. Foreign trade also stimulated local industrial development. By the middle of the Ming dynasty, Guangzhou had become one of the most industrially developed cities in China. During parts of the Ming dynasty (notably from 1522 to 1567) and since 1760 in the Qing dynasty, Guangzhou remained the only port open to foreign trade in China's policy of self-imposed isolation.

In the aftermath of the Opium War, Guangzhou, along with four other treaty ports, was designated open to foreign trade. With that came more overt foreign influences—such as banking, shipbuilding in Huangpu, and industries—culminating in extraterritorial rights of Shamian to the British and the French. As Guangzhou entered the twentieth century, it experienced rapid growth, especially since the 1920s and 1930s, when transport links were greatly improved with the construction of the Guang-San (Guangzhou–Sanshui), Guang-Jiu (Canton–Kowloon), and Jing-Guang (Beijing–Guangzhou) railways, as well as several trunk roads, together with improvements in water transport. Guangzhou's population of 0.85 million in 1901 grew to 1.30 million in 1936. Since 1949 Guangzhou's pivotal status as the southern metropolis has not diminished—indeed, it has expanded under the open policy. The continued historical importance of Guangzhou is inextricably linked to several favorable geographical factors.

Guangzhou is well situated in the subtropical part of Guangdong at the northern fringe of the fertile and populous Pearl River Delta (Figure 12.1). The year-round growing season is conducive to the production of a wide range of agricultural products; indeed the delta is famed for its fish, silk-mulberry, sugar, vegetables, and flowers. A close symbiotic relation has been developed between Guangzhou and the delta: many light industries in the city, such as sugar manufacturing, canned goods, and textiles, depend on the delta for their raw materials and the delta supplies most of Guangzhou's fresh and live subsidiary food products. In return, the delta forms an important part of Guangzhou's extensive market for its manufactured goods. The relation has recently been accentuated given the emerging role of the towns in the delta in value-added development and tertiary economic activities.

The proximity of Guangzhou to Hong Kong and Macau, as well as to Shenzhen and Zhuhai Special Economic Zones, is a critical factor that allows it to benefit from the peculiar advantages of these centers of international finance, commerce, tourism, transport, and communication. The locational advantage of Guangzhou as a "southern window" is reflected in the biannual Canton Fair that has been held since 1957. Guangzhou's strengths in foreign trade and contact are recognized within China, as extensive and close domestic links have been established with every province, *shi,* and autonomous district, many of which have opened representative offices, sometimes factories, in the city. As a consequence, the resource development of many other parts of China, as Guangzhou's wide hinterland, has been intensified.

Another factor in Guangzhou's favor is its excellent transport links. Guangzhou is at the confluence of the Xi, the Bei, and the Dong and through the Pearl River system is connected to the South China Sea. Its outport of Huangpu is one of the best, with a deep-water and lengthy coastline suitable for docking. While waterways traditionally made Guangzhou a natural collection and distribution center, its central role has lately been heightened by progressive improvements in land and air transport, further affirming its status as the "southern gateway."

Since 1978 Guangzhou has been benefiting from overseas Chinese, particularly those from Hong Kong and Macau, who have invested in factories, hotels, trade, and other economic activities. Their direct investments as well as their frequent visits have stimulated Guangzhou's market, consumption, and production, injecting a new vitality to the city.

Finally, in terms of human resources the concentration of educational and research institutions in Guangzhou has facilitated urban development. As a cultural center, Guangzhou has not only a constellation of hundreds of institutions of higher learning but also more than half of the high- and middle-level technical expertise in the province. This trained work force has greatly assisted in the research and manufacture of new products and in providing communication and consultant services in advancing Guangzhou's economic development.

The Urban Structure

The pattern of development in Guangzhou is clearly influenced by several physical factors. Constrained because of separation by the river on the west and hilly terrain on the north, the city has developed essentially in southerly and easterly directions along the Pearl River toward its mouth. This horizontal orientation follows major directions of water and land transport, reinforced by rapid port developments at Huangpu in recent years. In broad terms, following largely administrative delineations, the urban structure may be divided into three sectors.

The first cluster refers to the old city, the best developed and most densely populated part of Guangzhou *shi*. It consists of two subparts: three urban districts north of the Pearl River (Dongshan, Yuexiu, and Liwan) and Haizhu and Fangcun south of it (Figure 12.2). This area witnesses the heaviest concentration of administrative, commercial, financial, and industrial activities. It has been estimated that Liwan, Yuexiu, Dongshan, and Haizhu alone account for more than half of Guangzhou *shi*'s industrial units, value of production, and work force. Of these industrial units, more than 500 were public enterprises, with a concentration in textiles, electric machines, chemicals, and rubber manufacture. Street workshops concentrate on hardware, garment, and daily goods production.

Yuexiu, Dongshan, and Liwan manifest some of the problems faced by large cities in China. In these three districts, the average density of building reached 60 to 80 percent, the population density ranged from 27,000 to 55,000 persons per square kilometer, and the density of traffic averaged 287 motorized vehicles per kilometer—all ranking indicators in Chinese cities. In the most crowded areas, population density reached 120,000 persons per square kilometer. Because of the excessive concentration of population, industry, commerce, and other activities, the area suffers from acute housing shortages, traffic congestion, and land-use conflicts, all imposing restrictions on development. The area is also afflicted by environmental degradation and pollution and low public health standards. These problems are most serious in Liwan. Its inhabitants have the dubious distinction of experiencing the shortest life expectancy in Guangzhou.

Active steps have been taken to redevelop these urban districts. To preserve industrial activities, it has been recognized that there should be high-rise development, reduction of industrial land, and expansion of green space. Residential precincts should be developed with a view to combining commercial development, economic production, and daily living, again emphasizing the need to go high-rise. Haphazard development characterizes the buildings in these districts, however, which are typically low-rise (average 1.9 stories), old (more than half are at least forty years old), and unfit for occupation (10 percent). Thus redevelopment has proved both difficult and expensive. The problem is compounded as many properties are in private hands or owned by overseas Chinese. Recently different approaches have been tried in an effort to pool resources from various sources for the purpose of speeding redevelopment.

To the south of the Pearl River, Haizhu is another old part of the city, a main industrial area. Most of the industrial development since 1949 has centered in this district, in particular in Nanshitou and Chigang. There are more than 5,000 factories, of which 48 had more than 1,000 workers, specializing in such lines as textiles, papermaking, bicycles, sewing machines, and watches. Haizhu district is surrounded on three sides by the waterways of the Pearl River and thus enjoys convenient water transport. It is also blessed with developable land and offers a good basis for industrial development. It must, however, exercise restraint on any further increase of industrial land use, control environmental pollution, and upgrade technology and facilities. In view of the poor living conditions and the deteriorating environment, many workers live north of the Pearl River and contribute to the daily traffic congestion in the bridge areas at peak hours through their commuting. There is thus an urgent need to improve the basic infrastructure and facilities in the district.

Fangcun, situated southeast of the city and beside the main Pearl River waterway, was incorporated into the city only in 1985. It is the main heavy industrial area of Guangzhou. The major heavy industries are metallurgy and shipbuilding, which can be further expanded by including relocated industries from the more congested parts of the city. With its convenient transport facilities, the area around Hedong is especially suitable for further development.

The second cluster of development centers around Tianhe, incorporated since 1985. Situated about 10 km from the city center, Tianhe includes the subdistricts of Wushan, Shipai, Yuancun, and Tianhe. The first two subdistricts have a concentration of institutions of higher learning, whereas Yuancun has seen industrial development since the 1950s, particularly in chemicals, glass, canned goods, and textiles. Tianhe lately has been rapidly developed with a large and modern sports stadium as the focus of attention. Increasingly the emphasis of development will center on education, research, and sports; chemical industries in Yuancun will be subject to strict control or relocated. The third cluster, involving the development of an industrial park in Huangpu, warrants a separate account.

The Huangpu ETDZ

Situated 25 km from the city center, Huangpu began to accelerate development, in 1984, as a designated Economic and Technical Development Zone with a total area of 9.6 sq km. In contrast to a Special Economic Zone, an Economic and Technical Development Zone is created to serve the needs of a city—in particular by importing advanced technologies and expanding productive capacities. Its productive structure is research-oriented with a view to achieving technological improvements. The market is both domestic and overseas; hence the mix of value-added and import-substitution industries. Thus the Huangpu zone was created primarily to improve the industrial structure and quality of products in Guangzhou. (Zhang and colleagues have observed that Guangzhou's improving indexes of economic productivity have been realized so far by quantity rather than quality.)[1] Secondarily, the zone is intended to be a collection point of information about economic development and technology for dissemination to other parts of the country.

Subdivided into six industrial areas, the ETDZ is specifically geared to developing four types of investment: microelectronics, communication technology, biotechnology, and efficiency products like optical fiber. Seven lines of industrial production can be considered for their relatively small investment but large payoff: food products, toys, Chinese and Western patent medicine, fashion, furniture, domestic appliance, and instruments. Existing enterprises depending on imported technology for improvement include the petrol industry, refined chemicals, automobiles, and construction. Finally, there are imported systems, such as telecommunication and pollution treatment, designed to improve urban services.[2]

By 1987, satisfactory progress had been reported of development: sixty-four enterprises with Chinese and foreign investment from thirty countries were engaged in a wide range of production, including quality production of artificial heart valves, integrated circuits, high-grade health food, intelligent toys, goose liver pâté, and silklike embroidered products.[3] Infrastructure continued to be improved, and Nanwei administrative district was developed on schedule.

Development of the ETDZ is not without its share of difficulties, however. Sigel noted in 1986 that the zone lacked a sound economic base and manpower, that it needed enormous capital for development without fully capitalizing on the city's strengths and potential, that Huangpu was externally oriented with relatively weak links to other parts of China, that as much as one-third of the investment had been consumed in infrastructure, that the overall objective of using the zone to revitalize technology in Guangzhou might be jeopardized by the strict directive that each enterprise must be responsible for its financial loss or benefit and that many of the enterprises set up so far were not large consumers of land, public services, or environmentally polluting and could be located, in fact, in more central parts of the city.[4] These caveats underline the inconsistency between theory and practice and between the choice of development strategies in the parent city and the ETDZ. They must be carefully resolved if the development objectives of the zone are to be realized.

By the end of 1989 when the zone had been in operation five years,

318 development projects had been signed with foreign and domestic firms and infrastructure investment worth 1.2 billion *yuan* had been completed. In addition, 115 foreign companies had invested $160 million in the zone. Completed industrial output reached a value of 1.46 billion *yuan* with a profit of 348 million *yuan*. The high-grade products that started in 1987 further expanded and fetched in the five-year period foreign exchange totaling $328 million. In terms of the value of production output, profit level, and foreign exchange earned, the ETDZ is unrivaled in China.[5] In view of the zone's favorable investment climate including sound management practices and the increasing interest of Taiwanese entrepreneurs in Chinese investments, Huangpu along with the city as a whole is reported to have attracted close to one hundred Taiwanese firms, primarily in footwear, toys, and watchmaking.[6] Furthermore, the zone planned to sell 50,000 sq m of land toward the latter part of 1990, following the framework being tried in other open cities.[7]

Emerging Problems

For decades since 1949, the relative lack of public investment in infrastructure and uncoordinated development have left Guangzhou with a legacy of urban ills. Under the open policy, the city has been rapidly transforming itself with accelerated development along many fronts, with the result that some of the problems related to both the urban system and management are exacerbated. This section focuses on conflicting land use, housing shortages, and inefficient transport as examples of the difficulties that can be traced to decidedly different ways of organizing Chinese cities compared with other countries.

Land Use

Apparent irrationalities in land use in Guangzhou mirror a general malaise of Chinese cities, which until recently have emphasized production and industry at the expense of amenities and life improvement. An underlying problem of land-use management is reflected in the distribution of land use by category (Table 12.2). Industrial land (30.32 percent) is by far the largest user; 15 percent would have been reasonable as judged by the experience of other countries. Based on a 1982 survey, a total of 41.6 sq km was devoted to industrial land use in Guangzhou urban districts with the exception of Huangpu and Baiyun. The concentration of factories in the urban area is extremely high, as 56 percent of

Table 12.2   Land-Use Pattern in Guangzhou: 1982

INDICATOR	INDUSTRY	COMMERCE	HOUSING	SCHOOL	HOSPITALS/ CLINICS	ROAD	GREENERY	OTHERS	DONGSHAN, YUEXIU, HAIZHU, HUANGPU, AND BAIYUN	
									UTILIZED LAND AREA	TOTAL LAND AREA
Area (sq km)	41.60	5.56	12.22	16.33	1.45	3.60	1.20	55.1	137.2	1,345.3
Percentage	30.32	4.05	8.91	11.90	1.06	2.63	0.87	40.0	100.0	

Source: Li Xuedian, "Several Questions Related to Land-Use Management in Guangzhou," *Guangdong Social Science Studies* 2 (1987): 80.

all industrial units in Guangzhou *shi* were found in the urban area. On average, twenty-six factory units were found within 1 sq km. A direct consequence of this high concentration of factory units is the juxtaposition of factories with residential areas, temples, schools, and other uses.

Table 12.2 also shows, by contrast, relatively small proportions of land being devoted to hospitals, housing, and commerce, creating special difficulties in these activities. The 4.05 percent allotted to commercial land use is a glaring inadequacy. Official statistics reveal that between 1952 and 1981, retail volume increased almost six times but during the same period there was only a minimal increase in area for commercial use. Within the urban area, many sections are suitable for commercial use but factories have taken over. This inadequacy had been keenly felt in recent years. With the rapid economic development, tertiary economic activities associated with the open policy have been increasing 13 percent a year in production value. Public services are also far from meeting real demands. It has therefore been observed that the pattern of land use is highly irrational and conflicting—hampering urban transport, polluting the environment, and taxing the welfare of the inhabitants.[8]

At the same time, it is paradoxical that within urban Guangzhou serious underutilization of land exists. In fact, the 1982 survey revealed that 25.68 sq km of land, accounting for 18.72 percent of the total urban area, remained empty. The average height of buildings is only 1.89 stories for the urban area, with much potential for more intensified development. Traditionally not only houses but most factories, office buildings, and production-oriented structures were built to low heights. This tendency has recently been markedly reversed as even casual visitors cannot fail to be struck by the new high-rise hotels, office buildings, and residential districts.

The failure to coordinate land-use planning and to take advantage of Guangzhou's natural setting is evidenced in land on either bank of the Pearl River. Potentially a scenic area suitable for residential and commercial use, the riverside has been used for factories and transport (and not efficiently even at that). The shore is full of factories, warehouses, and jetties but has been much underused: many sections are wastefully employed as garbage heaps and for storage of building materials. These uses have destroyed the attractiveness of the place and squandered a valuable urban resource.[9]

The root causes of land-use mismanagement in Guangzhou may be attributed to the facts that it does not have a body of laws governing land use and no system of land rent is practiced. In the absence of a proper authority duly constituted for land-use planning, control, and management, the city has been helplessly vulnerable to demands for land by central and provincial agencies. Since these agencies are often allotted more land than is necessary, there is serious underuse or wastage. These higher-level public agencies have not been deterred from bidding for land over real demand because land is provided free to them.

To combat the problem, a system of land rent or taxes, differentially applied by location and other physical attributes, must be designed. It is, of course, recognized that under a socialist order, private ownership of land is prohibited but payment for the right to use land is allowed. Indeed, the Chinese Constitution stipulates: "Land in the city belongs to the government. Land in the villages and rural areas of the city is in collective possession, unless otherwise spelled out by law as belonging to the government." As Guangzhou has both types of land, it is necessary to work out a system whereby use of such land by the government and collective enterprises should be compensated for by payment of rent. Thus since 1978, in keeping with urban reforms called for by the open policy, land possession and the right to land use have been distinguished. The latter is seen to bring substantial revenue to the government through the collection of land rent. It remains to be seen how effectively this proposal has been applied to Guangzhou.[10]

In 1986 the Chinese government enacted the Law for Land-Use Management. Despite the existence of rules and regulations pertaining to urban land use, they do not apply to central and provincial units—hence posing considerable difficulties to the city administration in land-use control and planning. This perennial problem may have a solution, however, as Guangzhou set up in 1986 a National Land Bureau. This new body must be strengthened if it is to become a proper authority with sufficient legal power and expertise in land-use management to tackle a particularly thorny issue.

Housing

The problem of shelter is one of the most difficult besetting inhabitants in Guangzhou. An acute housing shortage has been felt for decades and is clearly reflected in several key statistics. In 1949 the average living space per person was 4.5 sq m, a figure that was progressively eroded until 1983, when it was bettered for the first time at 4.9 sq m. In 1988 it jumped to 7.29 sq m, reflecting heightened housing construction activity. The reason for this set of figures is not hard to find. Between 1949 and 1976, the annual increase of new housing provision as measured by area was negligible, always well below 2 percent. For the period 1977–1985, however, the figure jumped to 7.48 percent.

Another way of explaining the low housing construction activity is the low proportion of investment it was accorded in relation to total basic construction until 1981. Prior to 1981, housing accounted for a meager proportion ranging from 6.09 to 13.01 percent of basic construction investment from 1950 to 1980. Since 1981, it has risen to over 20 percent every year, reaching a level of 29 percent in 1988.[11] Thus, against a population increase of 89 percent as compared with a 17 percent increase of new housing space in the period 1949–1960, the average living space per person could only decrease. Even in the period 1961–1976, when population actually declined by 18 percent as opposed to a 27 percent increase in new housing provision, the living space per person still fell short of the 1949 average.[12]

Within the old city area there is a clear distinction between districts with respect to the quality of the living environment. In terms of living space and the general environment, Dongshan is the best, as it was previously inhabited by middle-class capitalists and the rich and over half of its households have an average living space of 6.0 sq m per person. The other three districts, namely Haizhu, Yuexiu, and Liwan, are heavily populated. In Yuexiu and Liwan, indiscriminate industrial development since 1949 has seriously affected the living environment.

A recent study of Guangzhou further shows that residential mobility is not a key factor in shaping social areas. In fact, the housing shortage is closely related to a housing allocation system based on the construction and allocation of housing by production/work units. People working for large factories or powerful administrative entities with the financial resources to build dwelling units will have their housing needs satisfied. Those working for small work units will have little or no housing; these people tend to rely on overburdened and overcrowded municipally owned housing.[13] Not surprisingly, under such a system the quality of housing is closely related to occupational groups and some are better housed than others.

A primary reason for the acute housing shortage and the low standard of repairs can be traced to the prevailing notion that housing is an administrative good rather than a commercial good. Consequently, there is a huge element of government subsidy and rents are pegged at artificially low levels. In 1984, for example, the standard of rental per month was 0.26 *yuan* per square meter, accounting for merely 35.9 percent of the real costs in depreciation, repairs, and maintenance. Based on the results of a sample household survey, it was found out that housing rental as a proportion of family income amounted to 11.1 percent in 1956, 7 percent in 1966, and 2.94 percent in 1982. When this is further deducted from a 40 percent government subsidy, the real cost to the family income was only 1.77 percent. As might be expected, the burden on the government has been growing heavier by the year. Low rental has also deprived most housing of needed repairs, shortening its lifespan. Indeed, housing classified as unfit for human habitation increased from 4.04 percent in 1978 to 5.12 percent in 1982.[14]

Clearly one of the first steps to reverse the situation would be to promote housing as a commercial good. Given the low rental charged each family every month, there is a vast stock of funds available for home purchase. Housing construction can be accelerated by including enterprise and individual efforts to complement the government's building programs. At the same time, rents must be raised to more realistic levels to cover necessary costs. When housing provision is made by many channels, the present vicious cycle of low rents, heavy subsidy, poor maintenance, and scarce supply will be broken. It will be replaced by a growing housing market where people pay realistic but affordable rent and where home purchase is a viable option for those who can afford it and for overseas Chinese who may invest for themselves or their relatives in Guangzhou.

Of course, other steps should be taken to improve the housing situation. Increase in population in the urban area must be well controlled to minimize any undue pressure on an already tight housing market. Polluting industries should be resited to locations outside the city, while the old city renews and improves the environment. To persuade urban residents to relocate in the outskirts, these locations must be made attractive by raising housing standards above those generally prevailing in the urban area. Other things being equal, future housing construction in the urban area should be geared to high-density usage involving generally (but not exclusively) high-rise developments. Finally, government expenditure on housing construction should increase or at least stabilize at the level of 20 to 25 percent of the basic construction investment.[15]

Transport

Problems surrounding urban transport in Guangzhou are serious and quite conspicuous, even to the casual visitor. Although these problems have existed for many years, the recent rapid development has exacerbated them. A few facts and figures should bring home the severity of the situation. Between 1939 and 1984, Guangzhou expanded its built-up area 3.7 times and increased its population 1.24 times, both rather modest gains, but mechanized vehicles and nonmechanized vehicles soared by 81 and 44.4 times respectively. The compound effect is keenly felt in traffic as road surface increased in the same period merely 1.2 times in area and 0.74 times in length—hardly an effort to meet the explosive growth of vehicles of all types.[16]

That the authorities in Guangzhou have been remiss in tackling its transport problems is implied in an examination of comparative statistics among Chinese cities. Of the ten largest cities in China, Guangzhou ranked the lowest, in 1984, in both area of road space per person (1.28 sq m compared with Beijing's 3.67, the highest) and length of road in relation to built-up area (1.96 km per square kilometer of built-up area compared with Beijing's 7.26, again the highest).[17] Consequently, traffic congestion went from bad to worse and the speed of public vehicles declined from an average of 20 km per hour in 1965 to 12 in 1984 (6–9 km per hour on some busy roads). While Guangzhou has the highest ratio of mechanized vehicles in relation to population (1 to 24) among Chinese cities, the increase in public transport has not kept up with demand. Public buses increased from 235 in 1949 to 1,435 in 1988, averaging one bus per 2,433 inhabitants. As a result, only 11.7 percent of the inhabitants take public transport. The widespread ownership of bicycles provides personal mobility but contributes to severe traffic jams.

Guangzhou suffers not only from having a large number of vehicles on very limited road space, but these vehicles are themselves problematic. According to estimates undertaken by the authorities, many of the vehicles were imported but already reported scrapped elsewhere and 60 percent of all motor cars were older than fifteen years. Not surprisingly, vehicles are characterized by high gas consumption and low efficiency; the lack of adequate parking facilities leads to indiscriminate parking on roads and sidewalks, further obstructing traffic.[18]

As Guangzhou is a riverine city, it may be expected that water transport will play a vital role in the movement of people and goods. Table 12.3 shows, however, that water transport has declined in relative importance since 1965: it now accounts for only 10 percent and 28 percent of the passenger and goods movement respectively. Water transport has not been developed further because of limited mechanization of Huangpu harbor and the lack of funds and space for expanding the old harbor in

Table 12.3   Comparative Importance of Transport Modes in Guangzhou

YEAR	TOTAL GOODS MOVEMENT (1,000 TONS)	ROAD (%)	WATER (RIVER AND OCEAN) (%)	RAIL[a] (%)	AIR (%)
1965	3,225.1	33.11	37.98	28.90	0.01
1981	7,955.2	65.25	17.95	16.78	0.02
1984	12,480.0	64.00	28.00	8.00	0.02

Source: Guangzhou Planning Committee, "Report on the Survey of Transport," p. 268.

[a]The goods handling volume in 1965 and 1981 was based on ten stations in Guangzhou, whereas the 1984 figure was based on five stations.

the urban area. Still another constraint is silting, which adversely affects any growth in water transport.

As in land use and housing, a more basic problem afflicts urban transport: the lack of a system of management. At present, the city has a multiplicity of agencies and bodies responsible to varying levels of authority. There are more than twenty transport enterprises at central and provincial levels and almost ten entities at the city level, all competing for power and resources without coordination. Their autonomy makes a mockery of any plans for transport planning and control. The crux of the difficulty lies in the fact that central and provincial agencies are not subject to the control of city authorities. Not surprisingly, therefore, some of the transport developments have not been supported by corresponding municipal services and amenities.

To combat these problems, the multilevel conflict of authority must be resolved—a daunting task indeed. Before this is achieved, a transport coordinating agency should be established with responsibility for collecting and reviewing all transport plans from different bodies. Any conflict would be reported back to the bodies concerned, with a request for change. In this way proposals for transport development could be incorporated within a comprehensive urban development plan. At the same time, the increase of mechanized vehicles must be strictly controlled by instituting license fees for vehicles and more stringently controlling and phasing out obsolete vehicles. Moreover, water transport can be elevated in importance by increasing funds to clear waterways of silt, employing tax incentives to promote warehouse construction, and enhancing harbor and other facilities as one of fourteen open cities. A related development is accelerated containerization of Huangpu harbor to increase its cargo handling capacity.[19]

Dai, on the other hand, has envisaged further transport improvement in Guangzhou in two phases.[20] In the first phase, stretching to 1990, emphasis should be put on improving public transport, strengthening transport control, maximizing the existing road network, and gradually limiting bicycle traffic. In short, the approach is to ameliorate transport problems within present constraints. In the next phase, stretching to 2000, the city should devise a system of urban transport and modernize public transport by developing an underground railway and light surface railway. Mass rapid transit is one technological answer to the movement of people within the urban area. Fiscal and coordinated planning with other facets of urban development must precede any development of these otherwise promising ideas.

Rural/Urban Relations

As Guangzhou is rapidly transforming itself, the relation of the city to the rural area has been a focus of attention so that development in both places can be accelerated. This issue may be examined from three perspectives.

Development of Rural Counties

From the standpoint of the economic development of the rural counties, it is noteworthy that traditionally they have pursued a self-sufficient "natural economy model" with the production of staples as the backbone and a relatively low production of subsidiary food products. This economic approach accounted for 75.6 percent of the arable land devoted, in 1980, to food grain production. The dominance of food grains in the county economies springs from a heavy responsibility of contributing 29 percent of the food grain production to the central government. Compared with Shanghai's 17 percent, the provincial average of 24.6 percent, and the national average of 26.9 percent, the required contribution of Guangzhou's rural counties is viewed as excessively high and a burden to the local economy.[21] Consequently, with the exception of vegetables, for which Guangzhou *shi* is self-sufficient, most of the subsidiary foodstuff has to be imported from other provinces and regions (Table 12.4).

Several observers are unanimous in their suggestion that the rural

Table 12.4   Proportion of Agricultural Subsidiary Goods in
Guangzhou Urban District Supplied by the City's
Rural Counties and Elsewhere: 1982

TYPE OF FOOD	FROM RURAL COUNTIES UNDER GUANGZHOU (%)	FROM OTHER PROVINCES OR REGIONS (%)
Pork	36.8	63.2
Beef	10.2	89.8
Mutton	0.2	99.8
Chicken	60.2	39.8
Duck	9.5	90.5
Goose	22.9	77.1
Eggs	19.8	80.2
Milk	100.0	0.0
Average	23.0	77.0

Source: Guangzhou Social and Scientific Research Center (ed.), *Guangzhou Economic Center Studies* (Guangzhou: Institute of Social Sciences of Guangzhou, 1984), vol. 3, p. 411.

counties must reorient their development strategies if they are to develop more rapidly.[22] First, the food grain responsibility to the central government has to be progressively reduced in order to free the counties concerned of "staples as the backbone" approach. Second, the counties should utilize the foreign exchange earned from their rural enterprises to import feed and food grains. Third, production should be promoted for poultry, livestock, the dairy industry, aquaculture, and other local subsidiary food products that are economical in the use of land and high in value of output. Fourth, integrated enterprises of agriculture, industry, and commerce should be developed. These enterprises will enhance the commercial value of agricultural products, minimize the need of middlemen, reduce rural/urban and agricultural/industrial differences, and absorb excess rural labor. It has been estimated that in the eight rural counties of Guangzhou, there is a total labor force of 1.2 million, of whom only 60,000 are employed in the industrial and service sectors, leaving more than 400,000 who can seek more active employment opportunities.

Development of Satellite Towns

Guangzhou's rural/urban relations may also be examined through the development of satellite towns. Early development of satellites during the First Five-Year Plan (1953–1957) was closely related to the objective of redistributing certain land uses, particularly industries, to the suburbs to minimize pollution. This measure led to the development of Nanshitou, Chigang, Lujiang, Hedong, Yuancun, and Shahe on the urban periphery. All these towns have since been virtually integrated with the urban area of Guangzhou. Lack of coordination has prevented a system of satellite towns from being planned and developed to decentralize population and economic activities to dispersed locations, to redistribute productive capacity over a wider area, and to accentuate the centrality of the parent city while alleviating its problems.

To realize these planning objectives, it has been proposed that, for Guangzhou, satellite towns should have a population of 200,000 to 500,000 each and be located at a distance of 20 to 80 km from the parent city, or within two hours of driving. In some cases, the maximum distance can be extended but should not be longer than 100 km. These distances are considered to be effective for satellites exercising their intended roles without being absorbed by the parent city and yet benefiting from their symbiotic relation.

On the basis of these assumptions, six satellites are envisaged as good candidates for development: Huangpu, Shiqiao, Zengcheng, Xinhua, Jiekou, and Qingcheng. Huangpu, described earlier, has the highest development potential because of its industrial and entrepreneurial base, its proximity (25 km) to Guangzhou, and its natural harbor. Its population of 148,851 in 1988 is anticipated to grow to 250,000 or even 300,000 by the end of this century. The next three towns are all located in densely populated counties characterized by a strong economy and relative wealth. Consequently, both population and economic development in these towns are expected to grow rapidly to 150,000 or even 200,000. Jiekou and Qingcheng may not compare as well in favorable factors for economic development. Their leading position to the north of Guangzhou has provided them with good potential for steady growth to centers of 100,000 to 150,000 inhabitants. Thus by the century's end these six satellites could conceivably form the backbone of a system of urban communities with close relations to Guangzhou. They in turn would be surrounded by towns of 50,000 to 100,000 inhabitants, which are yet surrounded by urban places of 10,000 each.[23]

Development of an Economic Region

The third level of discussion takes into account different propositions for the effective operation of a Guangzhou economic region. These propositions stem from the realization that the present administrative region of Guangzhou *shi* is too restrictive, with some counties too small in area, to develop its potential fully. Economic articulation is primarily toward the north and east, as Guangzhou is devoid of any land under its jurisdiction to the west. Xinfeng in the far northeast, under its administrative control prior to redrawing of administrative boundaries in 1988, is not really that close to Guangzhou in economic interaction. But the impact of the loss of four counties, namely Longmen, Xinfeng, Qinyuan, and Fogang, to Guangzhou *shi* in that year is yet to be evaluated. For instance, the artificiality of Guangzhou's administrative boundaries is reflected, in part, by the fact that many of its warehouses, factories, dockyards, residences, and subsidiary food production centers are located in counties in Nanhai and Dongguan outside its administrative boundaries, causing problems and affecting the pace of development.

Two models of Guangzhou economic region have been proposed with the aim of achieving a higher degree of economic rationalization. The first proposition involves five *shi* and eighteen counties: Guangzhou, Foshan, Jiangmen, Shenzhen, and Zhuhai *(shi)* and Longmen, Conghua, Huaxian, Zengcheng, Sanshui, Nanhai, Panyu, Shende, Dongguan, Gaoming, Heshan, Enping, Kaiping, Taishan, Xinhui, Doumen, Zhongshan, and Bao'an (counties). The second proposition is even more extensive, encompassing seven *shi* and thirty counties, building on the *shi* and counties already identified in the first model.[24]

Several factors motivated the proposition for a geographically more extensive Guangzhou economic region. One is the exploration for oil in the South China Sea, which is certain to boost the economic region as a service center. It will stimulate petrochemical industries and indirectly spur tertiary economic activities. Another factor is the industrial and technological coordination within production units in the economic region that will relieve pressure on Guangzhou itself, thus allowing it to further develop tertiary economic enterprises and technology-intensive light industries. Third, as the sovereignty of Hong Kong and Macau will revert back to China, political integration will facilitate economic links of the economic region with overseas and assist in the inflow of investment and technology. Already the economic region delineated above (in either version) is characterized by a relatively high degree of urbanization at 30 percent, a high degree of commercialized agriculture and light industry, wide-ranging external links, and well-developed water transport including the Huangpu harbor. It is therefore not unreasonable to speculate that the Guangzhou economic region may one day become one of the most important developed regions in the world.[25]

Conclusion

Guangzhou under the open policy has witnessed rapid and momentous changes, both functionally and physically. It is still in the throes of a transformation process that is presenting the city with new challenges and opportunities. On the one hand, new functional roles for the city and a multiplicity of new demands have sharpened many of the long-standing problems of service provision, and people's expectations are being raised to new heights as they become increasingly aware of the socioeconomic situation in other cities, especially Hong Kong and Macau. On the other hand, opportunities present themselves for finding new ways of organizing and managing the city, essentially in resolving the contradictions of allowing greater economic efficiency under a socialist order.

In the wider context of rapid change and development in the Pearl River Delta, Guangzhou must seek a role that will accentuate its centrality and leadership position in a system of urban places. As many of these centers are developing a capacity in the industrial and service sectors, Guangzhou should capitalize on its comparative advantage and development potential in large-scale and technology-intensive projects, such as its harbor and airport. Development should proceed along the lines of a division of labor among different-sized urban places so that they will all grow economically or otherwise in concert and not in competition. In this way, Guangzhou's traditionally key position as the southern metropolis will surely be further consolidated and expanded.

Notes

1. Zhang Lie, Ma Junlin, and Ye Duandi, "On Guangzhou's Economic and Technical Development Zone's Characteristics and Measures for Rapid Development," in Guangzhou Economic and Social Development Research Center (ed.), *Exploring the Question of Developing Guangzhou's External Economy and Foreign Trade* (Guangzhou: Zhongshan University Press, 1985), pp. 199–211 (in Chinese).

2. Zhu Senlin, "Several Questions Related to the Development of Guangzhou's Economic and Technical Development Zone," in Guangdong Economic

Society (ed.), *Research on the Strategies for Developing Guangdong's Economy* (Guangzhou: Guangdong People's Press, 1986), pp. 73–83 (in Chinese).

3. Liu Zhihuang, "Guangzhou Economic and Technical Development Zone," *China Trade and Investment* (February 1987), pp. 27–28.

4. Louis Sigel, "Guangzhou Economic and Technical Development Zone and Open Policy," *Guangzhou Yanjiu* 4 (1986): 47–51 (in Chinese).

5. "Five Years of Glorious Results in Guangzhou's Economic and Technical Development Zone," *Shenzhen Special Zone Daily,* 12 December 1989.

6. "Guangzhou Strengthens Attraction to Taiwanese Investment," *Ta Kung Pao,* 12 April 1990.

7. "Guangzhou Relaxes for Foreign Investment," *Ta Kung Pao,* 19 April 1990.

8. Two articles are noteworthy for their forward-looking ideas about land-use management in Guangzhou: Li Xuedian, "Several Questions Related to Land Use Management in Guangzhou," *Guangdong Social Science Studies* 2 (1987): 80–84; and Zhang Guixia, "Questions Related to Land Use in Guangzhou," *Tropical Geography* 6(2) (June 1986): 120–125 (in Chinese).

9. Zhang, "Questions Related to Land Use," p. 121.

10. Li, "Several Questions."

11. See *Guangzhou Economic Yearbook,* various years.

12. Zhang Guixia and Zhang Yingqi, "Housing Construction in Guangzhou and Its Future," paper presented at the Conference on Questions Related to the Acceleration of Housing Construction in Guangzhou, Guangzhou, November 1984 (in Chinese).

13. Anthony G. O. Yeh, Xu Xueqiang, and Hu Huaying, "Social Areas of Guangzhou," paper presented at the annual meeting of the Association of American Geographers, Toronto, 19–20 April 1990.

14. Peng Kunren, "Active Management of Housing Construction in Guangzhou Through Its Commercialization," paper presented at the Conference on Questions Related to the Acceleration of Housing Construction in Guangzhou, Guangzhou, November 1984 (in Chinese).

15. Zhang and Zhang, "Housing Construction," and Peng, "Active Management."

16. Dai Feng, "A Preliminary Study on the Financial Resources for Road Construction in Guangzhou," paper presented at the annual meeting of the Guangzhou Urban Economics Society, Guangzhou, December 1984 (in Chinese).

17. State Statistical Bureau, *Chinese Cities Statistical Yearbook* (Beijing: New World Press, 1986), pp. 35–50, 263–270.

18. Guangzhou Planning Committee and Guangzhou Economic Research Center, "Report on the Survey of Transport and Mobility in Guangzhou," in Guangzhou Economic and Social Development Research Center (ed.), *Develop-*

ment Strategies for Guangzhou's Economy and Society (Guangzhou: Popular Science Press, 1986), pp. 256–276 (in Chinese).

19. Ibid., pp. 266–276.

20. Dai, "A Preliminary Study."

21. Zhu Bingheng, "Models of Development for the Xian Within Guangzhou," *Guangzhou Yanjiu* 2 (1982) (in Chinese).

22. There is broad agreement in the strategies espoused by recent studies published independently, as detailed in this paragraph. See Zhu, "Models of Development"; Wang Liwen, "Questions Related to Guangzhou's Present Agricultural Development and 'City-Oriented Agriculture,' " *Guangzhou Yanjiu* 2 (1982): 1–6; and Guan Xihao and others, "Building an Externally Oriented Urban Agricultural Industry," *Guangzhou Yanjiu* 4 (1986): 26–31 (in Chinese).

23. Zhong Ting, "On the Basic Guidelines of Constructing Satellite Towns in Guangzhou," *Guangzhou Yanjiu* 8 (1986): 16–20. See also Fang Qingfang, "On the Construction and Development of Satellite Towns in Guangzhou," *Guangzhou Yanjiu* 4 (1987): 26–29. The debate on how (and, indeed, whether) Guangzhou should develop satellite towns is far from over, however. Much more conservative views about the need for satellite towns in Guangzhou are found in Ma Minjie, "Guangzhou Should Not Develop Satellite Towns Within This Century," *Guangzhou Yanjiu* 4 (1987): 30–32 (in Chinese).

24. Xu Zice and others, "Propositions for a Guangzhou Economic Zone: Delimitations, Characteristics and Development Trends," *Guangzhou Yanjiu* 1 (1983): 10–17 (in Chinese). See also Wu Yuwen (ed.), *Economic Geography of Guangdong* (Beijing: Xinhua Press, 1985), p. 393 (in Chinese).

25. Xu and others, "Propositions," p. 15.

13 Shenzhen: Special Experience in Development and Innovation

KWAN-YIU WONG, REN-QUN CAI, AND HAN-XIN CHEN

SHENZHEN'S PHENOMENAL GROWTH from small frontier town to the largest Special Economic Zone in China is unprecedented and is very much the product of planned development under the open policy and the drive for modernization. The significance of the Shenzhen experience is not only in urban and economic growth but also in its being a test case for numerous reforms and innovative measures quite foreign to a socialist country. Thus, despite the startling rapidity of its development and its relatively small size (compared with the established cities and metropolises), the growth of Shenzhen has significant implications for the whole country and its experience has drawn widespread attention all over the world.

Shenzhen was originally named Bao'an county. Since the establishment of the People's Republic, the county's frontier position has made it a restricted area which, to a large extent, has suffocated its development and resulted gradually in its lagged growth behind other counties in the Pearl River Delta. Despite Bao'an's fairly advantageous geographical position as the southern gateway of China, the adoption of an isolationist policy and the severing of economic ties with Hong Kong had negative effects on its development. Bao'an remained a small town of 20,000 people with a weak industrial base, low agricultural and industrial production, and none of the facilities of a modern city.

It was not until the end of 1978 that renewed hopes for the development of Bao'an began to emerge. In December of that year, at the Third Plenary Session of the Eleventh Central Committee of the Chinese Communist Party, it was stated that an important strategic policy for the development of the country was to open up to the outside world and to stimulate domestic economic reforms: the concept of Special Economic Zones (SEZs) began to be formulated. To prepare the area for establishment as an SEZ, Bao'an county was upgraded to municipal status (and renamed Shenzhen municipality) and put under the direct rule of the Guangdong provincial government in 1979.

264

In August 1980, the "Regulations on Special Economic Zones in Guangdong Province" were formally approved and promulgated by the Standing Committee of the National People's Congress, and a decision was made to delineate certain areas in Shenzhen for the establishment of an SEZ. Thus Shenzhen municipality (or city) as we know it today is composed of two sections: the Shenzhen SEZ with an area of 327.5 sq km and the non-SEZ section of Shenzhen, which was renamed Bao'an county (Figure 13.1). Shenzhen municipality has a total area of 2,020 sq km.

The change in the city's status, together with the immense size of the Shenzhen SEZ, has created a unique situation for development. As noted earlier, Shenzhen was a small town in the pre-1978 era, with a population of about 20,000 and an annual industrial output of less than $10,000 from twenty-six small factories.[1] The designation of the area as an SEZ is almost equivalent to building a whole new city—an undertaking which would require enormous capital input for infrastructure, the import of large numbers of skilled and semiskilled labor, as well as foreign/domestic investment in various economic activities. The transformation of the city within the last decade, as witnessed in its phenomenal growth in population and the expansion of various economic sectors, is, therefore, a unique experience.

Shenzhen's Environment for Development

Geographical Location

Shenzhen's geographical location is undoubtedly one of the factors that has led to its selection as an SEZ and to its subsequent phenomenal growth. As a laboratory to test the "special zone experiment," a location open to the world at large is essential for the flow of capital, technology, management skills, materials, products, and information. In this respect, Shenzhen is favored with a coastal location and at the same time commands the position as the gateway to South China. Above all, geographical proximity to Hong Kong gives Shenzhen an added advantage unsurpassed elsewhere in China. Hong Kong's position as a leading financial and manufacturing center can provide Shenzhen with diverse information, banking, insurance, and other financial services as well as expertise in modern production and management techniques. Furthermore, geographical proximity allows Shenzhen to make good use of

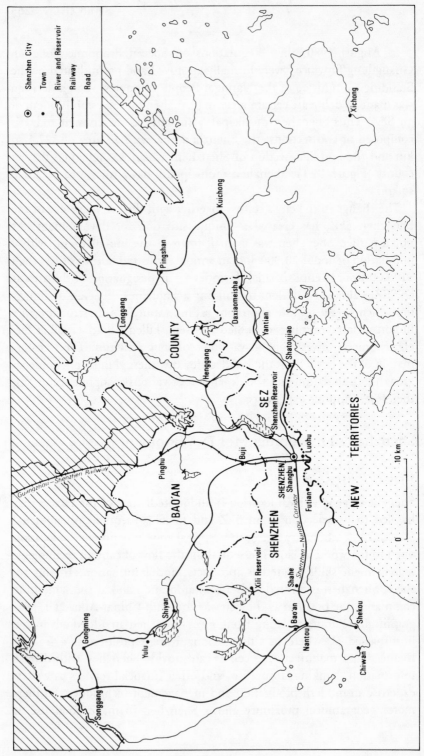

Figure 13.1 Shenzhen Municipality (Shenzhen SEZ and Bao'an County)

Hong Kong's fine harbor and port installations to facilitate the import of raw materials and equipment as well as the export of products. Currently, much of Shenzhen's external transport goes through Hong Kong and this situation is certain to last for quite some time.

Geographical proximity and kinship relations have also been instrumental in attracting the Chinese in Hong Kong to invest in economic production and service industries, to construct and purchase properties, and to patronize the various tourist spots that have flourished in Shenzhen. The significance of this factor is indicated by the fact that, over the years, the bulk of the total investment in the Shenzhen SEZ has come from Hong Kong and has undoubtedly contributed tremendously to Shenzhen's rapid development.[2] The relationship between Hong Kong and Shenzhen is by no means one way, however, for Shenzhen is an important supplier of fresh vegetables and other food products to Hong Kong. Furthermore, Hong Kong's water supply depends partly on the Dong Jiang–Shenzhen water scheme, which has proved essential for the teeming population's domestic use as well as for industrial usage.

Recent developments promise even closer ties between the two areas, as various measures have been implemented to facilitate movement between Hong Kong and Shenzhen. These include, for example, the opening of more border checkpoints, the simplification of entry procedures to China, the increase in transportation links, and the operation of the "Second Line" that separates the SEZ and the non-SEZ areas in China, thus further relaxing entry to the SEZ from outside. As closer economic ties between Hong Kong and Shenzhen are to be expected, it is fair to conclude that Shenzhen's locational advantage in close proximity to Hong Kong will continue to play a crucial role in the future development of the city.

Land Resources

Shenzhen is renowned for being the largest SEZ with an area far exceeding any of the export-processing zones in the developing world. Planned as an integrated and comprehensively developed zone covering primary, secondary, and tertiary activities, land must be available to meet the needs of various construction and development programs. Extensive flat land requiring little reclamation or leveling is essential in reducing development costs and expediting the progress of construction.

Shenzhen is fortunate in being endowed with abundant land resources, much of which are suitable for large-scale urban and economic

Table 13.1   Classification of Land in Shenzhen SEZ

LAND TYPE	AREA (HA)		AREA SUITABLE FOR URBAN DEVELOPMENT (HA)
Flat land	7,260	(22.2%)	7,260
Built-up area	1,740	(5.3%)	1,740
Rolling/undulating	5,730	(17.5%)	2,000
Low-lying	1,460	(4.4%)	—
Hilly	15,910	(48.6%)	—
Water surface	650	(2.0%)	—
Total	32,750	(100.0%)	11,000

Source: Wong and Chu, *Modernization in China*, p. 198.

development. According to estimates made by the Shenzhen government, out of the total land area of 32,750 ha in the Shenzhen SEZ, about one-third (that is, 11,000 ha) is capable of supporting sizable development and construction programs (Table 13.1). Of this area, 9,800 ha has been defined for planning purposes. Such an extensive area provides abundant opportunities and potential. The almost continuous stretch of flat and low-lying land along the Shenzhen–Nantou corridor (extending from Shenzhen town westward through Shangbu, Futian, and Shahe to Shekou and Nantou), where the soil is well structured and leveling is a relatively easy task, offers great potential for large-scale urban development (Figure 13.1).

Outside this area where concentrated development is most likely, Shenzhen's other land resources provide opportunities for a variety of other uses—for instance, the rolling, hilly regions in the north and east are often endowed with great scenic beauty favoring the development of tourist or holiday resorts. Outside the SEZ, vast stretches of agricultural land in Bao'an county are suitable for farming as well as for aquaculture, providing an important base of food production for the city as well as for export. All in all, these abundant land resources constitute the basis for a balanced program of urban development.

Natural Endowment

Apart from the abundance of land for development, Shenzhen is endowed with other natural resources. Building materials such as fine freshwater sand, high-quality granite, marble, and limestone, all required for the rapid development of the city, are readily available locally. Granites and limestones underlie more than half the area of Shenzhen. Apart from the Wushigu quarry, which is now being jointly developed with a Hong Kong company and mainly export-oriented, a number of smaller quarries are in operation to supply local needs.

To support the rapid rate of urban development, Shenzhen is fortunate, in contrast to Hong Kong, to be relatively free from the problem of water supply for both industrial and domestic uses. Shenzhen has a number of river systems, and numerous reservoirs (for example, Shenzhen reservoir and Xili reservoir) have been constructed to supply water to development areas. An additional source of supply is from underground water. In terms of electricity supply, Shenzhen, like many other Chinese cities, experiences frequent power failures. Yet Shenzhen is fortunate to be in close proximity to the Shajiao coal-fired power plant and to have the Daya Bay nuclear power station under active construction. These facilities should prove significant in the long-term development of the city.

The environment of Shenzhen also provides ample opportunities for development of the tourist industry. Shenzhen is endowed with scenic attractions both in the hilly regions and along the coast. Scenic spots in the undulating and hilly regions—set amidst a man-made reservoir such as Shenzhen reservoir, Xili, and Bijia Shan Silver Lake—are well known to most vacationers. In the east, the fine beaches of Xiaomeisha and Dameisha offer great potential for development. In the inland area, the presence of hot springs offers an additional attraction (as in Yulu). The potential for the development of holiday resorts and tourism in Shenzhen is therefore great.

Investment Environment

Being bestowed with the status of a Special Economic Zone is certainly an important factor in Shenzhen's rapid development in the last decade. As Shenzhen was one of the earliest cities to be opened to the outside world and is indeed the largest SEZ in China, it is natural that a huge amount of capital has been injected in the city to improve its investment environment and thereby attract the necessary capital and technology for development. Even though the result may fall short of expectations, efforts to streamline the administrative structure, to provide the required infrastructure, to develop a sound legal and financial system, and to offer preferential treatment and various incentives to investors are unmistakable.

In other words, all-out efforts are being made to create for Shenzhen an environment conducive to foreign investment and consequently to urban and economic development. Thus, in the initial years of the implementation of the open policy, Shenzhen, by virtue of its early start and the powers it possessed to offer concessionary terms to foreign investors, has been able to attract the lion's share of foreign capital in China for development. As of December 1981, for example, 50.6 percent of the total foreign direct investment in China was being attracted to Shenzhen.[3] Although such an advantage is gradually being diluted as more cities and regions are opened up to foreign investment, the momentum of the early start in accelerating the city's economic takeoff should not be underestimated. Furthermore, the huge capital investment in infrastructure (amounting to ca. 4.5 billion *yuan* by 1985) has played an important role in the development of such an extensive area as Shenzhen.

Although the central government has indicated that the cities must rely on their own sources of funding for infrastructure and development, Shenzhen has been able to obtain a larger share of funding from the state (particularly at the start in 1979 and 1980) and has been able to finance its development through a thriving entrepôt and consumer goods trade. As a result, Shenzhen has been able to lay a solid physical foundation to support the rapid urban and economic development of the last decade. Further improvements in the administrative structure, as well as in the financial and legal systems, would certainly be helpful for the creation of an even better investment environment.

Models of Development

Free Zones

The original formulation of Shenzhen's development and growth was very much based on the concept of the free zone system, a concept which embraces a variety of forms ranging from customs-bonded warehouses/factories and export-processing zones to free ports or comprehensive free-trade zones.[4] Shenzhen's model of development, however, does not seem to fit in any of these categories. Unlike the export-processing zones of developing countries, the Shenzhen SEZ is a comprehensive economic development zone of considerable size—not small enclaves within a city engaged in modern export processing of manufacturing production. On the other hand, in comparison with free port cities such as Hong Kong and Singapore, the scope of operation of the Shenzhen SEZ is much more limited. Thus although it evolved from the free zone concept, the Shenzhen SEZ has developed into a unique model of its own, particularly in light of its socialist setting.

While Shenzhen's form of development may be different, its objectives and strategies are not much divergent from the other members of the free zone family. Foreign capital is being attracted by means of concessionary terms and preferential treatment. Export-oriented economic activities are encouraged to achieve and accumulate foreign exchange earnings. The promotion of international economic cooperation and the subsequent attainment of technology transfer and domestic linkage are also sought after. The stimulation of employment and regional development are further common objectives. Although foreign investors are taking a somewhat cautious approach to this new system in China, its adoption has undoubtedly contributed to the city's accelerated growth in the last decade.

At the same time, one cannot deny that its operation is confronted with a host of problems. Bureaucratic/administrative complexity and inefficiency, inadequate infrastructure, and the lack of a sound legal and financial system are some of the well-known problems. In China, the proliferation of open cities and regions during the last few years has gradually eroded the original advantages of the Shenzhen SEZ, which is now becoming increasingly less "special." As a result, many of the objectives behind the original conception of development have not been accomplished, an outcome which has serious implications for the future growth of the city. Thus the initial model of development has fallen short of expectations within a decade. New strategies and new concepts of development are, therefore, being explored.

In light of the inherent problems of the Special Economic Zone, a new type of investment zone, known as the Bonded Industrial Zone, was conceptualized in 1987 and put into action in 1988. The Shatoujiao Bonded Industrial Zone—the first of its kind in China—is designed to provide an even better investment environment than the Special Economic Zones and open cities. It has five major characteristics: goods moving directly to and from Hong Kong will be duty free; all applications for investment will be processed within one week by the administrative committee of the zone without having to go through a number of departments before approval; overseas investors can recruit their own work force without going through the Shenzhen Labor Bureau; the zone will be managed by its own regulations; and products from the zone are basically meant to be exported only.

The whole idea is designed to attract additional foreign investment by providing better incentives and reducing the long and tedious application procedures now faced by many overseas companies. It is also hoped that more high-technology industries will be attracted. Construction work for the 200,000-sq-m site started in December 1987; total investment from the Shenzhen municipal government is estimated to be around 300 million *yuan*. Regulations for administering the Shatoujiao Bonded Industrial Zone were announced by the Shenzhen municipal government on 1 July 1988.[5] New hopes of reviving investment interest in Shenzhen are expressed, but the result of this new model of development remains to be seen.

Experiments in Modernization

Both the Special Economic Zone and the Bonded Industrial Zone are common international concepts, especially in the developing countries. They are relatively foreign systems to socialist countries, however, particularly to China, which has closed its doors to the outside world for a long period of time. Therefore, the models chosen for Shenzhen following the implementation of the open policy are meant rather as laboratories to test whether such concepts can be put into effect in China to speed the process of modernization the country so urgently needs. As a result, a number of innovative measures have been tested in Shenzhen and subsequently introduced to other parts of China. Thus not only has Shenzhen shown certain unique features of development compared with other cities, but its experience also has implications for future urban development in China. Since these innovative measures initiated in Shenzhen have been discussed elsewhere,[6] here we shall mention only the more important ones.

One pioneering feature is the introduction of contract labor and a new wage system whereby workers and staff are hired on contract rather than permanently and a job-specific and floating wage rate replaces the rigid system of fixed salaries. The Bonded Industrial Zone is given even greater autonomy in recruiting and managing its staff. This has resulted in breaking the "iron ricebowl" and improving labor discipline and productivity. Another well-known practice first tried in Shenzhen is the tender system in construction works whereby tenders are invited from all over the country and the job is awarded to the most cost-effective construction team. This became a common practice in Shenzhen as early as 1982 after being initiated in July 1981. Other praiseworthy reforms in Shenzhen include the commercialization of the housing stock and the introduction of the home purchase scheme for its workers. This is an important change from the original practice of heavy state subsidies of workers' housing and has led to a new attitude: workers should receive less subsidy but higher wages. This practice and the changing attitude toward housing will have far-reaching effects on the housing policy in China.

Another innovative move in Shenzhen is the launching of land sale reform which aims to make the best use of available land for development. Replacing and supplementing the former leasing system, future land transactions in Shenzhen will be through public tender, land grant, private treaty, or public auction. The first piece of government land was sold by tender on 9 September 1987.[7] The first land auction ever in the People's Republic took place in Shenzhen on 1 December of the same year. More sites were put on sale by various means in 1988, thus taking a great step forward in the reform of land and land management in the city as well as in China.

A number of other practices now common in China have been working in Shenzhen for years—for example, the separation of commercial functions from the state and government departments, the enactment of laws and increasing emphasis on the role of the legal system, and the democratic election of factory managers. Shenzhen has been performing very well in these aspects compared with other cities of China. It is thus fair to conclude that Shenzhen has become a pacesetter for the process of modernization in China. Clearly its experience will be of great value to urban and economic development in other parts of the country.

Population Growth and Characteristics

Shenzhen's development has been characterized by a high rate of urbanization and population growth within the last decade. Although such phenomenal urban growth is quite unusual in most developing nations or in other parts of China, it is not totally unexpected in Shenzhen. In choosing a small frontier town for establishment of a Special Economic Zone, clearly efforts were made to attract people from other parts of China to join the work force in Shenzhen and partake in the city's economic construction programs. The influx of migrants to Shenzhen within a relatively short period of time is, therefore, understandable.

Before 1978, what is now the Shenzhen SEZ could be considered a rural settlement with a relatively small urban population concentrated mainly in Shenzhen town and Nantou. According to figures cited by Zheng and colleagues,[8] of the total population of 68,166 in 1978, only 40 percent could be classified as urban. Since the designation of the SEZ, the proportion of urban population began to increase rapidly. Of the total population of 84,057 at the end of 1980, about 57 percent was classified as urban.[9] The 1982 Chinese census also provided figures on urban and rural population in Shenzhen; but due to the adoption of a different definition for urban population, they cannot be directly compared with previous figures. By employing the conventional definition of urban, however, it is estimated that the percentage share of urban population in Shenzhen in 1982 increased to about 70 percent.[10]

Rapid urbanization is accompanied by a high rate of urban growth. Table 13.2 shows the increase of population in Shenzhen since its designation as an SEZ. Several points are particularly noteworthy. First, most of the population growth occurred in the SEZ section of the city, the main center of attraction for the migrants. The non-SEZ section (that is, Bao'an county) has a fairly stable population, registering only a slight increase over the years. From 1979 to 1987, population in the SEZ increased by 305 percent, an average growth of 27,000 persons a year. During the same period, population in Bao'an county grew by only 11 percent, an annual increase of around 3,400 people. Due to the originally small population base and low natural increase rate, most of the population growth in the Shenzhen SEZ has been achieved by the massive influx of migrants, which accounts for over 90 percent of the net increase.[11] The main causes of this migration are the economic opportunities, higher wages, and better amenities and environmental conditions that are being perceived as prevalent in the SEZ.

The second point to note is that the ratio of working population to total population has shown a notable increase over the past few years. This indicates that increasing numbers of the new migrants are jobholders, reflecting the availability of employment opportunities in this developing city. In fact, Shenzhen has recruited many professionals and work-

Table 13.2   Population Growth in Shenzhen Municipality:
                1978–1987

YEAR	SHENZHEN	SEZ		NON-SEZ
Permanent Population				
1978	333,600			
1979	312,600	70,900	(23,300)[a]	241,700
1980	320,900	84,100	(26,500)	236,800
1981	333,900	98,300	(38,500)	235,600
1982	354,500	128,600	(66,800)	225,900
1983	405,200	165,000	(107,600)	240,200
1984	435,200	191,400	(154,400)	243,800
1985	478,600	231,900	(193,100)	246,700
1986	514,500	257,400	(221,300)	257,100
1987	556,055	286,927	(273,600)	269,128
Temporary Population				
1985	402,900	237,900		165,000
1986	421,133	231,300		189,800
1987	598,410	312,677		163,032

Source: Shenzhen SEZ Yearbook (1985–1988).

[a]Figures in parentheses are working population.

ers from other parts of the nation, including a substantial number of
transfers from other units, particularly state-owned enterprises. Apart
from the permanent population, Shenzhen has nearly an equal number
of temporary residents, both in the SEZ and in Bao'an county. In the
early years, most of these temporary residents were construction workers
recruited for the various development projects. In 1987, of the total
number of 598,410 temporary residents in the whole of Shenzhen, 50
percent were engaged in manufacturing activities, 16 percent in construction, 12 percent in agriculture, and 11 percent in commercial and
service industries.[12] Considerable internal movement also occurs within
the Shenzhen municipality as many residents of Bao'an county have
moved to the SEZ to take up jobs as manual workers or service personnel.
It has been estimated that about 13 percent of the manual workers in the
Shenzhen SEZ in 1985 came from Bao'an county.[13]

Due to the very nature of Shenzhen's development and the fact that
most of the population is made up of migrants of working age,
Shenzhen has a relatively young age structure. At the beginning of 1986,

the median age in Shenzhen was 23.8 and the average age 27.9 (compared with the figures of 22.5 and 27.2, respectively, recorded in the 1982 census).[14] This is mainly because Shenzhen has attracted a young labor force to work in the newly introduced light industrial sector. Young female workers are particularly noticeable in such industries as electronics, textiles, and garments, which form the backbone of Shenzhen's manufacturing structure today.

In the near future, Shenzhen's population is expected to maintain a fairly rapid growth rate. According to the revised Social and Economic Plan of the Shenzhen SEZ, the zone's target population is set at 800,000 by the year 2000. As most of the increase in population will continue to be accounted for by migration, particularly of the working population, the actual growth in Shenzhen's population in the years to come will depend, to a large extent, on the prevalence of employment opportunities which, in turn, rests on the city's ability to maintain a steady rate of economic growth—and this will depend, to a certain degree, on Shenzhen's success in attracting foreign investment to actively engage in its development programs. The future growth and distribution of population in Shenzhen are therefore quite uncertain and partly reliant on factors beyond the direct control of the government.

Shenzhen's rapid increase in population, its substantial numbers of temporary residents, and the nature and structure of its population will inevitably bring about a variety of problems. The provision of housing, medical, recreational, educational, and other facilities to the permanent residents is already a great burden to the government. Providing services to the temporary residents further aggravates the situation. Other social problems arising from the large number of young, single, female workers of courtship age have already become apparent.[15] Problems of social stratification, too, should not be overlooked.[16] In short, the anticipated growth of more than 700,000 people within two decades in the Shenzhen SEZ is indeed a rare experience and will undoubtedly tax the resources of the city and at the same time engender social and environmental problems.

Economic Development

Economic Structure

As a result of rapid urban development since the adoption of the open policy and the designation of the Special Economic Zone, Shenzhen's economic structure has witnessed significant changes. In 1979, the largest economic sector, in terms of employment, was in agriculturally related activities, followed by the commercial and service sector. Manufacturing, employing about 5,600 persons, was a distant third. With the development of the city, as one might expect, agriculture's dominance began to decline. On the other hand, both the manufacturing and the commercial/service sectors recorded fast rates of growth, particularly the former. From 1979 to 1987, manufacturing employment increased more than twenty-six times.[17] Most of the increase occurred within the SEZ section of the city. Also worth mentioning is the construction industry, which registered booming growth in the early stages of the city's development as a result of the need to provide infrastructure and construct a large number of capital development projects. This increase has slackened, however, and in fact has begun to show a decline since 1985.

After almost a whole decade of evolution, the primary objective of developing Shenzhen into a manufacturing production center has largely been accomplished. The economic structure of the city, in terms of employment at the end of 1987, is depicted in Table 13.3. The importance of manufacturing is evident: it employs almost half of the work

Table 13.3   Employment Structure by Economic Sector in Shenzhen: 1987

ECONOMIC SECTOR	SHENZHEN MUNICIPALITY (IN 1,000S)	SHENZHEN SEZ (IN 1,000S)	% IN SEZ
Agriculture, fishing, forestry	10.9	4.0	36.7
Manufacturing	148.0	121.2	81.9
Construction	26.2	24.9	88.5
Transport and communication	15.0	14.8	95.0
Commercial, material supply, storage	49.6	43.9	98.7
Housing, real estate	28.5	28.1	98.6
Health, sports, social services	7.2	6.1	67.9
Education and cultural activities	11.2	7.6	89.1
Research and technical services	1.4	1.3	87.8
Finance and insurance	5.5	4.9	92.9
Government and community	18.8	16.5	84.7
Geological survey and exploration	0.5	0.5	100.0
Total	322.9	273.6	84.7

Source: Shenzhen SEZ Yearbook, 1988, pp. 488–489.

force, followed by the commercial/service, housing/real estate, and construction industries. Again, the figures indicate that most of the employment is being generated within the SEZ rather than in Bao'an county; the only exceptions are agriculture, fishery, and forestry.

One of the major objectives of setting up the Shenzhen SEZ is to attract foreign investment to boost the city's economic growth. Thus the amount and direction of foreign direct investment have important implications for the economic structure of the city. It has been found that in the early stages of Shenzhen's development, most of the foreign investments were channeled into such areas as housing/real estate and tourism in which the period of return is short and the profit margin high—rather than in manufacturing, which usually requires a large capital outlay and a long period of return.[18] With the gradual maturing of the economy, however, the pattern of foreign investment has changed over the past decade. As indicated in Table 13.4, by the end of 1987 manufacturing accounted for almost two-thirds of the total realized foreign investment in Shenzhen, with another one-quarter going to the financial and insurance sector. Foreign investment in real estate and tourism, on the other hand, has declined considerably. Again the SEZ attracts almost all the foreign investment. Overall, Shenzhen has basically been developed as a manufacturing, financial, and commercial center in South China.

Table 13.4   Actual Amount of Direct Foreign Investment in
Shenzhen: 1987

ECONOMIC SECTOR	SHENZHEN MUNICIPALITY ($ MILLION)	SHENZHEN SEZ ($ MILLION)
Agriculture, fishery, forestry	2.32	2.31
Manufacturing	252.16	244.44
Construction	2.39	2.26
Transport and communication	4.32	4.00
Commercial etc.	3.87	3.87
Housing, real estate	4.54	4.54
Finance and insurance	102.47	102.47
Others	32.42	29.91
Total	404.49	393.80

Source: Shenzhen SEZ Yearbook, 1987, pp. 481–482.

Manufacturing Development

Although the Shenzhen SEZ was originally to be developed as a comprehensive economic entity, industrial growth has been accorded top priority and industrial production will be the backbone of Shenzhen's economy. It has been reiterated by the mayor of Shenzhen and other government officials that since manufacturing is the fundamental production activity on which the generation of economic benefits for the city depends, industry should be attracted by all possible means. In the early years of development, the lack of an efficient administrative, legal, and financial system and inadequate infrastructure have deterred many potential investors from putting large sums of capital into manufacturing undertakings. As a result, most of the investments in manufacturing were confined primarily to small enterprises engaging in intermediate processing or assembly work.

Since 1981, however, a number of developments have helped to change the picture. Notable among these were the enactment in November 1981 of four sets of SEZ provisional regulations governing labor and wages, entry and exit, business registration, and land administration, as well as a complete reorganization of the administrative structure in 1982. Furthermore, the drafting of the Social and Economic Development Plan and the organization of various meetings on industrial development by the Shenzhen government have made the objectives and directions of growth quite clear. The importance of industrial production has been strongly emphasized. Consequently, an increasing amount of foreign direct investment has entered the manufacturing sector, which by now has attracted the largest proportion of overseas capital. At the same time, the value of industrial production has risen to a new high level every year, as shown in Table 13.5.

Several features are worth noting from Table 13.5. First, the value of industrial production has been increasing at a fast rate ever since the adoption of the open policy. Due to the overheated economy and the financial squeeze in 1985, however, the rate of growth has slackened in recent years. Second, most of the industrial production comes from the SEZ section of the city, which now accounts for some 87 percent of the total value of production—indicating that growth of manufacturing in Shenzhen is led mainly by the SEZ. For reasons already mentioned, the takeoff period of industrial development was in 1981; only since that year has the value of industrial production exceeded that of agricultural production.

Table 13.5   Value of Industrial Production in
Shenzhen: 1979–1987

YEAR	SHENZHEN MUNICIPALITY (MILLION YUAN)[a]	SHENZHEN SEZ (MILLION YUAN)[a]
1979	60.61	29.66
1980	84.44	51.21
1981	242.82	202.53
1982	362.12	299.12
1983	720.41	577.02
1984	1,814.51	1,474.75
1985	2,674.29	2,355.51
1986	3,565.08	3,111.04
1987	5,762.89	4,990.11

Source: Shenzhen SEZ Yearbook (1985–1988).

[a]At 1980 constant value.

Industrial Location. Industrial development in Shenzhen can generally be classified into three broad regions: the Shenzhen SEZ; the Shekou Industrial Zone; and industrial districts in other parts of the municipality (that is, in Bao'an county). (See Figure 13.2.) The former two
entities belong to the SEZ section of the city and enjoy a high degree of
autonomy in dealing with foreign investment. However, there are some
complications in this structure. Shekou, although physically part of the
SEZ, has gained the status of a separate zone managed by the China
Merchants' Steam Navigation Company (CMSN) of Hong Kong. Nego-
tiations for development are often handled in Hong Kong and CMSN
has the authority to make decisions on overseas investment projects in
Shekou. In fact, apart from certain indigenous industries in Luohu and
Shenzhen town, Shekou is the first industrial district in Shenzhen to be
developed systematically. With regard to industrial districts in Bao'an
county, the special zone policy in China allows a certain degree of flexibility in its implementation by offering preferential treatment to firms
setting up in districts adjacent to, but outside the confines of, the SEZ.
Thus, although disadvantaged by their inferior infrastructure, districts
such as Shajing, Pinghu, Buji, Longgang, and Henggang have all been
planned as comprehensive industrial estates which have the positive
effect of spreading manufacturing development more evenly throughout
the city.

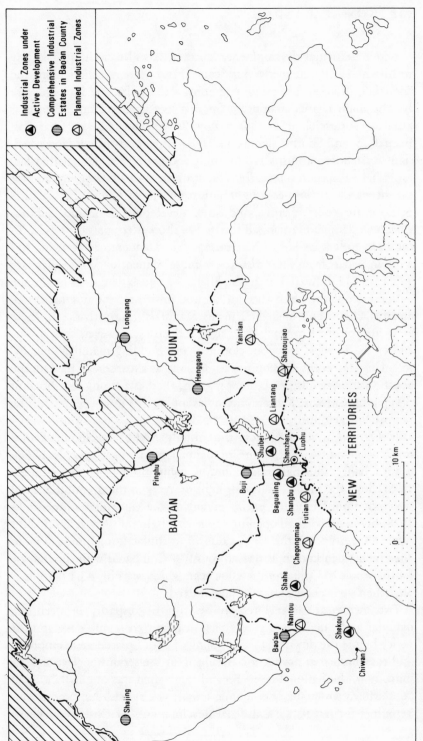

Figure 13.2 The Location of Industrial Districts in Shenzhen

Active industrial development, however, is still concentrated largely within the SEZ, particularly in the central and western sections along the Shenzhen–Nantou corridor. Topography, accessibility, and infrastructure are the main factors accounting for this locational pattern. The most intensively developed areas are now in Shekou, Shahe, Shangbu, Bagualing, and Shuibei (Figure 13.2). Apart from sufficient land provisions for modern and space-consuming industries, standard flatted factories have also been constructed (for example, in Bagualing) to cater for the needs of smaller-scale light industrial enterprises. Other districts planned for comprehensive industrial development include Nantou, Chegongmiao, and Futian, all situated in the western part of the city. In the east, industries are to be developed in Liantang, Shatoujiao, and Yantian. Apart from these districts, it must be mentioned that there are also a few old industrial centers in Shenzhen which date from before the designation of the SEZ. They are located in or near the original urban areas of Luohu and Shenzhen town. Manufacturing activities in these areas are confined to small-scale light industries, however, such as arts and crafts, textiles, footwear, clothing, and building materials. Finally, following the recent development of Chiwan as a rear service base for the South China Sea oil exploration program, there is a strong likelihood of developing Chiwan, Mawan, and adjacent regions into a center for the petrochemical industry.

Industrial Structure. From the initial period of development until today, the industrial structure of Shenzhen has been heavily biased toward light industrial production. A comparison of statistics (Table 13.6) shows the predominance of light industry in the overall industrial structure throughout the entire period of the city's development. In 1978, before the official opening of the city, light industry accounted for some 83 percent of the total value of manufacturing production in Shenzhen, then known as Bao'an county.[19] Compared with the statistic for the whole of China for the same year, which was only 43.1 percent,[20] Shenzhen's percentage was very high indeed.

Two factors are largely responsible for the disparity between the national and Shenzhen figures. First, China's economic development policy before the downfall of the "Gang of Four" placed great emphasis on heavy industrial production, resulting in the serious neglect of light industry at the national level. Second, Shenzhen was originally a small border town whose major economic activity was agricultural production. Resources for large-scale industrial development, particularly of heavy

Table 13.6   Changes in the Industrial
Structure of Shenzhen:
1978–1987

YEAR	PERCENTAGE OF TOTAL VALUE OF PRODUCTION	
	LIGHT INDUSTRY	HEAVY INDUSTRY
1978	82.9	17.1
1979	86.7	13.3
1980	83.5	16.5
1981	93.8	6.2
1982	87.9	12.1
1983	79.9	20.1
1984	81.0	19.0
1985	81.7	18.3
1986	80.8	19.2
1987	79.4	20.6

Source: Shenzhen SEZ Yearbook (various years).

industry, were very limited. As a result, statistics for Shenzhen's industrial production revenue in 1978 show that food products accounted for almost two-thirds of the total.[21]

With the beginning of economic takeoff in 1981, the share of light industry in the total value of manufacturing production in Shenzhen increased to about 94 percent. Several factors are found to be responsible for such growth in the light industrial sector. First, changes in China's economic policy since 1978 have led to a readjustment of the economic development strategy, shifting the emphasis to light rather than heavy industry. Figures for the whole of China show that the share of light industry in total manufacturing production increased from 43.1 percent in 1978 to 51.3 percent in 1981.[22] Second, in the initial period of development of the SEZ when details of the investment environment were not well known outside China, investors were not prepared to engage in heavy industrial production that required considerable capital expenditure. On the other hand, labor-intensive light industries such as electronics found favor among overseas investors who can capitalize on the cheap labor resources in the area. Third, due to the lack of an efficient administrative and legal system in the formative period, government officials have given greater consideration to the interests of potential investors than to the city's needs or development goals. As a result, a large number of small-scale light industries, some polluting and obsolete, were introduced into Shenzhen to make quick profits from a minimum amount of capital input.

With the gradual maturing of the economy, the share of light industry in the total value of manufacturing production began to drop to an average of about 80 percent in recent years. The percentage is still much higher than the national figure, however, for only about 47 percent of China's industrial production is in the light industrial sector.[23] In the immediate years to come, it is expected that Shenzhen's industrial structure will still be dominated by light industry.

Even within the light industrial sector, changes in the main types of manufacturing have been very noticeable since the establishment of the SEZ. In 1978, production was dominated by the food processing industry, followed by building materials, timber, paper, and textiles.[24] Production from the electronics industry was negligible. In the wake of the establishment of the SEZ, however, the electronics industry has witnessed meteoric growth. (Capital and expertise come largely from neighboring Hong Kong.) In 1987, the electronics industry accounted for 45 percent of the total value of manufacturing production in Shenzhen (Table 13.7). It also occupies a significant position at the national level. Shenzhen's electronics production ranks second only to Shanghai and accounts for about 6 percent of the national total value of production. In terms of the export of electronics products, Shenzhen ranks first among Chinese cities, contributing about 67 percent of Guangdong province's export and about 15 percent of the national export of electronics products.[25]

More traditional industries in Shenzhen, including textiles and garments, the mechanical industry, and food and beverages, although overshadowed by the electronics industry, still remain core components in the city's industrial structure. Nevertheless, despite the gradual diversification of industries in Shenzhen since the establishment of the SEZ, electronics will remain the leading industry for years to come. But even within the electronics industry there are great opportunities and a growing trend toward product diversification and sophisticated production techniques.

Achievements in Economic Development

Compared with other major cities in China, Shenzhen's economic development suffers from a late start, a weak economic base, and a peripheral location. Even so, the implementation of the open policy has allowed

Table 13.7   Value of Production by Major Types of Industries in
Shenzhen: 1987

TYPE OF INDUSTRY	VALUE OF PRODUCTION (MILLION *YUAN*)	% OF TOTAL
Electronics	2,601.91	45.15
Textiles and clothing	593.73	10.30
Mechanical and machinery	409.41	7.10
Food and beverages	315.08	5.50
Petroleum, chemical, pharmaceutical	255.05	4.40
Metal and metal products	249.06	4.30
Education, sporting goods	245.42	4.30
Feedstuff	204.25	3.50
Plastics	200.76	3.50
Paper and printing	155.12	2.70
Building materials	120.89	2.10
Others	412.21	7.15
Total	5,762.89	100.00

Source: Shenzhen SEZ Yearbook, 1988, pp. 471–472.

Shenzhen to take advantage of its close locational and social ties with Hong Kong to undertake a course of rapid urban and economic development unprecedented elsewhere in China. Perhaps one of its major achievements is its success in attracting foreign capital. In the initial phases of the open policy, as noted earlier, the power to offer concessionary terms to foreign investors was confined to a few localities, notably the SEZs. It has been reported, for example, that Shenzhen alone accounted for 50.6 percent of total direct foreign investment in China as of December 1981.[26] As the open policy gathered momentum, it is not surprising to find that foreign investment gradually spread to other open coastal cities and metropolises and Shenzhen's percentage share was reduced accordingly. Nevertheless, Shenzhen still leads the nation in the amount of direct foreign investment actually realized, exceeding Beijing and Shanghai by more than 150 percent and accounting for some 17 percent and 44 percent of the national and Guangdong provincial total respectively.[27] It is, therefore, fair to conclude that Shenzhen has made positive contributions to the attraction of foreign capital to China, particularly from Hong Kong and Macau.

In terms of employment generation, although Shenzhen's work force is quite insignificant compared with the national total, there is little doubt that economic development in Shenzhen within the last decade has enlarged job opportunities—as witnessed by the continual growth of employment figures and by the large number of temporary residents engaged in various economic activities in the city (see Table 13.2). A high proportion of this employment is in production activities, particularly in manufacturing, which has helped to establish a firm economic base for the city.

As an SEZ, Shenzhen is responsible for promoting international economic cooperation and technical exchange. Thus the introduction of advanced foreign technology and scientific management methods is of vital concern. Apart from serving as a window to import foreign technology, it has also been emphasized that the SEZ should establish strong backward and forward linkages with the rest of the economy of China. Thus enterprises in Shenzhen are expected to import, digest, and absorb high-level technology from foreign firms and then diffuse this knowledge to other parts of the country. At the same time, these enterprises are encouraged to utilize resources and technical know-how available in the hinterland regions of China. Shenzhen has also provided domestic linkage in the sense that incentives are offered to induce Chinese firms from various parts of the country to invest in the city. Through their interaction with foreign firms, a higher degree of technical exchange can be achieved. As a result, a substantial number of development projects in Shenzhen are associated with the central government ministries and domestic firms from various provinces in China.

Although effective technology transfer and domestic linkage take time to accomplish, Shenzhen has already paved the way for their ultimate achievement. Among the various forms of foreign financial participation, it is the cooperative development and equity joint-venture projects that provide the best opportunities for the accomplishment of these aims. In Shenzhen, they accounted for 94 percent of the total direct foreign investment in 1987.[28] Finally, the various reforms and innovative measures noted earlier have produced significant impacts on China, and Shenzhen has become the pacesetter for the process of modernization in China's coastal open cities.

Problems and Prospects

The designation of Shenzhen as one of the cities to test the concept of Special Economic Zones in a socialist country—and its subsequent phenomenal growth—will undoubtedly bring about a variety of problems which require careful scrutiny. Developing from a small frontier town with a very weak economic base, Shenzhen is grossly inadequate in capital and infrastructure. To make the place attractive to foreign investors, certainly resources must be spent on infrastructure construction. Due to the extensive size of the SEZ and the city, however, the problems of insufficient transport and communication linkages and an unreliable electricity supply remain unsolved. Despite much effort, Shenzhen has not been able to produce economic returns commensurate with the capital costs invested in its development. It has been reported that the Shenzhen SEZ has cost the government 4.5 billion *yuan* but has attracted only $700 million of foreign capital.[29]

These problems have made the original objectives of developing Shenzhen into an industrial-based and export-oriented economy difficult to achieve within a short period of time. Thus in the initial phase of the city's development when capital is inadequate to support growth, a lot of effort has gone into the commercial, trade, real estate, and tourism businesses to accumulate the capital required for infrastructure and industrial development. As a result, capital on "productive" and export-oriented activities has been relatively neglected and the ability to accumulate foreign exchange from export has been rather modest. In fact, dependence on such a trade-based economy has drained large amounts of foreign exchange—as exemplified by the huge volumes of imported foreign goods (durable consumer goods, such as electrical appliances, and clothing) on sale at Shenzhen in its early stages of development at a price lower than elsewhere in China. Moreover, the incentives offered to overseas investors tend to outstrip the foreign exchange earnings. Exemption from duties, licenses, fees, the long tax holiday, the repatriation of profits in full, low wages, and land utility charges all tend to negate the purpose of accumulating foreign exchange. A reorientation of the development program has been under way since 1985, however, and many of the problems have been rectified. Perhaps an economy based on industrial production, as well as an outward-looking and export-oriented economic structure, will be fully implemented in the not-too-distant future.

Other major problems encountered in the course of Shenzhen's development are well known: the absence of well-trained professional management staff, the lack of coordination between departments, unclear division of responsibilities, and power struggles among officials and units. The administrative structure is not always clear to foreign investors (the relationship, for example, between the Shenzhen SEZ and the She-kou Industrial Zone). Moreover, to develop Shenzhen into an export-led economy means breaking into the international market and competing with other developing economies in Asia. In the face of keen competition from the four "Little Dragons" of Asia (Hong Kong, Singapore, Taiwan, and South Korea) and given the protectionism prevailing in many developed nations of the world, the road ahead will not be an easy one. The need to compete for foreign capital is equally acute. A survey by a Japanese firm,[30] for example, indicates that the cost of running a business in Shenzhen is as high as in Hong Kong, but the investor will certainly find that the latter has a lot more to offer than the former.

Rapid economic development often brings about a phenomenal rise in land values and rents as well as the price of commodities. Moreover, Shenzhen has a rather confusing currency system with renminbi *(yuan)*, the foreign exchange coupon, and the Hong Kong dollar all in circulation at the same time. The varying demands on these currencies have resulted in black-market exchange rates and illegal transactions. Stories of white-collar crime, especially bribery, illegitimate trading, and smuggling, have often made the news and are familiar to most people. Also of relevance is Shenzhen's close relationship with Hong Kong, its main source of overseas investment. Clearly the future economy of Hong Kong will have an important impact on the development of Shenzhen.

In conclusion, the rapid growth of Shenzhen in recent years is very much the result of the open policy and the establishment of the Special Economic Zone. The Shenzhen experience has created much criticism, however. It has been charged, for example, that China has been paying too much and getting too little from the SEZ experiment, that an "entrepôt" rather than an export-oriented economy has developed, and that achievements in foreign exchange earnings and technology transfer have been unsatisfactory. Nevertheless, the experience provides valuable lessons for the future. Judging from recent developments in China, Shenzhen as well as the other SEZs are no longer enjoying the special privileges they were once accorded. The opening of other coastal cities and economic development zones has undercut the allure of Shenzhen and made the SEZs increasingly less "special." Apart from the need to draw up long-term plans and development strategies in light of the current situation, the policies and attitudes of the central government will have major implications for Shenzhen's future growth.

Notes

1. Renqun Cai, "A Discussion on the Choice of Locations and Some Rational Scale of Development of Special Economic Areas in China," *Tropical Geography* 1 (1981): 54–59 (in Chinese).

2. Kwan-yiu Wong, "China's Special Economic Zone Experiment: An Appraisal," *Geografiska Annaler* 69(B) (1987): 27–40.

3. James B. Stepanek, "Direct Investment in China," *China Business Review* 9 (1982): 5.

4. Kwan-yiu Wong and David K. Y. Chu, "Export Processing Zones and Special Economic Zones as Generators of Economic Development: The Asian Experience," *Geografiska Annaler* 66(B) (1984): 1–16.

5. *South China Morning Post,* 18 July 1988.

6. See, for example, Wong, "China's Special Economic Zone Experiment."

7. *Wen Wei Po,* 9 September 1987.

8. Tianxiang Zheng, Heguang Chen, and Qingquan Wei, "Some Population Problems in the Construction of the Shenzhen Special Zone," in *Jingji Tequ Dili Wenji* [Geographic essays on economic zones], vol. 1 (Guangzhou: Zhongshan University, 1981) pp. 20–24 (in Chinese).

9. Ibid.

10. Yen-tak Ng, "Planned Population and Labor Introduction in Shenzhen," in David K. Y. Chu (ed.), *The Largest Special Economic Zone of China—Shenzhen* (Hong Kong: Wide Angle Press, 1983), pp. 39–47 (in Chinese).

11. Xiangming Chen, "Magic and Myth of Migration: A Case Study of a Special Economic Zone in China," *Asia-Pacific Population Journal* 2(3) (1987): 57–76.

12. *Shenzhen SEZ Yearbook,* 1988, p. 49.

13. Chen, "Magic and Myth," p. 71.

14. *Shenzhen SEZ Yearbook,* 1987.

15. See, for example, Eva B. C. Li, "Implications of the Open Policy on Welfare in China," in Kwan-yiu Wong, Chong-chor Lau, and Eva B. C. Li (eds.), *Perspectives on China's Modernization* (Hong Kong: Centre for Contemporary Asian Studies, Chinese University of Hong Kong, 1988), pp. 157–171.

16. David K. Y. Chu, "Population Growth and Related Issues," in Kwan-yiu Wong and David K. Y. Chu (eds.), *Modernization in China: The Case of the Shenzhen Special Economic Zone* (Hong Kong: Oxford University Press, 1985), pp. 131–139.

17. *Shenzhen SEZ Yearbook,* various years.

18. See, for example, Kwan-yiu Wong (ed.), *Shenzhen Special Economic Zone: China's Experiment in Modernization* (Hong Kong: Hong Kong Geographical Association, 1982), p. 28.

19. Yongming Wu and Zhaoqui Yi, "Problems of Industrial Allocation in

Shenzhen and Zhuhai Special Zones," *Jingji Tequ Dili Wenji*, vol. 1 (Guangzhou: Zhongshan University, 1981) (in Chinese).

20. *Xinhua News Agency*, 11 January 1982; see also S. Feuchtwang and A. Hussain (eds.), *The Chinese Economic Reforms* (Beckenham, Kent: Croom Helm, 1983).

21. Wu and Yi, "Problems of Industrial Allocation."

22. *Xinhua News Agency*, 11 January 1982.

23. *Almanac of China's Economy*, 1987, p. III–3.

24. Wu and Yi, "Problems of Industrial Allocation."

25. *Shenzhen SEZ Yearbook*, 1988, p. 62.

26. James B. Stepanek, "Direct Investment in China," *China Business Review* 9(5) (1982): 20–27.

27. *Almanac of China's Economy*, 1987, pp. III–62–3; *Shenzhen SEZ Yearbook*, 1988, p. 481.

28. *Shenzhen SEZ Yearbook*, 1988, p. 481.

29. *Ming Pao* (Hong Kong), 16 October 1986.

30. *Hong Kong Economic Journal*, 16 October 1986.

14 Taizhong: A Geographical and Developmental Appraisal

YEU-MAN YEUNG AND DAVID K. Y. CHU

SITUATED IN THE NORTH central area of the Taizhong Basin, Taizhong is located in the heart of the developed region of western Taiwan, 197 km south of Jilong and 207 km north of Gaoxiong. With a population of about 0.7 million, Taizhong is the third-largest city in Taiwan after Taibei and Gaoxiong.

The evolution of Taizhong as a city may be divided into four periods. The city began as a frontier settlement in the early Qing dynasty.[1] During the reign of Yongzheng (1723–1735), Han migrants began to arrive in larger numbers and to shape the character of the settlement. Active urban development commenced only in the 1860s, however, and by 1889 the planned area of the city had reached 364 ha. The second period is one of vigorous economic and infrastructural development under the Japanese when Taiwan was ceded to Japan in 1905. Taizhong was designated a city in 1920 when its population was in the region of 25,000. By 1940, its population had soared to 62,500, an indication of a period of rapid growth. The third period of Taizhong's development coincided with the restoration of Taiwan in 1945 to Chinese rule. Taizhong *shi* had an administrative area of 164.43 sq km, with an east–west span of 14.2 km and a north–south extent of 11.3 km. The entire city was divided into eight districts which had a population of 260,902 in 1958. The developed areas, however, covered only 12 sq km with a mere population of 188,000. The remaining 38.8 percent, representing the rural population, lived in the Taizhong administrative region. In the latest period, characterized by rapid urbanization and industrialization, the city's population soared to 741,337 in 1988.

Geographical Environment

According to the regional delimitation of Taiwan, the central region includes Taizhong *shi*, Taizhong *xian*, Zhanghua *xian*, Nantou *xian*, Miaoli *xian*, and Yunlin *xian*. The region had an area of 1.05 million square kilometers and a population of 5.0 million by the middle of 1988. This, however, is an administrative region. Different schemes have been advanced to include the actual economic hinterland of Taizhong *shi* (Figure 14.1).[2]

The first proposes that the Taizhong region should include Taizhong *xian*, Zhanghua *xian*, and Nantou *xian* with an area of 7,387.6 sq km and a population of 3.72 million (including Taizhong *shi*) by the middle of 1988. Because of the proximity of these three *xian* to Taizhong *shi* and their dependence on it, this scheme including the hinterland of Taizhong *shi* is seldom challenged. The second scheme divides Taiwan into three big regions: Taibei, Taizhong, and Tainan. According to this scheme, the Taizhong region would include Xinzhu *xian*, Miaoli *xian*, Yunlin *xian*, Jiayi *xian*, and Hualian *xian* in the east. This delineation surely has the maximum possible coverage of the hinterland of Taizhong and is therefore controversial. Nevertheless, the Taizhong Harbor Bureau has insisted on using this delimitation.[3] A more realistic and less controversial scheme adds Miaoli and Yunlin *xian* to Taizhong, Zhanghua, and Nantou *xian* as the hinterland of Taizhong *shi*. Since this is the scheme used by the Taiwan government to delimit the central region, we have adopted it for the analysis of the hinterland of Taizhong *shi* in this chapter.

This region includes the Taizhong Basin and the northern Jianan Plain. The Taizhong Basin, measuring 48 km north to south and 14 km east to west, is the depressed basin between Ali Shan and Dadu Plateau as well as Bagua Plateau. Its area is approximately 400 sq km. Its northern portion slopes gently from northeast to southwest. Its southern part slopes gently from southeast to northwest, with the lowest point near Wuri, an exit of the basin and a confluence of all streams in the basin which form Dadu Xi. In the north of the basin is Miaoli, an undulating plateau; in the south and west are alluvial plains. As noted, Dadu Xi flows from Wuri into a river delta in Zhanghua. In its estuary is the delta of the largest river in Taiwan, Zhuoshui Xi, which stretches to Zhanghua *xian* and Yunlin *xian*. The eastern parts of Yunlin *xian* and Nantou *xian* are hilly areas.[4]

The region has a warm climate and receives adequate insolation. Its low relief and adequate rainfall are conducive to growing paddy and sugarcane. In addition, tobacco, sweet potatoes, wheat, green manure, flax *(Linum usitatissimum)*, corn, peas, vegetables, and fruits are grown. Since 1969 industry has become increasingly important in the region.

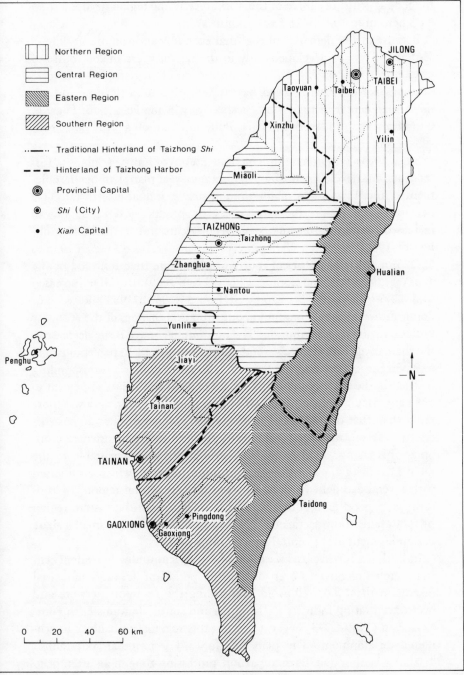

Figure 14.1 The Hinterland of Taizhong Harbor and Taizhong *Shi*

Indeed, agriculture's share of the work force in the region declined from 44.3 percent in 1981 to 21.23 percent in 1988.[5]

Because of the demands of the rural economy and community life, a settlement system developed early in the Japanese era in the course of economic development and the evolution of a transport network. Taizhong *shi* and Zhanghua *shi* have developed into the leading and second urban center of the system, respectively, while Fengyuan, Lugang, Qingshui, Yuanlin, Beidou, Dajia, Puli, and Nantou are the other subsidiary centers.

Since 1953, Taiwan has implemented a series of four-year plans to foster economic development. By 1980, six four-year plans had been implemented and Taiwan was maintaining a steady annual growth rate of 9 percent. As a result, the gross domestic product (GDP) of Taiwan increased tenfold during the twenty-eight years and reached $40.3 billion by 1980. Moreover, GDP per capita increased from $100 in 1950 to $2,275 in 1980. The series of four-year plans were then followed by the Ten-Year Economic Development Plan (1980–1989); the GDP increased to $122.6 billion and per capita GDP to $6,183 in 1988.[6] Rapid economic growth not only brought about structural changes of the economy but also regional redistribution. The prominent change is the decrease in the share of agriculture in the total output value from 36 percent in 1952 to 9 percent in 1980 and 5.2 percent in 1988; there was a corresponding increase in the share of industry from 18 percent in 1952 to 46 percent in 1982 and 51.9 percent in 1988.[7] The growth of heavy industry was more rapid than that of traditional light industry. Moreover, Taiwan has successfully transformed itself from a self-reliant to an export-oriented economy. This change in the economic structure is more favorable to the rapid growth of the northern and southern regions, which are blessed with several excellent harbors. The central agricultural region, by contrast, lacks good natural harbors and is severed from the eastern region by mountains. Both factors have helped to account for the smaller share of development in the central region (Table 14.1).

Indeed, the relative backwardness of the agriculturally dependent central region was obvious even during the period of Taiwan's industrial takeoff in the 1960s. To avoid overloading the transport network and overconcentrating industry in the north and south, Taiwan's Fifth Four-Year Plan (1969–1973) began to rectify this regional imbalance in economic development. The plan put forward a proposal to establish Taizhong Harbor and Taizhong export-processing zone in an attempt to

Table 14.1 Gross Domestic Product of Taiwan by Region: 1966–1988

REGION	1966	%	1971	%	1976	%	1981	%	1988	%
Northern	122,510	44.4	214,519	47.1	365,690	52.2	544,891	51.4	1,527,770	51.3
Central	60,030	21.8	90,796	19.9	136,232	19.4	203,654	19.2	559,933	18.8
Southern	83,634	30.3	136,839	30.1	182,341	26.0	286,730	27.1	824,102	27.7
Eastern	9,661	3.5	13,253	2.9	16,854	2.4	24,485	2.3	66,414	2.2
Taiwan	275,835	100.0	455,407	100.0	701,117	100.0	1,059,733	100.0	2,978,219	100.0

Source: Department of Residential and Urban Development, Economic Construction Committee of Executive Assembly (1982) and (1989), *Statistics on Urban and Regional Development.*

Note: GDP at 1976 NT$ million.

make Taizhong *shi* the economic center of the central region.[8] Statistics of 1976, 1981, and 1988 reveal that the relative decline of the central region has been arrested (Table 14.1). Moreover, the rate of development of the central region has increased to a level more commensurate with the national trend. Thus, the emergence of Taizhong is closely related to its geographical environment and socioeconomic conditions, especially the policy to redress regional imbalance implemented since 1969.

The Expanding City

The population of Taizhong *shi* increased drastically in the course of its rapid economic growth and reached 741,337 by 1988. With the expansion of city functions, the nonagricultural sector has increased in importance at the expense of the agricultural sector, resulting in a decrease in agricultural population. In 1988, the labor force engaged in agriculture of Taizhong *shi* was only 12,800 out of a total of 278,000, representing 4.61 percent of Taizhong *shi*'s working population. The corresponding figure for tertiary production was 57.6 percent; secondary production comprised 37.92 percent.[9]

In terms of age structure, 65.7 percent of the employed were of working age (16–64) while 29.5 percent and 4.8 percent of the entire working population were below 14 and above 65 years old respectively. With regard to education, 14.2 percent of the inhabitants above 6 years old attained the tertiary level. Those having attained upper secondary, lower secondary, and primary education made up respectively 26.7 percent, 18.9 percent, and 34.1 percent of the total population; whereas 1.3 percent were private students and 4.8 percent were illiterate.[10] As several institutions of higher learning are located in Taizhong, it has a sound basis for labor supply as well as research and development.

With respect to land use, the original built-up areas of Taizhong *shi* were concentrated in the inner urban districts, covering an area of about 10 sq km (Figure 14.2). Xitun, Nantun, and Beitun were originally agricultural areas. As the built-up areas became increasingly saturated in the course of industrial and commercial growth together with population increase, it was necessary to identify new sites for further industrial development in suburban Beitun and Xitun.

A land-use survey conducted by Pannell in 1970 shows that the central business district of the built-up areas of Taizhong *shi* was a mixed commercial-residential area containing a number of skyscrapers.[11] Adjacent

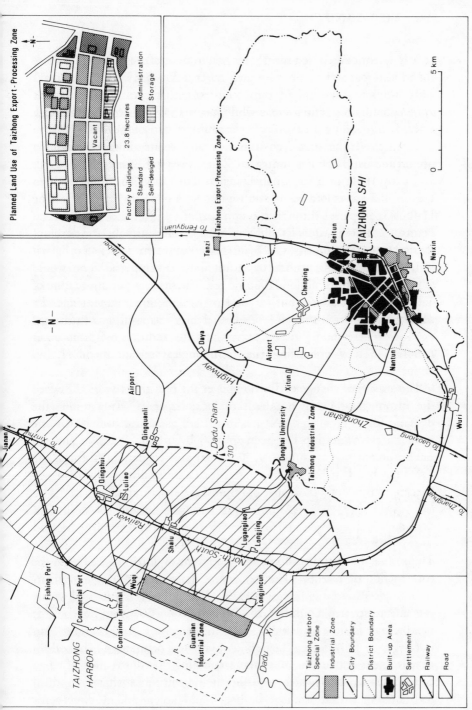

Planned Land Use of Taizhong Export-Processing Zone

Factory Buildings
Standard
Self-desiged

Vacant

23 8 hectares

Administration
Storage

TAIZHONG HARBOR

Fishing Port
Commercial Port
Container Terminal
Wuqi
Guanlian Industrial Zone

To Xinzhu
Jianan

Qingshui
Luliao
Shalu
Lugangliao
Longjing
Longjincun

Dadu Xi

Railway
North-South

Qingquanli
Airport

Dadu Shan
310

Donghai University
Taizhong Industrial Zone

To Taibei
Daya
Highway

Tanzi
Chenping

Taizhong Export-Processing Zone

To Fengyuan

Beitun
TAIZHONG SHI
Neixin

Airport
Xitun

Nantun
Zhongshan

Wuri
To Gaoxiong
To Zhanghua

Taizhong Harbor Special Zone
Industrial Zone
City Boundary
District Boundary
Built-up Area
Settlement
Railway
Road

0   5 km

Figure 14.2 The Location of Taizhong Harbor, Taizhong *Shi*, and Taizhong Export-Processing Zone

to it is a district occupied mainly by government offices, including those for educational and community uses. Further outward is a zone of small-scale industries and mixed industrial-residential uses. The outermost zone contains residential areas while heavy industries concentrate in a linear fashion along the railway in the southern part of the city.

To improve the urban environment and create more employment opportunities, Taizhong Industrial Zone was established in the 1970s and early 1980s near suburban Donghai University. The zone, with an area of 402 ha, is located on the western side of Dadu Shan. Taizhong Harbor Road passes through the northeastern part of the zone whereas Nantun Road cuts across its southern part. By one estimate, the developmental cost of the zone was NT$600/*ping* (equivalent to 3.3 sq m). That is to say, the total investment required to develop the zone would amount to NT$943 million (1980 value). The most important feature of Taizhong Industrial Zone is its modern working environment and the accompanying high-standard residential areas as well as recreational facilities. These should attract technicians and industrialists from other regions, thereby enhancing the technological advancement of Tai-zhong.[12]

The structural change of Taizhong over the past thirty years has raised the income and living standards of local residents. As a result, the demand for external transport has increased, as has car ownership. The need for car ownership has been spurred by urban expansion and the establishment of new suburban industrial and residential districts. On the other hand, it has become easier for factories in the suburban districts to recruit workers because of improved transportation.

Taizhong Harbor

The key factor in the economic development of Taizhong has been the construction of Taizhong Harbor, one of Taiwan's ten largest construction projects started in the early 1970s. The harbor is not located within the administrative boundary of Taizhong *shi,* however, but on the nearby coast in the northwest. In fact, the construction of Taizhong Harbor began in 1937 during the period of Japanese occupation. The scale of development at that time was small, including the construction of a pair of wrist-shaped breakwaters in its north and south, six wharves, and fif-teen buoys. The anticipated harbor would accommodate twenty-one oceangoing ships of below 10,000 dwt and was planned to be completed within ten years. Construction was halted after only three years because of the outbreak of World War II.[13] Consequently, freight sent to or from the Taizhong region had to be shipped through the harbors of Jilong in the north or Gaoxiong in the south until October 1976. In view of serious problems of silting, the port facilities left by the Japanese could accommodate only fishing boats and small ships even during high tides, while at low tide they could be operated only near the wharves.[14]

In the late 1960s, after a period of rapid economic development in Taiwan, the cargo-handling capacity of the harbors of Jilong and Gaoxiong was approaching its limit. Moreover, the major industries of Taiwan were concentrated mainly in the areas near the two harbors. To ameliorate the overconcentration of industry, to relieve the burden on the transport network in the adjacent areas of Jilong and Gaoxiong harbors, and to accelerate economic development in the central region, the Construction Bureau of Taizhong Harbor was established in November 1969 to develop the harbor.

The entire project was divided into stages of development. It took ten years (1969–1978) for the first phase, which included the construction of a commercial and fishing port. Construction of an industrial port would take place in the second and third phases from 1979 to 1986. Taizhong Harbor has now become a multipurpose commercial, fishing, and industrial port. The harbor reaches the southern coast of Dajia Xi in the north, the northern coast of Dadu Xi in the south, the Harbor Road and its extension in the east, and Taiwan Strait in the west. It has a total area of 3,970 ha. Work on the first phase, which envisaged a cargo-handling capacity of only 2.8 million revenue tons, commenced in October 1973. It was formally opened for commercial use three years later. On 1 July 1976, the Construction Bureau was reorganized into the Taizhong Harbor Bureau, which was responsible for the further expansion of the harbor. Officially, the first stage was completed in 1986 with a planned freight-handling capacity amounting to 14.6 million revenue tons of cargo.[15] In 1988, it handled 1,646 ships totaling 1.69 million net registered tonnage (NRT) and 13.71 million revenue tons of cargo.[16]

Since Taizhong Harbor is an artificial port built on the estuary of a sandy beach, construction work encountered a number of problems. Two of them stemmed from the natural environment: the control of the accumulation of drift sand and the protection of harbor facilities and operation from the monsoons. Since Taizhong Harbor is located in the south of Dajia Xi where Taiwan Strait experiences a lengthy period of north-easterly monsoons paralleling the coast, the northerly sea waves and long shore drifts carry voluminous coastal sand from Dajia Xi and the coast in the north and deposit it as drift sand at Taizhong Harbor. The harbor thus faces serious problems of silting. To prevent the deposition of drift sand and the silting of the harbor, a sandbreak was built north of the harbor to capture the drift sand in the deposition area. Furthermore, the deposition area must be cleared by dredgers every year to prevent it from saturation. Some 0.8 to 1.0 million cubic meters of silt sand must be dredged annually if the configuration of the coast is to be stabilized.[17] Fortunately, the dredged sediments could be used to form large pieces of reclaimed land for establishing an industrial district adjacent to the harbor. The other major problem, as noted, is wind. Monsoon winds with speeds over 40 km per hour are experienced in Taizhong Harbor from November to March. The consequential sandstorms adversely affect construction work and other operations in the harbor. To reduce the problem, a windbreak forest of 1.9 million horsetail trees *(Casuarina equisetifolia)* must be planted between the harbor and the deposition area.[18]

The enormous scale of the project called for enormous investments. The total investment for the three phases of the first stage amounted to NT$19.5 billion (about US$50 million at 1986 value).[19] Considering the huge investments, the project is justifiable only if significant economic benefits can be reaped. Besides the unquantifiable factor of the balance in regional economic development, the major economic benefits of Taizhong Harbor include reduced costs of internal transfer of freight, the decongestion costs of Jilong and Gaoxiong harbors, and the economic value of the reclaimed land formed from the dredged sand.

In 1980 one estimate put the imported or exported cargo to or from the hinterland handled by Taizhong Harbor at 4.7 million revenue tons (about 3 million metric tonnes). Consequently, a total of NT$920 million was saved since freight need not be transported to Jilong or Gaoxiong for loading and unloading. In addition, the savings attributable to the relief of congestion in Jilong and Gaoxiong harbors were estimated to be about NT$10 billion.[20] It was also learned from a visit to the Taizhong Harbor Bureau in 1983 that the 6 million revenue tons of cargo handled in 1982 had already saved freight owners NT$1.6 billion (125 km was saved on average for each metric ton of freight) formerly spent in transferring cargo to Jilong or Gaoxiong.[21] Thus the economic benefits to the hinterland of the central region would be even more remarkable judged by the actual number of ships and freight handled in 1988.

By 1980 the land reclaimed from the construction of Taizhong Harbor amounted to about 650 ha. The government of Taizhong *xian* estimated that land value of registered areas was NT$1,300/sq m on average. The total value of the reclaimed land would therefore be NT$8.45 billion.[22] An additional 810 ha of land was formed when the first stage of development was officially completed in 1986.[23] The economic benefits of the reclamation stand at about several billion (NT$). Of course, the realization of these benefits depends on whether the reclaimed land is used efficiently or not.

To enhance the efficiency of Taizhong Harbor so that the harbor and the city complement each other, as well as to avoid overconcentration in Taizhong *shi* in the future, four rural towns between Taizhong Harbor and the city (Qingshuizhen, Shaluzhen, Wuqizhen, and part of Longjing Xiang) were designated as parts of a special zone. Residential and industrial districts were set up in the zone: Guanlian Industrial Zone is one of these districts; Youshi Industrial Zone is another. In 1984, some 75,645 jobs in the secondary sector, representing 37.63 percent of all gainfully employed persons in Taizhong *xian,* were offered in Guanlian and Youshi industrial zones.[24]

Although the investment required for the construction and maintenance of Taizhong Harbor has been enormous, the economic benefits will be considerable if the limitations imposed by the natural environment can be overcome and the harbor put to efficient use.

The Taizhong Export-Processing Zone

The Taizhong export-processing zone is not situated within the administrative boundary of the city. Located in Tanzi of Taizhong *xian,* it is 9 km from the center of Taizhong *shi* (Figure 14.2). The area was formerly the site of the Tanzi Sugar Plant and was originally earmarked for the establishment of Tanzi Industrial Zone. However, in order to achieve balanced regional development of Taiwan's industry and to ameliorate the outmigration of population from the central region, it was decided, in August 1969, that the area should be developed into an export-processing zone. This is the third such zone in Taiwan after the establishment of Gaoxiong zone in December 1966 and Nanzi zone in January 1969.

Construction work on the Taizhong export-processing zone, undertaken by the Taiwan Land Development Trust Company, began in August 1969 and was completed the following year. The zone covers an area of 23.8 ha, of which 14.23 ha is allocated for exporting industries, 2.87 ha for administrative and service functions, 0.76 ha for female dormitories, and 5.63 ha for roads and greenery. The Sino-American Fund invested NT$26.4 million in the zone.[25] Four standard factory buildings and four standard flatted factory buildings have been erected in the area. These buildings were divided into 120 units of factory space having a total area of 91,105 sq m and catering to the needs of more than twenty-nine exporting factories. In addition, thirteen firms have built factories providing 51,951 sq m of space for their own use. The planned targets for the zone were to attract fifty exporting firms involving $7.5 million of investment, to produce $30 million of goods for export per year, and to employ 10,000 local workers as well as attract 150 foreign technicians.[26]

The scale of the Taizhong export-processing zone is smaller than that of Gaoxiong and Nanzi (69 and 90 ha respectively) because the zone was established far from the harbor and the international airport. It mainly depends on the north–south railway and Taizhong airport for external links. In addition, one of its objectives was to enhance the development of the economically backward central region. Indeed, it has taken several years for the export-processing zone to achieve its development targets. The earliest targets achieved were the amount of investment (1972), total value of exports (1974), and the number of workers employed (1976). Although the number of exporting firms established (forty-six as of 1988) still falls short of the target of fifty, the occupancy rate of factory buildings is satisfactory.

The major industries of the Taizhong export-processing zone are electronics (twenty firms), optical instruments (six firms), precision instruments (three firms), machinery (three firms), leather goods (three firms), and plastic products (three firms). Some of these enterprises are technologically advanced and entail technology transfer and technical cooperation. They have made the industrial structure of the central region more diverse and provide training for many workers. Furthermore, the zone has imported an increasing volume of components from adjacent tax areas so that the difference between total exports to and total imports from foreign countries has been enlarging. (Total exports in 1987–1988 were $610.2 million whereas total imports were $257 million.)[27] The industrial growth of areas outside the export-processing zone has been greatly enhanced by these trends.[28] Thus the overall performance of the Taizhong export-processing zone is remarkable.

A Triangular Spatial Relationship

From the foregoing account, it can be discerned that the locational principles governing the development of Taizhong *shi,* Taizhong Harbor, and the Taizhong export-processing zone are based mainly on regional interests and provincial needs. Less attention has been paid to the spatial relationships among them.

From a theoretical viewpoint, the optimum spatial arrangement is one in which the export-processing zone, the harbor, and the city are fully integrated as a unit. Even if geographical conditions limit this possibility, they at least should be administered under the same regional or local government to coordinate their development. For instance, Gaoxiong is a successful example where the city, harbor, and export-processing zone are integrated. Why, then, are Taizhong *shi,* Taizhong Harbor, and the Taizhong export-processing zone separately developed in a triangular relationship?

It is obvious that Taizhong *shi* existed before the harbor and the zone, and Taizhong Harbor had to be built along the coast. On the other hand, both the harbor and the export-processing zone were established in 1969 to achieve more balanced regional development. The harbor is located northwest of the city, however, while the export-processing zone is at Tanzi in the northeast. This is undoubtedly an irrational spatial arrangement. Moreover, the timing of their development was so poor that the harbor could be used only six years after the export-processing zone was established. Consequently, the zone had to rely on the already heavily laden north–south railway as well as on Jilong and Gaoxiong harbors during the earlier period of its development. At present, the harbor and the zone still cannot share the customs and warehousing facilities due to a physical separation of 28 km.

Economies of scale cannot be fully realized, either. In fact, industrial growth in the Taizhong Harbor Special Zone has remained slow and its population has been out-migrating since the harbor's establishment. Population growth rate for the area as a whole from 1977 to 1979 was – 0.8 percent (–12.4 percent for Qingshuizhen, 14.67 percent for Shaluzhen, –5.43 percent for Wuqizhen, and 0.1 percent for Longjing Xiang).[29] It was planned that the Taizhong Harbor Special Zone would develop into a new town of 0.5 million inhabitants by 1991 in the course of industrial growth.[30] By that time the zone's frontier of development would reach Taizhong *shi*. Clearly this planned development is irreconcilable with the negative population growth of the area in recent years. It is probably because of the administrative autonomy of the *xian*, the harbor, and the city that the Taizhong Industrial Zone was established adjacent to the Taizhong Harbor Special Zone while the export-processing zone was located further inland.

Lack of data for the 1980s makes it impossible to substantiate this hypothesis. But if these issues were put under the responsibility of a single government body—and if regional and local interests, as well as the characteristics, costs, and benefits of various projects were fully considered—it is doubtful that the spatial arrangement would be the same.

Conclusion

As a highly artificial city, Taizhong *shi* does not have favorable geographical conditions such as a natural harbor or rich natural resources such as minerals and ores. Its development can be traced to the Taiwan government's decision to establish another economic center in the central region in order to ameliorate regional imbalance. Essentially it was designed to redress the concentration of economic development and wealth in Taibei in the north and Gaoxiong in the south. The development of Taizhong Harbor and the export-processing zone since 1969 has followed this design. Although the result over the past ten or more years has been satisfactory, the location and administration of Taizhong *shi*, the harbor, and the export-processing zone are still so discrete that the potential for unified growth has not yet been fully exploited.

For Taiwan as a whole, however, the development of Taizhong has already contributed much to a change in the regional balance of population and economic growth. Population out-migration is no longer a problem for the region. Indeed, the Taizhong region is now one of the three regions in Taiwan experiencing net in-migration.[31] (The other two are Taibei and Gaoxiong regions.) Thus it can be said that the Taizhong region now possesses the basic economic conditions for more rapid economic growth. However, its administrative framework must be modified if the region is to play a greater role in promoting economic development in the future.

One possible change is to expand the administrative boundary of Taizhong *shi* until it reaches the coast so that Taizhong Harbor is put under its jurisdiction. The Taizhong special zone would also fall into its ambit. Another change is to delegate the administration and planning of the Taizhong export-processing zone to Taizhong Harbor in order to improve coordination. In the long run, it would benefit the development of the whole region if the export-processing zone and its adjacent areas were put under the administration of Taizhong Harbor and the city.

No one can dispute that Taizhong *shi* and the harbor have performed a vital stabilizing role in the urban system, regional development, and population redistribution of Taiwan. Their future growth and further contribution to the development of the central region and Taiwan, however, hinge on the administrative changes suggested here. Indeed, with these changes the future prospects of both Taizhong *shi* and the harbor are quite promising.

Notes

1. Data on the historical development of Taizhong come mainly from sections about Taizhong in Chen Zheng-xiang (ed.), *Taiwan Dizhi* (Taibei; Fu-min Geographical Institute of Economic Development, 1960); data for the modern period, unless otherwise specified, are taken from *Republic of China Yearbook*, various years.

2. C. W. Pannell, *T'ai-chung, T'ai-wan: Structure and Function*, Research Paper no. 144 (Chicago: University of Chicago, Dept. of Geography, 1973), pp. 18–25.

3. Fieldwork in 1983; and *Taiwan Ribao*, 18 October 1982.

4. Chen, *Taiwan Dizhi*.

5. Department of Residential and Urban Development, Economic Construction Committee of Executive Assembly, *Statistics on Urban and Regional Development*, 1989.

6. In 1980, US$1 was exchanged roughly for NT$36; in 1988 US$1 equaled NT$28.

7. Chen, *Taiwan Dizhi; Republic of China Yearbook*, 1989.

8. Xu Yan-sun, "The Construction of Taizhong Harbor and Economic Development of the Coastal Region," *Bank of Taiwan Quarterly* 31 (1) (1982): 208; and Economic Division, Management Department of Export-Processing Zone, *The Export-Processing Zone in the Past 15 Years*, 1981, p. 17.

9. Department of Residential and Urban Development, *Statistics*.

10. Ibid.

11. Pannell, *T'ai-chung, T'ai-wan*.

12. Xu, "The Construction of Taizhong Harbor."

13. Chen Ming-zheng, "The Construction of Taizhong Harbor in Taiwan," *Bank of Taiwan Quarterly* 29 (3) (1978): 129–144.

14. Bureau of Taizhong Harbor, *Taizhong Harbor,* 1981, p. 9; and fieldwork in 1983.

15. *Republic of China Yearbook,* 1986, p. 824.

16. *Republic of China Yearbook,* 1989.

17. Xu, "The Construction of Taizhong Harbor"; but the figure obtained in fieldwork done in 1983 is 3 million.

18. Ibid.

19. *Republic of China Yearbook,* 1986.

20. Sun Dang-yue, *The Impact of Port Zhanghua on Taizhong* (Taibei, 1981), pp. 47–48.

21. Fieldwork in 1983.

22. Sun, *Impact of Port Zhanghua.*

23. *Republic of China Yearbook,* 1986.

24. Fan Ai-wei, "Development of Industrial Zones and Export-Processing Zones in Taiwan," in Du Wen-tian (ed.), *Essays on Industrial Development of Taiwan* (Taibei: Lianjing Publishing Company, 1976).

25. Economic Division, *The Export-Processing Zone in the Past 15 Years,* p. 22.

26. Ibid., pp. 26, 27, 32.

27. *Republic of China Yearbook,* 1989.

28. For details see, for example, Xue Yi-zhong, "On the Attraction of Industry to Taizhong Harbor Special Zone," *Huagang Dixue,* 2 (1982): 67–79.

29. Department of Residential and Urban Development, *Statistics,* pp. 24–25.

30. *Taiwan Ribao,* 18 October 1982.

31. Liu Zheng-zheng, "The Relationship Between Economic Growth and Spatial Distribution of Population in Taiwan," *Bank of Taiwan Quarterly* 40 (1) (1989): 322–361.

15 Conclusion and Synthesis

YUE-MAN YEUNG AND XU-WEI HU

IN THIS CHAPTER we tie together the various city studies presented in earlier chapters. This task is necessitated by the fact that not all the coastal open cities are included in this volume and only two of the cities in the Special Economic Zones have been subjects of inquiry. This is also the place to present some comparative statistics among the major coastal cities—in this case, following the format of the companion Chinese volume, twenty major cities. And, finally, given the political events of June 1989, it is highly proper that we assess recent developments here. Now that the dust has almost settled, the modernization and development roles to which Chinese coastal cities have been assigned can be duly weighed in the context of broad policies and development.

Special Economic Zones

Since the adoption of the open policy in 1978 in China, its coastal cities have been cast in the role of spearheading development. Particularly important in the early phase of this development strategy have been the Special Economic Zones (SEZs) in Shenzhen, Zhuhai, Shantou, and Xiamen, which have witnessed extremely rapid growth. The value of industrial output of these four SEZs amounted to 22.57 billion *yuan* in 1988, or 10.7 times the corresponding value in 1980, an annual rate of increase of 34.5 percent.[1] Of the four, Shenzhen's growth has been particularly rapid: the value of industrial output has reached 7.73 billion *yuan*, or 151.5 times the value in 1980, an annual growth rate of 87.3 percent. Simply comparing the 1985 and 1988 figures, we find that the annual growth rate registered 71.8 percent.

The massive growth of export-led foreign exchange earnings has become a mark of distinction of export-oriented economic structures of SEZs in recent years. The four SEZs generated in 1989 a total of $3.5 billion in export value, which quadrupled the value in 1985. The value of industrial output by foreign investors accounted for 51 percent of the total value of industrial output in the four SEZs. Shenzhen's generation of foreign exchange soared from $11 million in 1980 to $2.17 billion in 1989, making it second only to Shanghai of all cities in China in its ability to earn foreign exchange. The total value of foreign exports through the four SEZs reached $14.17 billion in 1988—2.9 times the value in 1985 and representing an increase in China's total export value from 18 percent in 1985 to 29.8 percent in 1988. In 1988, too, direct foreign investment reached $0.93 billion, of which Shenzhen and Zhuhai accounted for 70 percent. Between 1979 and 1988, these two SEZs alone attracted a total of $3 billion worth of foreign investment, of which $2.26 billion went to Shenzhen.

Shenzhen and Zhuhai, both sharing the geographical advantages of being close to Hong Kong and situated on level land, have grown rapidly as brand-new cities in economic development as well as population. In 1988, both cities had within their urban area a total of 513,000 inhabitants (Shenzhen, 322,000; Zhuhai, 191,000)—an increase of 126,000 inhabitants from 1985, an annual rate of increase of 9.8 percent in the three-year period. Since they were conferred the status of SEZs, Shenzhen and Zhuhai have attracted basic infrastructure investments totaling 20 billion *yuan*. After several years of development and construction, the basic infrastructure is being improved all the time. At present, both cities lead China in terms of transport, telecommunications, housing, water supply, gasification, and the general level of urban services.

Xiamen and Shantou, situated in southern Fujian and eastern Guangdong, may be regarded as the hub of the homes of many overseas Chinese. Intimate links—economic, social, and other contacts—have been forged especially with overseas Chinese in Southeast Asia. As these cities carry a special meaning and attraction to overseas Chinese, their growth has been quite rapid. Because of its proximity to Taiwan, where many early migrants from Fujian have settled, Xiamen has stood to benefit markedly from intensified cultural contacts between two sides of the Straits of Taiwan in recent years. Xiamen is poised to become a major investment center for Taiwan. Since the 1989 State Council approval of Xinglin and Haicang as development zones outside the city but within the Xiamen SEZ set aside solely for Taiwanese interests, particularly petrochemical and textile companies, the response has been most encouraging. Xiamen officials have approved more than 370 Taiwanese investment projects, 130 alone in the first eight months of 1990.[2] As a result of the collapse of the Taibei stockmarket and lower corporate profits, however, Taiwanese investment in China tapered off sharply in the second half of 1990.[3]

As development in the SEZs has progressed, their area has been progressively expanded. In the beginning when the four SEZs were established, the total area delineated for their use was 338.37 sq km. Later Zhuhai increased its area from 6.7 to 121 sq km, Shantou increased its from 1.67 to 52.6 sq km, and Xiamen increased its from 2.5 to 131 sq km—all huge increases in land for development. Only Shenzhen has remained within its original area of 327.5 sq km. In 1988, Hainan province came into being with the establishment of the Hainan Special Economic Zone. With a total area of 33,920 sq km, representing the whole island, it has become the largest SEZ. The five SEZs together now encompass a total area of 34,552 sq km.

Situated at the northern and southwestern tips of Hainan Island are Haikou and Sanya, respectively, having become important gateways to the Hainan SEZ. In particular, Haikou is the main port city on the island and the political, economic, and cultural center which will determine the pace and character of development in the new SEZ. In view of its relatively late start, the Hainan SEZ has not been able to match the rate of development in the other four SEZs. As it has been accorded even more special terms for development, however, and has been permitted to adopt an even more open policy, Haikou is reported to have experienced notable improvements since 1988. The special conditions allowed for the Hainan SEZ include experimental schemes not tried before in other SEZs. Such schemes are permitted as long as they are recognized as effective internationally and suitable to China—such as the recognition and guarantee of economic freedom of individuals and enterprises, the practice of market economy following the guidelines of national macroeconomic policies compatible with the trends in international markets, and freedom of movement of capital, individuals, and goods in and out of the Hainan SEZ. These measures have been designed to make the zone most attractive to foreign investors.

Modernization Roles

In 1984, when the fourteen open coastal cities were declared, the policy was explicitly formulated to favor investors from overseas and the territories of Hong Kong, Macau, and Taiwan over domestic interests. At present, with the exception of Wenzhou and Beihai, every open coastal city has developed an Economic and Technological Development Zone within the urban area having easy access to the port to attract foreign investment and technology. Over the past several years, these twelve open cities have each invested at least 1 billion *yuan* in the construction and development of basic infrastructure in these zones. The capital outlay has concentrated in leveling land, construction of standardized factories and housing, modern road networks, communication facilities, water supply and discharge systems, electricity, gas, and the like. In a majority of cases, sizable infrastructures have been provided, thereby creating a relatively favorable investment climate and realizing the expected economic gains.

From the standpoint of recent development in open coastal cities, the rate of growth in small and medium-sized cities has exceeded by and large that in very large cities such as Shanghai and Tianjin. Nevertheless, because of their stronger economic structures, more extensive hinterlands, superior technological bases, and hence higher absorptive capability, very large cities are better positioned to compete for technology-intensive, capital-intensive, export-oriented (or import-substitution) projects. Moreover, the ETDZs of these cities have proved to have a greater drawing power for foreign investment than similar zones in smaller cities.

The relative strengths of very large cities in attracting foreign investment may be reflected in several developments in Shanghai such as the construction of the Baoshan Iron and Steel Mill, the Volkswagen Automobile Company, and other major projects. Ranking first among Chinese cities in foreign direct investment, Shanghai was able to attract $1.318 billion, representing 12.9 percent of China's total. Another example of effective foreign investment is Shanghai's Hungqiao ETDZ with an area of not even 1 sq km but a total investment of $0.66 billion, including $0.38 billion in foreign investment, making it the foremost development zone in China. Likewise, the Minhang Development Zone had all recent development projects financed by foreign investors; 82 percent of these projects involved advanced technology and export-oriented manufacturing. Minhang is the leading development zone in China in terms of export-led foreign exchange earnings and generating economic benefits.

ETDZs in Tianjin, Dalian, and other very large cities are also developing well and becoming increasingly attractive to foreign investors. Among the fastest growing of the very large coastal cities is Guangzhou, where medium-sized industries have seen rapid growth in recent years. Much of this growth can be traced to its peculiar geographical advantages and its favorable policies designed by the central government. In 1988, as much as 10.1 percent of China's total foreign trade passed through Guangzhou. Similar progress has been reported in development zones in Fuzhou, Qingdao, and Yantai. Although Yantai's ETDZ was established in 1985, economic returns on investment have been so satisfactory that repayment of mortgages is running ahead of schedule. In 1989, this zone repaid capital plus interest to the central government totaling 5.5 billion *yuan.*[4]

To strengthen the role of coastal open cities as agents of foreign exchange and domestic links, considerable efforts have been devoted to improving ports and constructing new land transport facilities during the past decade. In Shanghai, for instance, China's busiest port, the berthing facilities of its Huangpu Jiang have been completely saturated for a long time. Shanghai now plans to build new port facilities on the southern side beyond the mouth of Chang Jiang. It relies on Ningbo to take the overflow traffic of ships in the 50,000 to 100,000-dwt class. In addition to Ningbo, the harbors of Dalian, Qinhuangdao, Qingdao, Lianyungang, and Zhanjiang, are all blessed with natural factors for the development of deep-water seaport facilities.

Qinhuangdao, the largest port in the country for the export of energy resources, has the second largest throughput capacity after Shanghai. Apart from the existing Jingshan double-tracked and Jingqin electrified railways, the first phase of a modern, dedicated railway for moving coal from Datong in Shanxi to Qinhuangdao has recently been completed. Dalian and Tianjin are well known as the gateways from the sea to Northeast China and North China. Recently their importance has been accentuated by the completion, in 1990, of the Dalian–Shenyang and Tanggu–Tianjin–Beijing high-speed expressways. Lianyungang, as fully revealed in Chapter 6, has an exceedingly extensive hinterland, with the Longhai and Lanxin railways connecting the city to the extreme northwest of China. In 1990, the Lanxin railway was connected with the rail system in the Soviet Union, thereby rendering, in effect, Lianyungang as the eastern beachhead of the continental land bridge across Europe and Asia.

In the twenty cities—fourteen open cities plus six with SEZ status or located as port cities in an SEZ—the total throughput in 1988 reached 409.43 million tons, representing over 90 percent of the total tonnage

Table 15.1 Selected Indicators for Chinese Coastal Cities

CITY	SHI AREA (SQ KM)		URBAN AREA (SQ KM)		SHI POPULATION (IN 1,000S, YEAR END)		URBAN POPULATION (IN 1,000S, YEAR END)		NONAGRICULTURAL URBAN POPULATION (IN 1,000S, YEAR END)	
	1985	1988	1985	1988	1985	1988	1985	1988	1985	1988
Dalian	12,574	12,574	1,062	2,915	4,852.6	5,065.4	1,629.1	2,329.0	1,378.0	1,663.3
Qinhuangdao	7,523	7,523	363	363	2,281.6	2,394.1	436.0	478.2	307.5	345.1
Tianjin	11,305	11,305	4,276	4,276	8,084.0	8,434.3	5,380.9	5,621.7	4,202.5	4,419.0
Yantai	18,433	13,507	835	835	8,195.0	6,136.1	717.3	778.4	327.0	422.5
Qingdao	10,654	10,654	244	1,103	6,267.2	6,491.0	1,251.3	2,006.8	1,162.3	1,371.3
Lianyungang	6,327	6,327	830	830	3,006.3	3,197.3	459.4	499.1	288.0	330.7
Nantong	9,140	8,001	244	121	7,447.2	7,624.0	411.0	436.6	308.8	308.1
Shanghai	6,186	6,341	351	749	12,166.9	12,624.2	6,983.0	7,326.5	6,871.3	7,228.6
Ningbo	9,365	9,365	1,033	1,033	4,877.4	5,030.6	1,021.1	1,061.9	552.3	533.0
Wenzhou	11,784	11,784	187	187	6,291.9	6,529.7	530.6	552.1	372.2	391.2
Fuzhou	11,968	11,968	1,043	1,043	4,888.6	5,142.1	1,189.5	1,251.3	784.2	846.2
Xiamen	1,516	1,516	555	555	1,026.7	1,076.8	546.4	579.5	343.7	370.1
Shantou	10,346	10,346	245	245	9,202.4	9,517.6	760.8	801.1	488.8	526.8
Shenzhen	2,021	2,021	328	328	478.6	601.4	231.9	321.9	189.6	280.0
Zhuhai	1,630	1,266	654	654	414.7	466.0	155.0	190.7	88.8	124.6
Guangzhou	16,632	16,632	1,444	1,444	7,103.9	5,769.1	3,288.8	3,490.9	2,569.5	2,811.3
Zhanjiang	12,471	12,471	1,460	1,460	4,772.6	5,049.4	920.9	989.0	335.5	373.7
Beihai	275	275	275	275	175.9	1,162.0	175.9	190.1	119.0	137.5
Haikou	218	218	218	218	289.6	334.0	289.6	334.0	209.2	247.1
Sanya	1,887	1,887	1,887	1,887	321.7	341.6	321.7	341.6	70.5	88.9

continued

CITY	OUTPUT VALUE OF SHI INDUSTRY (BILLION YUAN, CONSTANT 1980 YUAN)			OUTPUT VALUE OF URBAN INDUSTRY (BILLION YUAN, CONSTANT 1980 YUAN)		
	1985	1988	1985–1988 INCREASE (%)	1985	1988	1985–1988 INCREASE (%)
Dalian	10.646	14.825	39.3	8.245	12.207	48.1
Qinhuangdao	1.185	1.967	66.0	0.920	1.494	29.8
Tianjin	28.580	36.256	26.9	27.745	33.630	21.2
Yantai	6.750	8.887	31.7	1.923	3.248	68.9
Qingdao	9.937	16.001	61.0	7.845	11.331	44.4
Lianyungang	1.984	2.946	48.5	1.329	1.867	40.5
Nantong	8.531	14.251	67.0	3.441	4.622	34.3
Shanghai	83.227	99.677	19.8	65.321	70.033	07.2
Ningbo	8.906	14.961	68.0	4.368	6.278	43.7
Wenzhou	3.270	5.075	55.2	1.572	2.247	42.9
Fuzhou	3.790	6.950	83.4	3.181	5.742	80.5
Xiamen	2.141	4.590	114.4	2.070	4.513	118.0
Shantou	3.180	6.655	109.3	1.336	3.160	136.5
Shenzhen	2.704	8.881	228.4	2.356	7.731	228.1
Zhuhai	0.594	2.446	311.8	0.380	1.929	407.6
Guangzhou	16.143	24.579	52.3	14.378	21.967	52.8
Zhanjiang	1.576	3.510	122.7	0.802	1.928	140.7
Beihai	0.223	0.644	188.8	0.223	0.331	48.4
Haikou	0.371	0.894	141.0	0.371	0.894	141.0
Sanya	0.063	0.137	117.5	0.063	0.137	117.5
Total	193.801	274.132	41.5	147.869	195.289	32.7
Country total	829.451	1,212.710	46.2			

Table 15.1 (continued)

CITY	THROUGHPUT HANDLED BY PORT (1,000 TONS)		VALUE OF FOREIGN EXPORT TRADE ($1,000)		VALUE OF FOREIGN IMPORT-EXPORT TRADE ($1,000)		FOREIGN DIRECT INVESTMENT ($1,000)	
	1985	1988	1985	1988	1988	IMPORT TRADE	1985	1988
Dalian	43,810	48,530	5,467,250	5,005,170	8,190,570	3,185,400	14,860	213,460
Qinhuangdao	44,190	58,120	1,138,980	1,308,820	1,803,410	494,590	1,410	5,250
Tianjin	18,560	21,090	1,152,740	1,529,470	2,344,390	814,920	69,210	344,010
Yantai	6,890	7,800	173,330	110,080	620,320	510,240	25,960	9,150
Qingdao	26,790	31,530	2,341,520	2,591,760	4,745,160	2,153,400	18,990	39,580
Lianyungang	9,290	11,140	35,050	285,500	1,263,790	978,290	500	10,480
Nantong	17,540[a]	20,200[a]	4,090	134,680	534,850	400,170	11,470	27,000
Shanghai	112,910	133,200	4,908,540	7,323,950	18,654,040	11,330,090	108,790	1,321,780[b]
Ningbo	10,410	20,020	291,310	378,030	761,180	383,150	3,690	12,230
Wenzhou	2,460	2,900	—	56,130	83,070	26,940	1,300	1,040
Fuzhou	3,380	5,150	236,610	491,050	1,255,040	763,990	15,160	36,630
Xiamen	3,180	4,690	165,280	574,040	1,364,800	790,760	73,280	164,090
Shantou	2,030	3,790	191,840	671,120	1,443,260	772,140	33,140	103,640
Shenzhen	2,590	7,340	4,264,740	11,914,100	21,567,420	9,653,320	329,250	444,290
Zhuhai	1,150	1,310	323,800	1,013,870	2,228,730	1,214,860	91,040	217,620
Guangzhou	17,720	32,650	1,781,160	4,021,560	11,311,530	7,289,970	155,310	255,190
Zhanjiang	12,740	16,530	619,210	1,585,180	2,248,740	663,560	30,410	40,350
Beihai	550	640	62,360	86,800	135,710	54,910	1,800	1,940
Haikou	1,710	2,410	40,700	97,630	458,630	360,700	11,830	29,560
Sanya	930	590	—	—	—	—	—	9,750
Total	321,290	409,430	23,203,510	39,172,940	81,014,640	41,841,400	997,400	3,287,040
Country total			27,350,000	47,520,000	102,790,000	35,270,000	4,647,000	10,059,000

CITY	PER CAPITA URBAN LIVING SPACE (SQ M/PERSON)		PER CAPITA SHI PAVED ROAD SURFACE (SQ M/PERSON)		URBAN TELEPHONE OWNERSHIP (PER 100 INHABITANTS)	
	1985	1988	1985	1988	1985	1988
Dalian	4.9	5.7	3.7	3.1	2.5	3.3
Qinhuangdao	5.4	7.9	6.2	9.2	2.9	4.9
Tianjin	5.0	6.4	1.9	4.6	2.7	3.8
Yantai	5.6	7.0	2.2	6.3	2.0	6.1
Qingdao	5.4	6.1	3.7	3.1	1.6	3.3
Lianyungang	5.5	6.4	1.6	4.7	1.7	2.6
Nantong	4.8	5.7	3.3	3.8	2.6	3.8
Shanghai	5.4	6.3	1.9	2.3	3.9	5.0
Ningbo	7.6	7.1	0.8	3.3	2.2	4.9
Wenzhou	5.2	7.8	1.1	2.5	2.2	3.7
Fuzhou	6.1	7.3	1.3	3.5	2.6	3.8
Xiamen	6.3	7.2	2.5	6.0	1.8	3.8
Shantou	4.4	5.1	1.4	2.1	1.2	4.5
Shenzhen	11.8	10.4	17.5	18.2	4.8	22.1
Zhuhai	8.8	12.8	13.6	15.2	4.7	12.2
Guangzhou	5.6	7.3	1.4	1.9	3.1	5.9
Zhanjiang	7.5	8.1	1.1	1.8	1.1	2.2
Beihai	5.9	6.7	3.6	4.6	1.2	2.2
Haikou	5.0	7.4	2.4	5.9	1.7	3.5
Sanya	6.3	8.5	2.7	1.6	0.4	0.8

[a] Calculation is based on river transport, not inclusive of sea traffic.

[b] Figure derived from *China's Provincial Historical Statistical Compendium.*

Sources: State Statistical Bureau (ed.), *Chinese Urban Statistical Yearbook, 1986, 1989; China's Provincial, Autonomous Region, Special Municipality, Historical Statistical Compendium, 1949–1989.*

handled by China. In addition, these twenty cities accounted for a GVIO amounting to 274.13 billion *yuan,* representing 22.6 percent of the national total. The value of foreign trade reached $81.02 billion, representing 78.8 percent of the national total; direct foreign investment was worth $3.29 billion, representing 32.7 percent of the national total (see Table 15.1). These statistics bring home the catalytic and critical roles that China's coastal cities have clearly assumed in the economic transformation and modernization of their country.

Developments since June 1989

In the wake of the events of June 1989, Western industrialized nations applied economic sanctions against China. Without a doubt, they adversely affected China's economy, leading to short-term dislocations and delaying the process of modernization. More specifically, foreign loans were curtailed and foreign exchange earnings sharply declined resulting from much subdued tourism and reduced export of service industry. Overall, though, the economic sanctions have not fundamentally affected China's economy and the difficulties have been overcome.[5]

In fact, foreign trade maintained its steady development in 1989. According to statistics of the Customs Department, foreign trade in that year reached a total of $111.6 billion, an 8.6 percent increase over 1988. Total export trade value reached $52.5 billion, a 10.5 percent increase over 1988. Owing to the central government's repeated declarations of support for the open policy, the SEZs and ETDZs have continued to make progress in attracting foreign investment to develop export-oriented, value-added enterprises. In 1989, the total value of new contracts signed involving direct foreign investment reached $5.6 billion, a 5.6 percent increase over 1988. Actual foreign investment amounted to $3.3 billion in 1989, an increase of 4.1 percent over 1988.

With a view to maintaining and further expanding the open policy, a series of measures were adopted in 1990 to encourage and attract foreign investment. In April, the Third Session of the Seventh National People's Congress passed the "Revised Ordinance for Chinese–Foreign Cooperative Joint Enterprises": nationalization and levy will not ordinarily apply to such enterprises; the chairman of the board of directors may be elected or chosen by agreement; and in certain industries the period of cooperative venture may be left unspecified. In May, the State Council stipulated two more measures: "Temporary Regulations Concerning the Use,

Lease, and Transfer of Government Land in Cities and Towns in the People's Republic of China" and "Methods for Regulating the Opening and Development of Large Plots of Land by Foreign Investors." The first enactment clearly provided for the use and transfer of different types of land for lease periods ranging from forty to seventy years; the second was designed for the convenience of foreign investors interested in comprehensive and long-term development involving large tracts of land. In August, the State Council enacted "Rules Concerning Encouragement of Investment by Overseas, Hong Kong, and Macau Chinese." The objective here is to provide favorable terms and convenience for investment by Chinese in various categories. It is clear from these enactments that the government has gone to great lengths to signal the world that a climate of favorable investment prevails in China.

Beyond these statutory enactments, top government officials took a decisive step to demonstrate their determination to deepen China's reform and expand its open policy by announcing, in April 1990, their endorsement of an ambitious plan (mooted since 1986 by Shanghai) to accelerate development in an area east of Huangpu Jiang, simply called Pudong, with the adoption of policies similar to ETDZs and SEZs.[6] Pudong, a 350-sq-km area of relatively isolated and undeveloped land, has a present population of 1.10 million and a certain industrial base. Plans for improving the transport network between Pudong and the bustling downtown section across the river are being actively pursued: two road tunnels have been completed; Nanpu Bridge and a new port at Waigaoqiao are being constructed. The mayor of Shanghai has announced a favorable policy of ten concessions and views Pudong as a colossal engineering project stretching to the next century.[7] Not only will it become a major development area within Shanghai, but it will also aspire to be the industrial, trading, and financial center of the Chang Jiang Delta region. Pudong will play much the same role for Jiangsu and the surrounding provinces that Hong Kong has played for Guangdong.

Indeed, Pudong is perceived as China's first free-trade zone, modeled after Hong Kong, hence the term "socialist Hong Kong."[8] Widely seen as an agent for Shanghai's economic renaissance, Pudong is dependent on a huge infusion of funds to realize its development goals. It has been estimated that over the next forty years, $80 billion will be needed for funding the development schemes, a figure that may be compared with the total foreign investment of $50 billion in China over the past decade of reforms.[9] After a subdued response from abroad, the first stage of development at an estimated cost of $10 billion will probably have to rely on domestic funding. Pudong officials have indicated that 26 to 30 billion *yuan* will be spent on infrastructural developments in the next five years. Meanwhile, 20 billion *yuan* has been secured from central government grants and local resources, but the municipality still needs another 10 billion *yuan* to complete ten major projects during the first three to five years.[10] The realization of Pudong's development goals depends critically on an adequate transport infrastructure, for the present system is failing and sorely outmoded.[11] Foreign bankers and entrepreneurs have also advised that radical reforms should be implemented before foreign investment is committed. In any event, Dupont as the first foreign company in Pudong has agreed to invest $25 million to build a factory producing agricultural chemicals.[12] The municipality also announced that it had approved 161 overseas-funded ventures in the first ten months of 1990, a total contracted investment of $220 million.[13]

Proponents of Pudong have argued for its development as a launching pad for Shanghai on its path to economic rejuvenation, which is important for China's overall development. Moreover, it is viewed as a counterbalance to the exceedingly rapid development of Guangdong in recent years. There is little doubt that with Pudong's development, the major focus of the open policy will in the 1990s shift to Shanghai and the Chang Jiang Delta. Shanghai will be given the opportunity to reassert its former premier role as a pacesetter and pioneer of development in China.[14]

Even before the Pudong project is fully launched, repercussions are being felt in other coastal cities and various plans have been spawned in anticipation of keener competition from Shanghai. Tianjin officials, for instance, have considered how to gain new concessions from the central government to enable the city to compete with Pudong. It has sought permission to establish a bonded area (where imports would be tax-free provided they are used for reexport) and the right to have foreign banks open branches. A new Leading Group on Foreign Investment has been set up to plan a strategy for attracting investment from abroad. Eventually the city would like to develop, beyond the bonded warehouses it already possesses, a large area similar to Pudong that can be turned into a free port.[15]

Ningbo has mounted, on the other hand, a two-pronged strategy. Plans were provided in May 1990 for leasing land in a 60-sq-km industrial development zone to foreign enterprises with fifty-year transferable leases which could be mortgaged to raise funds for infrastructure development and construction work. Japanese and Taiwanese companies, including a subsidiary of Japan's Nippon Steel, were committed to setting up ventures in the zone. In addition, a second industrial zone would be established in the Beilun harbor area, 20 km west of Ningbo, with tax concessions and other benefits applicable to foreign investment not unlike terms prevailing in the Special Economic Zones. Ningbo, the birthplace of Chiang Kai-shek, has been popular with Taiwanese investors.[16]

Fears of being overshadowed by Pudong's planned developments have prompted counterstrategies by still other coastal cities. There was a plan by the Hainan SEZ to lease 30 sq km of land at Yangpu, the island's deepest-water port, to a Japanese consortium led by the construction giant Kumagai Gumi (Hong Kong).[17] Tianjin and Dalian have sought permission from the central government to set up large-scale development zones as parallels to Pudong. Guangdong officials, likewise, feel threatened and hope to capitalize on the province's traditional links with Hong Kong to create a "major economic base" by linking Shenzhen, Huizhou, and Guangzhou into a mega-zone that would rival Pudong as an industrial and commercial center. In a bold attempt to lure Taiwanese investors from Fujian and Shanghai, the Zhuhai SEZ has set up a special zone in the city's western district offering land-use rights for seventy years gratis to industrial users.[18]

From the design of Pudong and subsequent proposals from Tianjin and Dalian, there appears to be great interest in expanding China's open policy in the direction of free-trade zones analogous to the Hong Kong experience. The free-trade policy of Hong Kong appears to have been appreciated for its positive effects on the territory's rapid economic growth in recent decades and its economic modernization and internationalization. A conceptual design has been proposed to evolve families of free-trade zones centered around a number of coastal cities. While they would have all the characteristics expected of such zones, they would come under the macromanagement of the central government and thus under socialist ideology. Seven such clusters of free-trade ports/zones have been proposed around Haikou, Shenzhen, Xiamen, Shanghai, Qingdao, Tianjin, and Dalian.[19]

In all these recent developments or new conceptual designs, it is beyond question that China's open policy and the coastal cities' role in furthering this policy have, if anything, been strengthened and expanded. In June 1990, the central government announced that four more ports—two seaports and two river ports—would soon be opened. The two seaports are Yangpu Harbor and Qinglan Harbor on Hainan Island; the river ports are Yantian in the Shenzhen SEZ and Da'an in Jilin province, which is important for trade with the Soviet Union. These will be over and above the 143 ports that China has opened to the world. It was also suggested that dozens more ports might be opened to foreign countries over the next two years.[20]

With the passage of time, Japan has led other nations in the resumption of loans to China. As well, the European Economic Community recently announced the termination of economic sanctions against China. Thus the external political climate has gradually improved. The countervailing tendency is the shortage of capital for investment, both domestically and internationally. The central government has curtailed the flow of funds to development zones in recent years. The yearly total of such mortgage loans from the central government of more than 1 billion *yuan* in 1985 declined to 0.3 billion *yuan* in 1989 and 0.1 billion *yuan* in 1990, posing difficulties to new infrastructure projects in the zones.[21]

There appears to be a a tight global market, too, for funds which China has to compete with other nations. Certain new factors are not in China's favor: the current momentous changes within the Soviet Union, the fall of communism in Eastern Europe, German unification, and the Mideast situation. These dramatic political changes have given rise to either political uncertainty or alternative investment locales—both of which have the effect of holding back foreign investment in China. Furthermore, the ASEAN countries have offered bold concessionary terms to compete actively for foreign investment. As a result, greater attention has been paid to controlling the outflow of investment funds from China, particularly to Hong Kong. It has been estimated that over the past five years, Chinese firms have invested several billion dollars in the territory, an amount which exceeded investments by Hong Kong entrepreneurs in China.[22]

Finally, after massive investment in infrastructure and industrial development over the last ten years, the open policy is beginning to bear fruit. To be sure, there are still problems and challenges which confront planners and policymakers in resolving the contradictions between economic modernization and political reform. For example, there is still too much bureaucratic interference in economic decisions, administrative efficiency leaves much to be desired, and the price system is badly in need of reform and rationalization. But with the rectification of these inadequacies and continued improvement of the investment environment, China's coastal cities do present a sanguine prospect for future growth and development.

Notes

1. *"Yuan"* refers to constant 1980 *yuan* throughout this chapter.

2. Tai Ming Cheung, "The Taiwan Beachhead," *Far Eastern Economic Review,* 15 November 1990, pp. 76–77.

3. Tai Ming Cheung, "The Water Margin: China-Taiwan Trade Growth Suffers a Setback," *Far Eastern Economic Review,* 15 November 1990, pp. 76–77. There are other problems faced by SEZs despite ten years of impressive progress. See Wu Shibin, "Special Economic Zones Being Confronted by Ten Challenges," *Hong Kong and Macao Economic Digest* 11 (1990): 49–52.

4. Lu Guoguan, Zhou Zhenping, and Zhang Weidi, "Development Zones in Coastal Cities Have Become Most Active Economic Belts," *Shenzhen Special Zone Daily,* 14 September 1990 (in Chinese).

5. He Ping, "Conceptual Designs for Developing the Economy of the Coastal Region—I," *Wen Wei Po,* 9 May 1990 (in Chinese).

6. Kwok Cheung Hi, "Pudong: Shanghai's Future Glory," *Wah Kiu Yat Po,* 2 June 1990 (in Chinese); and Kong Fung, "Cross-Century Developments in Shanghai's Pudong," *Wah Kiu Yat Po,* 9 June 1990 (in Chinese).

7. These concessions are detailed in "Preferential Policies for the Development of Pudong," *New China Quarterly* 17 (August 1990): 61.

8. Jaime A. Florcruz, "Zhu's Grand Plan: Shanghai's Leader Seeks to Rebuild His Crumbling Metropolis," *Time,* 24 September 1990, pp. 24–25. Pudong has also been called China's "Special Economic Zone with socialist characteristics" and a quasi-Special Economic Zone. See Willy Wo-Lap Lam, "Deng Steps In to Push for More Reform," *South China Morning Post,* 8 May 1990, and "Shanghai Economic Zone 'Boost for Reform,' " *South China Morning Post,* 19 April 1990.

9. Guy Dinmore, "Investors Urge Reform to Tap Waiting Billions," *South China Morning Post,* 29 October 1990.

10. Geoff Crothall, "Shanghai Still Needs $16 Billion for Pudong Projects," *South China Morning Post,* 16 November 1990; see also Tai Ming Cheung, "Clogged Arteries: Shanghai's Revival Hinges on Better Transport," *Far Eastern Economic Review,* 4 October 1990, pp. 68–69, and Eva To, "Pudong May Not Get Enough Foreign Funds," *South China Morning Post,* 17 October 1990. See also Geoff Crothall, "Mainland Bank Pledges $7.5 b to Fund Pudong Development," *South China Morning Post,* 7 December 1990. The reopening of the

Shanghai Securities Exchange in December 1990 after a break of more than forty years is expected to help raise funds from overseas sources. See Sondra Wudunn, "Shanghai Exchange Opens," *South China Morning Post,* 20 December 1990.

11. Tai, "Clogged Arteries."

12. Tai Ming Cheung, "Pudong's Investment Lures," *Far Eastern Economic Review,* 4 October 1990, pp. 68–69.

13. Crothall, "Shanghai Still Needs $16 Billion."

14. "China Adjusting Its Relevant Policy Tilting Gradually Toward Shanghai," *Wen Wei Po,* 30 July 1990 (in Chinese).

15. John Kohut, "Tianjin Bids for New Concessions," *South China Morning Post,* 22 May 1990.

16. Geoff Crothall, "Ningbo to Lease Land in Zone to Foreigners," *South China Morning Post,* 18 April 1990.

17. Kent Chen, "Coastal Cities to Gain from Lease Decision," *South China Morning Post,* 18 April 1990.

18. Geoff Crothall, "Pudong Status Starts Internal Economic War," *South China Morning Post,* 28 May 1990.

19. Tan Hui, "Free Port: New Options in China's Open Policy," *Hong Kong and Macao Economic Digest,* November 1990, pp. 35–37 (in Chinese).

20. Wang Xiangwei, "State to Open Four Ports," *China Daily,* 10 June 1990.

21. "Seeking Breakthroughs in Developing Development Zones: Toward Regional Cooperation," *Wen Wei Po,* 7 May 1990 (in Chinese).

22. He Ping, "Conceptual Designs for Developing the Economy of the Coastal Region—II," *Wen Wei Po,* 10 May 1990 (in Chinese); also "Seeking Breakthroughs."

INDEX

Production Notes

Composition and paging were done on the
Quadex Composing System and typesetting
on the Compugraphic 8400 by the design
and production staff of University of
Hawaii Press.

The text typeface is Garamond and the
display typeface is ITC Garamond.

Offset presswork and binding were done by
The Maple-Vail Book Manufacturing Group.
Text paper is Writers RR Offset, basis 50.